MIDDLEPLOTS™ 4

MIDDLEPLOTS® 4

A Book Talk Guide
for Use with Readers Ages 8–12

By JOHN T. GILLESPIE
and CORINNE J. NADEN

R. R. BOWKER®
A Reed Reference Publishing Company
New Providence, New Jersey

Published by R. R. Bowker,
A Reed Reference Publishing Company

Printed and bound in the United States of America

Middleplots 4 is part of Bowker's Booktalking Series of "plots" books.

The covers of these books are designed to correspond to the complexity of the plots contained in each volume. The "roads" on the *Primaryplots* cover therefore are very simple; those on companion volumes *Middleplots, Juniorplots,* and *Seniorplots* are increasingly intricate. Circles, squares, and other geometric shapes that highlight capital letters also move from the simple to the elaborate, reflecting the ascending age levels of the readers.

Library of Congress Cataloging-in-Publication Data

Gillespie, John Thomas, 1928–
Middleplots 4 : a book talk guide for use with readers ages 8–12 / by John T. Gillespie and Corinne J. Naden.
p. cm.
Includes bibliographical references and index.
ISBN 0-8352-3446-0
1. Young adult literature—Book reviews. 2. Youth—Books and reading. 3. Young adult literature—Stories, plots, etc. 4. Book talks. I. Naden, Corinne J. II. Title. III. Title: Middleplots four.
Z1037.A1G518 1993
028.5'35—dc20 93-21146
CIP

Contents

Preface

Helping youngsters select books for their reading pleasure is one of the most enjoyable responsibilities of teachers and librarians. There are many methods that can be used, but perhaps the most potent is actually talking about the books one wishes to recommend to either an individual patron or to groups. This technique is known as "booktalking."

The primary purpose of this volume is to help librarians and teachers supply reading guidance by way of the book talk. A secondary purpose is to serve as a collection-building tool. The introduction, "A Brief Guide to Booktalking," is reprinted from the companion volume *Seniorplots* (Bowker, 1989) and provides hints and aids for the would-be booktalker.

This book is a successor to the three books previously issued in the *Introducing Bookplots* series. They are *Introducing Books* (Bowker, 1970) by John Gillespie and Diana Lembo, *Introducing More Books* (Bowker, 1978) by Diana L. Spirt, and *Introducing Bookplots 3* (Bowker, 1988) also by Diana L. Spirt. Although *Middleplots 4* differs somewhat in scope, treatment, and coverage from these three books, it, too, is intended for use with readers ages 8 to 12. The changes in *Middleplots 4* reflect the desire to make it comparable in arrangement and content with three companion titles: *Primaryplots* for readers ages 4 to 8, *Juniorplots* for readers ages 12 to 16, and *Seniorplots* for readers ages 15 to 18.

In addition to the usual author, title, and subject indexes, this volume contains cumulative indexes (again by author, title, and subject) to the books summarized in this and the preceding three volumes. These indexes will facilitate the use of the volumes as an integrated set.

The eighty plots in *Middleplots 4* have been divided by subjects or genres popular with middle grade readers. They are (1) Adventure and Mystery Stories; (2) Humorous Stories; (3) Fantasy and Science Fiction; (4) School and Friendship Stories; (5) Personal and Social Problems; (6) Family Life; (7) Other Lands and Times; and (8) Interesting Lives.

Various methods were used to choose the books to be highlighted. A basic criterion was that each had to be recommended for purchase in several standard bibliographies and reviewing sources. In addition to criteria involving quality, an important consideration was the desire to provide materials covering a variety of interests and needs at different reading levels. In spite of these concerns, some of the selections remain personal and, therefore, arbitrary. Particular emphasis was placed on titles published between 1988 and 1993.

The individual titles are analyzed under six headings:

1. *Plot Summary*. Each plot briefly retells the entire story. The summary includes all important incidents and characters, while trying to retain the mood and point of view of the author.

2. *Thematic Material.* This section enumerates primary and secondary themes that will facilitate the use of the book in a variety of situations.

3. *Book Talk Material.* Techniques are given on how to introduce the book interestingly to young adults. Passages suitable for retelling or reading aloud are indicated and pagination is shown for these passages for the hardcover edition. It was found that pagination in the hardcover edition was usually the same in the paperback.

4. *Additional Selections.* Related books that explore similar or associated themes are annotated or listed with identifying bibliographic information. Approximately seven titles are given per book.

5. *About the Book.* Standard book reviewing sources (for example, *Booklist*) are listed with dates and pages of reviews. Also, listings in *Book Review Digest* and *Book Review Index* are given when available so that additional reviews can be located if needed.

6. *About the Author.* Standard biographical dictionaries (for example, *Something about the Author* and *Contemporary Authors*) were consulted to locate sources of biographical information about the author. When this section does not appear, no material was found. However, the user also may wish to consult other sources, such as periodical indexes *(Readers' Guide, Education Index, Library Literature),* jacket blurbs, and material available through the publisher.

The detailed treatment of the main titles is not intended as a substitute for reading the books. Instead, it is meant to be used by teachers and librarians to refresh their memories about books they have read and to suggest new uses for these titles.

This volume is not meant to be a work of literary criticism or a listing of the best books for young adults. It is a representative selection of books that have value in a variety of situations.

The authors have had many helpers in preparing this book, but special thanks should be given to Catherine Barr, Senior Editor at Bowker.

Introduction: A Brief Guide to Booktalking

by John T. Gillespie

There is basically just one purpose behind booktalking—to stimulate reading and a love of literature through delivering tantalizing, seductive introductions to books. There are, however, often many different secondary purposes, for example, to introduce specific authors, titles, or themes of books; to develop a specific aspect of literary appreciation; to further a particular school assignment; to present yourself to students; or to encourage visits to and use of the library.

Book talks generally fall into two main categories, informal and formal. The informal book talk consists of the spontaneous introduction to books that goes on every day in the library with single or small groups of students often in reply to such questions as "Could you suggest some good books for me to read?" The formal book talk is explored here in this brief introduction.

Before preparing a specific book talk, three "knows" are helpful. First is to know your audience as well as possible—age and grade levels, the range of abilities and interests, and levels of maturation and sophistication. Second is a knowledge of books. This comes in time through reading about books, in book reviewing journals and other secondary sources, but more importantly from reading the books themselves. It is wise to begin a card file with brief notes on each book read. Although these are never as detailed as the coverage of each title in *Middleplots 4,* certain topics should be covered. Basically these are: a brief plot summary; a list of a few key passages, particularly at the beginning of the book, that would be suitable for retelling or rereading to an audience; a note on the major subjects or themes covered; and other related book titles that come to mind. As this file grows it can be used to refresh one's memory of books and thus save rereading time and also serve as a source to create new book talks by "mixing and matching" titles to create a variety of interesting new combinations of titles and themes.

Third is a knowledge of the many aids, such as *Middleplots 4,* available to help in preparing and delivering a book talk. Some of the most valuable aids are described at the end of this introduction.

Before choosing the books to be presented, a preliminary framework should be established. First, the physical conditions should be studied (place, time, purpose, number of attendees). Second, the length of the talk should be determined. Most book talks last 15 to 25 minutes depending on such factors as the number of books to be introduced and the attention span of the audience. An average length is about 20 minutes. In a classroom period of 40 to 45 minutes this allows time for housekeeping chores (for example, announcements, attendance taking), the book talk itself, browsing through the books presented and additional titles, checking out books, and so on.

Deciding on the number of titles to be presented is next. Some booktalkers like to give short one- or two-minute "quickies" whereas others feel more comfortable spending longer periods on each title, supplying more details of plot or character and perhaps retelling or reading a key self-contained incident. Still others mix both techniques. The conditions of the book talk and the preference of the booktalker in the end determine the style used. Also, if a large number of books is to be introduced, a bibliography can be prepared and distributed to students to prevent confusion and give them reading guidance for future visits to the library. This bibliography should contain names of authors, titles, and a brief "catchy" annotation for each.

In preparing the talk, a connecting link or theme should be identified. This could be as general as "Books I think you would enjoy reading" or "Some titles old and new that are favorites of young people your age" to something more specific such as American Civil War novels or family crises as portrayed in fiction. The more specific topics are often suggested by a classroom teacher and are assignment-oriented. Regardless of the nature of the theme or subject, it supplies a structure and connecting link to give a oneness and unity to the book talk. It is used to introduce the talk, act occasionally as a bridge from one book to the next, and serve as a conclusion to round out the presentation.

Next choose the books themselves. Although this seems an obvious point, each book should have been read completely. The ultimate outcome or denouement in a book will often determine the material to be presented in introducing the book. Lacking this knowledge, the booktalker might misrepresent the contents or give an inaccurate or incorrect interpretation. One should believe in the value of each title to be presented—feel that the book is worthy of being introduced and that it will supply enjoyment and pleasure to the intended audience. The booktalker does not necessarily have to dote on each title and must at times introduce examples of a genre he or she does not like. It is sufficient that one choose good books that will enlighten and entertain the audience regardless of the personal preference of the presenter. Be sure the selection represents the interests and reading levels of the group—some difficult, some average, some easy; some old titles, some new; some fiction, some nonfiction; and so forth.

One should determine the method and content of each book introduction after choosing the theme and the books themselves. There are several ways of introducing books. The most frequently used is a brief description of the plot to a certain climactic moment. Words of caution: Do not give away too much of the plot, stick to essential details (for example, avoid introducing subplots or subsidiary characters), and try not to overwork this technique or else students will find the "cliff-hanger" endings ultimately frustrating. The second method is by retelling or reading a specific self-contained incident or incidents that give the flavor of the book. This can be the most satisfying for the audience because a "complete" story has been told and yet one hopes a desire for more has also been implanted. One must be very cautious about reading from the book and use this technique sparingly, only when the author's style cannot be produced otherwise. Some booktalkers eschew reading from the book entirely and instead memorize the passages because reading from the book interrupts the immediate eye contact with the audience and can lessen or destroy the rapport one has with the group. Therefore, passages to be read must be chosen very carefully, and should be short and fulfill a specific purpose when simple retelling will not suffice. A specific interesting character can be introduced fully and placed within the context of the book. Using the setting or atmosphere of the novel is a fourth method. Science fiction or fantasies with their often exotic, fascinating locales lend themselves frequently to such introductions.

Make sure you are honest in interpreting the book. To present, for example, *The Red Badge of Courage* as an exciting, action-filled war story is both a disservice to the book and a misrepresentation to the audience.

Some people write down their book talks and memorize them; others simply prepare them mentally. A rehearsal, however, is necessary to test pacing, presentation, timing, and sequencing. Perhaps friends, family, or colleagues can be an initial test audience. Tape recorders, or better yet video recorders, are also helpful in preparation. Though rehearsals are necessary, always try for sincerity, naturalness, and a relaxed atmosphere in the delivery. Because initial nervousness can be expected, be particularly careful to know thoroughly the beginning of the talk. Once one becomes used to the audience and the surroundings nervousness usually disappears. Introduce the theme quickly in a way that bridges the gap between the experience and interests of the audience and that of the contents of the books you wish to introduce. Be sure to mention both the author and the title of the book (often twice—once at the beginning and once at the end of the presentation), show off the book (dust jacket and covers can help sell a book and supply a visual reminder of the book), and then display the book (usually by standing it up on the desk). Try to adhere to principles of good public speaking—include the entire audience in your eye contact; don't fidget, rock, play with elastic bands or create other distractions; speak slowly with good intonation and use pauses effectively; and move quickly from one book to the next.

Fortunately there are many excellent guides to help one become a good booktalker. Joni Richards Bodart, a master booktalker, has written extensively on the subject. Bodart's *Booktalk! 2* (Wilson, 1985), an update of *Booktalk!* (Wilson, 1980), gives extensive guidance in preparation and delivery of book talks and supplies many brief examples. Sequels, *Booktalk! 3* (Wilson, 1988), *Booktalk! 4* (Wilson, 1992), and *Booktalk! 5* (Wilson, 1993), give additional sample book talks for a variety of age levels from toddlers to senior citizens. Bodart's 30-minute videotape *Booktalk* (also available from Wilson) supplies both tips and actual presentations.

Hazel Rochman, staff reviewer for young adults at *Booklist,* also has a fine book and videotape on booktalking (both released in 1987). They are called *Tales of Love and Terror: Booktalking the Classics Old and New.* The book is available from American Library Association Publications and the tape from Library Video Network. Both are geared to booktalking with young adults but nevertheless are useful for booktalkers working with younger students. Also available from ALA is Elinor Walker's *Book Bait* (ALA, 1988), which gives detailed notes on some adult books popular with young adults. *Primaryplots* by Rebecca L. Thomas (Bowker, 1989) and its sequel *Primaryplots 2* (Bowker, 1993) are book talk guides for use with children ages 4 to 8. *Middleplots 4,* for use with readers ages 8 to 12, is a successor to *Introducing Books* (Bowker, 1970) by John Gillespie and Diana Lembo, *Introducing More Books* (Bowker, 1978) by Diana L. Spirt, and *Introducing*

Bookplots 3 (Bowker, 1988), also by Diana L. Spirt. Also suggested are two series of book talk guides for older students. They are *Juniorplots* (Bowker, 1967) by John Gillespie and Diana Lembo, which contains an introduction on booktalking by Doris Cole; *More Juniorplots* (Bowker, 1977) by Gillespie with a special section on booktalking by Mary K. Chelton; *Juniorplots 3* (Bowker, 1987); *Juniorplots 4* (Bowker, 1993) and *Seniorplots* (Bowker, 1989). The last three were coauthored by John Gillespie and Corinne Naden.

Many public and school library systems also hold workshops or mini courses on booktalking and some of the veteran booktalkers in one's area can be invited to give advice and demonstrations. Booktalking is an exciting way to introduce books to young people, and it's always worth the effort.

1

Adventure and Mystery Stories

YOUNG readers, like their adult counterparts, enjoy escapist literature involving mysteries and tales of adventure. In this section, there are eleven such spellbinders that take the reader from the Catskills in New York State and the American Far West as far away as New Zealand and England, even ancient Egypt. Regardless of the setting, each scores high on quality writing and enjoyable reading.

Bellairs, John. *The Chessmen of Doom*
Dial, 1989, $13.95 (0-8037-0729-0); pap., Bantam, $3.50 (0-553-15884-8)

This is the seventh novel written by John Bellairs that features Johnny Dixon and Professor Childermass. The series began with *The Curse of the Blue Figurine* (pap., Bantam, 1984, $3.50) and *The Mummy, the Will and the Crypt* (Dial, 1983, $12.95; pap., Bantam, $3.50). Each title in the series is an exciting mystery adventure enlivened with large doses of fantasy and the occult. The straightforward plots move swiftly from one crisis to another, but the writing often contains a humorous play on words or a literary reference that adds a subtle touch to each incident. *The Chessmen of Doom* is written in the third person, and its locales are Maine and Massachusetts. The series is enjoyed by both girls and boys in grades 5 through 8.

Plot Summary

It is May in the mid-1950s in the small town of Duston Heights, Massachusetts, and elderly, somewhat eccentric Professor Roderick Childermass, a history teacher at nearby Haggstrum College, has just received an unusual letter from his recently deceased brother, Peregrine. It states that Roderick has inherited Perry's estate in Maine and $10 million if he fulfills specific conditions to be revealed later. The note also includes a strange four-line riddle in rhyme that makes reference to stars, a chessboard with pale-colored chessmen, and a room without light.

The Professor discusses this mysterious legacy with the Dixons, his friends across the street, and their young grandson, Johnny, who is living with them while his father serves in the Korean War. Johnny, a bright, bespectacled youngster, and Professor Childermass have formed a close friendship and have already shared many hair-raising adventures.

Within a few days, Perry's lawyer sends news about the conditions of the will: Roderick must spend the summer, June 15 through Labor Day, at the estate and keep it in good order without hired help. Roderick agrees and invites Johnny and his friend, Byron Ferguson, a.k.a. Fergie, to join him. After a few days of preparation including assembling camping gear, the three adventurers take off in the Professor's ancient Pontiac. At a small town named Stone Arabia, they get directions to the nearby Childermass estate. The property is enormous and is bordered on one side by the large island-dotted Lake Umbagog. Within the grounds are an abandoned astrological observatory, a huge monument in the shape of a column, an eerie family crypt with massive bronze doors, and the large family mansion capped on one corner by a tall tower. After the moving-in proceedings are completed, the three relax around an open fire. Suddenly the Professor jumps up. He has seen someone staring at them through a window. Although a search of the grounds is fruitless, the three see that someone has opened the gates of the tomb.

The next day while the boys play ball, the Professor explores the room in the turret. It is windowless, and among its contents is a chessboard, two of the elements mentioned in his brother's enigmatic poem. That evening, after a modest dinner at the only restaurant in Stone Arabia, the three return home to find the tomb doors again ajar. Inside, they find Perry's coffin open and empty. The next day the police are summoned, but no clues are uncovered.

Several days pass without incident until one night, after attending a movie in town, the three encounter a sinister, oddly dressed man who is accidentally jostled by the Professor. The ill-tempered stranger drops the case he is carrying. The contents, delicately carved ivory chessmen, obviously very rare and of museum quality, spill out onto the sidewalk.

On returning home, they discover light shining through cracks in the tower room. In their absence, someone has entered the mansion and left the light burning. During the night, Johnny is visited in his bedroom by a ghostlike apparition that whispers, "Don't let him do it. Stop him if you can."

Events become even more ominous the next morning, when the Professor reads in an old newspaper that the British Museum was robbed of some ivory chessmen only two weeks before.

That night Johnny is again visited by the ghost, which he now believes to be that of Peregrine Childermass. The ghost again begs him to prevent an unknown future event and adds mysteriously, "Crazy Alice has the key."

To relieve the growing tension, the Professor suggests a camping trip to Lake Umbagog. One day, without the Professor's permission, the two boys explore the lake in their rented rowboat. They land on an island with a solitary cabin. Peering through the windows, they see on a table the set of stolen ivory chessmen. This adventure is never mentioned to the Professor.

The next few weeks are uneventful. Whoever has been trying to frighten them into leaving the mansion has at least temporarily given up. The night skies, however, provide a different kind of excitement, with increasingly violent showers of meteors and sightings of giant comets that narrowly miss crashing to earth.

One evening, after a visit to town, the three return to the estate during a particularly spectacular and frightening celestial shower to find that all the lights are on in the mansion and that they are blocked from entering by an invisible wall. Two burning comets appear headed for earth. As they miraculously veer off into space, a terrific earthquake occurs, the lights go out, and the invisible barrier disappears.

The boys now realize that the strange celestial phenomena are somehow related to the mansion, the chessmen, and the mysterious stranger. They tell the Professor about their island adventure and, after some basic sleuthing, discover the stranger to be Edmund Stallybrass, a reclusive new resident. The three decide to explore his island by boat. Unfortunately, shortly after leaving the dock, they encounter such heavy fog and rain that they become lost and are grounded on the shores of an unknown island. Through the fog, they see, as in a mirage, a stone chapel that contains three coffins. Each has one of their names on it, along with an inscription indicating that each was drowned in the lake. All three race back to the lake and the safety of their rowboat. The boat accidentally overturns, but they are able to cling to it throughout the night until a police boat rescues them in the morning.

This latest occurrence convinces the Professor that, for the safety of the boys, they must return home, even though it is still a few days before Labor Day. Johnny and Fergie, however, are convinced that the Professor is far from abandoning the search for a solution to all these mysterious events, particularly when at home he is visited regularly by Dr. Coote, a friend who is a noted authority on magic and the occult. During one of these visits, Johnny and Fergie hide in the Professor's house and overhear talk of Stallybrass, his use of medieval chessmen to perform ceremonial magic, and a plan that the Professor and Dr. Coote have devised to return to Perry's estate on January 15, when there will be an eclipse of the moon and the necessary planetary alignment to ensure the successful performance of powerful magical rituals.

On the night of the 15th, the boys secretly board a train for Stone Arabia. Unfortunately, at the station, they are kidnapped by Stallybrass, who takes them to the underground crypt of a deserted church. They see the Professor and Dr. Coote lying in coffins, both under a powerful spell cast by the wizard Stallybrass. Johnny and Fergie are tied up, and all four are left to die in the sub-zero cold in the vault.

Miraculously, salvation comes in the form of an unusual woman dressed in tatters, who enters the crypt claiming she is a witch in search of scrapings from skulls and coffin wood for her potions. Johnny suddenly realizes that this is Crazy Annie, although she is incensed when he calls her this, stating that she is Mrs. Tripp, Anna Louise Tripp to be exact. By using her counteractive spells, she is able to waken the Professor and Dr. Coote. The Professor discovers that Mrs. Tripp owns a magical brooch shaped like a key that is able to combat evil spells. With the key, all five set off for the mansion and a final confrontation with Stallybrass.

They find him in a turret room surrounded by ritualistic paraphernalia including the chessmen, a human skull, and astrological devices. After blocking off himself and the room with an invisible shield the five cannot penetrate, he explains the purpose of his scheme. Through his years working as a medievalist in the British Museum, he discovered parts of rituals that could command the paths of comets. Peregrine Childermass had discovered similar, more complete versions and had invited Stallybrass to his mansion in Maine to combine their explorations into the occult. When Stallybrass found that Perry intended to use his work only to frighten humankind into living better lives, he murdered him, because his own plan was to assume world power after destroying large parts of the earth by bombardments of comets. Just as he is about to cause a rain of destruction from the skies, Mrs. Tripp, through the use of her key brooch, evokes the powers of light and goodness in time to thwart his plan and cause Stallybrass to be thrown from the tower to his death.

Although the Professor lost his inheritance when he left his late brother's estate before Labor Day, he receives a reward of £3,000 from the British

Museum for the return of the chessmen. Johnny and Fergie happily accept the Professor's invitation to accompany him to London to receive the reward in person.

Thematic Material

Although the boys and the Professor show great courage and resourcefulness throughout the book, this novel is intended to entertain and provide vicarious thrills rather than to develop moral values. Although short on characterization, this thriller contains good atmosphere, excellent use of setting, and lots of tension and suspense. The writer's cliff-hanging chapter endings and such stereotypical chill-producers as creaking floorboards, ghostly visitations, and empty coffins are used effectively in this tale of goodness overcoming the foulest of evildoers.

Book Talk Material

An explanation of Edward Gorey's suitably macabre illustrations for the dust jacket and frontispiece would produce interest in reading the book. Some thrilling passages are: the Professor receives his brother's letter and the riddle (pp. 3–5); the three arrive at Perry's estate (pp. 14–17); the Professor sees a face at the window (pp. 21–23); the discovery of the empty coffin (pp. 28–31); Johnny is visited by Perry's ghost (pp. 38–40); and the boys visit Stallybrass's island (pp. 57–61).

Additional Selections

Sam and Robert are convinced that their new neighbor is the real Frankenstein in Elizabeth Levy's *Frankenstein Moved In on the Fourth Floor* (Harper, 1979, $12.89; pap., $3.95). The sequel is *Dracula Is a Pain in the Neck* (Harper, 1983, $12.89; pap., $3.95).

The five youthful members of Shannon Gilligan's Millerton Detective Gang decide to protect the precious gems at a science exhibition because they believe that a robbery has been planned in *There's a Body in the Brontosaurus Room* (pap., Bantam, $2.99). An earlier title in this series is *The Clue in the Clock Tower* (pap., Bantam, 1991, $2.95).

In one of Scott Corbett's many "trick" books, *The Disappearing Dog Trick* (pap. Scholastic, 1983, $2.50), Korby and Fenton plan a secret night of camping, and then their dog disappears.

Three of the teammates on the Southside Sluggers search for three valuable baseball cards in a story that combines mystery and baseball, *The Great Baseball Card Hunt* (Simon & Schuster, 1992, $12) by Daniel A. Greenberg.

In Philippa Pearce's *The Way to Sattin Shore* (pap., Puffin, 1985, $3.95), the gravestone of Kate's father mysteriously disappears in this English story of a girl's search for the cause of her father's death.

Several books disappear from the Chickertown Library book sale in Avi's *Who Stole the Wizard of Oz?* (Knopf, 1981, $7.99; pap., McKay, David, 1990, $3.99).

Sixth-grader Susannah and her friends investigate strange fires at Miss Quigley's house that begin after she adopts Theresa, a foster child, in *Susannah and the Purple Mongoose Mystery* (Dutton, 1992, $15) by Patricia Elmore. Another in this series is *Susannah and the Blue House Mystery* (Dutton, 1980, $10.25; pap., Scholastic, 1990, $2.75).

About the Book

Book Report, May 1990, p. 44.
Booklist, November 15, 1989, p. 657.
Horn Book Guide, July 1989, p. 87.
Kirkus Reviews, January 12, 1989, p. 1744.
School Library Journal, October 1989, p. 114.
VOYA, February 1990, p. 369.
See also *Book Review Index,* 1989, p. 63; 1990, p. 62.

About the Author

Holtze, Sally Holmes, ed., *Fifth Book of Junior Authors and Illustrators.* Wilson, 1983, pp. 26–27.
Olendorf, Donna, ed., *Something about the Author.* Gale, 1992, Vol. 68, pp. 23–25.
Straub, Deborah A., ed., *Contemporary Authors* (New Revision Series). Gale, 1988, Vol. 25, pp. 50–51.

Boston, Lucy M. *A Stranger at Green Knowe*

Illus. by Peter Boston. Harcourt, 1961, $9.95 (0-15-281762-2); pap., $3.95 (0-15-281762-2)

Lucy M(aria) Boston (1892–1990) did not begin to write until she was over 60 years of age. Part of the inspiration to write came when she moved into a manor house at Hemingford Grey in Huntingdonshire, England. This became the model for the magical Green Knowe, the locale of the six novels in the series that has become a landmark in children's literature and a model for excellence in fantasy writing. The first title is *Children of Green Knowe* (pap., Harcourt, $3.95), first published in 1954, in which the owner of the manor house, the understanding and loving Mrs. Oldknow, is visited by her great-grandson Tolly, who is able to communicate and mingle with three children who lived in Green Knowe during the seventeenth century. In its sequel, *The River at Green Knowe* (pap., Harcourt, $3.95), Green Knowe is taken over for the summer by a family that includes young Ida Biggin and a governess, Miss Bun. Ida is joined by two refugee children, a Polish boy, Oskar, and a Chinese youngster, Ping. Together, the three share mystical adventures exploring the river that runs past the house. The third novel, *A Stranger at Green Knowe*, winner of the 1961 Carnegie Medal, is the only one in which elements of fantasy are not used directly, although the spell of the mansion and its grounds is still pervasive. In this novel, Ping comes to Green Knowe to visit Mrs. Oldknow. Ping, Tolly, and Mrs. Oldknow reappear in subsequent volumes in the series. The last, *The Stones of Green Knowe* (1976, now out of print), is set in 1120 and tells of the construction of the house. The character Tolly is modeled on the author's son, Peter, who brilliantly illustrated each of the Green Knowe books. These books are enjoyed by better, more introspective readers in grades 5 through 7.

Plot Summary

The gorilla, growing up in the rain forests of the Congo, is only two years old and therefore still considered a child. He loves to play with his young sister and accept affection from his mother and the other females. Most of all, he admires and tries to copy the actions of his courageous and caring father, the leader of the group, the Old Man. This massive, powerful gorilla guides his family to luxuriant feeding areas and refreshing watering holes and in return demands only obedience to his commands. When his oldest son challenges this authority, a fierce battle ensues. The Old Man emerges triumphant, and the son limps off into the jungle with his mate to form his own family.

The gorillas have few natural enemies, but one day the young gorilla senses danger in the air. The Old Man hastily begins moving the family to another feeding ground, but the menace keeps getting closer and closer. Suddenly the trap is sprung, and a group of natives led by a white hunter named Blair attacks the family. They are intent on capturing young animals for zoos in England. Before he and his sister are captured, the young gorilla sees both his mother and the courageous Old Man killed by the natives' arrows and the bullets from the white man's guns. The young gorilla, named Hanno after the sixth century B.C. Carthaginian navigator who explored the Atlantic coast of Africa and first reported seeing gorillas, is heartbroken by the death of his beloved sister, who could not endure the trauma of the capture and loss of her family. Hanno, however, survives and is soon transported to London, where he becomes one of the prize fixtures in the Regent's Park Zoo.

Eleven years pass, and Hanno is now a massive, full-grown gorilla radiant in his strength and well-formed body. Although he still chafes at life in captivity, he has established a bond and formed a neutrality pact with the Keeper, who admires this magnificent specimen of virility and physical power.

Into the Monkey House, one day, comes a group of youngsters on a field trip from the International Relief Society's Intermediate Hostel for Displaced Children. Among them is eleven-year-old Ping, a Chinese war refugee who has spent the past five years in various relief camps after surviving an enemy attack that destroyed both his family and home in Burma. He is so impressed with Hanno's size and majesty that when the rest move on to the Lion House, Ping begs permission to remain behind. From the Keeper, he learns a great deal about Hanno's habits and his past. He feeds him a peach, a gesture the Keeper tells him Hanno won't forget.

Ping is a lonely but enterprising youngster who longs for the stability and love of a family. The summer before had been one of the few joyful periods of his life—he was invited, together with another refugee, Oskar, to spend time with young Ida Biggin at the lovely manor house Green Knowe in the Midlands. This summer the owner, Mrs. Oldknow, is back in residence at Green Knowe, but Ida makes a personal plea to the old lady. Mrs. Oldknow, whose great-grandson Tolly will not be spending his usual summer with her, contacts Ping and invites him to take Tolly's place. The boy is overjoyed. Ping fondly remembers the great house and garden both surrounded by a moat fed from the local river and the bridge that leads from the house to the estate's dense, lush bamboo grove and nearby Toseland Thicket.

On the train to Green Knowe, Ping reads a fellow passenger's newspaper and learns that Hanno escaped from the London zoo the night before. In fact, Hanno, who curled up in an empty lorry to rest, has now been transported to the very part of England where Ping is headed.

At Green Knowe, Ping and Mrs. Oldknow form an immediate friendship. She is kind and understanding and he polite and anxious to be accepted. Ping begins to explore the thicket and receives permission to build a hut in the bamboo grove. The following day, when he returns to his private sanctuary with a picnic and provisions given him by his benefactor, his solitude is broken by the discovery that another being is sharing his refuge—Hanno. Ping suppresses his initial fear and begins feeding the magnificent animal he has never forgotten. Hanno responds to his kindness with friendly grunts and gestures. Ping cannot bring himself to tell anyone, even his beloved Mrs. Oldknow, about Hanno's presence in the thicket. Instead, for the next two days, he secretly takes food to Hanno and feels a guilty sense of wonder and kinship during the hours he spends with the awe-inspiring creature.

The pursuers, who have been joined by Blair, the famous hunter and gorilla expert, have traced Hanno to the area around Green Knowe and arrive to question Mrs. Oldknow. In spite of Ping's assurances that Hanno is not hiding in the thicket, Blair and company plan to come back the next day for a thorough search.

That night, there is a fierce electric storm that fells a large tree, forming a second bridge from the thicket to the mansion and garden. With Ping's help, Hanno manages to cross this bridge in the morning and hide in the garden, eluding the hunters searching the bamboo grove. However, at this moment, a crazed cow that has escaped from a local farm races into the estate grounds and charges Ping. Hanno catapults from the garden and throws the cow over his mighty shoulders, killing her seconds before Ping would have been gored. The commotion arouses the hunters. Blair appears. Hanno, remembering his ancient enemy, attacks. There is a gunshot, and Hanno falls dead with a bullet through his heart. Ping is inconsolable until he realizes that in Hanno's case it was better to die free than live as a slave in captivity. Mrs. Oldknow forgives Ping for deceiving her about Hanno's presence and, to show how much she loves this courageous little waif, offers him a permanent home at Green Knowe.

Thematic Material

Whereas the other books in this series deal with the continuity of the past and present, this book's central theme is the oneness of life and the unity between human and so-called beast. In addition, this is a heartwarming story that stresses the need for compassion and understanding toward all living things. It also explores the nature and value of freedom as well as the terrible crime of cruelty toward animals, whether perpetrated by hunters or well-intentioned zookeepers. Ping's ethical dilemma and the boy's loneliness and longing for a stable family are two other important subjects. The book is also instructive in the amount of gorilla lore it contains. The author's poetic, lyrical writing style is another highlight. In an autobiographical note in the English edition of the novel, she states: "I believe children, even the youngest, love good language, and that they see, feel, understand, and communicate more, not less, than grownups. Therefore I never write down to them, but try to evoke that new, brilliant awareness that is their world." This book is a shining example of that commitment.

Book Talk Material

With a small group, one could use the many black-and-white illustrations to arouse interest. Some important passages are: the quarrel between the Old Man and his rebellious son (pp. 18–21); the Old Man and his family try to avoid the hunters (pp. 26–30); Hanno and his sister are captured (pp. 30–34); Ping sees Hanno at the zoo (pp. 38–40); the Keeper tells Ping about Hanno, who is fed a peach (pp. 46–50); Ping reads about Hanno's escape (pp. 58–60); and from his bamboo hideaway, Ping encounters Hanno in the thicket (pp. 90–95).

Additional Selections

An African-American girl and an Australian boy are so shocked at the treatment baboons receive in their African research station that they kidnap two of them and go live with them in the jungle in *Rescue! An African Adventure* (Dial, 1992, $14) by Victor Kelleher.

A Polynesian boy conquers his fear of the sea in the Newbery Medal winner *Call It Courage* (Macmillan, 1968, $13.95; pap., $3.95) by Armstrong Sperry.

Eric Knight tells of a four-hundred-mile journey through Great Britain by a faithful collie in *Lassie Come Home* (Holt, 1978, $16.95).

The last wolf in England, Greycub, must outwit the frightening horror of death at the hands of the Hunter in Melvin Burgess's *The Cry of the Wolf* (Tambourine, 1992, $13).

In the fantasy *Between the Cracks* (Dial, 1992, $14) by Joyce Wolf, eighth-grader Bentley, a feisty young girl, and friend Charles meet a villainous magician, Mordicus, and his talking raven, Klack.

The Lemming Condition (Harper, 1976, $13) by Alan Arkin is a modern parable in which young Bubber, while finding out about his species, also reveals a great deal about how humans behave.

Jim Hawkins sets out for the adventure of a lifetime in the classic story by Robert Louis Stevenson of pirates and murder most foul, *Treasure Island* (many editions available).

About the Author

Chevalier, Tracy, ed., *Twentieth-Century Children's Writers* (3rd ed.). St. James, 1989, pp. 119–121.

Commire, Anne, ed., *Something about the Author.* Gale, 1980, Vol. 19, pp. 38–45.

de Montreville, Doris, and Hill, Donna, eds., *Third Book of Junior Authors.* Wilson, 1972, pp. 44–45.

Kirkpatrick, D. L., ed., *Twentieth-Century Children's Writers* (2nd ed.). St. Martin's, 1983, pp. 110–111.

Locher, Frances C., ed., *Contemporary Authors.* Gale, 1978, Vols. 73–76, pp. 72–73.

Senick, Gerard J., ed., *Children's Literature Review.* Gale, 1978, Vol. 3, pp. 20–29.

Ward, Martha, ed., *Authors of Books for Young People* (3rd ed.). Scarecrow, 1990, p. 74.

Conrad, Pam. *Stonewords: A Ghost Story*

Harper, 1990, $14 (0-06-021315-9); pap., $3.95 (0-06-440354-8)

Since the mid-1980s Pam Conrad has written a number of excellent novels for young people. Among them are *Prairie Songs* (pap., Harper, 1987, $3.95), set in turn-of-the-century Nebraska, in which an adolescent girl witnesses the gradual mental deterioration of a fragile young wife who can't adjust to frontier life; and *My Daniel* (Harper, 1989, $12.89; pap., $3.95; condensed in *Juniorplots 4,* Bowker, 1993, pp. 23–28), a structurally challenging dual-level novel, part of which takes place in contemporary New York and involves a visit to the Museum of Natural History by an eighty-year-old grandmother, Julia Summerwaite, and her two grandchildren. The other part, evoked by memory, is set in Nebraska many years before and tells the story of the discovery of a dinosaur skeleton by Julia and her brother. *Stonewords,* subtitled *A Ghost Story,* involves two Zoes, one a modern girl and the other a girl who died in a fire over a hundred years before. There is suspense, mystery, time travel, and a series of revelations at the end that leaves the reader frightened but satisfied. It is read by youngsters in grades 5 through 8.

Plot Summary

Eleven-year-old Zoe has a friend, a best friend named Zoe Louise. But it is a strange friendship, for one girl lives in the present and one in the past. Zoe lives in the house where Zoe Louise used to live long ago. The two girls are connected to each other by a back staircase in the house. They are ghosts in each other's lives.

Zoe has been aware of Zoe Louise for a long time. She first saw the other girl soon after she came to live with her loving grandparents—Grandma and PopPop—and their fat old dog, Oscar. Grandma and PopPop are unaware of Zoe Louise's existence. Only Oscar knows. No one else sees or hears her.

Zoe lives with Grandma and PopPop because her own mother is peculiar and perhaps, in fact, just a little bit crazy. That's what everyone says. Her mother just dumped Zoe with her grandparents when the little girl was four. Now and again her mother turns up. When she does, she always wants to visit the nearby cemetery, and she takes Zoe with her. Grandma tells Zoe that her mother had years ago fallen in love with the stoneword on a tombstone—Zoe—and she always said she would one day name her own daughter after that person.

Most of the time Zoe and Zoe Louise get along very well. Zoe notices, however, that as she grows older, Zoe Louise never seems to change. Although Zoe Louise was older to begin with, by the time Zoe is nearly eleven, both girls appear to be about the same age.

Zoe Louise keeps telling Zoe that her birthday is coming and that her Papa is bringing her a pony. Zoe gets tired of hearing the story.

One day Zoe's mother turns up and wants to go out in the woods for some honeysuckle vines. Zoe goes with her. She comes upon what her mother calls memory roses, planted, she says, "when that little girl died." Over one hundred years ago.

Soon after, PopPop discovers that the playhouse he fixed up for Zoe has been vandalized. Zoe is certain that the vandal is Zoe Louise. When she asks the girl about the destruction, Zoe Louise merely says that she got tired of waiting for Zoe to come back one day, so she kept "moving the furniture around until she got it right." Suddenly Zoe Louise says that her Papa is coming and she must get home. But she has her shoes off, so she grabs Zoe's sneakers. Zoe puts the other girl's scuffed-up shoes in her pockets, and suddenly her feet begin to move on their own. They run right after Zoe Louise. And for the first time, Zoe follows Zoe Louise up the back stairs and sees the home of her friend.

Zoe becomes curious about her mother's talk of a young girl who died so many years ago and what she sees and hears in Zoe Louise's home. Sometime later, Zoe comes upon some old newspapers in the basement of her grandparents' home. They date from the late 1800s. She reads them to see if they contain the story of the death of an eleven-year-old girl.

When Zoe once again goes up the staircase to look for Zoe Louise, she sees a long, black dress hanging against the wall. It is a funeral dress. "Oh, Zoe Louise," Zoe cries. She knows that Zoe Louise is actually dead. It shouldn't matter, she realizes, that an eleven-year-old girl died over a hundred years ago. But it does matter to Zoe, and part of her says that it isn't too late to change things.

The next day Zoe goes to the old cemetery and finds the tombstone bearing the name of Zoe Louise's mother, but she can't find a tombstone with the date of Zoe Louise's death. Maybe there is still time.

Back in the basement, going over the old newspapers once again, Zoe is confronted by Zoe Louise, who has never looked more terrible. Zoe begs her to go home, but she refuses. Instead, Zoe Louise snatches Oscar and runs off.

Zoe chases after her friend and confronts her. When Zoe Louise runs to the bluff overlooking the water, Zoe senses that the cliff is giving way. She tackles her friend, and they both end up on the grass. Oscar is saved too. Zoe Louise is angry because her party dress is soiled.

Later, PopPop tells Zoe of a story he read in the old newspapers she found. It says that an eleven-year-old named Zoe Louise suffered an untimely death in a fire in the kitchen of her home. Now Zoe knows what she must do. She once again goes up the back staircase into Zoe Louise's world. She watches in horror as her friend lights her birthday candles and her clothes catch fire. While Zoe Louise struggles against the flames, Zoe calls to her. Finally, even though she is about the same size as her friend, Zoe picks her up and carries her to safety. It is an act of strength, and of love.

Zoe doesn't remember how long she stays in the stairwell where she has carried Zoe Louise to safety. But when her friend looks into her eyes and doesn't see her, Zoe knows that she has succeeded. Zoe Louise is now alive in her own time. They are no longer ghosts to each other.

The staircase never works again for Zoe. And Zoe Louise never returns. One strange thing does happen, though. On her mother's next unexpected visit, Zoe asks her about the memory rosebushes and the little girl who died. Her mother says doesn't know what she's talking about.

Thematic Material

This story has a strange, other-world quality that speaks of the pull of loneliness and the power of love. Zoe is a sensitive child but unafraid as she reaches out into another dimension to save the friend she has grown to love. It is also the story of a warm and loving relationship between grandchild and grandparents, and how a sensitive child adapts to and reacts to a mother who is in some ways more child than parent. This is a book for the more thoughtful reader, who will be rewarded with its messages of friendship, love, and caring.

Book Talk Material

Young readers will be attracted by the growth of friendship and the interaction between Zoe and her friend of another time. See: Zoe Louise first appears (pp. 13–14); Zoe Louise is naked in the snow (pp. 24–25); Zoe first goes up the staircase (pp. 36–39); Zoe Louise wrecks the playhouse (pp. 57–62); Zoe finds the old newspapers and begins to unravel the strange tale (pp. 81-84).

Additional Selections

Natalie Babbitt's *Goody Hall* (pap., Farrar, $3.50) features a mystery involving robbers, diamonds, a missing father, and a new tutor in the Goody family.

An unusual will and an equally unusual group of legatees highlight Ellen Raskin's Newbery Medal-winning puzzler, *The Westing Game* (Dutton, 1978, $15.95; pap., Puffin, $3.99).

Ivy, from a poor family, helps Martha emerge from her cocoon in Zilpha Keatley Snyder's *The Changeling* (Macmillan, 1985, $12.95; pap., Dell, $3.95).

In Evelyn Wilde Mayerson's *The Cat Who Escaped from Steerage* (Scribner, 1990, $12.95), Chanah is a nine-year-old Polish girl emigrating to America in ship's steerage, where she is trying to keep a cat hidden.

Eighth-grader Casey wonders if her friend Mackenzie is really psychic or if it is coincidental that her predictions come true in Stephanie S. Tolan's *The Witch of Maple Park* (Morrow, 1992, $14).

In Chris Brodien-Jones's fantasy, *The Dreamkeepers* (Macmillan, 1992, $13.95), two children visiting their grandparents in Wales become involved in a struggle between the forces of good and evil.

A wizard named Zebulum and his talking crow move into a dilapidated castle only to meet its resident ghost in Sarah Hayes's *Crumbling Castle* (Candlewick, 1992, $13.95).

About the Book

Booklist, March 1, 1990, p. 1338.
Center for Children's Books Bulletin, May 1990, p. 211.

Horn Book, September 1990, p. 600.
Horn Book Guide, January 1990, p. 254.
Kirkus Reviews, February 23, 1990, p. 103.
School Library Journal, May 1990, p. 103.
VOYA, January 1990, p. 101.
Wilson Library Bulletin, January 1991, p. 15.
See also *Book Review Digest,* 1990, p. 379; and *Book Review Index,* 1990, p. 168; 1991, p. 190.

About the Author

Commire, Anne, ed., *Something about the Author.* Gale, 1988, Vol 52, pp. 29–31.
Holtze, Sally Holmes, ed., *Sixth Book of Junior Authors and Illustrators.* Wilson, 1989, pp. 64–66.
May, Hal, ed., *Contemporary Authors.* Gale, 1987, Vol 121, pp. 110–111.
Senick, Gerard J., ed., *Children's Literature Review.* Gale, 1989, Vol 18, pp. 86–89.

George, Jean Craighead. *On the Far Side of the Mountain*

Dutton, 1990, $14.95 (0-525-44563-3); pap., Puffin, $3.99 (0-14-034248-6)

Jean George's father was an entomologist and her twin brothers, wildlife ecologists. It was natural, therefore, for her to develop a flair for nature writing. With her husband, John L. George, she first produced such now out-of-print titles as *Volpes, the Red Fox* and *Meph, the Pet Skunk.* Then, on her own, she wrote such excellent titles as the 1973 Newbery winner *Julie of the Wolves* (Harper, 1974, $14.95; pap., $3.95; condensed in *More Juniorplots,* Bowker, 1977, pp. 213–217). This is the story of a young Inuit girl's oppressive life in Barrow, Alaska, the horror of her arranged marriage, and her amazing journey of escape alone across miles of arctic tundra to what she hopes will be freedom. *My Side of the Mountain* (Dutton, 1988, $14.95; pap., $4.95; condensed in *Introducing Books,* Bowker, 1970, pp. 144–147) was first published in 1959 and tells the story of an adolescent Thoreau, Sam Gribley, who decides to live off the land on a wild piece of family property in the Catskill Mountains in New York State. This first-person account covers one year of hardship, deprivation, and finally triumph. It is filled with fascinating details on wildlife and takes an unsentimental view of nature. The sequel begins two years later. Sam, still in the Catskills with his peregrine falcon, Frightful, faces a crisis when his sister joins him in his solitary retreat. Both books are enjoyed in grades 4 through 8.

Plot Summary

Teenager Sam Gribley loves the wilderness, so much so that, before this book opens, he has run off to live alone in the wilderness of the Catskill Mountains of the eastern United States. In this continuation of the wilderness saga, Sam still lives off the land in the midst of the natural surroundings he loves, but he is no longer alone. His beloved falcon, Frightful, is with him, and so is his pesty younger sister, Alice.

In the beginning, Sam was reluctant to have Alice share his peace and quiet. However, some time ago, when their parents and brothers and sisters left the wilderness to return to civilization so that their father could find work on the docks, thirteen-year-old Alice refused to go with them. To Sam's surprise, his parents agreed to let Alice remain with him, on their own, for a year. His mother reasoned that Alice could continue her education through correspondence courses, and she would be safer in the woods than in the mean city streets. Now, as time has passed, even Sam the loner grudgingly admits to himself that, as ornery as Alice can be, it's nice to have her to talk to once in a while. An added benefit is that Alice's scientific mind, with its constant search for new inventions, keeps him on the alert. For instance, Alice wants Sam to read a book about making electricity with water mills so that they can have some light in their mountain retreat. Sam refuses to go that far. He doesn't want light or electricity or anything that isn't natural to the woods.

One day, a man who calls himself Leon Longbridge, the conservation officer, disturbs Sam's wilderness. Longbridge tells Sam he has learned that the boy is harboring a member of an endangered species—Frightful, the peregrine falcon. Longbridge says he must confiscate the bird. She will be taken to the university where she will be cared for and bred. Although Sam protests, he is helpless to save Frightful and distraught at her loss. Not only will Sam miss her and her help in finding food, but he fears that Frightful will die because she is so bonded to him.

Alice was not in their camp when Longbridge arrived, so Sam leaves her a note about Frightful and goes off to be by himself for a while. When he returns, he can tell that Alice has come back, although she seems to have run off once again. At first Sam is unconcerned. But as days go by with no signs of her, he realizes that his sister has really left their mountain retreat. He speaks about Alice's disappearance to his friend Bando, who teaches English in a nearby college on the Hudson River and stays in the mountains on vacations.

Sam remembers how Bando cared for him during his first months on the mountain, making sure he came to no harm. Now Sam must make sure that his sister is safe, wherever she has gone and whatever she has decided to do. With Bando, he sets off to track Alice, who apparently is traveling in the company of her pet pig, Crystal.

Alice left her brother a cryptic message about "thinking waterfalls," so Sam uses some tracking methods of his own to follow his sister and her pig. He discovers a compass she made to determine her direction in the forest, and although Sam doesn't know exactly where Alice is heading, reasoning leads him in the direction of the Helderbergs. These mountains are not as spectacular as the Catskills or Adirondacks, but they have lots of waterfalls. They also reportedly harbor a nest of goshawks, the most aggressive of all birds of prey. Yes, Sam decides, that's exactly where Alice would go.

Following his sister's trail as well as unmistakable signs of Crystal's foraging, Sam, with Bando's help, ends up in the small mountain town of Livingstonville. There they get news of Alice that leads them to the Monroe Farm, where they find Crystal. Alice has left her pig for safekeeping while she continues her journey.

Before Sam sets out on the last part of his tracking, he and Bando learn from the local librarian that there is a great deal of interest in the area concerning hawks and falcons. This is quite unusual. Bando reasons that since these birds are rare, they are precious, and precious things are worth a lot of money. The librarian tells them that a man from Saudi Arabia has been in the region inquiring about such birds. Arab sheiks especially prize falcons and will pay very high prices for them.

Sam soon learns more distressing news. Leon Longbridge, who took Frightful away is not a conservation officer at all. He obviously used that deception to capture Frightful and surely is about to sell her. While Bando goes in search of the real authorities, Sam looks for Alice. All signs indicate that she is camped right in the midst of the men who are attempting to steal these valuable birds.

Sam does find Alice safe and sound. The true authorities come to the rescue and capture the would-be falcon-nappers. In the commotion, Alice is lost again. Where has she gone? This time Sam finds her in the act of stealing a baby goshawk from the nest of these most aggressive birds! He can't believe that she would attempt such a foolhardy act, but she explains that she did it for him, to make up for the loss of Frightful. Sam's heart melts when she places the small, beautiful bird in his gloved hands.

But Sam knows he cannot accept Alice's gift. The baby bird must be returned to its nest and family. While they wait for nightfall to do so, Sam hears a familiar "Creee, creee" sound. He knows it is Frightful. She is safe and free! Alice tells Sam that she found Frightful being held captive and cut her free.

Sam knows that all he has to do is to whistle and Frightful will come and alight on his fist. She will be his again. Frightful looks down from her rock and waits for the whistle. With all his heart, Sam wants to call her. But he cannot. Why? Alice asks him. Because if she is free, Frightful will breed, Sam tells her, and there will be wild peregrines on the cliffs again. Although it breaks his heart, Frightful must be free.

Sam and Alice return the baby goshawk to its nest. Later, Bando tells Sam that a miller in the nearby town knows how to convert a water mill to electricity. Sam says he'll look into it. It's time, and it would make Alice happy.

Sam also thinks he might see about getting a falconer's license so that he can raise these rare birds and return them to the wild. He feels qualified because he knows what it's like to set one free.

Thematic Material

This is a nature story that shows the true love of the wild of two resourceful young people. Both Sam and his sister are portrayed as unusually independent youngsters who feel completely at home in nature in all its forms. Their inventiveness and ingenuity, as well as Sam's reluctant concessions to "modern inventions," are a refreshing change in the computerized, electrified, often glitzy world of the late twentieth century. The pair's independence may take some getting used to for the average reader, as will their parents' acceptance of their life in the wilderness.

Book Talk Material

The various ways that Sam and Alice adapt to their life in the wilderness will serve as a fascinating introduction to this nature-loving book. See: Alice's mill (pp. 17–18); Sam tries to make a sling (pp. 29–30); Alice and Sam learn from the beavers and also build a millhouse (pp. 41–53); Sam finds Alice's first compass (pp. 68–70); and Sam learns to think like a pig (pp. 81–91).

Additional Selections

A young white boy and an old black sailor are shipwrecked on a Caribbean island in *The Cay* (Doubleday, 1987, $13.95; pap., Avon, $3.50) by Theodore Taylor.

Big Red (Holiday, 1956, $15.95; pap., Bantam, $3.99), James A. Kjelgaard's classic story, tells about Danny and his champion Irish setter. Sequels include *Irish Red* (Holiday, 1951, $15.95; pap., Bantam, $3.50).

In *Run Far, Run Fast* (pap., Blue Heron, 1989, $6.95) by Walt Morey, recently orphaned Mick Lyons escapes the authorities and rides the rails.

Two brothers explore an abandoned amusement park and begin a search that leads to danger and excitement in Willo Davis Roberts's *Scared Stiff* (Macmillan, 1991, $13.95).

Flynn, his little sister, and their cat spend two harrowing days floating in a crate lost on the high seas in a novel set in Australia, *Adrift,* by Allan Baillie (Viking, 1992, $14).

Matthew talks to a red-tailed hawk who, over a period of years, helps him explore his senses and the beauty of nature in the pensive novel *Matthew's Meadow* (Harcourt, 1992, $14.95) by Corinne Demas-Bliss.

Downwind (pap., Dell, 1987, $2.75) by Louise Moeri is the dramatic story of a near-disaster at a nuclear power plant.

About the Book

Booklist, April 1, 1990, p. 1550; September 15, 1990, p. 111.
Center for Children's Books Bulletin, June 1990, p. 238.
Horn Book, July 1990, p. 454.
Horn Book Guide, January 1990, p. 242.
Kirkus Reviews, April 1, 1990, p. 498.
New York Times Book Review, May 20, 1990, p. 42.
School Library Journal, June 1990, p. 120.
See also *Book Review Digest,* 1990, p. 650; and *Book Review Index,* 1991, p. 294.

About the Author

Block, Ann, and Riley, Carolyn, eds., *Children's Literature Review.* Gale, 1976, Vol. 1, pp. 89–94.
Chevalier, Tracy, ed., *Twentieth-Century Children's Writers* (3rd ed.). St. James, 1989, pp. 381–383.
Estes, Glenn E., ed., *American Writers for Children since 1960: Fiction* (Dictionary of Literary Biography: Vol. 52). Gale, 1986, pp. 168–174.
Fuller, Muriel, ed., *More Junior Authors.* Wilson, 1963, pp. 99–100.
Kirkpatrick, D. L., ed., *Twentieth-Century Children's Writers* (2nd ed.). St. Martin's, 1983, pp. 318–320.
May, Hal, and Straub, Deborah R., eds., *Contemporary Authors* (New Revision Series). Gale, 1989, Vol. 25, pp. 156–158.
Olendorf, Donna, ed., *Something about the Author.* Gale, 1992, Vol. 68, pp. 78–85.
Ward, Martha, ed., *Authors of Books for Young People* (3rd ed.). Scarecrow, 1990, p. 264.

Hildick, E. W. *The Case of the Dragon in Distress: A McGurk Mystery*
Macmillan, 1991, $13.95 (0-02-743931-3)

This English writer, who has had a long and prolific career writing for young people, is primarily known for his books in series. His first dealt with a milkman named Louie and began in 1965 with *Louie's Lot,* in which Louie tests all the young applicants who want to accompany him on his rounds by such means as encounters with vicious dogs and trying to decipher patrons' handwriting. At present, Hildick is best known for two other series. The first involves the Ghost Squad, four lively ghosts who communicate with a youthful confidant and are able to solve and sometimes prevent crimes. The series began with *The Ghost Squad Breaks Through* (Dutton, 1984, $12.95). There are several additional titles available. The second series involves the young detective Jack McGurk and the group of fellow sleuths known as the McGurk Organization. The first in this series, *The Nose Knows* (o.p.), was published in 1973. Subsequent titles begin with *The Case of the* . . . . In 1990, this series changed course and began including elements of fantasy. In the first of these, *The Case of the Dragon in Distress,* for example, the McGurk group travels to twelfth-century England and encounters a damsel in distress, dungeons, castles, and an ancestor of Jack's called The McGurk, whom the boy must free so that he will be born one day. The second McGurk fantasy is *The Case of the Weeping Witch* (Macmillan, 1992, $13.95). These books are enjoyed by readers in grades 4 through 7.

Plot Summary

It is only the first week of summer vacation, but McGurk, head of the McGurk detective group, is already getting antsy. Joey Rockaway knows why—the usual reason, no case to work on. The McGurk Organization, composed of McGurk, Joey, Wanda Grieg, Willie Sandowsky, Brains Bellingham, and Mari Toshimura, is pretty adept at solving mysteries.

Before this adventure, the group had become fascinated with castles, long-ago England and King Arthur and the Knights of the Round Table. They had even designed shields for each member. When their teacher heard about their interest, she made the Age of Chivalry the main topic in history class for a few weeks. All the students really got into life in the twelfth century. And all this propels the McGurk group into their tightest adventure ever.

It starts with Brains Bellingham and his black boxes. Brains comes to a McGurk meeting with a flat black box for each of the six members. He explains that the boxes are battery-operated transmitting/receiving sets—walkie-talkies—and Brains has been working on them so that all of the members can keep in constant touch. Trouble is, whatever Brains did has caused the boxes to work only at night. However, McGurk thinks that's fine; now they can all keep in touch after they've gone to bed.

Joey tests his black box that evening as soon as he gets in bed. All he can bring in is a faint hiss. He falls asleep, but when he wakes up, he and the whole McGurk group have been transported back to twelfth-century England! And they are immediately caught up in a hotbed of castle intrigue.

At first the group thinks that the castle is being protected by a fiery dragon that is guarding a captured princess. But the dragon turns out to be a phony; inside the dragon skin are Gwyneth and Gareth, twins who, the young detectives later learn, have themselves been transported back in time from seventeenth-century England. The twins explain that the princess in the castle is not a captive at all; she is the evil Melisande the Bad. The twins are her prisoners and must do her bidding. Melisande also has other prisoners, whom she keeps in the dungeon.

The McGurk group is escorted to the castle, where they meet Princess Melisande. She doesn't *look* evil, with her bright blue eyes and silvery-gold hair. In fact, her lady-in-waiting, Lady Polly, looks far more threatening than Melisande. But McGurk and friends quickly learn just how evil the princess really is. For one thing, she hangs people from trees if they don't obey her. And for another, she drinks human blood. She is not a vampire. Instead, she gets leeches to suck the blood out of people, and then she eats the leeches! This news leaves the young detectives understandably distressed.

They are also disturbed by a tour of the dungeons. The prisoners look pale and emaciated. Perhaps the astounding story of the blood-sucking leeches really is true. The young detectives learn that one of the prisoners is Prince Geoffrey, the son of the king of England. Another is an Irish chieftain named McGurk, an ancestor of the modern McGurk, who quickly realizes that if prisoner McGurk doesn't get out of the dungeon alive, detective McGurk might not even exist.

But how to escape? It's not going to be easy. The evil princess is currently fascinated with all sorts of scientific marvels—like zippers on windbreakers—that the young detectives are able to show her. Eventually, of course, they are going to run out of amusements. Then, surely it will be the dungeon—and the leeches—for them.

Gareth and Gwyneth tell them about a secret passage in the castle, a passage that the twins themselves discovered when they were back in their own century.

At first the detectives and the twins try to escape from the castle under the dragon skin. Alas, Joey loses his shoe, and they are all discovered. They end up in the dreaded dungeon waiting to be tortured.

With the help of information the twins learned in their own time and Mari's voice-throwing ability to disarm the guards, the plucky young detectives discover the long-hidden secret passageway. They cannot free the other prisoners, who are too weak to escape on their own, but the newcomers vow to find the king of England and enlist his aid. They will return for the prisoners.

With McGurk in charge, the detectives and the twins find their way through the hidden passage and out of the castle. They set off in search of King Henry II of England, who is nearby at his hunting camp. When they reach the camp, they are taken to the tent of the king, who, they are surprised to see, has red hair and freckles. He is most grateful for their news and vows to effect a rescue of Prince Geoffrey and all the other prisoners. He also vows to reward the young detectives upon his return.

In the meantime, the McGurk Organization deserves a rest. They have had a busy time of it. Before they drift off to sleep, McGurk tells them that at least they did what they set out to do. Mission accomplished!

At once the black boxes, which they are still carrying, begin to crackle and sputter. A voice booms: "You have just uttered the final magic words, Sir Jack McGurk! Thy mission is, well and truly, accomplished!"

Joey wakes up in his own bed at dawn.

Could it have been a dream? If so, it appears that it was a dream all six members of the McGurk Organization shared. Later that morning (in the twentieth century), they realize that they all had exactly the same experience.

Brains declares that he has either discovered a time machine or a dream machine. The debate goes on. Isn't it funny, Wanda says, how much Princess Melisande looked like their archenemy Sandra Ennis; even their names are similar. They recognize other characters too.

Even if they can't quite decide what happened to them, they figure that King Henry must have successfully rescued the other prisoners in the

central characters in the other series. In *Eat Your Poison, Dear* (Macmillan, 1986, $13.95; pap. Avon, $3.50), Sebastian discovers that a flu epidemic crippling his eighth-grade classmates is really a case of premeditated food poisoning. *Dew Drop Dead* combines a fine mystery story with a more serious theme about homeless people when a homeless man becomes a suspect in a murder. These series are enjoyed by readers in grades 4 through 6.

Plot Summary

Thirteen-year-old Sebastian Barth lives in rural Connecticut, in the town of Pembroke. As the story opens, Sebastian has been leading a rather happy life. He has his own radio show for kids at the local radio station where his father is the station manager; his mother runs a successful restaurant in the area, so he eats well; and he has two best friends: David Lepinsky, whose father, Josh, is a writer; and Corrie Wingate, whose father is a minister. Even though David regards Corrie as "Sebastian's girl-friend," the three of them get along well together for the most part, and they all enjoy a mystery.

Life starts to fall apart for Sebastian, however, when he loses his job at the station because of cutbacks. Worse yet, it looks like his father may lose his job too. If that happens, they may have to leave the area. This has begun to cause friction between Sebastian's parents, since his mother does not want to give up her successful restaurant business.

To escape the tension at home, Sebastian takes his bike and persuades David and Corrie to ride with him out to the Dew Drop Inn, now boarded up and apparently abandoned. Both David and Corrie are glad to get out of their respective homes for a while. David's father has "writer's block" and is difficult to live with, and Corrie's father is upset because so few people have responded to his desire to help the homeless in the area with a food-and-shelter program at the church.

At the Dew Drop Inn, the three young people see that a window has been forced open, and they decide to investigate. After some argument about the legality of their actions, they decide that in the best interest of police work they should go inside and look around. Corrie suggests they have a new mystery for David's father—*Dew Drop Dead.* They laugh and enter the inn.

The laughter stops upstairs when they come upon a body in one of the rooms. The three beat a hasty retreat, and once outside the inn decide that they must report what they have seen to Police Chief Alex Theopoulos. The chief, along with his new deputy, Rebecca Quinn, are skeptical about their story at first but agree to investigate. When Alex and Rebecca return from the inn, they report that there was no body!

The three young people are stunned. They are certain they saw a man in a red-and-black hunting shirt. They are also certain the man was dead.

Alex and his deputy agree to return to the inn the next day to investigate more thoroughly. The three children accompany them. They find evidence of people living there, who Corrie says must be some of the homeless people her father is concerned about, but no dead body.

Sebastian is determined to prove that they saw something, and he resolves to go back to the inn. In the meantime, the boys agree to help Corrie work with the youth group giving out food and clothes to homeless people. Sebastian is amazed to discover how many people need help even in rural Connecticut. Reverend Wingate, Corrie's father, brings a number of them into the church as a temporary shelter until help can be found for them. Among them are loud, demanding Estelle Barker and her children; a man named Raymond Elveri, who is estranged from his family; and a man who looks like a caged animal and keeps repeating, "I am Abraham." Corrie takes a special interest in him, coaxing him to eat.

Sebastian and David return to the Dew Drop Inn and begin to search the area looking for clues to prove their story. What they find is a body—the dead man they had seen earlier. They are certain it is the same body, even though the red-and-black shirt is missing.

The police investigate once again; this time the body is where the boys reported it to be. When Sebastian and David go to the church to tell Corrie what they discovered, a new shock awaits them. Draped on one of the church chairs is the red-and-black shirt they had first seen on the dead man. The boys speculate that someone in that room is the murderer.

Corrie is shocked when Abraham, whom she has befriended, is charged with the murder.

Some good police work by Alex and Rebecca, plus some more sleuthing by Sebastian and David, uncover the truth. Abraham is not guilty of murder, because there was no murder. The dead man was Kevin Moore, a troubled young homeless man and a heavy drinker. He and Abraham had been camping out at the abandoned Dew Drop Inn. Kevin, intoxicated, froze to death one night. Abraham, already a confused individual, was in the inn when Sebastian and his friends snooped around. Scared, he carried the body into the woods, taking Kevin's shirt for warmth.

Where is Abraham now? Corrie asks the police chief. Abraham has been released. He is "somewhere out there."

Later, the three young sleuths learn that Abraham is really Bill Conroy, and his sister and her husband are the owners of the abandoned Dew Drop Inn. They deserted the inn and left the area to get away from her brother, a disturbed man who has spent most of his adult life in institutions. The sister leaves a family photograph with Corrie, who hopes that someday he will come back and she can give it to him.

Later that day, the mystery solved, Sebastian has a talk with his mother and father. He discovers that they had considered buying the abandoned Dew Drop Inn as a new career for his father if he loses his job. However, the inn isn't for sale. Corrie's father has convinced the county to buy it and turn it into a permanent shelter for the homeless. As for the future of the Barth family, they'll just wait and see.

Thematic Material

This is a pleasant, low-key mystery with a strong underlying theme of the need to care about others. Sebastian and his friends are perhaps a bit more thoughtful and introspective than most young teens, but their feelings, especially Corrie's care for Abraham, are nicely drawn and believable. The problems of people without means to support themselves and the turmoil that shakes a family when loss of livelihood is threatened are all-too-realistic themes in the 1990s.

Book Talk Material

The book jacket gives a nice, eerie quality to this entertaining mystery. Young readers should especially enjoy the following scenes: Sebastian, David, and Corrie see the body at the Dew Drop Inn (pp. 21–25); they tell the police chief about their discovery (pp. 26–30); Corrie meets Abraham (pp. 70–72); Sebastian and David find the body again (pp. 87–90); Abraham is charged with murder (pp. 119–120).

Additional Selections

Sheepdog Sebastian helps his owner recover a necklace in *Sebastian (Super Sleuth) and the Hair of the Dog Mystery* (Macmillan, 1982, $10.95) by Mary B. Christian. Also use sequels like *Sebastian (Super Sleuth) and the Time Capsule Caper* (Macmillan, 1989, $10.95).

The Roberts family believes a ghost is in their house in Peggy Parish's *Haunted House* (Peter Smith, 1991, $16.25.; pap., Dell, $3.25). There are many other adventures of Jed, Bill, and Lisa Roberts in print including *Clues in the Woods* (pap., Dell, $3.25).

Two young cousins are held prisoner in a lonely country estate by a spiteful governess and an evil co-conspirator in Joan Aiken's *The Wolves of Willoughby Chase* (Doubleday, 1989, $13.95; pap., Dell, $3.50; condensed in *Introducing Books,* Bowker, 1970, pp. 106–109). Also use such sequels as *Black Hearts in Battersea* (pap., Dell, 1981, $1.75) and *Nightbirds on Nantucket* (pap., Dell, 1981, $1.75).

In Eve Bunting's *The Hideout* (Harcourt, 1991, $14.95; pap., $4.95), Andy stages his own kidnapping to collect the ransom and visit his dad in England.

Anthony Monday with librarian McEells and her brother summer on a remote island and discover a mystery involving an object that can destroy the world in John Bellairs' *The Mansion in the Mist* (Dial, 1992, $15; pap., Puffin, $3.99), a sequel to *The Lamp from the Warlock's Tomb* (Dial, 1988, $14.95; pap., Bantam, $3.50).

In Peg Kehret's *Horror at the Haunted House* (Dutton, 1992, $14), Ellen enters a house and finds she is suddenly haunted by the ghost of a woman who died three years before.

Henry Coffin, son of a famous detective, helps a sixteen-year-old girl locate her missing mother in the suspenseful *Coffin on a Case* (Harper, 1992, $13; pap., $3.95) by Eve Bunting.

About the Book

Book Report, September 1990, p. 49.
Booklist, March 1, 1990, p. 1343.
Horn Book Guide, January 1990, p. 259.
School Library Journal, April 1990, p. 120.
VOYA, June 1990, p. 104.
Wilson Library Bulletin, June 1990, p. 117.
See also *Book Review Index,* 1990, p. 384; 1991, p. 433.

About the Author

Chevalier, Tracy, ed., *Twentieth-Century Children's Writers* (3rd ed.). St. James, 1989, pp. 470–471.
Commire, Anne, ed., *Something about the Author.* Gale, 1982, Vol. 19, pp. 110–111.
Holtze, Sally Holmes, ed., *Sixth Book of Junior Authors and Illustrators.* Wilson, 1983, pp. 135–137.
Locher, Frances C., ed., *Contemporary Authors.* Gale, 1982, Vol. 105, pp. 231–232.
Senick, Gerard J., ed., *Children's Literature Review.* Gale, 1985, Vol. 9, pp. 54–60.
Straub, Deborah A., ed., *Contemporary Authors* (New Revision Series). Gale, 1982, Vol. 22, pp. 208–209.
Telgen, Diane, ed., *Something about the Author.* Gale, 1993, Vol. 71, pp. 90–94.

Mahy, Margaret. *Underrunners*
Viking, 1992, $14 (0-670-84179-X)

Margaret Mahy is considered to be New Zealand's foremost contemporary writer of children's literature. She writes for a variety of audiences. Her first picture book, *The Dragon of an Ordinary Family* (Dial, 1992, $14), was illustrated by Helen Oxenbury and was published in 1969. In a later picture book, *A Lion in the Meadow* (Overlook, 1992, $13.95), a mother refuses to take her son seriously when he says there is a lion in the meadow. Both these early works explore a theme that is popular in many of her works, the close relationship between fantasy and reality. This is also true in many of her novels for older readers. In *The Haunting* (pap., Dell, 1991, $3.25), for example, Barney, an eight-year-old boy, receives frightening supernatural messages stating "Barney is dead" and discovers that he has inherited psychic powers from Cole, an uncle who reappears after being presumed dead for many years. *Memory* (Macmillan, 1988, $14.95; pap., Dell, $3.50; condensed in *Juniorplots 4,* Bowker, 1992, pp. 76–81), a novel for older readers, explores the nature of memory as it involves a disturbed teenager and a bag lady he befriends. *Underrunners* is a realistic novel set in contemporary rural New Zealand. In spite of a rather slow beginning, the pace accelerates about halfway through, and suddenly the reader in involved in a suspenseful, fast-paced adventure story. It is suitable for youngsters in grades 5 through 8.

Plot Summary

Tristram Catt, Tris for short, lives in rural New Zealand with his laid-back father, a free-lance landscape architect, in a house at the end of a deserted peninsula that juts out into the sea. The house was constructed on poles by his father, Randall Catt, and unfortunately shows the primitive amateurism of its well-meaning but often impractical builder. Most of the generator-driven appliances malfunction, drains are clogged, the chickens roam freely and lay their eggs anywhere, the goat, Bessie, frequently gets loose and munches goodies from the garden, and, in general, a benevolent disorder reigns. These circumstances and a desire to be free led Tris's mother to leave their home almost two years previously to start a new life in Australia. Tris has never really recovered from being deserted, and every day he checks the mailbox, looking in vain for a letter from his mother. When he remembers his life in town before they moved to this house, he realizes painfully that, even then, his mother wanted to pursue her own career. When Tris remembers those days, he tends to confuse his mother with Dearie Tyrone, a woman who lived next door and who frequently took care of him. He vaguely remembers that Dearie had many marital problems of her own and also had to take care of her own three children, Tod, Damon, and Cissy, the youngest, who was two years older than Tris.

Recently, Tris's freewheeling father has found an attractive, charming widow, Victoria Emanuel, who has both a three-year-old daughter, Rosie, and a yen to get closer to Randall. Tris is fearful that a marriage will take place, not because he dislikes Victoria, who has nicknamed him Ratty from *The Wind in the Willows,* but because in his insecurity he doesn't wish to share his loving father with someone else.

As Tris walks home from school with friend Sylvia Collins (rich Elaine Partridge is picked up by car, and the bratty Morley twins have bicycles), they are stopped by a man in sunglasses driving a yellow Lotus Elan who asks the way to Featherstonehaugh (pronounced Fanshaw) Children's Home. Tris passes it every day on his way home and therefore gives directions easily to the stranger.

After Sylvia's house, Tris still has a long walk home, but he is never alone. His imaginary friend, Selsey Firebone, a brave galactic warrior, keeps him company, and the two have animated conversations about their war against the dreaded space conquerors, the Veng. Tris's secret path home lies first beside the fence that surrounds the children's home, and then across the grassy dunes pockmarked with entrances to small caves, called underrunners, that are caused by interior soil erosion and frost heaves. In one of these underrunners, Tris's secret hideaway, he has hidden some provisions such as canned goods, packages of peanuts, and cans of Coke.

While passing the children's home, Tris's conversation with Selsey is interrupted by a young girl inside the fence who, between sneezes—caused, she explains, by her hay fever—is busily digging a tunnel under the fence. She calls Tris by his name. He is embarrassed to think that she learned this by listening to his many out-loud talks with Selsey. The girl is plain looking, very thin, and has close-cropped black hair. Before Tris can continue the conversation, she disappears.

On the way to school the next day, Tris again sees the strange waif digging at the fence. She introduces herself as Winola, a name she claims means friendly princess, and tells him that she has been in the home for one week and is building an escape tunnel in case the man who is following her should learn of her whereabouts. Tris thinks this story rivals his relationship with Selsey but remains quiet.

The following day, Winola's tunnel is so advanced that she can squeeze through to freedom. She visits with Tris on the outside for a few minutes, and they talk about themselves and their concerns. Tris admires this tough, strong-willed girl who, in spite of a past chequered by stays in orphanages, still has the ability to feel compassion and a hope for better times.

In the dunes, Tris encounters the man who asked him directions to the children's home and notices that he has a pair of binoculars that are trained on the shelter.

Brian and Guy Morley, the school bullies, pick a fight with Tris on his way home from school the next day. He is being pounded unmercifully when Winola appears and drives them both off. A thankful Tris shows Winola the underrunner that he uses as his secret cave and the stores he has collected. He also mentions seeing the man from the yellow automobile. Winola suddenly stiffens and says that he is the man she fears. Now that he has found her, she can't return to the home. She decides she will stay in Tris's underrunner for safety.

For dinner that evening, Randall has invited Victoria and Rosie. Tris is so concerned about Winola being alone in the underrunner that he tells his father he too has a guest coming for dinner. It is Elaine Partridge, a classmate and the young daughter of the town's wealthiest residents. Randall is impressed, but Tris is apprehensive. Claiming he must meet the Partridges' car, he gathers up Winola and, after a quick briefing, introduces her as Elaine. Somehow it works. Winola plays the part with perhaps too much gusto, but the dinner is a success. Later that night, Tris hears the sirens of police cars at the children's home. Winola's disappearance has been discovered.

The next morning, Tris visits Winola in the underrunner. She tells him the stranger is actually her father, who is trying to locate their mother to patch up their off-and-on-again marriage. Winola, who knows her mother wants to be rid of this abusive man, swears she will never tell him of her whereabouts.

Back at Tris's home, the domestic situation reaches a climax for the boy after he sees his father and Victoria kissing passionately and finds Bessie, untied, eating at the plants in his special garden. Suddenly all his insecurities and hatred of the disorder and chaos around him surface. Screaming that he hates his home, he runs off and stumbles into the arms of Winola's father, who is now carrying a gun. Tris refuses to tell him where Winola is hiding. When Randall appears in the distance looking for his son, the stranger shoots, and Tris's father falls into tall grasses. The stranger then demands that Tris accompany him. Suddenly Winola appears, hoping to save Tris, but they both are forced at gunpoint into her father's car. There follows a nightmarish ride at top speed through lanes and streets to an old deserted house Tris vaguely remembers from his past. Winola clarifies the mystery. Her father is Orson Tyrone, and she is the daughter of Tris's next door neighbor and babysitter of years ago, Dearie Tyrone. Winola was once called Cissy but now uses her middle name. It was coincidence that brought her to the shelter near Tris's home—and she knew his name because she remembered him as a young child. Her old house remains in the family, even though Dearie abandoned it some time ago.

Orson locks them in the bathroom while he goes out to get food, and Winola and Tris try to escape by breaking the glass in the skylights. Orson returns and drags Winola down, causing deep cuts in both her hands, but she steadfastly refuses to reveal her mother's whereabouts. In a last attempt at freedom, she drops three antihistamine tablets she carries for her hay fever into his coffee, hoping they will make him drowsy. There is a sound at the door. Orson hears it, but in his semistupor seems to have lost the will to continue. He points the gun at himself. Tris's tears and entreaties not to kill himself bring him back to his senses, and he lowers the gun. The two youngsters rush past him and out onto the street. There they are greeted by Randall, sporting a bandaged shoulder from his wound, Victoria, and a host of policemen. Randall had remembered Orson from their earlier days on that street and, on a hunch, decided to look for the children there.

Within the next few days, Tris's life becomes much tidier. He hears from his mother in Australia, his father decides to get a regular job and have the house properly finished, and Winola is assigned to a loving foster home. Before she leaves, the two pledge lasting friendship. The imaginary Selsey Firebone is not heard from again now that Tris has a real friend.

Thematic Material

In many ways, Tris's world is like a landscape filled with underrunners—that is, seemingly solid on top but filled with unexpected hollows. The boy's insecurities, his worries, and his solitary existence are well portrayed, as is his journey to acceptance of life's realities without escaping into a fantasy world. This transition represents both a loss of innocence and a step toward maturity. Winola is a survivor whose resourcefulness and independence make for a fascinating characterization. This suspenseful thriller also deals with friendship, family problems, and father-son relations.

Book Talk Material

The cover shows Tris and Winola meeting at the mouth of his underrunner. Some interesting passages are: Tris and his alter ego, Selsey, first see Winola (pp. 6–9); Tris and his father are visited by Victoria (pp. 15–19); Tris and Winola talk seriously to each other (pp. 23–30); Tris meets the stranger in the dunes (pp. 49–54); Winola saves Tris from the Morley twins (pp. 67–71); Tris tells Winola about the stranger (pp. 78–80); and the Elaine Partridge hoax (pp. 87–93).

Additional Selections

Two youngsters flee from a cruel English stepfather to their mother's home in Ireland in Walter Macken's *The Flight of the Doves* (Simon and Schuster, 1992, $14; condensed in *More Juniorplots,* Bowker, 1977, pp. 137–140).

In Avi's *The Man from the Sky* (Morrow, 1992, $13; pap., $3.95), young Jamie Peters is on the track of a thief in rural Pennsylvania.

Philip and a streetwise youngster become involved in a robbery in contemporary London in Nina Bawden's *The Robbers* (Lothrop, 1989, $12.95; pap., Dell, $3.25).

In Mollie Hunter's *The Haunted Mountain* (Harper, 1972, $12.89), Mac Allister and son confront the Great Gray Man of the haunted mountain in a tale of old Scotland.

Meg discovers her new home in Ohio was once a stop on the Underground Railroad in Katharine Wilson Precek's *The Keepsake Chest* (Macmillan, 1992, $13.95).

Lisa and some homeless people living in the Florida Everglades band together to protect Dajun, a twelve-foot alligator, from destruction in *The Missing 'Gator of Gumbo Limbo* (Harper, 1992, $14; pap., $3.95) by Jean Craighead George.

In Patricia Pendergraft's *Brushy Mountain* (Putnam, 1989, $14.95), young Arnold finds himself in the position of saving the life of the meanest man in town.

In a reissue of the 1965 title by William Stevenson, *The Bushbabies* (Peter Smith, 1984, $16; condensed in *Introducing Books,* Bowker, 1970, pp. 128–131), East African authorities search for a white girl last seen with an old native man.

About the Book

Booklist, February 1, 1992, p. 1028.
Horn Book, March 1992, p. 204.
Kirkus Reviews, March 15, 1992, P. 395.
School Library Journal, February 1992, p. 108.
VOYA, April 1992, p. 32.
See also *Book Review Index,* 1992, p. 572.

About the Author

Bowden, Jane A., ed., *Contemporary Authors.* Gale, 1978, Vols. 69–72, pp. 391–92.
Chevalier, Tracy, ed., *Twentieth-Century Children's Writers* (3rd ed.) St. James, 1989, pp. 626–628.
Commire, Anne, ed., *Something about the Author.* Gale, 1978, Vol. 14, pp. 129–131.
de Montreville, Doris, and Crawford, Elizabeth D., eds., *Fourth Book of Junior Authors and Illustrators.* Wilson, 1978, pp. 248–50.
Kirkpatrick, D. L., ed., *Twentieth-Century Children's Writers* (2nd ed.) St. Martin's, 1983, pp. 504–506.
Lesniak, James G., ed., *Contemporary Authors* (New Revision Series). Gale, 1990, Vol. 30, p. 257.
Metzger, Linda, ed., *Contemporary Authors* (New Revision Series). Gale, 1984, Vol. 13, p. 342.
Olendorf, Donna, ed., *Something about the Author.* Gale, 1992, Vol. 69, pp. 140–146.
Senick, Gerard J., ed., *Children's Literature Review.* Gale, 1984, Vol. 7, pp. 176–188.
Ward, Martha, ed., *Authors of Books for Young People* (3rd ed.). Scarecrow, 1990, p. 475.

Newman, Robert. *The Case of the Watching Boy*

Macmillan, 1987, $13.95 (0-689-31317-9)

Young Andrew Tillett was first introduced to readers in 1978 in Robert Newman's *The Case of the Baker Street Irregular* (pap., Aladdin, $4.95) when he sought the aid of Sherlock Holmes to help solve the mystery behind the kidnapping of his tutor. This was followed by six other mysteries set in Victorian England in which Andrew is joined by his friend Sara Wiggins, the daughter of housekeeper Mrs. Wiggins; Andrew's mother, the successful actress Verna Tillett; and Scotland Yard inspector Peter Wyatt. Three other exciting titles in this series are *The Case of the Vanishing Corpse* (pap., Aladdin, $4.95), in which Andrew and Sara assist Scotland Yard in locating a missing corpse and recovering a cache of stolen diamonds; *The Case of the Murdered Players* (1985, Macmillan, $14.95), in which the life of Andrew's mother is threatened by a murderer intent on killing London's famous stage actresses; and *The Case of the Indian Curse* (1986, Macmillan, $12.95), a thriller involving the disappearance of an antique dealer and members of a murderous Indian cult called the Thuggee. A subplot in these mysteries involves the gradual realization by both Verna and Inspector Wyatt that they are in love. By the beginning of the present novel, they are now man and wife and living comfortably in a large flat in St. John's Wood, a fashionable residential area in north-central London. These stories are enjoyed by boys and girls in grades 4 through 7.

Plot Summary

One day, quite unexpectedly, Andrew Tillett is sent for by Dr. Bartram, the headmaster of the prestigious English boys' school he attends in rural Somerset only a few miles from the city of Bath. It is not Andrew's behavior that has upset the headmaster and other faculty members, however, but the actions of a slightly younger boy, Christopher Markham, who in the past week has been seen wandering alone on the Downs as if distracted and disturbed. Markham has a reputation for being a loner, but this recent strange behavior has his teachers particularly concerned. Dr. Bartram hopes Andrew can help determine its cause, because Andrew already has a reputation as a fine amateur sleuth and helper of his stepfather, Inspector Wyatt of Scotland Yard.

The next day, Andrew finds Markham on top of a tor overlooking the Downs, intently staring through field glasses at a solitary old stone house. He tells Andrew that several days ago he was approached on the Downs by an attractive woman who had alighted from her carriage to speak to him. She called herself Mrs. Grey and told him that her only child, three-year-old Michael, had been kidnapped by her wicked husband in an attempt to keep her from leaving him. Through a private detective, she had found out that the lad was being held prisoner in the stone house. She gave Markham the glasses and asked him to watch the house whenever possible to make sure the child was not taken away.

Within minutes, Mrs. Grey's coach appears. She readily accepts Andrew as another helper in her plan and explains that her boy's nanny will be away tomorrow, leaving only the gardener and his wife at the cottage, and she plans to rescue her son then with the help of the two boys and her coachman. The plan works. The next day, while Mrs. Grey distracts the servants by fainting on the front doorstep, the boys grab the boy from his play yard and give him to a waiting nurse. As the coach races off, the boys hurry back to school.

The following day, Detective Inspector Gillian appears at the school. As each of the boys enters chapel, his blazer is carefully examined. Because Markham's sleeve is missing a button, he is mysteriously taken out of line and brought before the headmaster. Sensing that this somehow involves the day before's events, Andrew accompanies him. In the headmaster's study, they meet a distraught young mother who is introduced as Mrs. George Vickery, the resident of the stone house. They also learn the horrible truth—yesterday, strangers kidnapped her baby son while she was in London following a false lead in her search for her husband, who had disappeared over a week ago while in Rumania on business. The blazer button had been ripped off during the scuffle with the young boy and had led the police to the school. Markham and Andrew had been duped by "Mrs. Grey" into becoming accomplices in a most heinous crime!

Andrew's mother, the actress Verna Tillett, and his stepfather, Inspector Wyatt of Scotland Yard, are contacted, and soon a full investigation is under way. Two gypsies, Jasper and Daniel Lee, who had camped close to the Vickery house on the day of the kidnapping, are questioned. They appear to be honest, but Wyatt is convinced they know more about the case than they admit.

After listening to a detailed description of the physical appearance of "Mrs. Grey"— her clothes, speech patterns, and mannerisms—Verna is able to identify her as an out-of-luck London actress named Coral Lumden. Taking Markham, Andrew, and Mrs. Vickery with them, the Wyatts return to Verna's London home, where Markham meets Andrew's sleuthing companion, Sara Wiggins, daughter of the housekeeper. Coral is tracked down and identified by the boys. She confesses to being hired by a man known as Mr. Benson and his coachman, a cockney, to help in their scheme but she does not know where either can now be found.

When Mrs. Vickery visits the Rumanian Embassy seeking news of her husband, the three youngsters accompany her and are startled to see the villainous coachman working in the embassy mews. Meanwhile, Wyatt's men have identified him as a lowlife criminal named Zack Macy. Wyatt and his helper, Sergeant Tucker, set up surveillance in a hotel suite across from the Rumanian Embassy and decide to pay a call on the ambassador. They are told that the ambassador, Count Rozarin, is dangerously ill and cannot see them. Instead they meet his extremely hostile first secretary, Colonel Katarov, and his aide, Captain Benesh, who claim they cannot help in locating George Vickery or Zack Macy. That night, an arch-criminal, Stub Pollard, is seen entering and leaving the embassy. Later the same night, before Pollard returns to the embassy, Macy is found murdered in the underworld area of Limehouse.

The next day, while Captain Benesh is escorting a heavily veiled woman out of the embassy, Wyatt and Tucker intervene and "accidentally" remove the veil to reveal a startled and soon-to-be-incarcerated Stub Pollard. Diplomatic immunity prevents Wyatt from searching the embassy, where he is convinced the boy Michael is being held prisoner. Wyatt is also amazed by the reappearance of the two gypsies, Jasper and Daniel Lee, who also seem to have placed the embassy under surveillance.

Sara, Andrew, and Markham decide to help the investigation. Disguised as street urchins, they appear at the embassy kitchen and so distract the chefs that Markham is able to slip upstairs. Peering in various rooms, he finally finds the bedroom where Michael is hidden. When they report their findings to Wyatt, Jasper overhears and suddenly, like a madman, rushes to the embassy followed by Wyatt, Tucker, and the youngsters. In a tense scene, Jasper is able to outwit a revolver-brandishing Benesh and carry the child to safety.

Explanations are in order and given. Jasper is actually George Vickery and also Prince Maximilian, heir to the throne of Rumania. He had kept this information from his wife, hoping to forestall the day when he would have to face reality and return to his homeland. However, when he did return, he found that his wicked stepbrother, John, was conspiring to usurp the throne by having him and his son Michael killed. After escaping an assassination attempt, he secretly fled Rumania and returned to England in the guise of a gypsy, hoping to subvert any further plots. Unfortunately, the loyal ambassador had been overcome by the treacherous Katarov and Benesh (alias Benson), who were supporters of John. But now the score has been settled, the villains are sent back to Rumania to face trial, Ambassador Rozarin can resume his post, Mrs. and Mrs. George Vickery can look forward to a future as King and Queen of Rumania, and, for young Andrew Tillett, another case has been solved.

Thematic Material

This is a true Victorian adventure story that authentically recreates the atmosphere and locales of London during the nineteenth century as well as the various strata of London's social life. In addition to a clever plot, cliff-hanging chapter endings, and a baffling mystery, the reader is treated to colorful settings, historically accurate details, and interesting characters who reflect the times in which they live. The plot also contains many examples of courage, devotion to duty, and the necessity to stand up to the forces of evil.

Book Talk Material

The cover shows a large picture of George Vickery in his gypsy disguise. Some passages that will stimulate interest are: Andrew talks with Headmaster Bartram about Markham (pp. 3–7); Markham tells about Mrs. Grey, and later Andrew meets her (pp. 11–21); the kidnapping (pp. 25–29); Andrew and Markham find out the truth (pp. 30–36); Verna identifies Mrs. Grey as Coral Lumden, and all set out to London to find her (pp. 46–52); and confronting Coral (pp. 63–72).

Additional Selections

A witness to a murder is not believed in *The View from the Cherry Tree* (Macmillan, 1975, $14.95; pap., $3.95), by Willo Davis Roberts.

In Sid Fleischman's Bloodhouse Gang series, a trio of young detectives uses deductive reasoning to solve baffling crimes in such mysteries as *The Case of the Cackling Ghost* (pap., Random, 1981, $1.50) and *The Case of Princess Tomorrow* (pap., Random, 1981 $1.50).

In a mystery set in the Old West, *A Deadly Promise* (Bantam, 1992, $16) by Joan Lowery Nixon, Sarah and her young sister, Susannah, solve a puzzling mystery and clear their father's name. This is a sequel to another fast-paced mystery, *High Trail to Danger* (Bantam, 1991, $15).

Supernatural events begin occurring to Cosmo Curtoys when he moves into his family home in England after his mother and older brother disappear in Joan Aiken's *The Shadow Guests* (Delacorte, 1980, $11.95; pap., Dell, $2.95).

In Carolyn Lane's *Ghost Island* (Houghton, 1985, $11.85), four campers are marooned on Ghost Island and soon discover how it got its name.

A slime-covered creature in a pool is stalked by Raymond and his friends, who also solve a mystery, in Drew Stevenson's *The Case of the Horrible Swamp Monster* (Putnam, 1984, $10.95). Another in this series is *The Case of the Visiting Vampire* (Putnam, 1986, $10.95; pap., Pocket, $2.50).

Two boys find a diamond ring in the woods and know that they are at the start of an adventure in David Kherdian's *The Mystery of the Diamond in the Wood* (Knopf, 1983, $9.99).

About the Book

Booklist, August 1987, p. 1751.
School Library Journal, September 1987, p. 183.
See also *Book Review Index,* 1987, p. 564; 1988, p. 599.

About the Author

Chevalier, Tracy, ed., *Twentieth-Century Children's Writers* (3rd ed.). St. James, 1989, pp. 718–719.
Commire, Anne, ed., *Something about the Author.* Gale, 1973, Vol. 4, pp. 161–164.
Holtze, Sally Holmes, ed., *Sixth Book of Junior Authors and Illustrators.* Wilson, 1989, pp. 206–208.
Kirkpatrick, D. L., ed., *Twentieth-Century Children's Writers* (2nd ed.). St. Martin's, 1983, pp. 575–576.
Metzger, Linda, ed., *Contemporary Authors* (New Revision Series). Gale, 1987, Vol. 19, p. 349.
Ward, Martha, ed., *Authors of Books for Young People* (3rd ed.). Scarecrow, 1990, p. 525.

Paulsen, Gary. *The Haymeadow*

Delacorte, 1992, $15 (0-385-30621-0)

In his autobiographical writings, Gary Paulsen says one of the brightest lights in his deprived childhood was receiving a library card, the passport to new worlds and new experiences. In recent years, he has transferred this love of reading to a love of writing and the production of a series of excellent outdoor adventures for young people. Among them are *Hatchet* (Macmillan, 1987, $14.95; pap., Puffin, $3.95; condensed in *Seniorplots,* Bowker, 1989, pp. 227–231), the story of Brian, a thirteen-year-old who is the sole survivor of a plane crash in a northern Canadian wilderness and finds himself facing the unknown with only the clothes he is wearing and a hatchet his mother gave him for his scout belt; and *Dogsong* (Macmillan, 1985, $11.95; pap., Puffin, $3.95; condensed in *Introducing Bookplots 3,* Bowker, 1988, pp. 189–193), a Newbery Honor Book in 1986, which retells the ordeal of a fourteen-year-old Eskimo boy, Russel, and his 1,400-mile trek by dog sled across Alaska in search of the song that represents himself. In a change of setting, mood, and pace, Gary Paulsen has also written the humorous *The Boy Who Owned the School* (Orchard, 1990, $12.95), about a different kind of survival when high-schooler Jacob Freisten falls hopelessly in love with the most beautiful and talented girl in his school. *The Haymeadow* returns to the outdoors Mr. Paulsen knows so well and another tale of endurance and courage. These novels are enjoyed by readers in grades 5 through 9.

Plot Summary

John Barron has just turned fourteen, and the weight of several previous generations of John Barrons lies heavily on his shoulders. The John Barron who was his great-grandfather moved from the East, staked out this huge 960,000-acre of land in Wyoming as his own and began sheep ranching. He was a tough, violent, man known to kill in the name of justice. He died at age 92 with his trusty six-shooter still at his side. This is the heritage passed down in the Barron clan, a family of strong, taciturn, hard-working men. John's father is no exception. Since John's mother died when he was only three, his father has cared only for the ranch, which has come under the ownership of eastern corporations. He shuns other people, and except for a monthly visit to his wife's grave and a few necessary trips into town, he has remained on the ranch. John is in awe and a bit frightened of this man and the traditions he represents.

It is June and time for Tink, one of the two hired men on the ranch, to move the sheep into the hills for the summer, where they will graze on the luxuriant grass of the haymeadow, a stretch of land several miles long nestled between two mountain ridges. However, these plans are suddenly changed. Tink falls ill and is taken to a doctor in town, who diagnoses cancer. John's father and the other hired hand, 35-year-old Horace Cawley, must remain on the ranch because eastern corporate representatives are due for an inspection. That leaves only young John to take over for Tink.

The boy is aghast at the responsibility and loneliness involved in this assignment. The thought of being almost three months with only a horse and four Border collies, Pete, Billy, Jenny, and Peg, while taking care of six thousand sheep fills the boy with dread and a fear approaching panic. Although his father assures him that Cawley will fill him in on the details and any problems John might face, the paralyzing dread won't leave. Yet at night, when John reflects on the Barron heritage, the legacy of his great-grandfather, and the fact that his father did his first haymeadow stint at age fifteen, John finds it impossible to say no.

Preparations get under way. John will be living in a trailer that resembles a covered wagon except with rubber tires. It is six feet by twelve feet, has a canvas top, and contains a small wood-burning stove, a bunk, wooden boxes used for shelves, and a Coleman lantern. Provisions, including stacks of canned goods, dog food, clothes, first aid supplies, and a rifle, are soon collected and stored inside. Originally they planned to tow the trailer with an old half-ton truck, but when it was found to be unserviceable, they decided to use Spud and Speck, two ranch horses, instead.

Soon the caravan leaves—Cawley on his horse, Roan, John driving the horse-drawn trailer, and the sheep being carefully guided by the four attentive dogs. They meet some problems when they must cross the main highway, but the rest of the three-day drive to the haymeadow is uneventful. John is unable to anticipate the problems he might encounter during the summer, and Cawley, who is the strong, silent type, doesn't volunteer any information, so that when Cawley leaves to return to the ranch, John still feels unprepared for his stay. One consolation is that someone will bring him fresh provisions in approximately six weeks.

The haymeadow is a beautiful grazing ground with a quiet stream meandering through it. After the trailer is parked close to its banks, John begins the task of unloading. He hears in the distance the dogs barking wildly, sheep bleating, and an ominous hissing sound. He races to the center of the noise and finds a rattler coiled to strike. Using a large rock, he manages to kill the snake, but not before it strikes a lamb. John knows he should shoot the wounded animal but instead tries to save it by cutting out the area infected by the poisoned fangs. In spite of his efforts, the lamb dies, and he must bury it. Within minutes there is another uproar—a skunk has wandered into the flock and Billy, one of the dogs, has cornered it. Again John enters the fray. The dog kills the skunk, but not before both he and John receive such a thorough spraying that they must wash in the river to try and rid themselves of the terrible odor. Next Pete, another of the dogs, tears the tender pads on one of his feet, and John must administer primitive first aid. This is followed by a sudden sheep stampede caused by the sight of a roving bobcat. The stampede leaves John's drying clothes in tatters and the few supplies he has unpacked scattered and trampled. John realizes that he has completely lost control of the situation and is entirely at the mercy of nature.

That night there is a violent mountain storm with a driving, pelting rain. John awakes to an ominous roar. A flash flood sweeps through the valley. The stream's banks overflow and erode, causing the trailer to tip over violently and slide into the water. John escapes to dry land. In the morning, he finds the waters have receded, but the contents of the trailer have been swept away. He begins a search of the banks and stream bottom and is able to retrieve many of the provisions, although the contents of the now-labelless cans remain a mystery. The one important item still missing is his rifle.

His sleep that night is once more disturbed by loud noises. A pack of ravenous coyotes is attacking the herd. He mounts Speck and, with the help of the dogs, drives them off, but not before several sheep have been killed. He knows the coyotes will return and that he must find the rifle if he is to protect the flock.

The next day, he puts the horses in harness and is able to right the trailer, dragging it to a position of safety. However, during the final pull, the board holding the harness rope rips loose and flies through the air, dealing John a crippling blow across the base of his shoulders. Although it momentarily knocks him unconscious, fortunately no bones are broken, and in spite of the excruciating pain, he continues his chores. In the shallow water where the trailer was, he finds the rifle and then begins the arduous chore of taking it apart, drying and greasing each part, and reassembling it. That night, he uses it to repulse another deadly assault from the coyotes.

John marks the passing days with notches on a willow stick. Amazingly, there are no other crises. He puts his camp in order, and apart from each meal being a mystery until the cans are opened, life settles into a more natural routine. He is now able to study the behavior of sheep and, for the first time, to appreciate his surroundings. During these moments, John begins to feel like the shepherds of ancient times who faithfully guarded their flocks.

One night during his third week, he is again awakened by the din of barking and bleating. It is joined by a more frightening sound, a bellowing growl. A black bear has invaded the flock. John, rifle in hand, tries to drive off the raging animal by firing at him from his horse. Unfortunately the shot goes wild and John, who accidentally slips from the horse, is clawed on the shoulder by the retreating animal. The wound is deep, but he must first care for Peg, who was also wounded in the attack. With his one free arm, he takes off his T-shirt, rolls the dog onto it, and drags her back to the camp, where he crudely sews her wounds together. Almost passing out from his own pain and loss of blood John then douses his wound with iodine and bandages his shoulder. When daylight comes, he gathers up the dead sheep, sixteen in all, and buries them.

As his shoulder mends and Peg returns to her flock-tending duties, John's life again becomes a quiet ritual. On the forty-seventh day, he sees in the distance a man on horseback followed by a pack animal. It is his father, who has brought him provisions.

That night they sit around the campfire. John's father seems to sense the experiences his young son has endured and is inwardly proud. This, and the magic of the surroundings, suddenly unleash a torrent of reminiscences from him. He tells John about the real nature of his great-grandfather and how he was really a ruthless bully. He also speaks of the love and loss he feels for his dead wife. In the dark of that night, a new bond is established between the two. The next morning, his father tells him that this is just the beginning. He will stay the rest of the summer in the haymeadow getting to know his son.

Thematic Material

This is an exciting survival story that also describes a boy's rites of passage from youngster to adult by overcoming terrible crises with courage and endurance. The complex relationship between an embittered father and his sensitive son is well portrayed. John's self-doubts and lack of confidence and his adult idol worship are conditions that many adolescents experience. The outdoor setting with both its beauty and savagery is depicted realistically. The reader also gets a truthful, detailed picture of the trials and satisfactions of sheep ranching and outdoor living.

Book Talk Material

There are several full-page drawings by Ruth Wright Paulsen that could be used with small groups. For example, the trailer is shown on page 37, and John on horseback on page 156. Some exciting incidents are: John thinks about his great-grandfather (pp. 16–18); John learns he will take Tink's place (pp. 19–22); Cawley and John prepare for leaving (pp. 33–39); they reach the haymeadow and Cawley leaves (pp. 71–77); the rattlesnake (pp. 80–84); trying to save the lamb (pp. 85–89); and the skunk attack (pp. 93–95).

Additional Selections

In the arctic regions, Matthew and his Eskimo friend set out to find Matthew's father in James Houston's *Frozen Fire* (Macmillan, 1977, $13.95; pap., $4.95).

In *The Grizzly* by Annabel Johnson and Edgar Johnson (pap., Harper,

1973, $3.95; condensed in *Introducing Books,* Bowker, 1970, pp. 195–198), a camping trip that was intended to bring father and son together ends in disaster.

Travis and his dog live through a difficult summer on the Texas frontier in Fred Gipson's *Old Yeller* (Harper, 1956, $19.95; pap., $3.95; condensed in *Juniorplots,* Bowker, 1967, pp. 133–135). A sequel is *Savage Sam* (pap., Harper, 1976, $4.95).

In *Some Fine Dog* (Holiday, 1992, $13.95) by Patti Sherlock, twelve-year-old Terry adopts a dog named Duffy who saves him when he is trapped on a mountain during a snowstorm.

Annie and her two brothers set out on a perilous hike across snow-covered mountains to find their father in P. J. Petersen's *Going for the Big One* (Delacorte, 1986, $14.95; pap., Dell, $2.95; condensed in *Juniorplots 4,* Bowker, 1993, pp. 168–173).

A juvenile offender, Cameron Powell, gets involved in clashes between local fishermen and Vietnamese newcomers in Texas in Mary Blount Christian's *Dead Man in Catfish Bay* (Whitman, 1985, $8.95).

In Patricia Welch's *The Day of the Muskie* (Faber, 1984, $11.95), Norm wants desperately to catch a large muskie and win a fishing boat.

About the Book

Booklist, May 15, 1992, p. 1679.
Center for Children's Books Bulletin, May 1992, p. 246.
Horn Book, July 1992, p. 456.
Kirkus Reviews, June 15, 1992, p. 783.
School Library Journal, June 1992, p. 139.
VOYA, June 1992, p. 99.
See also *Book Review Index,* 1992, p. 700.

About the Author

Chevalier, Tracy, ed., *Twentieth-Century Children's Writers* (3rd ed.). St. James, 1989, pp. 763–765.
Commire, Anne, ed., *Something about the Author.* Gale, 1981, Vol. 22, pp. 192–193; updated 1989, Vol. 54, pp. 76–82.
Garrett, Agnes, and McCue, Helga P., eds., *Authors and Artists for Young Adults.* Gale, 1989, Vol. 2, pp. 165–173.
Holtze, Sally Holmes, ed., *Sixth Book of Junior Authors and Illustrators.* Wilson, 1989, pp. 219–220.
Senick, Gerard J., ed., *Children's Literature Review.* Gale, 1990, Vol. 19, pp. 167–178.
Ward, Martha, ed., *Authors of Books for Young People* (3rd ed.). Scarecrow, 1990, p. 553.

Peck, Richard. *Blossom Culp and the Sleep of Death*
Delacorte, 1986, $14.95 (0-385-29433-6); pap., Dell, $3.25 (0-440-40676-5)

Although Richard Peck is probably best known for his realistic novels for teenagers, he has also written for a younger audience a series of adventure-fantasies on the lighter side starring the irrepressible Blossom Culp. She first appeared in *The Ghost Belonged to Me* (Viking, 1975, $13.95; pap., Dell, $3.25; condensed in *Introducing More Books,* Bowker, 1978, pp. 187–190; and *More Juniorplots,* Bowker, 1977, pp. 140–143). In this story, narrated by young Alexander Armsworth, readers are introduced to pre-World War I Bluff City, a small midwestern Mississippi River town, and to the spunky, outspoken Blossom Culp. Alexander and Blossom possess the unusual and sometimes unwelcome power to communicate with ghosts. In this novel, they solve the case of the disturbed ghost of Inez Dumaine, who will not rest until her body is exhumed and taken to the family vault in New Orleans. In *Ghosts I Have Been* (Viking, 1977, $13.95; pap., Dell, $3.25), Blossom takes center stage and narrates an episodic story in which she manages to shift the blame concerning Alexander's foiled Halloween attempt to overturn Old Mr. Leverette's outhouse onto her nemesis, Letty Shambaugh. Blossom also tames the ghost of a suicidal servant and in so doing travels to London and witnesses in hindsight the sinking of the *Titanic.* Following the third title, *The Dreadful Future of Blossom Culp* (Delacorte, 1983, $13.95; pap., Dell, $3.25), comes the present novel. All four are enjoyed by readers in grades 4 through 7.

Plot Summary

It is the beginning of November 1914 in the small midwestern town of Bluff City. The freshman class of the local high school, after cutting up worms in biology class, has moved on to English with Miss Blankenship and an introduction to *A Tale of Two Cities,* which, in spite of tales of tumbrels and guillotines that go "swoosh," fails to elicit a positive response. Among those present are the tiniest boy in the class, Collis Ledbetter; the handsome and blondest boy, Alexander Armsworth, son of the town's wealthy house builder; and snobbish, spoiled Letty Shambaugh, another of Bluff City's privileged because her family owns the local dry goods store. Letty is the president of a closed girls' club, the Sunny Thoughts and Busy

Fingers Sisterhood, S.T. and B.F.S. for short. In class, there is also fourteen-year-old Blossom Culp, feisty, plain-spoken, and intelligent. But because of her poverty, shabby appearance, and the fact that she is the daughter of a nocturnal bag lady who claims to be the town's clairvoyant, Blossom is also an outcast. Her social position does not trouble her greatly, although she would like more attention from Alexander, whose arms seem destined to be around Letty. However, Alexander and Blossom share a most unusual bond that they discovered in previous adventures. They have supernatural powers that enable them to communicate with ghosts and to travel through time.

On to history class where, before the teacher arrives, a group of the rougher boys roll little Collis in a window blind and hoist him aloft. Suddenly the door opens and in strides a monocled despot who introduces herself as Miss Augusta Fairweather, surely one of the world's greatest misnomers. Gossip has it that their former teacher, Mr. Lacy, was escorted out of town for philandering. No-nonsense Miss Fairweather claims she will teach history, starting with the Egyptians, as it really happened and not through the eyes of male chauvinist historians. Blossom is intrigued, Letty outraged, and Alexander bewildered. In the middle of a vivid description of ancient burial rites, the blind cord breaks and Collis hits the floor. Miss F. is not amused.

That night in Blossom's room, the attic part of the Culps' two-room shanty, she awakens from strange dreams when her mother arrives back from her nocturnal scavenging. Among the treasures the old witch has brought back are a dead rabbit, a live puff adder that immediately slithers into hiding, and an unusual carved red stone that looks like an Egyptian scarab.

The next day in history class, each student is given the assignment of finding a special topic on ancient Egypt and researching it. Looking for inspiration, Blossom visits the library and, using a movable ladder, climbs to a top shelf where the books on Egypt are kept. From her perch, she sees Alexander diligently scrubbing the library floor with a toothbrush. His explanation is that this is part of a hazing process involved in joining the secret boys' society, Iota Nu Beta. Blossom conveniently falls into Alexander's arms at the moment that Letty enters. Chalk up a point for Blossom!

To her amazement, Blossom is invited as a one-time guest to a meeting of the S.T. and B.F.S. at Letty's house to discuss what to do about Miss Fairweather's officious manner and the rumors that are circulating about her suffragette activities. Armed with a five-inch worm lifted from the biology lab, Blossom attends and, when snotty Mrs. Shambaugh brings in some finger sandwiches, delicately hides the worm under a slice of bread. Letty demonstrates her latest toy, a Ouija board, which spells out the word *Hathor* for Blossom before the planchette mysteriously breaks in two. Letty is upset but is valiantly trying to get the meeting back on course when Mrs. Shambaugh sees a large chunk of worm dangling from greedy Maisie Markam's face. A nauseated sisterhood flees amid screams and gagging.

That night, Blossom is gathering sassafras roots with her mother over by Old Man Leverette's property when she spies a group of boys around his outhouse. As part of the initiation ceremony, Alexander has been placed inside and must stay there until he has completely smoked a huge stogie. The boys leave. Blossom creeps up to the outhouse and, in a masculine voice, tells Alexander he must kiss Blossom the next day in school.

Back home in her bed, Blossom is woken by the sound of distant temple bells. Suddenly a beautiful young Egyptian woman appears. She introduces herself as the ghost of an ancient princess, Sat-Hathor, and commands Blossom to retrieve her mummified body and the items that have been stolen from her tomb by grave robbers, so that she can rest in peace. Suddenly Blossom has an assignment and a topic, the desecration of Egyptian tombs, for her school assignment.

After receiving a halfhearted kiss from Alexander the next morning, Blossom persuades Miss Fairweather to assign Alexander to co-research her topic. That evening at Blossom's home, the two are planning a search strategy when Princess Sat-Hathor materializes and repeats her demands. Alexander finds he too now has a mission.

In the wreckage left by an old tent circus after it disbanded last year, Alexander and members of Iota Nu Beta find an ancient piece of papyrus. Convinced this is where her mother found the scarab, Blossom and Alexander set out to explore the site. Under a bale of hay they discover the decaying remains of an Egyptian mummy obviously used as part of a sideshow exhibit. It is the earthly body of Sat-Hathor. They retrieve it and place it under Blossom's bed for safekeeping.

When the class's assignments come due, a few of Miss Fairweather's students bring in display items that obviously once belonged in Sat-Hathor's tomb and were found as circus debris, including a valuable chair from the Shambaughs. At the show-and-tell reporting session, to which parents are invited, Blossom and Alexander bring in the mummy as their *pièce de résistance.* Admiring mothers shower kudos on all the students as well as on Miss Fairweather and, to Mrs. Shambaugh's annoyance, volunteer to help in her suffragette activities. They also agree to contribute their few Egyptian artifacts so that they, along with the mummy, can be returned to their home in Egypt.

Blossom and Alexander are hoping this will be enough to satisfy Sat-Hathor, but not so. She wants all the contents of her tomb returned, or a terrible punishment will be visited on the youngsters. Blossom knows this task can only be accomplished one way. She learns that the tomb was plundered fifty years ago. Using their time-travel abilities, she and Alexander arrive at the tomb in time to frighten away the would-be grave robbers, making it possible for archeologists to discover the tomb intact later—except for the items and the body that are slated to arrive by freight shortly from the United States. Satisfied, Sat-Hathor is now free to sink peacefully into her eternal sleep of death. But an act of gratitude is forthcoming. During the annual November Homecoming parade, to which Letty and her club have contributed a garish float using an ancient Egyptian motif, with Letty highlighted as Cleopatra, there is a sudden clap of thunder and bolt of lightning. Letty and her sycophants scurry for safety as the float goes up in flames. Score another one for Blossom!

Thematic Material

This is an exciting, humorous ghost story in which a social outcast triumphs over injustice and snobbery. Blossom remains a proud individual, true to herself in spite of her background and pressures from her peers. This novel also evokes a gentler, more innocent period in our history before television and Nintendo, with such inconveniences as outdoor plumbing and such injustices as restricted voting rights. The artificial social manners of the middle class and the rigid tyranny that existed in many classrooms are presented as items for laughter. Teenage crushes, friendship, the need to preserve historical artifacts, ancient Egyptian culture, and the occult are interesting subjects also explored.

Book Talk Material

This novel is filled with many wonderfully funny and exciting episodes. Some are: *A Tale of Two Cities* is introduced along with Alexander, Letty, and Blossom (pp. 5–12); Miss Fairweather begins teaching history, and tiny Collis drops from above (pp. 14–24); Mama returns with items including the snake and the scarab (pp. 31–38); Blossom and Alexander in the library (pp. 42–47); the worm in the sandwich and the Ouija board (pp.

55–67); Alexander in the outhouse (pp. 68–75); and Princess Sat-Hathor first appears (pp. 77–87).

Additional Selections

Twelve-year-old Sarah is afraid that a ghost intent on revenge is haunting her Great-Aunt Margaret in *A Ghost in the House* (Scholastic, 1991, $13.95) by Betty Ren Wright.

The well-meaning ghosts of Horace, who was beheaded during our Revolution, and Essie, who drowned in an 1800s accident, live in an old house now a museum and share many adventures in Bill Brittain's *Who Knew There'd Be Ghosts?* (Harper, 1985, $14; pap., $3.95). This is followed by *Ghost from Beneath the Sea* (Harper, 1992, $14).

After Maggie Jones buys a strange catlike object at a garage sale, she is thrown back to the days of ancient Egypt and the boy-king Thutmose in Catherine Dexter's *The Gilded Cat* (Morrow, 1992, $14)

Much to the kidnappers' dismay, not only Amanda but all the Stanley children get kidnapped in *The Famous Stanley Kidnapping Case* (pap., Dell, $3.50) by Zilpha Keatley Snyder.

Katie has silver-colored eyes and the ability to communicate with animals in *The Girl with the Silver Eyes* (Macmillan, 1980, $14.95; pap., Scholastic, $2.95) by Willo Davis Roberts.

When the three Garrett children, including Kirby, go to live with their mother, Kirby's extrasensory perception is revealed in Lois Duncan's *A Gift of Magic* (Little, Brown, 1971, $15.95; pap., Archway, $3.50).

For younger readers, Abby and friend Potsie solve the mystery of missing Hyacinth in the lighthearted and amusing *Have You Seen Hyacinth Macaw?* (Delacorte, 1981, $11.95; pap., Dell, $3.25) by Patricia Giff.

About the Book

Book Report, September 1986, p. 35.
Booklist, April 15, 1986, p. 1226.
Center for Children's Books Bulletin, April 1986, p. 155.
Kirkus Reviews, February 1, 1986, p. 212.
School Library Journal, May 1986, p. 108.
Wilson Library Bulletin, March 1986, p. 51.

About the Author

Chevalier, Tracy, Ed., *Twentieth-Century Children's Writers* (3rd ed.). St. James, 1989, pp. 768–769.

Commire, Anne, ed., *Something about the Author.* Gale, 1980, Vol. 18, pp. 242–244; updated 1989, Vol. 55, pp. 126–138.

Gallo, Donald, *Presenting Richard Peck.* Twayne, 1989.
Garrett, Agnes, and McCue, Helga P., eds., *Authors and Artists for Young Adults.* Gale, 1989, Vol. 1, pp. 215–230.
Holtze, Sally Holmes, ed., *Fifth Book of Junior Authors and Illustrators.* Wilson, 1983, pp. 238–240.
Kirkpatrick, D. L., ed., *Twentieth-Century Children's Writers* (2nd ed.). St. Martin's, 1983, pp. 610–611.
Locher, Frances C., ed., *Contemporary Authors.* Gale, 1980, Vols. 85–88, pp. 458–459.
Metzger, Linda, ed., *Contemporary Authors* (New Revision Series). Gale, 1987, Vol. 19, pp. 366–370.
Sarkissian, Adele, ed., *Something about the Author: Autobiography Series.* Gale, 1986, Vol. 2, pp. 175–186.
Senick, Gerard J., ed., *Children's Literature Review.* Gale, 1988, Vol. 15, pp. 146–165.

Skurzynski, Gloria. *Trapped in Slickrock Canyon*

Illus. by Daniel San Souci. Lothrop, 1984, $13.95 (0-688-02688-5)

Gloria Skurzynski writes successfully in many genres and for various age groups. Among her nonfiction works is the highly praised *Robots: Your High-Tech World* (Macmillan, 1990, $15.95), a comprehensive look at how robots work and the part they play in industry, medicine, and space exploration. One of her stories for primary graders is *Honest Andrew* (pap., Harcourt, $1.95), about Andrew Otter, who learns that honesty must be tempered by tact. For middle graders, she has written the touching *Dangerous Ground* (Macmillan, 1989, $13.95), about Angela, who lives part time with her 78-year-old great-aunt, whom she fears has Alzheimer's disease; and *The Minstrel in the Tower* (Random, 1988, $6.99), the story of two youngsters' search for a lost uncle in Europe during the Middle Ages. This author, however, is perhaps best known for a series of fast-moving adventure stories set in the southwestern United States and collectively known as Mountain West Adventures. In addition to the present title, others in the series are *Caught in the Moving Mountain* (Lothrop, 1984, $11.95), about two boys held captive in mountainous Idaho, and *Lost in the Devil's Desert* (pap., Willow, 1992, $2.99) set in Utah. Because of their simple text, straightforward narrative, and breathtaking outdoor action, these novels are particularly suitable for reluctant or slow readers in grades 4 through 6. *Trapped in Slickrock Canyon* takes place during a Labor Day weekend and is told in alternating chapters by the two central characters, Gina and Justin.

Plot Summary

Twelve-year-old Gina is not thrilled at leaving her home in Denver and traveling with her father, Dylan, to visit her Uncle William and his son, twelve-year-old Justin, in the mountains of Arizona. But Gina's mother suddenly deserted her family three months before to pursue a career as a pottery maker in San Francisco. To help soften the hurt caused by this terrible loss, Dylan has arranged this summer vacation over a Labor Day weekend. Dylan and William are identical twins and get along famously, whereas Gina resents Justin's macho attitudes and affected cowboy talk that is intended to impress her with his manliness and supposed maturity. Justin, in contrast, is annoyed that his city-slicker cousin is privileged and pampered to the point of owning her own purebred Arabian horse.

When Dylan and William begin climbing the sheer sandstone face of Muleskin Cliff, Gina becomes so nervous and worried that the brothers ask Justin to take her on a hike to show her the petroglyph—an ancient Indian rock carving—he discovered in Slickrock Canyon when he was only eight years old.

As they approach the rim of the canyon, Justin hears an ominous buzzing sound and throws Gina and himself violently to the ground to avoid being seen. It is the sound of a rock saw being used by two vandals who are cutting the petroglyph out of its rock. Nearby, Justin and Gina see that someone else is watching this robbery and taking pictures. By the Jeep parked below, they identify him as an agent with the Bureau of Land Management. Unfortunately, at that moment the two thieves also spot him. One thief, who is called Jaggers by his partner, attacks the officer with such force that the BLM man falls off the cliff. Gina screams, revealing their whereabouts. Jaggers grabs his rifle and begins shooting at them as the two frantically run back into the canyon with the thief in hot pursuit. Somehow, through Justin's clever maneuverings, they lose their pursuer, but Gina falls into a pool of quicksand and must be rescued. As they stop for a moment to rest, they hear a distant roar that quickly grows in intensity. It is the sound of a flash flood catapulting through the canyon. As the swirling waters grow deeper, Gina accidentally finds a set of Moki steps, a series of holes carved in the rock by the ancient Indians for climbing purposes. As they climb to safety, a big log slams into Justin's foot, paralyzing him with pain. Gina uses her belt to help lift Justin to safety on a ledge a few feet above the swirling waters, now also being fed by a fierce, pelting rain.

In the safety of their small cave, Gina removes Justin's boot by cutting it with shards from her pocket mirror. Using techniques she has learned from her orthopedic surgeon father, she wraps the broken foot in bandages that she improvises from her T-shirt. As the storm continues and night approaches, the cave becomes freezing cold. Gradually, their mutual needs make the two forget their rivalries and differences, and like a latter-day Hansel and Gretel, they huddle together for warmth and comfort. Gina takes off her new $180 hiking boots, revealing painful blisters that have broken and are bleeding. Justin carefully washes them with water they have gathered. As they drift off into a fitful sleep, they share secrets about their plans for the future and their present problems. Gina tells Justin how lonely and deserted she feels because of her mother's departure, and Justin tells how he grieved when his best friend, Arlen, was killed in a motorcycle accident.

The following morning, they are awakened by the sound of an airplane engine. While Justin holds onto Gina, she stretches far out over the ledge and tries to signal the pilot by using her mirror to deflect sunlight. The effort is unsuccessful, and the plane flies off. There is now no alternative but for Gina to go for help. Slowly, she lowers herself down the Moki steps and into the canyon floor, which has been much changed by the rushing waters that fortunately have now subsided. Justin watches as Gina limps off into the distance.

Amazingly, the boy does not have too long to wait before help arrives. Gina is intercepted by her father and uncle who have been searching the area on horseback. Justin's rescue from the ledge is a complicated operation involving pulley, ropes, and a seat harness, but within hours he is safe on the ground, being driven to the hospital in Flagstaff where a cast is placed on his foot. The rest of the pieces of the puzzle are soon put together. The agent from the Bureau of Land Management, although badly injured, is recovering in the hospital, but Jaggers was drowned in the flooding. His accomplice, a man named Volkins, has been caught and awaits trial. The unharmed petroglyph will be removed from the stone for safekeeping in a museum. Best of all for Gina, her mother, who was notified after her daughter's disappearance, drives in from San Francisco. Although it appears that her parents' marriage cannot be saved, arrangements are made for Gina to spend all her summer vacations with her mother in San Francisco, except, of course, for some time each year when she will be with Uncle William and her newfound friend, cousin Justin.

Thematic Material

This is a suspenseful story of how two youngsters resourcefully survive severe hardships caused by nature and by the greed that leads two men to attempt murder. It is a story in which justice and courage triumph. Authentic details of the terrain of Arizona, its natural resources, phenomena, and history are nicely interwoven into the plot. A major theme is how adversity can bring people together so they can understand and accept their differences while learning to respect and eventually love one another. Another interesting aspect of this novel is the reversal of male/female role models that evolves. Gina begins as the submissive underdog in her relationship with Justin, but as necessity demands, she becomes the leader and eventually his savior. Family relationships are also explored, along with the nature of loss and friendship.

Book Talk Material

With small groups, some of Daniel San Souci's black-and-white illustrations could be used, such as the one on page 30 depicting the two vandals and the petroglyph. Special passages are: Gina and Justin are on the trail when Justin sees the vandals (pp. 11–18); Gina is terrified at seeing her father and uncle mountain climb (pp. 21–24); Justin describes finding the petroglyph (pp. 26–27); the vandals are confronted by the Bureau of Land Management agent (pp. 32–36); Jaggers begins shooting and the two youngsters flee (pp. 39–44); and the quicksand episode followed by the coming of the flood (pp. 45–48).

Additional Selections

While on an archeological dig in Arizona, Ben discovers a ring of "pot robbers" in Georgess McHargue's *The Turquoise Toad Mystery* (Delacorte, 1992, $9.95).

Twelve-year-old Evelyn, living on a ranch in central Florida, discovers her brother-in-law is a rustler in Vera Cleaver and Bill Cleaver's *The Kissimmee Kid* (Lothrop, 1981, $12.88; pap., Morrow, $3.95).

Marguerite Henry's *Born to Trot* (Macmillan, 1987, $8.95; pap., $3.95) is the Newbery Medal winner about an Arabian horse's journey to England.

During World War II, a young boy goes to live in a road workers' camp where his grandmother is the cook in Gary Paulsen's *The Cookcamp* (Orchard, 1991, $13.95; pap., Dell, $3.50).

In Ruth Riddell's *Ice Warrior* (Macmillan, 1992, $13.95), a lonely sixth-grade boy turns to iceboat racing for fun when he spends a cold winter in Minnesota with his new stepfamily.

Helen becomes involved in a mystery with drug smugglers in Rosemary Wells's *The Man in the Woods* (Dutton, 1984, $11.95; pap., Scholastic, $2.95).

In Bill Wallace's *Trapped in Death Cave* (Holiday, 1984, $13.95), Gary is convinced his grandpa was murdered to secure a map that indicated where some gold was buried.

About the Book

Booklist, June 15, 1984, p. 1486.
Center for Children's Books Bulletin, June 1984, p. 192.
School Library Journal, April 1984, p. 118.
VOYA, August 1984, p. 145.
See also *Book Review Digest,* 1985, p. 1480; and *Book Review Index,* 1984, p. 654.

About the Author

Commire, Anne, ed., *Something about the Author.* Gale, 1976, Vol. 8, pp. 190–92.
Holtze, Sally Holmes, ed., *Fifth Book of Junior Authors and Illustrators.* Wilson, 1983, pp. 294–295.
Lesniak, James G., ed., *Contemporary Authors* (New Revision Series). Gale, 1990, Vol. 30, p. 407.
Metzger, Linda, ed., *Contemporary Authors* (New Revision series). Gale, 1984, Vol. 13, p. 468.
Nakamura, Joyce, ed., *Something about the Author: Autobiography Series.* Gale, 1990, Vol. 9. pp. 319–334.

2

Humorous Stories

YOUNG readers enjoy books that produce laughter, particularly those that evoke humor from everyday occurrences with which they can identify. Ordinarily, many of these situations might be taken very seriously, but in the hands of skilled authors they become humorous, usually through the use of exaggeration. This section contains twelve titles. They cover such subjects as awaiting a new addition to the family, making a birthday present for Mom, and earning one's own spending money. In each case, however, there is an unexpected and humorous treatment of the situation, often resulting in out-loud laughter from the young reader.

Blume, Judy. *Fudge-a-mania*

Dutton, 1990, $12.95 (0-525-44672-9); pap., Dell, 1991, $3.50 (0-440-40490-8)

Using bright, snappy dialogue and honest, often amusing situations, Judy Blume has captured the delights and disasters of childhood in her novels and has become one of the world's most popular writers of books for young people. For example, in *Tales of a Fourth Grade Nothing* (Dutton, 1972, $11.95; pap., Dell, $3.50), the narrator, nine-year-old Peter Hatcher, tells of his many problems, the main one being a pesky two-year-old brother, Fudge, who is continually causing trouble and gaining a disproportionate amount of his parents' affection. Fudge became such a hit that the author has continued his adventures, still narrated by brother Peter. The first sequel is *Superfudge* (Dutton, 1980, $13; pap., Dell, $3.50) and the second is *Fudge-a-Mania,* in which Pete's family vacations in Maine. In an uncomplicated, direct plot, further wacky situations are chronicled. These books are very popular with readers in grades 3 through 6.

Plot Summary

Peter Hatcher has just completed the sixth grade and is looking forward to summer. That is, he would be looking forward to summer if his five-year-old brother, Fudge, didn't constantly drive him crazy. Fudge, whose real name is Farley, is a human hurricane and constantly in trouble. Currently, Fudge has decided to get married. Peter wouldn't really care about that so much except that Fudge has also decided on his bride. It is none other than Pete's schoolmate Sheila Tubman. Pete hates Sheila Tubman practically more than any other person in the entire world. She is bossy, a know-it-all, and a pest.

As though this isn't bad enough to ruin a summer, Pete's mother has even more devastating news. The Hatchers—Mom, Dad, Pete, Fudge, and the baby, Tootsie, along with Grandma Muriel—are going to Maine for three weeks in August. Ordinarily, that might be a desirable move. But—horror of horrors—they are going to share a house. Again, not terrific perhaps, but terrible? Yes, because they are going to share the house with none other than the Tubmans, including Sheila's grandfather, Buzzy Senior.

Pete doesn't feel he can endure three weeks even in Maine under such conditions. So he talks his best friend, Jimmy Fargo, into coming up to Maine for a few days to stay with them. Of course, he doesn't tell Jimmy about sharing the house with you-know-who. Jimmy doesn't have much use for Sheila either.

More bad news awaits when the Hatchers arrive in Maine. Pete had not asked too many questions when his mother popped the news about Maine, but he had sort of assumed that sharing a house with the Tubmans meant sharing an "attached house" with Sheila and family. Like a two-family house side by side, or upstairs and downstairs. But the reality is much worse. They are actually sharing the same house. Each family has its own bedrooms and bath, crowded as they are, but they share the kitchen and living room. Pete can't believe it!

He can't believe the ultimate pest that Fudge has turned out to be either, especially after his mother hires Sheila for seven dollars a day to baby-sit him. Right away, dumb Sheila opens up a window and lets Fudge's myna bird, Uncle Feather, escape. There is a big to-do all around the town about that. It is solved when Uncle Feather locates himself and comes home to his cage unassisted.

Things begin to look a little better, however, when Pete and Fudge meet five-year-old Mitzi, who is smaller than Fudge and seems to have a baseball glove permanently attached to her left hand. No wonder. It turns out her grandfather is none other than Big Apfel. Pete can't believe it. Big Apfel is right here in little Southwest Harbor, Maine, and he actually has a baseball game every Sunday with all the kids in town. Pete calls Jimmy long-distance right away with the great news.

"Who's Big Apple?" Jimmy wants to know.

Pete is astounded that Jimmy doesn't recognize Big Apfel, greatest center fielder of all time for the Boston Red Sox.

Jimmy is skeptical about the importance of this latest news, but he says his father will be driving him up to Maine.

While Pete waits for Jimmy's arrival and dreams of how he will star in the next baseball game and impress Big Apfel, life goes on in its chaotic fashion. Fudge is still planning his wedding to Sheila, and Grandma Muriel and Buzzy Senior, much to Pete's astonishment, seem to be hitting it off just fine.

One day Fudge and Pete go to the local library, and all thoughts of the upcoming baseball game go right out of Pete's head. For the lovely Isobel is working at the library, and Pete apparently is in love—not that he would admit that, of course.

Jimmy arrives with his weird painter father. Pete's mother is a bit dismayed to learn that Mr. Fargo plans to stay for a while too, with them! He sets up his painting equipment, including his canvas, right on the lawn. Anyone might have predicted this would cause trouble and it does. Especially when Tootsie trots right over Mr. Fargo's painting, leaving little blue footprints. Pete is sure a fight will ensue, but no—Mr. Fargo looks at the painting and thinks the baby feet are a wonderful idea. In fact, a whole new kind of art is born.

The day of the big game finally arrives. It doesn't turn out quite as Pete had hoped, however. All in all, he makes two errors on the first play of the game, knocks down Isobel as she is running the bases, and is on the losing end of a 26 to 8 score.

But that won't be the most amazing memory of the Maine vacation for Pete. More surprises are in store when Grandma Muriel and Buzzy Senior announce their coming marriage. They will be married right there on the lawn before the summer vacation ends. Fudge is going to be the "ring bear."

All Pete can think about is that Sheila Tubman is going to be his "stepsomething" for the rest of his life.

Actually, the wedding goes off pretty well with a big barbecue afterward. Maybe the summer vacation isn't so bad after all. But just to make sure, Pete makes a deal with Sheila. They both promise that even if they are sort of related now, they'll always hate each other. Then they shake on it.

Thematic Material

The wacky, offbeat Hatcher family offers hilarious adventures and constant surprises. The characters are wonderful fun, and Pete is a very likable boy beset by worries. There is never a dull moment in this fun-filled household, and Fudge is as irrepressible as ever. There is much good-natured bantering among family members, which should appeal to young readers. Judy Blume fans will love this truly humorous summer vacation adventure in Maine.

Book Talk Material

Readers will be delighted by some of the book's giggle-prompting scenes. See: Fudge announces his marriage (pp. 3–5); Uncle Feather flies the coop (pp. 27–40); Pete dreams up the poison-gas-in-the-toilets story (pp. 55–57); the Fudge-a-mania craze (pp. 58–67); and the wedding day (pp. 141–147).

Additional Selections

When Pete's father lets him have a dog, no one expects the miracle known as *Mishmash* (Houghton, 1962, $13.95; pap., Pocket, $2.95), a humorous novel by Molly Cone. One of the sequels is *Mishmash and the Big Fat Problem* (Houghton, 1983, $13.95).

Thad Smith goes to terrible lengths to prevent Maggie from telling his secret in Marjorie Sharmat's *Getting Something on Maggie Marmelstein* (Harper, 1972, $13.89). A sequel is *Maggie Marmelstein for President* (Harper, 1975, $13.89; pap., $3.50).

Ellen, a third-grader, seems well in control except when Otis Spofford begins teasing her in *Ellen Tebbits* (Morrow, 1951, $12.95; pap., Avon, $3.50) by Beverly Cleary.

Kitty tries to get rid of her mother's new boyfriend but later realizes she is wrong in *My War with Goggle-Eyes* (Little, Brown, 1989, $13.95) by Anne Fine.

Twelve-year-old Collette Murphy volunteers to be mother-for-a-day to help her pregnant mother in the hilarious novel, *Mother Murphy* (Scholastic, 1992, $13.95) by Colleen O'Shaughnessy McKenna.

Unlike his namesake, this present-day Hercules messes up even the most ordinary jobs, like watering the garden, in John Bendall-Brunello's *The Seven-and-One-Half Labors of Hercules* (Dutton, 1992, $10.95).

In Kathy Kennedy Tapp's *Den 4 Meets the Jinx* (Macmillan, 1988, $12.95; pap., Dell, $3.25), Adam's Cub Scout troop meets his sister, the jinx.

About the Book

Booklist, October 15, 1990, p. 441.
Center for Children's Books Bulletin, November 1990, p. 54.
Horn Book, January 1991, p. 94.
Horn Book Guide, July 1990, p. 40.
Kirkus Reviews, September 15, 1990, p. 1321.
New York Times Book Review, November 11, 1990, p. 29.
School Library Journal, December 1990, p. 98.
See also *Book Review Digest,* 1991, p. 194; and *Book Review Index,* 1990, p. 83; 1991, p. 94.

About the Author

Chevalier, Tracy, ed., *Twentieth-Century Children's Writers* (3rd ed.). St. James, 1989, pp. 99–101.
Commire, Anne, ed., *Something about the Author.* Gale, 1983. Vol 31, pp. 28–34.
de Montreville, Doris, and Crawford, Elizabeth D., eds., *Fourth Book of Junior Authors and Illustrators.* Wilson, 1978, pp. 46–47.
Estes, Glenn E., ed., *American Writers for Children since 1960: Fiction* (Dictionary of Literary Biography: Vol. 52). Gale, 1986, pp. 30–38.
Kirkpatrick, D. L., ed., *Twentieth-Century Children's Writers* (2nd ed.). St. Martin's, 1983, pp. 93–95.
Lee, Betsey, *Judy Blume's Story.* Dillon, 1989. Riley, Carolyn, ed., *Children's Literature Review.* Gale, 1976, Vol. 2, pp. 15–19.
Senick, Gerard J., ed., *Children's Literature Review.* Gale, 1988, Vol. 15, pp. 57–82.
Ward, Martha, ed., *Authors of Books for Young People* (3rd ed.). Scarecrow, 1990, pp. 68–69.
Weidt, Maryann. *Presenting Judy Blume.* Twayne, 1989.

Burgess, Barbara Hood. *Oren Bell*

Delacorte, 1991, $15 (0-385-30325-4); pap., Dell, $3.50 (0-440-40747-8)

This author has spent most of her life in Detroit, where she used to shop at the downtown branch of the J. L. Hudson Company, a setting important in the plot of *Oren Bell,* which begins in the year the department store closed. In this first novel, the story is told through the eyes of Oren, a black youngster in the seventh grade. The Bell family encompasses three generations, including a mother who is a cleaning lady at the department store. The story also involves a condemned house in Detroit, the ghost of a famous trumpeter, hidden treasure, heroes, and villains. The author has been so encouraged by the welcome this novel received that she is planning sequels. It is enjoyed by readers in grades 5 through 9.

Plot Summary

With humor, love, compassion, and a certain amount of weirdness, the Bell family of Detroit maintains a close family unit in a condemned house in a rundown section of the city. The family includes: seventh-graders Oren the underachiever and his powerhouse twin sister Latonya, who is in the running for king of the world; younger (and most weird) sister Brenda, who helps Oren with his math; Granddaddy, who spends many of his evenings under the influence of Red Rose wine; and Mama, who goes to work each day to keep the family together. Other main characters include a friendly veterinarian named Jack Daniels, from Lansing, who seems bent on becoming Mama's boyfriend; and cousins Dink and Dede, who live in the upstairs part of the old house with Aunt Grace. Since Aunt Grace believes she and the cousins are better than the rest of the family, the group doesn't socialize too much.

The Bell children go to S.S. Elementary School. So do friends Blue, Whitey, and Fred Lightfoot, who claims to be 100 percent American Indian. Their teacher this year is Ms. Pat Pugh, who immediately puts everybody on the buddy system. This is supposed to improve study and social skills. Smart Latonya gets familyless Fred Lightfoot for a buddy, and Oren is stuck with Wesley Wrigley Fry—a dumb white girl, for heaven's sake.

Besides having to contend with what happens *in* school, the Bell children have a hassle getting there because they have to pass the evil house next door. At the beginning of the school year, as always, Latonya makes them all perform a ceremony to protect them from the curse of the haunted house. Last year, Oren didn't follow Latonya's instructions correctly and they all had bad luck. This year he vows to do better. He manages to pass Latonya's complicated ritual—though Latonya doesn't know that he opened his eyes during the backward walk. Oren figures what Latonya doesn't know can't hurt them.

Not long into the school year, Ms. Pugh makes the startling discovery that the S.S. in their school name stands for Spiro Spill, and that good old Spiro, who died in 1918, actually built the house the Bells are renting. (Brenda believes this because she thinks his ghost is under her bed.) The house is cheap because the city may tear it down. Oren is dubious about the Spiro Spill news, but Ms. Pugh organizes a special musical program in the dead man's honor. Oren will play third-part trumpet in the school band.

Despite Granddaddy's declaration that the S.S. school band is the worst in all the country, the special ceremony comes off pretty well. This triumph is followed by the return of Skid the cat, who spends winters in the Bell house. After that, weird Brenda finds a dog about to have pups, and, what with one thing and another, the Bells need a veterinarian. That's where smiling Jack Daniels comes in. After that first visit, it doesn't look like they are ever going to get rid of him. He has definitely taken a shine to Mama, and she doesn't seem to mind all that much.

The puppies are born but one by one die, until Jack Daniels discovers the cause and is able to save one—whom they name Tuffcity. Things happen pretty quickly to the Bells after that. Brenda gets sick and is taken to Children's Hospital. Jack Daniels persuades the family that Granddaddy really should go to the veterans hospital, where he can get the care he needs because his drinking is really a problem. The S.S. Elementary School is going to be demolished, and the Bells and friends are sent off to Jefferson school, which much depresses Latonya. Mama is about to lose her job because her company is closing down, and the city sends a notice that the Bells must move. What next?

But it turns out that good times are coming after all. While searching around the old house, the Bell children discover a gold treasure left by Spiro Spill. Then Jack Daniels asks Mama to marry him and move the whole group to Lansing. When and if Granddaddy recovers, he will be welcome too. Oren decides he is not against this idea.

However, another surprise is in store. The condemned house in which they live is declared a historic dwelling. Perhaps the Bells can keep the house. Aunt Grace moves out, and music teacher Mr. Shell from the S.S. Elementary School proposes to open a music studio right on the top floor. Jack Daniels can get the land next door and open an animal hospital. Oren agrees with this idea, especially since Jack Daniels is going to need money to support his new family.

When all these grandiose schemes have been talked about, Oren decides to look at reality. He tells Latonya that some of this dream stuff might come true—one out of ten is a possibility. But wise Latonya tells her twin: "What you don't realize is, sometimes real stuff is just dream stuff while other times dream stuff is real as rain." Sounds good to Oren.

Thematic Material

This is a funny and warm novel of a poor black family in a poor section of Detroit whose members are held close by love and respect and a determination to face life square on. The Bells are fully aware of the squalor and danger of life around them; they just don't let it get them down. An endearing first novel.

Book Talk Material

Any of the following scenes will serve as a humorous introduction to the wonderful and weird Bell family: the reverse curse ceremony (pp. 4–10); the seventh grade meets Ms. Pat Pugh (pp. 19–23); Oren and Granddaddy have a talk (pp. 28–32); the Spiro Spill research team goes into action (pp. 51–59); and the memorable ceremony to honor Spiro Spill (pp. 66–70).

Additional Selections

The Mayberry family faces middle-class snobs when they move to Havenhurst in Lila Perl's *Me and Fat Glenda* (Houghton, 1972, $13.95; pap., Archway, $2.50). A sequel is *Hey, Remember Fat Glenda?* (Houghton, 1981, $13.95; pap., Archway, $2.50).

A loving black family including sixth-grader Koya Delaney, who loves to make people laugh, are portrayed in Eloise Greenfield's *Koya Delaney and the Good Girl Blues* (Scholastic, 1992, $13.95).

Akers and Marlena are convinced that their new friend, Uncle Shamus, an elderly black ex-con, has come back to Shanty Town to retrieve his loot in James Duffy's *Uncle Shamus* (Scribner, 1992, $13.95).

For the first time in her life, Maizon, a bright black girl, feels like a minority member when she attends a private Connecticut boarding school in Jacqueline Woodson's *Maizon at Blue Hill* (Delacorte, 1992, $14).

When sixth-grader Rachel Harper is saved from choking by her friend Cherry Hill, Rachel must take a back seat as Cherry basks in glory in Jacqueline Shannon's *I Hate My Hero* (Simon & Schuster, 1992, $13).

When Sarah and family move from the city to an old house in the country, the young girl meets Jethro, who claims he is a slave from Civil War times come back to life in Betty Levin's *Mercy's Mill* (Greenwillow, 1992, $14).

In a zany science fiction parody titled *Harry Newberry and the Raiders of the Red Drink* (Henry Holt, 1989, $14.95) by Mel Gilden, Harry tries to save the city of Yupitz from the attack of evil Bonnie Android.

About the Book

Book Report, May 1991, p. 40.
Booklist, May 15, 1991, p. 1791.
Center for Children's Books Bulletin, July 1991, p. 259.
Horn Book, May 1991, p. 196.
Horn Book Guide, September 1991, p. 105.
Kirkus Reviews, May 1, 1991, p. 602.
School Library Journal, April 1991, p. 116.
VOYA, April 1991, p. 26.
See also *Book Review Digest,* 1991, p. 269; and *Book Review Index,* 1991, p. 130.

About the Author

Olendorf, Donna., ed., *Something about the Author.* Gale, 1991, Vol. 69, pp. 25–26.

Conford, Ellen. *Can Do, Jenny Archer*

Illus. by Diane Palmisciano. Little, Brown, 1991, $11.95 (0-316-15356-7)

Ellen Conford has written children's books aimed at a variety of age groups. For middle and junior high students, she has written such humorous stories as *Genie with the Light Blue Hair* (Scholastic, 1989, $14.95; pap., $3.95; condensed in *Juniorplots 4,* Bowker, 1993, pp. 202–206), in which a fifteen-year-old girl finds that the power to have wishes granted by Arthur, one's own private genie, can produce unexpected problems; and *Seven Days to a Brand New Me* (Little, Brown, 1981, $14.95; pap., Scholastic, $2.95), the story of Maddy, who tries to follow directions in a self-help book so that she can conquer the handsome new boy in school. For a younger audience she has created the engaging youngster Jenny Archer, who appears in a series of brief beginning chapter books suitable for grades 2 through 4. In the first, *A Case for Jenny Archer* (Little, Brown, 1988, $10.95; pap., $2.95), Jenny becomes so involved with reading mystery stories that she begins imagining that the neighbors across the street are criminals. Others in this series include *Jenny Archer to the Rescue* (Little, Brown, 1990, $10.95) and *What's Cooking, Jenny Archer* (Little, Brown, 1989, $10.95). In the present volume, Jenny, who is not given to halfway measures, becomes fiercely competitive when she enters a tin-can-collecting contest. Like others in the series, it is charmingly illustrated by Diane Palmisciano.

Plot Summary

Sixth-grader Jenny Archer has always wanted to make a movie. Actually, she has wanted to ever since her teacher, Mrs. Pike, announced the can-collecting contest. The empty tin cans will be sold to a scrap-metal dealer. The money earned will buy a video camcorder and a TV monitor for the school. The person who collects the most cans will get to direct the first movie.

Jenny tells her practically best friend in the world, Beth Moore, that she can star in Jenny's movie if she wants to.

Beth replies, "What do you mean, *your* movie?"

It seems that Beth isn't thrilled with Jenny's idea, because she has her own ideas about collecting the most tin cans and directing the first movie. Jenny hadn't quite counted on that. A decided chill envelops their friendship, even though Jenny can't quite understand why. The two girls shake hands. "May the best collector win," they say. "As long as it's me," thinks Jenny.

Jenny goes into can collecting in a big way. She insists on going food shopping with Mrs. Butterfield, who looks after her while her mother is at work. Mrs. Butterfield is puzzled about Jenny's sudden interest in the grocery store until she sees all the cans of food that Jenny is collecting in the cart . . . then she puts her foot down, especially when Jenny wants to buy potted meat product! Whatever that is.

Relations with Beth are pretty cool as the collecting goes on. Jenny can't understand it. Why should Beth be mad at her just because she wants to win the contest so badly?

Then Jenny gets a really good idea. She begins to raid the plastic bins that neighbors put out for the recycling people to collect once a week. Unfortunately, Beth also has this great idea, and the two of them are in frantic competition to get the most cans. Jenny's can collection is growing, but her friendship with Beth isn't.

By the end of the week, Jenny is stumped for new ideas. Then she goes to visit her grandparents at their apartment house. There she gets another brilliant idea. She puts a notice on the bulletin board at the apartment house announcing her can collecting. Jenny figures she'll return the following week and there will be lots of cans from all the apartment dwellers. She's bound to win the contest.

But when Jenny returns to the apartment house, she is disappointed to discover that the super threw the cans out with the trash, probably because someone pasted a "Kittens for adoption" sign over hers.

Jenny almost gives up the contest then and there. But that isn't the "can do" spirit that Jenny Archer has always displayed. So when it's contest day, Jenny takes her cans to school and waits for them to be counted and the winner announced. She can't believe it. The winner is her own classmate, Wilson Wynn. Turns out Wilson's aunt is a veterinarian, and she has a kennel for boarding animals—lots of cans of dog food around.

Jenny is disappointed to find that she lost the contest, but she is very happy to learn that Beth unselfishly added her own can collection to Jenny's in hopes that Jenny would win because she wanted it so much. What an amazing thing to do, Jenny says. Beth is a true friend.

Someday, when Jenny Archer is a famous movie director and wins the Academy Award, the first person she is going to thank is Beth Moore.

Thematic Material

Jenny Archer is a likable, determined youngster whose grand ideas sometimes send her off in various scatterbrained directions. Her plans don't always work out, but she keeps trying, and sometimes, as in the contest with Beth, Jenny learns a valuable lesson about just how important a friendship can be.

Book Talk Material

Jenny's ideas for winning the contest are a good starting point for this story of competition among the young. See: Jenny and Beth first confront each other about the contest (pp. 3–4); Jenny goes shopping with Mrs. Butterfield (pp. 8–13); Jenny raids the recycling bins (pp. 19–28); the apartment house bulletin board idea (pp. 34–37); and Jenny gives up (pp. 44–46).

Additional Selections

A shop-and-swap business brings headaches to four enterprising youngsters in Jill Ross Klevin's *The Turtle Street Trading Co.* (Delacorte, 1982, $11.95). A sequel is *Turtles Together Forever* (Delacorte, 1982, $9.95).

In *Squashed* (Delacorte, 1992, $15.) by Joan Bauer, Ellie has grown a 600-pound pumpkin named Max that she plans to enter in the county fair.

Burton tries to foil a thief, Professor Sarry, and build a giggle machine that will make all his friends so happy they will forget their troubles in Dorothy Haas's *Burton and the Giggle Machine* (Macmillan, 1992, $13.95), a sequel to the equally hilarious *Burton's Zoom Zoom Va-Room Machine* (Macmillan, 1990, $13.95).

Valentine's Day approaches, and the love bug seems to be biting all Adam Joshua's friends, including Nelson and his dog, George, in Janice Lee Smith's *Nelson in Love* (Harper, 1992, $12). This is part of a good-natured series that includes *The Show-and-Tell War* (Harper, 1988, $11.95).

In a simple chapter book, *Mary Marony and the Snake* (Putnam, 1992, $12.95), by Suzy Kline, Mary is brave enough to pick up a snake but is fearful that her classmates will tease her about her stuttering.

At a magic shop, Jennifer picks up a talking toad, Bufo, whose kiss will change the receiver into an amphibian in a light, fast-moving fantasy, *Jennifer Murdley's Toad* (Harcourt, 1992, $16.95), by Bruce Coville.

In *Happy Burpday, Maggie McDougal!* (Little, Brown, 1992, $11.95) by Valiska Gregory, Maggie must improvise when she discovers that she has no money to buy a birthday present for best friend Bonkers.

About the Book

Booklist, December 1, 1991, p. 702.

Horn Book Guide, Spring 1991, p. 57.

Kirkus Reviews, December 1, 1991, p. 1531.

School Library Journal, December 1991, p. 80.

See also *Book Review Index,* 1992.

About the Author

Chevalier, Tracy, ed., *Twentieth-Century Children's Writers* (3rd ed.). St. James, 1989, pp. 228–229.

Commire, Anne, ed., *Something about the Author.* Gale, 1974, Vol. 6, pp. 48–49.

Evory, Ann, ed., *Contemporary Authors* (First Revision). Gale, 1979, Vols. 33–36, pp. 203–204.

Holtze, Sally Holmes, ed., *Fifth Book of Junior Authors and Illustrators.* Wilson, 1983, pp. 82–83.

Metzger, Linda, ed., *Contemporary Authors* (New Revision Series). Gale, 1984, Vol. 13, p. 117.

Senick, Gerard J., ed., *Children's Literature Review.* Gale, 1986, Vol. 10, pp. 87–100.

Ward, Martha, ed., *Authors of Books for Young People* (3rd ed.). Scarecrow, 1990, p. 143.

Cresswell, Helen. *Ordinary Jack: Being the First Part of the Bagthorpe Saga*

Macmillan, 1977, $14.95 (0-02-725540-9); pap., Puffin, $3.95 (0-14-031176-9)

Because of the vast variety of settings, moods, and characters Helen Cresswell has created in her many books for young people, this English writer has gained the reputation of being both unpredictable and daring. She has written over fifty juvenile novels plus many picture books, most of which, unfortunately, have not been published in this country. In *Dear Shrink* (Macmillan, 1982, $12.95), for example, she tells, in the form of a diary written by young Oliver Saxon, about the plight of three once-affluent youngsters who become homeless in London when their guardian dies. The novels in the Bagthorpe Saga represent a complete change of pace and tone and more closely resemble the zaniness of good television situation comedies (actually, these novels formed the basis of a popular BBC comedy series). *Ordinary Jack* has been followed by six sequels, two of which, *Bagthorpes Abroad* (Macmillan, 1984, $13.95; pap., Puffin $3.95) and *Bagthorpes Haunted* (Macmillan, 1985, $13.95; pap., Puffin, $3.95) were condensed in *Juniorplots 3* (Bowker, 1987, pp. 32–36). These novels contain a few English expressions perhaps unfamiliar to young readers, but this does not inhibit the fun and laughter they produce for readers in grades 5 through 8.

Plot Summary

The Bagthorpe family consists of eight members. There is Mr. Bagthorpe, the father, a pontificating television scriptwriter whom no one takes too seriously, and his wife, who vainly tries to maintain some semblance of order in the bedlam known as her household while ironically conducting a newspaper family advice column. They have four children. Three of them—the oldest, William; thirteen-year-old Tess; and Rosie, age eight—are bona fide geniuses and, like their parents, flaming eccentrics. In the middle at age eleven is Jack, normal, average, and, in his eyes, disgracefully ordinary. Fortunately for him, he has a friend in the family dog, a nondescript mutt appropriately named Zero, who also is something of a misfit. Also in the household are self-willed Grandma and her husband, perhaps the most fortunate of them all because he has a hearing problem or, as some suspect, is actually S.D. (selectively deaf). Mrs. Fosdyke, the general cook and housekeeper, has the good sense to live off premises. Nearby at The Knoll live the rest of the zanies: rich Uncle Russell Parker, his wife, Aunt Celia, and their precocious four-year-old daughter, the uncontrollable novice pyromaniac Daisy.

It is Grandma's seventy-fifth birthday, and the Bagthorpes are gathering for a gala dinner. Jack has a private conversation with Uncle Parker in which he complains about continually being bested by all his siblings. Only today, young Rosie severely trounced him at swimming, the last straw in a seeming endless parade of defeats and humiliations. Uncle Parker promises he will develop a scheme to make Jack a valuable, indeed distinguished, member of the clan.

In an unusual display of harmony and serenity, the birthday dinner begins, but within minutes a catastrophe occurs. Zero, who is playing under the dinner table with Daisy, is frightened by an exploding party cracker, becomes entangled in the tablecloth, and brings down the entire dinner, including a cake ablaze with candles. These, in turn, with Daisy's help, ignite a box of fireworks. After the firemen leave, the Bagthorpes realize that they are now minus a dining room. Undeterred, they decide that henceforth meals will be taken in the kitchen.

The next day, Uncle Parker reveals his plan to Jack. The boy will gain position in the family only if he can display a unique talent. Therefore, he must convince the family that he is a Prophet, a seer who is able to pierce the mysteries of the future. He must practice gazing into space, creating what Uncle Parker calls a Mysterious Impression, and utter prophecies. Uncle Parker makes Jack write down all the stages of this project in a book so there will be no slip-ups. The first assignment is to begin the next day, when Jack will reveal that in a vision he sees a Lavender Man Bearing Tidings. In the evening, Uncle Parker will visit wearing his new lavender suit with news that the Bagthorpes' au pair girl will arrive the next day from Denmark. Voilà! an instant prophet.

Unfortunately, the family is so used to ignoring Jack that his Mysterious Impression and frequent murmurings about lavender and so forth go practically unnoticed, particularly when his father steals center stage by breaking his arm trying to practice a head-standing yoga exercise. Nevertheless, the arrival of lavender-clad Parker with his news report does create the beginnings of the respect Jack longs for, although his father claims Jack simply needs a mental checkup.

Stage two is more elaborate; Uncle Parker admits that he is still working on details. He takes Jack into town and, in a shop specializing in the occult, purchases such items as a dowsing rod, tarot cards, incense, and a crystal ball, the latter with a seven-day return guarantee. With all this paraphernalia, Jack again tries to create a Mysterious Impression, but distractions dilute his attention-getting ploys. For example, on two different occasions, Zero runs off with the microphone of Mr. Bagthorpe's tape recorder, causing household crises and work stoppages. The gorgeous new arrival, the non-English-speaking Atlanta from Denmark, also creates many diversions, particularly for William, who is instantly smitten. The discovery of Jack using his crystal ball and his dowsing rod plus Grandma's enthusiastic endorsement of his incense in her yoga training do help a little, however. When Uncle Parker issues new instructions and Jack begins murmuring in a distracted way about a giant red-and-white bubble bearing tidings, and later includes mention of mysterious brown bears, the desired effect is gradually produced, and Jack receives some attention and respect—at least as much as possible in the Bagthorpe family.

Uncle Parker plans the grand denouement on the day Rosie's birthday is being celebrated with an elaborate outdoor picnic meticulously planned by Mrs. Fosdyke. In the midst of the festivities, a large red-and-white hot air balloon appears with two bears aboard, dropping visiting cards with "Jack Bagthorpe Appointed Prophet" printed on them. Unfortunately, at the moment Mr. Bagthorpe finds Jack's secret journal, the balloon loses altitude and lands in the meadow. The extraterrestrial bears are unmasked as two of Parker's cronies in costume and the whole plot exposed. In true Bagthorpe tradition, all is forgiven, Rosie is convinced she has had the best birthday party ever, and the family at last realizes that Jack is far from ordinary.

Thematic Material

The Bagthorpe books are intended for pure fun and enjoyment. The plot moves easily from one laugh-aloud slapstick situation to another. Interesting family relationships are also explored and a number of social customs gently spoofed, including a reminder of the dangers of vanity and overstuffed attitudes of self-importance. Readers will empathize with ordinary Jack and his attempts to gain respect and position. They will also realize that in the chaos of the Bagthorpe household, being ordinary and normal are desirable and admirable characteristics.

Book Talk Material

The problems of being average in a family of geniuses could be discussed as an introduction to this novel. Some important passages are: Jack discusses his problem with Uncle Parker (pp. 1–7); Grandma's birthday party and the fire (pp. 8–18); Uncle Parker tells Jack about his plan (pp. 27–35); Jack practices creating a Mysterious Impression on Mrs. Fosdyke (pp. 39–40); he causes consternation by calling Uncle Parker for advice (pp. 49–53); and his Lavender Man speech is interrupted by Mr. Bagthorpe's accident (pp. 60–65).

Additional Selections

Nils tries to follow the loony instructions he finds in a library makeover book in *Be a Perfect Person in Just Three Days* (Houghton, 1982, $12.95; pap., Bantam, $2.50); by Stephen Manes.

Olivia wonders about how intelligent she is, considering she has a super-bright brother and sister in Lila Perl's *Don't Ask Miranda* (Houghton, 1979, $12.95).

Bossy sixth-grader Douglas Fairchild and basketball freak Armando Rivera are forced to join the school's Special Discussion Group, known as The Twinkie Squad, with hilarious results, in Gordon Korman's *The Twinkie Squad* (Scholastic, 1992, $13.95).

In Avi's *S.O.R. Losers* (Macmillan, 1984, $11.95; pap., Avon, $2.75), the eighth-grade soccer team of the South Orange River school is very talented but unfortunately not in sports.

In an unusual story that is part realistic and part tall tale, the reader is introduced to an extraordinary hero in *Maniac Magee* (Little, Brown, 1990, $13.95; condensed in *Juniorplots 4,* Bowker, 1993, pp. 108–113), by Jerry Spinelli.

In Clive King's *Me and My Million* (Harper, 1979, $12.89), Ringo, a London street urchin, has some amazing and amusing adventures from a learning disability.

Adam Blessing and Brenda Belle Blossom are two outsiders whose problems stem from their families in *The Son of Someone Famous* (Harper, 1974, $12.89; pap., $3.95), by M. E. Kerr.

About the Book

Booklist, February 15, 1977, p. 895.
Center for Children's Books Bulletin, July 1977, p. 173.
Horn Book, June 1977, p. 312.
Kirkus Reviews, January 1, 1977, p. 4.
School Library Journal, February 1977, p. 62.
See also *Book Review Digest,* 1978, p. 285; and *Book Review Index,* 1977, p. 98.

About the Author

Chevalier, Tracy, ed., *Twentieth-Century Children's Writers* (3rd edition). St. James, 1989, p. 241–242.

Commire, Anne, ed., *Something about the Author.* Gale, 1971, Vol. 1, pp. 70–71; 1987, Vol. 48, pp. 58–67.

de Montreville, Doris, and Crawford, Elizabeth D., eds., *Fourth Book of Junior Authors and Illustrators.* Wilson, 1978, pp. 105–106.

Ethridge, James M., ed., *Contemporary Authors* (First Revision). Gale, 1967, Vols. 17–18, p. 116.

Evory, Ann, ed., *Contemporary Authors* (New Revision Series). Gale, 1983, Vol. 8, pp. 129–131.

Kirkpatrick, D. L., ed., *Twentieth-Century Children's Writers* (2nd ed.). St. Martin's, 1983, pp. 204–205.

Lesniak, James G., ed., *Contemporary Authors* (New Revision Series). Gale, 1992, Vol. 37, pp. 115–119.

Senick, Gerard J., ed., *Children's Literature Review.* Gale, 1989, Vol. 18, pp. 90–113.

Ward, Martha, ed., *Authors of Books for Young People* (3rd ed.). Scarecrow, 1990, pp. 157–158.

Crew, Linda. *Nekomah Creek*

Illus. by Charles Robinson. Delacorte, 1991, $14 (0-385-30442-0); pap., Dell, $3.50 (0-440-40788-5)

After trying folk singing and acting, Linda Crew married and settled on a farm in Oregon, where she raised three children. Getting to know a family of Cambodian refugees who worked on their farm inspired her first novel, *Children of the River* (Doubleday, 1989, $14.85). The river in the title refers both to the Mekong River in East Asia and the attitude that life also flows inexorably. The story centers on the Americanization of one of the girls in the family. Her second novel, *Someday I'll Laugh About This* (Delacorte, 1990, $14.95), grew out of many family experiences and deals with twelve-year-old Shelby and her troubled relationship with her cousin Kirsten. *Nekomah Creek* is her third book and another family story. The central character is fourth-grader Robby, who wants some peace and quiet to read and get away from his noisy, unconventional family, in which Mom works and Dad stays home to care for the kids. His desire for solitude is misunderstood by his teacher. She sends him to the school counselor, where there are further complications. The story is enhanced by good pen-and-ink drawings by Charles Robinson. This novel is enjoyed by readers in grades 4 through 6.

Plot Summary

Nine-year-old Robert Hummer—"Please call me Robby"—can't understand all the fuss his fourth-grade teacher, Mrs. Perkins, makes about his preference for reading books over playing sports. Since when is reading books a problem? he wants to know. But Mrs. Perkins thinks such things as soccer and "joining in" are important, even in Robby's small out-of-the-way school in Nekomah Creek, Oregon.

In fact, Mrs. Perkins is so concerned about him that she insists he go to see the school counselor, Mrs. Van Gent. Apprehensive after being warned by classmate Amber not to tell "nothing" to the counselor, Robby babbles on in an effort to show Mrs. Van Gent how perfectly normal his home life, and therefore Robby himself, is. Trouble is, Robby is acutely aware that his home life is a little unusual. First of all, he has twin siblings—a boy and a girl, which is pretty unusual in itself. They are practically still infants, and ever since their arrival, life in the Hummer household has been more chaotic than before, if that's possible. Robby admits that the house always looks as though a tornado has just struck, or is about to. Then there's his parents. His mother works, and his father doesn't. That is, his father stays home to tend the house and the twins, and his mother, who designs greeting cards and stuff, goes out to work. That's a little unusual, too, even in this modern era, only Robby and most of his friends don't think so. They're used to it. But as he tries to convince the counselor how normal his family is, they begin to look all the more abnormal, and just a little embarrassing.

When the annual auction rolls around, Robby is surprised to find that his father's donation this year is a romantic gourmet dinner for two, prepared by none other than Robby's father himself in the Hummer home! At first Robby thinks it's a great idea, especially when the dinner is auctioned off for $60, but then the class bully, Orin, declares Robby's father to be a wimp. Things take a turn down from there.

Not long afterward, Robby learns two disturbing facts. Mrs. Van Gent and her husband have won the dinner that Robby's father will prepare. And, through Mrs. Van Gent's intervention, his friend Amber has been taken from her family and placed in a foster home. Robby is convinced the counselor is coming to the gourmet dinner to spy on his own home life, which is a disaster as far as looks and conventionality go, and once she sees what chaos reigns in the Hummer household, she will take him and the twins away to foster homes too.

Life keeps getting worse. The twins come down with stomach flu, and so does Robby. The house gets more messy than usual. His mother and father sort of have words with each other because they're cranky from lack of sleep and kids throwing up all over the place. A foster home seems more plausible than ever. To make things even more miserable, Robby is attacked by bully Orin on his way home from school, and the present Robby has made for his father's birthday is destroyed. Then Robby learns his father has decided to take a casserole over to Orin's family because Orin's father has been injured in a logging accident. Robby can't believe it, but he can't let his father go through this alone either, so he goes with him. Robby discovers how unlike his own kind and fun-loving father Orin's father is. Later, Robby defends Orin when the bully is accused of stealing money at school. Orin couldn't have done it because he was attacking Robby at the time of the theft! The two boys don't become fast friends, but at least Orin stops picking on him and doesn't call his father a wimp anymore.

Before the night of the gourmet dinner, Robby confesses his fears of a foster home to his parents. They assure him that even though they may be a bit unconventional, no one is about to take their children away. Robby also learns the true reasons behind Amber's placement in a foster home. He feels a little bit better with those fears out of his mind, but he begs his parents to at least make things "nice" when the Van Gents come to dinner, just so he won't feel so "embarrassed."

The dread night of the gourmet dinner arrives, and so do Mrs. Van Gent and her husband. The house is so picked up and neat that Robby hardly recognizes it, although he lives in mortal fear that someone will open a closet door and half their belongings will come tumbling out.

The night starts off in rather stilted fashion, but wonder of wonders, Dr. and Mrs. Van Gent actually *like* his parents. They all hit it off splendidly and have a marvelous evening.

Robby comes to the end of the night with the realization that life, unlike many books, doesn't always have happy endings, but that's OK, too. No one is coming to take him away from his slightly wacky, but all-in-all pretty happy family. He feels safe and tired. Come to think of it, even soccer isn't so bad when you get the hang of it . . . not as good as reading books, of course.

Thematic Material

This is a humorous look at a warm, nutty, and slightly unconventional family. It captures the ups and downs of life in a small town with people who love and respect each other as a family unit but preserve their own individuality too. Here is a family that carries old-time values into a late-twentieth-century setting.

Book Talk Material

The exuberant happenings in the Hummer home will serve as a wonderful introduction to this delightful family. See: Robby tells the counselor about his family (pp. 17–21); Mom arrives home in the midst of jack-o'-lantern carving (pp. 24–27); the spaghetti dinner incident (pp. 68–73); Robby rebels (pp. 74–78); and the Halloween mess (pp. 92–105).

Additional Selections

Mack's truck ruins Morris's pushcart and the war is on, in Jean Merrill's *The Pushcart War* (Harper, 1992, $14.89; pap., Dell, $3.50).

The Dither family has a most unusual summer when Great-Aunt Emma arrives with her flying carpet in Sid Hite's *Dither Farm* (Henry Holt, 1992, $15.95).

The four somewhat spoiled and unpredictable Conroe sisters are sent off to Big Grandma's for a summer of misadventures in Hilary McKay's *The Exiles* (McElderry, 1992, $14.95).

When Gretchen diets and becomes the former "Hippo Hubbard," the results are mixed in Ilene Cooper's *The New, Improved Gretchen Hubbard* (Morrow, 1992, $14).

In Joel L. Schwartz's *How to Get Rid of Your Older Brother* (pap., Dell, 1992, $3.25), twelve-year-old Jay is tired of competing with his older brother, Louis, and would gladly help him disappear.

With the help of a former Notre Dame player, middle-grader Molly shows the class bully, Jason, how football is really played in Ann Sullivan's *Molly Maguire, Wide Receiver* (pap., Avon, 1992, $2.99).

Pat claims that he is naturally accident-prone, but he tries to avoid a mishap after making a bet that he can remain for an entire summer without a scratch in Bill Wallace's *The Biggest Klutz in Fifth Grade* (Holiday, 1992, $14.95).

About the Book

Booklist, October 15, 1991, p. 438.
Center for Children's Books Bulletin, September 1991, p. 5.
Horn Book Guide, Spring 1992, p. 64.
Kirkus Reviews, November 15, 1991, p. 1468.

School Library Journal, August 1991, p. 164.
See also *Book Review Digest,* 1992, p. 24; and *Book Review Index,* 1991, p. 203; 1992 (n.p.).

About the Author

Telgen, Diane, ed., *Something about the Author.* Gale, 1933, Vol. 71, pp. 52–53.
Trosky, Susan M., ed., *Contemporary Authors.* Gale, 1990, Vol. 133, p. 100.

Dahl, Roald. *Matilda*

Illus. by Quentin Blake. Viking, 1988, $14.95 (0-670-82439-9); pap., Puffin, $4.50 (0-14-034294-X)

Roald Dahl's madcap adventure stories for youngsters horrify as many parents as they delight their children, because they deal with the dark side of human nature, in which many adults are cruel oppressors and the young heroes and heroines must resort to the most outrageous stratagems to achieve justice, freedom, and, sometimes, revenge. For example, in *James and the Giant Peach* (Knopf, 1961, $17.95; pap., Puffin, $3.95), the orphaned James escapes the trials of living with an oppressive aunt and uncle by entering a magically grown huge peach and discovering a new world populated by insects. *Charlie and the Chocolate Factory* (Knopf, 1991, $15; pap., Puffin, $3.50; condensed in *Introducing Books,* Bowker, 1970, pp. 60–63) tells of a young boy from a poor family who not only wins a contest to tour the Wonka Candy Factory but ends up inheriting it. Roald Dahl's two books of memoirs are also popular with young readers. The first, *Boy: Tales of Childhood* (Farrar, 1984, $13.95; pap., Puffin, $4.95; condensed in *Introducing Bookplots 3,* Bowker, 1988, pp. 71–76), takes the reader through Dahl's childhood in Wales to age twenty, and *Going Solo* (Farrar, 1986, $14.95; pap., Puffin, $4.99; condensed in *Seniorplots,* Bowker, 1989, pp. 281–285), for an older audience, continues the story through his Royal Air Force days in World War II. In *Matilda,* we meet an amazing girl who is able to rid her school of a hateful headmistress and also restore a teacher's rightful inheritance. Quentin Blake's illustrations complement the text wonderfully. It is enjoyed by readers in grades 4 through 6.

Plot Summary

Although her parents are simply too dumb and preoccupied with themselves to notice, their daughter, Matilda, by the age of five, is a genius. She spoke perfectly before she was two, taught herself to read at three, and by the time she was ready for school, was checking adult books out of the library on a regular basis. She had already enjoyed *Great Expectations* by Charles Dickens as well as such classics as *The Grapes of Wrath* by Steinbeck and Jane Austen's *Pride and Prejudice.*

Her doltish parents took no notice. They found her to be a nuisance anyway and paid little attention to her except to berate, belittle, and otherwise make her life miserable. Her father's only interest was in her older brother, because he was to take over the family's used-car business one day. Matilda knew her father was a crook, but naturally she said nothing. However, she does get back at her parents in small ways for their abuse, like the time she puts Superglue on the rim of her father's porkpie hat, and the only way it can be removed is along with a lot of his hair.

Through this terrible treatment and dull existence, Matilda remains a sweet-tempered, loving child. She is quite excited about starting school, even though her parents couldn't care less if she had an education. In fact, they are so careless about it that Matilda is five and a half by the time she enters school. Her mother, who overeats and watches telly all day, thinks education is a waste of time anyway.

Matilda's first teacher is Miss Honey, whom she likes immediately. On the very first day, Miss Honey casually tests her pupils to see how advanced they are and is astounded to discover that Matilda is surely a genius. When she goes to the headmistress to ask that Matilda be put immediately in a higher grade where her astounding ability can be nurtured, Miss Trunchbull, the headmistress, an authentic holy terror and terrible person, laughs at her.

But Miss Honey knows that Matilda is an extraordinary child, so she allows her to study separately from the rest of the class and in many ways encourages the child to learn more and grow. A great bond of love and friendship develops between the two. Miss Honey even goes to Matilda's home to get her parents interested in fostering the education of this delightful child. Her parents are not interested, to say the least.

Although Matilda loves school and her friendship with Miss Honey, all the children live in terror of Miss Trunchbull, who is not above picking up little boys by the ears or little girls by their braids and flinging them about. One day when the headmistress comes into their classroom to see how they are progressing, she accuses Matilda of putting a slimy newt into her water glass. Matilda, who is innocent of this, becomes incensed at being so unjustly accused.

That is when the first miracle occurs. Matilda concentrates all her brain power on tipping over the glass right onto Miss Trunchbull. She concentrates with all her might, and it works!

Later Matilda tells Miss Honey of her new power. Miss Honey is astounded, if skeptical. She asks Matilda to come home with her for some tea and to discuss this most unusual development. Matilda is shocked to see the poor shack where Miss Honey lives, with practically no furniture, no running water, and little else. Miss Honey explains that her own home, left to her when her father died, has been taken over illegally by her mean aunt, who helped to raise her after her mother's death. The aunt was terribly cruel and abusive, and Miss Honey is forced to live in these impoverished circumstances. Her father's will has mysteriously disappeared, and that is why she has been left out in the cold. Matilda is amazed to hear this story and even more amazed to discover that Miss Honey's cruel aunt is none other than the dreaded Miss Trunchbull.

Matilda decides to use her magic powers to gain back Miss Honey's rightful inheritance. The next time Miss Trunchbull enters the classroom, a piece of chalk mysteriously hops up to the blackboard and begins to write. It tells Miss Trunchbull to give Jenny (Miss Honey) back her house and get out of there. She does!

With Miss Trunchbull gone and a new head of the school installed, Matilda is promoted to the top grade to take advantage of her astounding talents. Miss Honey moves into her rightful home, and the bond between the teacher and the little girl grows ever stronger.

One day Matilda returns to her home to find that her parents are packing for Spain. The whole family has to get out of the country because of her father's crooked used-car dealings. Matilda does not want to go. She runs to Miss Honey, who returns with her to Matilda's home. With very little effort, they persuade the parents to let her stay and live with Miss Honey. As Matilda's family drives away, Matilda jumps right into Miss Honey's arms for a hug.

Thematic Material

Preposterous, outlandish, and great fun! A zany, exaggerated comedy that young readers will thoroughly enjoy. It takes all the small annoying traits of adults and blows them up far larger than life. The children are satisfyingly clever, good-natured, honest, and picked on. This funny novel incorporates all the wishes of children—to outsmart their elders, get sweet revenge for mean behavior, and so forth—into a most satisfying romp.

Book Talk Material

Almost any scene in the book is an introduction to the zany world of superintelligent Matilda. See: preschool Matilda at the library (pp. 15–21); Matilda puts Superglue in her father's hat (pp. 30–37); Matilda's first day at school with Miss Honey (pp. 66–81); Miss Trunchbull picks on Bruce Bogtrotter (pp. 117–133); Matilda moves the glass (pp. 162–169); and Matilda practices to help Miss Honey (pp. 210–214).

Additional Selections

Two boys sneaking out at night to attend late-night movies are featured in the zany *The Snarkout Boys and the Avocado of Death* (Lothrop, 1992, $12.95; pap., NAL, $3.50; condensed in *Juniorplots 3,* Bowker, 1987, pp. 145–148) by Daniel M. Pinkwater.

An orphan, Maniac, is part-time savior, part tall-tale hero, and full-time wonder who changes the lives of those he meets in Jerry Spinelli's *Maniac Magee* (Little, Brown, 1989, $14.95; pap., Harper, $3.95; condensed in *Juniorplots 4,* Bowker, 1993, pp. 108–113).

In an easy chapter book by Duncan Ball, the reader meets *Emily Eyefinger* (Simon & Schuster, 1992, $13), a young girl who performs good deeds like solving a bank robbery by using the eye she has on one of her fingers.

A spunky rag doll enlists the help of other toys to help save their nursery school in Terrance Dicks's easily read *Sally Ann on Her Own* (Simon & Schuster, 1992, $14).

Pushy Maxine thinks she is on the way to becoming a world-famous inventor after she devises such gadgets as a hamster-driven pencil sharpener in David Getz's *Almost Famous* (Henry Holt, 1992, $13.95).

When her disliked stepfather shrinks to four and a half inches because he takes the wrong drugs, nine-year-old Mallory finds he is at last in her control in Barbara Dillon's *My Stepfather Shrank!* (Harper, 1992, $13).

Mitzi's mother is going to marry Walter, whose son thinks he is a dinosaur, in Barbara Williams's *Mitzi and the Terrible Tyrannosaurus Rex* (Dutton, 1982, $10.95; pap., Dell, $1.95). Also use *Mitzi and Frederick the Great* (pap., Dell, $2.50).

About the Book

Center for Children's Books Bulletin, October 1988, p. 30.
Emergency Librarian, March 1989, p. 42.
Horn Book, January 1989, p. 68.
Kirkus Reviews, August 15, 1988.

New York Times Book Review, January 14, 1987, p. 31.
School Library Journal, October 1988, p. 70.
Wilson Library Bulletin, February 1989, p. 84.
See also *Book Review Digest,* 1989, pp. 362–363; and *Book Review Index,* 1988, p. 192; 1989, p. 191.

About the Author

Block, Ann, and Riley, Carolyn, eds., *Children's Literary Review.* Gale, 1976, Vol. 1, pp. 49–52.
Chevalier, Tracy, ed., *Twentieth-Century Children's Writers* (3rd ed.). St. James, 1989, pp. 255–256.
Commire, Anne, ed., *Something about the Author.* Gale, 1971, Vol. 1, pp. 74–75; 1982, Vol. 26, pp. 50–61.
de Montreville, Doris, and Hill, Donna, eds., *Third Book of Junior Authors.* Wilson, 1972, pp. 73–74.
Kirkpatrick, D. L., ed., *Twentieth-Century Children's Writers* (3rd ed.). St. Martin's, 1983, pp. 216–218.
Lesniak, James G., ed., *Contemporary Authors* (New Revision Series), Gale, 1991, Vol. 32, pp. 107–109; 1992, Vol. 37, pp. 123–131.
Senick, Gerard J., ed., *Children's Literature Review.* Gale, 1984, Vol. 7, pp. 63–84.
Ward, Martha, ed., *Authors of Books for Young People* (3rd ed.). Scarecrow, 1990, p. 166.

Danziger, Paula. *Not for a Billion Gazillion Dollars*

Delacorte, 1992, $14 (0-385-30819-1)

Paula Danziger is known for her zany but often touching novels about the trials and tribulations of young people growing up. These books are also known for having among the most unusual-sounding titles in the field. For example, her first book was *The Cat Ate My Gymsuit* (Delacorte, 1974, $14.95; pap., Dell, $3.25), named after the excuse that overweight, bored Marcy Lewis uses to get out of attending odious physical education. Ten-year-old Matthew Martin was first introduced in *Everyone Else's Parents Said Yes* (Delacorte, 1989, $13.95; pap., $3.50), in which the youngster manages to alienate both his sister and all the girls in his class by his constant practical jokes. The situation, however, is reversed when it becomes time to celebrate his eleventh birthday. *Make Like a Tree and Leave* (Delacorte, 1990, $13.95; pap., Dell, $3.50) tells how irrepressible Matthew continues to get into trouble at home and at school, at the same time trying to save some property from a developer. The third title, *Earth to*

Matthew (Delacorte, 1991, $13.95; pap., Dell, $3.50) is followed by *Not for a Billion Gazillion Dollars*. In this installment, Matthew's summer becomes filled with money-making schemes after his parents tell him he must earn half of the money needed to buy the computer program he wants. These funny, lighthearted stories are enjoyed by readers in grades 4 through 6.

Plot Summary

The summer stretches boringly before eleven-year-old Matthew Martin. Two things have gone wrong. His parents will not let him have the computer program he says he needs so desperately. No amount of pleading, getting on his knees, cajoling, and promising will move Mr. and Mrs. Martin. The computer program is simply too expensive—a couple hundred dollars; Matthew is always saying that he needs things and then tossing them aside soon after he gets them; and besides, Matthew is, to say the least, irresponsible about money. He owes practically everyone in his soon-to-be-seventh-grade class. His parents think Matthew has some growing up to do. Matthew figures he is growing up in other ways, at least. Last year he couldn't even stand girls; now he spends a good deal of time thinking about exploring the possibility of kissing Jil! (that's how she spells her name) Hudson, his very first girlfriend. But that's also his second summer problem. Jil!'s mother is having a baby, and Jil! must accompany her to the lake for the whole summer to await the infant's arrival. What a bummer.

Matthew thinks his parents are unreasonable about the subject of money, especially since they are sending his pain-in-the-neck older sister, Amanda, away to camp just because she wants to be an actress. His mother explains that camp in general is a good idea for thirteen-year-old Amanda right now, and besides Amanda herself is paying part of the tuition with money she has earned.

That gives Matthew the idea of coaxing his parents into promising the new computer program if he earns half the cost. He has no idea how to do it, because the truth is that Matthew, just on the verge of leaving little-boy status behind, really is quite irresponsible about money.

But he vows to try. His initial venture, lawn mowing, is kind of a disaster. First, he runs the mower into the cow ornament on Mrs. Levy's lawn. Then Mrs. Levy has an emergency and must run off, leaving her two young children in Matthew's not-too-capable hands. Actually, he manages quite well, although he ends up with baby "everything" all over him. He decides baby-sitting is not for him.

Next, Matthew and his best friend, Joshua, try windshield washing.

They have seen it done on street corners in New York City. It's easy. When a car stops for a light, you run up and clean the windshield and then wait for the driver to hand over some change. But this isn't New York City, it's small-town Califon, New Jersey, and Matthew's parents quickly hear that the two boys are out in the streets with cars whizzing by. They are not happy. Windshield washing is declared off limits.

Just when things are at their darkest, a little light dawns with the return of Jil! Both she and her mother were miserable out at the lake because the water is polluted and no one can go swimming. Matthew starts to think about kissing again.

Matthew, Joshua, and Jil! form a committee of three, with much prodding from Jil!, to put their heads together on a marvelous make-money project that will use Matthew's skills on the computer. Jil! will be in charge of finances; Joshua will be publicity and promotion; Matthew will develop and design cards and posters on the computer; and they will sell them to businesses around town. The IMA CARD, INK enterprise is born.

It isn't easy, and Matthew doesn't grow up about money overnight, but the business is successful. At last the day comes when Matthew has the couple hundred dollars for his expensive computer program. Along with his parents, he goes to the computer store. The clerk pulls the program off the shelf. Matthew has taken so long to earn the money that the program is now on sale. It is eighty dollars cheaper than the original price!

For a moment, Matthew is tempted back to his old ways—what else can he buy? Then he remembers a public television program that he and Jil! had seen earlier, showing a little girl who had to go without milk because her family was so poor.

Matthew tells his parents he is going to donate the rest of his money to UNICEF to help children like that little girl. And he really means it.

Matthew's parents are very happy that he is growing up. Matthew's happy because that puts them in a good mood, and a good mood means he can ask a favor.

"Can we go to the ice cream store and try out three of their new flavors?" he asks.

Mrs. Martin says some things never change. But Matthew knows they do. In the meantime, the three set out for ice cream with Matthew Martin leading the way.

Thematic Material

This is a lighthearted, amusing look at a boy on the verge of growing up. Matthew bounces back and forth between silly kid and young man with a serious thought or two. His perplexity over his feelings about Jil! are honest and will be understood by young boys of this age group. It is also the story of a close family group and of parents trying hard—sometimes without too much success—to keep their children from repeating their own mistakes, such as when Mr. and Mrs. Martin tell Matthew about their own early troubles with credit cards. Matthew's relationships with his schoolmates ring true and will be shared by all young readers.

Book Talk Material

Boys and girls will be amused by Matthew's antics as he swings back and forth between childhood and the beginning of young manhood. See: Matthew argues with his parents in vain about the computer program (pp. 1–7); Matthew thinks about renting out his sister's room (pp. 8–15); the baby-sitting almost-disaster (pp. 26–47); Matthew and Joshua try windshield washing (pp. 55–60); his parents talk to him about money (pp. 69–73); the business idea is born (pp. 88–92).

Additional Selections

Twelve-year-old Mitch seeks fame and fortune when he goes to Miami to enter a national baking contest in Jamie Gilson's *Can't Catch Me, I'm the Gingerbread Man* (Lothrop, 1982, $12.95; pap., Pocket, $2.75).

A boy breaking into television commercials finds he must pose in an ad for underwear in Betty Miles's *The Secret Life of the Underwear Champ* (Knopf, 1981, $8.99; pap., $2.95).

Keith Robertson's *Henry Reed, Inc.* (Viking, 1958, $14.95; pap., Dell, $3.25), told in diary form, is the story of Henry, a young entrepreneur, and his summer in New Jersey. A sequel is *Henry Reed's Baby-Sitting Service* (Viking, 1966, $14.95; pap., Dell, $3.25).

When Leroy's obnoxious cousin comes to live in Leroy's town, the young boy must learn to cope in Patricia Giff's *The Winter Worm Business* (Delacorte, 1984, $8.95; pap., Dell, $2.95).

Doug's family, preparing for his sister's wedding, doesn't know that he must be a goat sitter in the clubhouse in *Me, My Goat, and My Sister's Wedding* (Houghton, 1985, $13.95; pap., Pocket, $2.75) by Stella Pevsner.

When Billy bets he can eat fifteen worms a day, his friends and family devise ways to cook them in Thomas Rockwell's *How to Eat Fried Worms* (Franklin Watts, 1973, $13.50; pap., Dell, $3.50).

Seven humorous stories by such popular writers as Lloyd Alexander and Scott Corbett are included in *Just for Fun* (Dutton, 1977, $8.95), edited by Ann Durrell.

About the Book

Booklist, September 1, 1992, p. 56.
Kirkus Reviews, October 1992, p. 1253.
School Library Journal, September 1992, p. 250.

About the Author

Chevalier, Tracy, ed., *Twentieth-Century Children's Writers* (3rd ed.). St. James, 1989, p. 262.
Commire, Anne, ed., *Something about the Author.* Gale, 1984, Vol. 36, pp. 62–65; 1991, Vol. 63, pp. 24–31.
Holtze, Sally Holmes, ed., *Fifth Book of Junior Authors and Illustrators.* Wilson, 1983, pp. 92–94.
Lesniak, James G., ed., *Contemporary Authors* (New Revision Series). Gale, 1992, Vol. 37, pp. 131–135.
May, Hal, *Contemporary Authors.* Gale, 1985, Vol. 115, pp. 122–123.
Senick, Gerard J., ed., *Children's Literature Review.* Gale, 1990, Vol. 20, pp. 49–56.

Delton, Judy. *Angel's Mother's Wedding*

Illus. by Margot Apple. Houghton, 1987, $13.45 (0-395-44470-5)

Judy Delton is a prolific writer of both picture books for very young readers and novels for the middle grades. In the former area, she is well known for her stories about Rabbit. For example, in *Hired Help for Rabbit* (Macmillan, 1988, $14.95), Rabbit, who is tired from working in the garden all day, hires Squirrel to do his cooking. Among the series created for an older audience are those featuring Angel and those with Kitty as the central character. In the first book about Kitty, *Kitty in the Middle* (Harcourt, 1979, $14.95), she and her two friends share episodic adventures while living through the war in 1942. The prequel, *Kitty from the Start* (Houghton, 1987, $12.95), tells how Kitty enters the third grade in a strict Catholic school and forms friendships with Margaret Mary and Eileen. Angel appears in 1983 in *Back Yard Angel* (Houghton, 1983, $13.95; pap., Dell, $2.95), the story of how ten-year-old Angel O'Leary must take care of her younger brother, Rags. In *Angel's Mother's Boyfriend* (Houghton, 1986, $12.95; pap., Dell, $2.95), the two youngsters are dismayed to discover that their mother has a boyfriend who is a clown. *Angel's Mother's Wedding* traces the wedding ritual hilariously from bridal shower to the actual wedding. Another in this genial, cheerful, easy-to-read series is *Angel's Mother's Baby* (Houghton, 1982, $12.95). These series are enjoyed by readers in grades 3 through 5.

Plot Summary

Angel O'Leary is a born worrier. And heaven knows she has enough to worry about. In three months, her mother is going to marry a clown. That's not the problem, however, for Angel loves her soon-to-be-stepfather, Rudy, and he really is a clown, with his own television show. The problem is that the wedding is three months off and Angel's friend Edna—who knows *everything*—has informed Angel that three months is scarcely enough time to plan a wedding. What about the invitations? The minister? The wedding cake? Angel had no idea that a wedding was such a complicated affair. And it's obvious to her that her mother hasn't even thought about it. Angel is afraid they'll have a wedding and no one will come.

Before Angel can delve into the mysteries of planning a wedding, other complications arise. Her nearly five-year-old brother, Rags, overhears Rudy, whom he adores, saying that what he'd really like as a wedding present is a new car, because the one he has is old and shabby looking. But since he knows no one will give him a new car, maybe he could just settle for a new paint job. Ah, thinks Rags, this is something I can do. He tells no one of his marvelous plans. So, when Angel is supposed to be babysitting but is instead off bike riding with Edna, Rags takes a can of red paint to Rudy's blue car. The result is a disaster and a new worry for Angel. But Rudy, amiable as always, thinks the strangely painted car might be just the thing to pull the float he is planning for the upcoming Memorial Day parade.

Angel and Rags get involved in helping prepare the float, and thoughts of wedding plans are temporarily put aside. But all their work seems for nothing when Memorial Day arrives with a soaking rain. Not to worry, says Rudy. March they do, drenched to the skin. It turns out to be a Memorial Day the little Wisconsin town will long remember. Despite the rain, the large crowd enjoys the floats and marchers. At one point, when the parade is stopped, as it frequently is, Rudy tells Rags to get the dogs, out of their cages and onto their chairs on the float. Rags has been practicing this great animal act for a long time. Rags gets the borrowed dogs onto their chairs and is about to begin his act when the parade, and their float, moves forward quickly. The sudden movement scares the dogs, and off they go in all directions through the audience. The entire parade stops while everyone, including the police, rounds up the dogs. Rudy decides they better forget the whole dog show idea. That ends the parade, but everyone is laughing.

Finally, after Memorial Day, Angel is able to discuss the upcoming wedding with her mother. The affair will be small, her mother explains calmly. Angel will be a junior bridesmaid, her mother's friend Alyce will the maid of honor, and Rags will be the ring bearer. Angel is glad her mother at least has made some plans about the wedding even if she is far too calm about it to quell Angel's anxieties.

Angel and her mother shop for the perfect wedding dresses. Alyce can't go with them at the appointed time. She will shop for her own dress later. Angel's mother finds just the right dress in teal blue for herself and a lovely pale lavender dress for Angel. But Angel thinks it's a mistake not to have Alyce shop with them. The truth is that Alyce is scatterbrained. Surely she will buy something too fancy on her own and ruin the whole wedding. Another worry.

Wedding plans get into high gear with a shower, which both Angel and Rags attend. Despite herself, Angel rather enjoys all the activities. Later, their mother informs Angel that Rudy loves them both so much that he wishes to adopt them. This is certainly fine with Rags and it is OK with Angel too, until she realizes adoption means taking Rudy's last name. His name is Pappadopolis. Is she really ready to go through life as Angel Pappadopolis? Something else to worry about.

Now Rags has his own problem. He is very concerned because his bear suit hasn't arrived. Rags understands his role in the wedding to be the "ring bear." He is puzzled as to why a bear should be the one to carry the ring, but he's perfectly willing to play the part if that's what his mother and Rudy want. However, when the suit does arrive, he is very disappointed to see it is just an ordinary pair of pants and a jacket! Surely a mistake has been made. They have sent the wrong suit. But in all the excitement going on in the household, no one will listen to his complaints.

On the day of the wedding, the house fills up with guests, including Rudy's parents. Naturally, Alyce is late for the ceremony. When she does finally arrive, Angel's worst fears are surpassed. Alyce hasn't bought something too fancy for the wedding. No indeed, she has bought the exact same teal dress that Angel's mother is wearing!

The strange wedding ceremony begins with the "ring bear" heading the procession. Suddenly Rags begins to crawl on all fours and then twirls in the air like a prancing bear! He reasons that if his mother made a mistake and gave him the wrong suit, the least he can do is to play the part of a bear. Angel believes he has lost his mind.

Of course, the prancing ring bear is nothing compared to the maid of honor and the bride marching down the aisle in exactly the same dresses. Angel is mortified.

However, what seems to be a mess of a wedding changes for Angel when they get to the part where her mother and Rudy say a few words. When Rudy talks about how much his new family means to him and gives Angel a locket with her new initials on it, all the disasters and all the worries about becoming Angel Pappadopolis fade away. She dearly loves this gentle, kind man who is now her father.

After the wedding, Rags has a chance to tell everyone how hard it was to be a bear without a bear suit with real fur. Now that she understands, Angel is glad her brother is not going entirely crazy. But Rags still doesn't understand why, if his mother wanted him to be a ring bear, she didn't want him to look like one.

Rags decides that no one seems to understand him. Angel knows how he feels, but somehow, right now, it doesn't matter a bit.

Thematic Material

This is a truly funny and warm story of people becoming a family. Angel is a highly likable character going through the pains and worries of growing up, for whom the future is full of potential disasters. The affection the family members have for each other is real and endearing. Rudy is the kind of new father any child would love to have. The wedding scene with its many upsets, including Rags's bear antics down the aisle, is a laugh-out-loud adventure. To be enjoyed by all readers in this age group, the story speaks of childhood and growing up and love and friendship and family.

Book Talk Material

Young readers will especially enjoy the book's many amusing episodes that only enhance Angel's list of worries. See: Edna explains the countless plans that go into a wedding to an amazed Angel and Rags (pp. 4–11); Rags "makes" Rudy's wedding present (pp. 32–51); the Memorial Day parade (pp. 60–65); Angel is convinced the wedding is off (pp. 70–72); Angel discovers she will be a Pappadopolis (pp. 86–94).

Additional Selections

To cement their friendship, Jimmy and Zander agree to face three dares together in Nancy Lamb's hilarious *The Great Mosquito, Bull and Coffin Caper* (Lothrop, 1992, $12).

In Eth Clifford's *Help, I'm a Prisoner in the Library* (Houghton, 1989, $13.95; pap., Scholastic, $2.95), two young girls take refuge from a blizzard in a library and are locked in.

Katie John's friend Sue says Katie's new home is haunted, and they set out to explore this claim in Mary Calhoun's *Katie John* (Harper, 1960, $12.89; pap., $3.50), one of many titles in this series that includes *Katie John and Heathcliff* (pap., Harper, $3.50).

Rosy, who is anxious to impress fellow student Blaine, exaggerates her family history in *Rosy Cole Discovers America!* (Little, Brown, 1992, $13.95) by Sheila Greenwald. This is the seventh adventure about Rosy and her Upper East Side school in Manhattan; another is *Rosy's Romance* (Little, Brown, 1989, $12.95; pap., Pocket, $2.75).

Veronica, trying to get her companions to accept her, says a new girl is already her special friend in Nancy K. Robinson's *Veronica Meets Her Match* (Scholastic, 1990, $12.95), one of a series about Veronica that includes *Veronica Knows Best* (Scholastic, 1987, $12.95; pap., $2.75).

Instead of getting the attention she wants from her family, Leona only gets into trouble in Juanita Havill's *It Always Happens to Leona* (Crown, 1989, $12.95).

James and his friends are running a successful summer pet care business when suddenly their profits begin disappearing in *Critter Sitters* (Holiday, 1992, $13.95) by Constance Hiser.

About the Book

Booklist, October 1, 1987, p. 318.

Center for Children's Books Bulletin, January 1988, p. 87.

Horn Book, September 1987, p. 610.

School Library Journal, November 1987, p. 104. See also *Book Review Digest,* 1987, p. 447; and *Book Review Index,* 1987, p. 190; 1988, p. 205.

About the Author

Commire, Anne, ed., *Something about the Author.* Gale, 1978, Vol. 14, pp. 54–55.

Evory, Ann, and Metzger, Linda, eds., *Contemporary Authors* (New Revision Series). Gale, 1983, Vol. 8, p. 140.

Holtze, Sally Homes, ed., *Fifth Book of Junior Authors and Illustrators.* Wilson, 1983, pp. 97–98.

May, Hal, and Straub, Deborah A., eds., *Contemporary Authors* (New Revision Series). Gale, 1989, Vol. 25, pp. 91–92.

Nakamura, Joyce, ed., *Something about the Author: Autobiography Series.* Gale, 1990, Vol. 9, pp. 127–140.

Lowry, Lois. *Attaboy, Sam!*
Illus. by Diane de Groat. Houghton, 1992, $13.95 (0-395-61588-7)

Lois Lowry's first book for young readers was *A Summer to Die* (Houghton, 1977, $13.95; pap., Bantam, $2.95), a powerful story of guilt and grief involving the death of an older sister. This novel, published in 1977 and based on an incident in the author's life, won that year's International Reading Association's annual award given to a young writer of promise. Since that time, the author has produced a number of books with serious themes such as the Newbery Medal winner *Number the Stars* (also condensed in this volume), and *Rabble Starkey* (Houghton, 1987, $12.95; pap., Dell, $3.25; condensed in *Juniorplots 4,* Bowker, 1993, pp. 71–76), the affecting story of a young girl's problems being the daughter of a poor but loving single mother.

Interspersed with these somewhat serious works came a series about the laid-back Krupnik family of Boston and their precocious, dynamic daughter, Anastasia. She was first introduced in *Anastasia Krupnik* (Houghton, 1979, $12.95; pap., Bantam, $2.75), during which this articulate, sophisticated ten-year-old fourth-grader toyed with the idea of becoming a Catholic to change her name, developed a crush on young basketball enthusiast Washurn Cummings, and reluctantly adjusted to the arrival of a family addition. Anastasia faithfully keeps two lists in her private notebook: "Things I Love" and "Things I Hate." Naturally, the prospect of a new baby in the house ranked high on the second list! Her entertaining, often hilarious, adventures continue through many sequels, such as *Anastasia on Her Own* (Houghton, 1985, $13.95; pap., Dell, $2.95) in which Anastasia, now a seventh-grader, faces both romantic and household crises; and *Anastasia's Chosen Career* (Houghton, 1987, $13.95; pap., Dell, $2.95) in which at age thirteen she begs to go to a charm school to correct her freaky looks. Throughout all these stories, her new baby brother, Sam, plays a secondary role as a lovable but frequently pesky fly in her ointment. In *All About Sam* (Harcourt, 1988, $12.95; pap., Dell, $2.95), he emerges as a central character with a description of his childhood from birth to about the age of three. Some of the incidents are new, while others found in earlier books are retold from Sam's point of view. They include his liberating Anastasia's goldfish by flushing it down the toilet, his guilt at shoplifting a package of gum, difficulties in toilet training, and his fear of attending nursery school. His delightful saga continues in *Attaboy, Sam!* All these books are popular with readers in grades 4 through 7.

Plot Summary

In addition to bright, resourceful, and sensitive Sam, age almost three, the Krupnik family of Cambridge consists of his thirteen-year-old sister, Anastasia; Dad, a.k.a. Myron Krupnik, the renowned National Book Award-winning poet and Harvard professor of English; and Mom, Katherine, a successful illustrator of children's books.

It is only one week away from Mrs. Krupnik's thirty-eighth birthday. When Dad announces he has been unable to find a bottle of her favorite perfume, Je Reviens, in department stores, Mom admits she would rather forget her advancing years. Because it's the thought that counts, she suggests that instead of store-bought presents, homemade gifts are the best. Quick-witted Sam decides he will secretly concoct his own special perfume for his mother, using the smells of her favorite things. Without divulging any information about this project, he asks Anastasia for a spare container. She directs him to the family's recycling bin, where he retrieves a large grape juice jar.

Remembering that his mother loves the smell of his father's pipes, he creeps into his dad's study and takes one of the lesser-used, not-to-be-missed ones from the rack. Gently he lowers it into the bottle, pouring in a glass of water to dissolve the fragrance. The bottle and contents are hidden in his toy box, which he renames the Lab.

Anastasia gets a baby-sitting job caring for the Parishes' two-month-old Alexander. Sam, who has overheard Mrs. Krupnik say that she loves the smell of little babies, gets permission to tag along, intent on obtaining another specimen for his perfume jar. On their way to the Parishes', the two pass the house of their neighbors, the Sheehans, in whose driveway is a large cardboard box containing kittens being offered for adoption. Sam would love to own one of them, particularly a lovely furry gray one, but he knows his father "is 'lergic."

During her baby-sitting chores, Anastasia changes Alexander's poop-filled diaper and wipes up after he has thrown up. Alexander reluctantly decides these must be the smells of young babies and places two tissues containing specimens in a Ziploc bag brought specially for the occasion.

Sam generously helps his sister write a special birthday poem, but his chief concern is identifying ingredients for the perfect perfume. When Mrs. Krupnik mentions that she loves the smell of her chicken soup, Sam secretly fills another Ziploc bag with a generous amount and adds it to the jar. Satisfying her love of the smell of clean hair causes some problems when, at nursery school, Sam is caught chopping clumps of his hair and placing them in another bag. He doesn't mind being seated in the time-out chair as a mild punishment, because another necessary component has been found.

The aroma of freshly baked bread is another favorite smell, and so, when Sam visits the family's friendly neighbor, Gertrustein, Sam's version of Mrs. Gertrude Stein, he brings back a sample of yeast, which, according to Mrs. Stein, is an important component in all bread recipes. During this excursion, he steals another peek at the kittens and again longs to bring the little gray one home.

After a class field trip to the Boston aquarium, Sam brings home a Ziploc bag of water and some seaweed from the tidepool area to satisfy his mother's craving for the smell of the sea. By this time the concoction is emitting a terrible stink and beginning to bubble and hiss. Sam is convinced that by Friday this will miraculously become a luxurious perfume. But for the moment he asks his mother not to enter his room because of the birthday surprise it contains.

It is Thursday, and Sam becomes so fearful that his beloved kitten will soon be adopted that he commits a naughty act. He creeps over to the Sheehans and, pretending he has his parents' permission, tells Mrs. Sheehan he has come to adopt the gray cat. She is pleased and even gives him a bag of cat food as a bonus. Sam steals back to his house, and, undetected, gets bowls for water and food, and some sand from his sandbox for the cat's potty, then moves his pet into his powerfully smelling bedroom. That evening, Anastasia and Sam bake a surprise birthday cake for their mother.

The next day, after nursery school, Sam helps his mother prepare the table for the special birthday dinner, to which Gertrustein has been invited. Fearful that the noxious fumes will asphyxiate the kitten, he moves him to the safety of the spare bedroom.

When Mr. Krupnik gets back from school, he asks Sam and Anastasia to meet him in his study. There, he sheepishly unveils a painting of his wife he has done for her birthday. He realizes that it is far from satisfactory, and all three agree that poor Mr. K. is a lousy painter. Afterward, Anastasia reads the poem she has delicately copied on a piece of cardboard, and all three are unanimous in proclaiming tactfully that she is an equally lousy poet. It's Sam's turn. He takes them up to his room to give them a whiff of his creation. Candidly, Dad says it reminds him of his visit to New York after a seventeen-day strike of garbage collectors, and Anastasia says it smells like the school locker that had been opened after a student had barfed in it five days before. All three are ashamed of the presents they have to offer. Suddenly, the jar explodes, covering Mr. Krupnik, his painting, Anastasia, her poem, and Sam with a thick purple liquid and evil-smelling streaks of the debris that had been part of Sam's perfume. Sam has an idea on how to save the situation and rushes to the spare bedroom.

That night after dinner, the little kitten is given to Mrs. Krupnik accompanied by a poem the three have written in which Mr. Krupnik promises to control his sneezing. Last, Sam offers a name for the family's new pet—Purrfume. Attaboy, Sam!

Thematic Material

This is an affectionate comedy about a close, understanding family in which each member is respected and loved. Sam emerges as a wonderfully earnest, inventive, literal-minded youngster whose problems in growing up are universal. The humor evolves naturally out of simple situations, and the author shows once again that she knows how children feel and also what makes them laugh.

Book Talk Material

Some of the wonderful drawings by Diane de Groat, including the cover, which illustrates all the main plot elements, could be used with small groups. Some entertaining passages are: Sam tries his hand at typing (pp. 1–5); Sam decides to produce the perfume (pp. 9–11); after visiting Anastasia, Sam finds the grape juice jar and begins his collection (pp. 12–20); Sam sees the kittens (pp. 25–26); he collects Alexander's smells (pp. 28–33); he gets some yeast from Gertrustein (pp. 49–53) and adds the tidewater to his collection (pp. 64–69).

Additional Selections

Socks, a cat, ceases to be the center of attention when a new baby arrives on the scene in Beverly Cleary's *Socks* (Morrow, 1973, $11.95; pap., Avon, $3.50).

Homer is a well-meaning youngster whose adventure with an out-of-control doughnut machine is world famous. This is only one of the funny incidents in Robert McCloskey's *Homer Price* (Viking, 1943, $13.99; pap., Puffin, $3.95).

During her attempts to rescue a kitten, third-grader Anna meets an eccentric elderly woman, Mrs. Sarafiny, in *Anna and the Cat Lady* (Harper, 1992, $14) by Barbara M. Joosse.

Josie is a feisty young heroine who gets into trouble regularly and sometimes has to lie to get out of it in a light-hearted British series by Magdalen Nabb. Two titles are *Josie Smith* (McElderry, 1989, $12.95) and *Josie Smith at School* (McElderry, 1991, $12.95).

After a week of rehearsing, Max Malone decides he is not up to his goal of being a TV megastar in Charlotte Herman's *Max Malone, Superstar* (Holt, 1992, $14.95), one of a humorous series that includes *Max Malone Makes a Million* (Holt, 1991, $13.95).

Jenny is an active, curious, and pesky five-year-old who experiences typical childhood concerns in Bonnie Pryor's humorous *Jumping Jennie* (Morrow, 1992, $14).

Sara Fine goes to any length to convince her parents that she really needs a dog in the humorous *Dog Crazy* (Morrow, 1992, $13) by Eve B. Feldman.

About the Book

Booklist, February 15, 1992, p. 1106.
Center for Children's Books Bulletin, April 1992, p. 213.
Horn Book, July 1992, p. 451.
Kirkus Reviews, March 1, 1992, p. 326.
School Library Journal, May 1992, p. 114.
See also *Book Review Digest,* 1992, p. 1222; and *Book Review Index,* 1992, p. 559.

About the Author

Chevalier, Tracy, ed., *Twentieth-Century Children's Writers* (3rd ed.). St. James, 1989, pp. 610–611.
Commire, Anne, ed., *Something about the Author.* Gale, 1981, Vol. 23, pp. 120–122.
Estes, Glenn E., ed., *American Writers for Children since 1960: Fiction* (Dictionary of Literary Biography: Vol. 52). Gale, 1986, pp. 249–261.
Holtze, Sally Holmes, ed., *Fifth Book of Junior Authors and Illustrators.* Wilson, 1983, pp. 198–199.
Metzger, Linda, ed., *Contemporary Authors* (New Revision Series). Gale, 1984, Vol. 13, pp. 333–336.
Olendorf, Donna, and Telgen, Diane, eds., *Something about the Author.* Gale, 1993, Vol. 20, pp. 134–137.
Senick, Gerard J., ed., *Children's Literature Review.* Gale, 1984, Vol. 6, pp. 192–197.
Ward, Martha, ed., *Authors of Books for Young People* (3rd ed.). Scarecrow, 1990, p. 451.

Myers, Walter Dean. *Me, Mop, and the Moondance Kid*
Illus. by Rodney Pate. Delacorte, 1989, $13.95 (0-440-50065-6)

This author has produced an amazing number of high-quality novels for both elementary and junior high school readers. Almost exclusively, his main characters are black youngsters growing up in inner city neighborhoods such as Harlem or areas of New Jersey, both settings being places where the author has lived. Two of his better known novels for readers in grades 6 and up are *Scorpions* (Harper, 1988, $13; condensed in *Juniorplots 4,* Bowker, 1993, pp. 90–95), the tragic story of a twelve-year-old boy who reluctantly inherits the leadership of a Harlem street gang from his brother, who is in prison; and *Hoops* (Delacorte, 1981, $13.95; pap., Dell, $2.95; condensed in *Juniorplots 3,* Bowker, 1987, pp. 249–253), the story of a young boy who hopes to use his extraordinary ability in basketball as a ticket out of Harlem. In *Me, Mop and the Moondance Kid,* the "me" is the eleven-year-old narrator, T. J., who tells an easygoing story involving adoption and Little League games. A sequel, *Mop, Moondance and the Nagasaki Knights* (Delacorte, 1992, $14), also contains baseball action, this time involving foreign teams plus the youngsters' continued worries about their adoptive families. The Mop books make good reading for youngsters in grades 4 through 6.

Plot Summary

T. J. (which stands for Tommy Jackson), his younger brother Billy, known as Moondance, and Miss Olivia Parrish, called Mop, are best friends. They have been best friends for most of their eleven years, in the case of T. J. and Mop, because most of those years have been spent at the Dominican Academy for orphaned children. But now T. J. and Moondance have been adopted. Mop is hoping she will soon be adopted, too, especially since the word is out that the Dominican Academy is about to close, which means that any children not adopted by that time will be sent to another orphanage far away.

Mop, being Mop, retains an upbeat attitude. In fact, she is certain that if she performs well as the catcher for the Elks, the academy baseball team, then the coaches, Jim and Marla Kennedy, who are childless, will want to adopt her. T. J. is not quite so sure. Every time Marla Kennedy shows up, Mop does something stupid like dropping pizza on her clean shirt or punching some guy out for making a smart remark. But that's Mop.

T. J. is having problems with the baseball team anyway. He knows he's the star player, the champion, the best they've got, but perhaps he's just trying to impress his new dad a little too much. Dad boasts about how he almost had a career in the majors. Every time Dad watches an Elks' game, the ball just seems to slip through T. J.'s fingers, or he strikes out on three pitches. T. J. just can't figure it. In addition, it's a little embarrassing because Moondance is so good.

Besides the problems with the baseball team and Mop's possible adoption, they are worried about what will become of Taffy, the llama, when the academy is closed. Not everyone wants a llama as a pet, even T. J. must admit.

The Elks enter the baseball season hoping to win at least one game, which would equal their record of last year. They do get some extra coaching help from Peaches the wino and Sister Carmelita, who used to do some pitching herself when she was known as Titi.

Wonder of wonders, the Elks win a game! T. J., star that he is, doesn't actually contribute to this win, and Dad's jaw gets a little tighter watching from the stands. But the Elks are happy just the same.

Jim Kennedy's job keeps him from doing the coaching, so Marla takes over. This makes Mop more anxious to impress her than ever. Marla seems to be doing a good job, because the Elks win three more games, once again without much contribution from T. J.; and miracle of miracles, they end up facing a three-game championship against the powerful Eagles! This is not going to be easy, especially because the Elks pitcher, who is none other than Moondance, seems to have an aversion to throwing a ball anywhere near the batter for fear of hitting him or her. Once again, Peaches comes to the rescue by constructing a cardboard dummy of a batter and teaching Moondance to get the ball closer and closer.

The Elks are ready! Game 1: Eagles 1, Elks 0. In the second game, T. J. actually catches a ball. The Elks win.

Now it's the all-important game 3. First, the Eagles coach tries to get Mop out of the catching position, claiming that it's too hot for a girl to catch, according to the Children's Welfare Association. Marla the coach is a little worried that he might be right, but Mop sets her straight. "Fight for me," she tells Marla, "I'm worth it." Marla tells the Eagles coach that Mop is going to catch—that's it.

In game 3, Mop scores and the game is tied. The bases are loaded, and guess who's up! T. J. would rather be anywhere else in the world. Two strikes. The Eagles pitcher throws the ball, and T. J. is too afraid to move. It smacks him right in the back. He isn't hurt, but a run scores and the Elks win the championship.

That isn't the only miracle. There are more to follow. The academy is going to be turned into a day-care center, and Taffy the llama can stay as mascot. Dad is pretty pleased with the Elks win. And Mop gets adopted by the Kennedys.

The only blot on this happy time is when Sister Carmelita, who is a little prone to accidents, shows them an example of her fine pitching—there goes the stained-glass window!

Thematic Material

This is a funny, fast-moving story of friendship, family life, and Little League baseball. The illustrations indicate that T. J. and Moondance are black and Mop is white, but otherwise little is made of race relations in the story. The children's genuine affection and caring for each other are well drawn, and T. J.'s numerous excuses for his poor performances on the baseball field are truly amusing. This is a story rich in the joys of friendship and family life.

Book Talk Material

Conversations between T. J. and Mop or among the members of the Elks baseball team will serve as hilarious introductions to this amusing sports story. See: how Mop got her name (pp. 9–10); the first game with the Lions (pp. 19–24); Mop drops the pizza after the game (pp. 38–40); Moondance loses his bear (pp. 46–49); Peaches the wino gives the kids some pointers (pp. 49–54); and Mop explains how come Moondance can pitch so well (pp. 65–66).

Additional Selections

A group of youngsters searching for missing cats encounter the homeless in Jill Pinkwater's *Tails of the Bronx* (Macmillan, 1991, $14.95).

Yellow Bird and Me (Ticknor & Fields, 1986, $12.95) by Joyce Hansen is the story of a black girl growing up in the Bronx and her friendship with Yellow Bird, who suffers from dyslexia.

In Mary Stolz's *Stealing Home* (Harper, 1992, $14), Thomas is sharing a messy existence in Florida with his grandfather and cat, Ring, until Great-Aunt Linzy moves in.

A group of black kids are featured in Brenda Wilkinson's *Definitely Cool* (Scholastic, 1993, $13.95), in which Roxanne is worried about starting junior high school.

A thirteen-year-old black girl whose father is dead is afraid her older sister is drifting away from the family, as revealed in a series of diary entries in *Sister* (Harper, 1990, $14; pap., $3.50) by Eloise Greenfield.

Ten-year-old Doris is living a protected life in an inner city community until an unconventional boy, Amir, moves into the neighborhood in Joyce Hansen's *The Gift-Giver* (Houghton, 1980, $13.85; pap., $4.95).

In *Buster's World* (Dutton, 1989, $12.95) by Bjarne Reuter, a novel set in Copenhagen, Buster's magic tricks get him in and out of trouble.

About the Book

Book Report, January 1989, p. 38.
Booklist, February 1, 1989, p. 941.
Emergency Librarian, May 1990, p. 25.
Horn Book, January 1989, p. 73.
Kirkus Reviews, November 15, 1988, p. 1677.
School Library Journal, December 1988, p. 110.
See also *Book Review Digest,* 1989, p. 1191; and *Book Review Index,* 1989, p. 590; 1990, p. 584.

About the Author

Chevalier, Tracy, ed., *Twentieth-Century Children's Writers* (3rd ed.). St. James, 1989, pp. 707–708.

Commire, Anne, ed., *Something about the Author.* Gale, 1982, Vol. 27, p. 153; updated 1985, Vol. 41, pp. 152–155.

Evory, Ann, ed., *Contemporary Authors* (First Revision). Gale, 1979, Vols. 33–36, pp. 592–593.

Holtze, Sally Holmes, ed., *Fifth Book of Junior Authors and Illustrators.* Wilson, 1983, pp. 225–226.

Kinsman, Clare D., ed., *Contemporary Authors* (First Revision). Gale, 1973, vols. 33–36, p. 638.

Metzger, Linda, and Straub, Deborah A., eds., *Contemporary Authors* (New Revision Series). Gale, 1987, Vol. 20, pp. 325–330.

Sarkissian, Adele, ed., *Something about the Author: Autobiography Series.* Gale, 1986, Vol. 2, pp. 143–156.

Senick, Gerard J., ed., *Children's Literature Review.* Gale, 1982, Vol. 4, pp. 155–160; 1989, Vol. 16, pp. 134–144.

Peck, Robert Newton. *Soup's Hoop*

Delacorte, 1990, $13.95 (0-385-29808-0); pap., Dell, $3.25 (0-440-40589-0)

Robert Peck often uses rural Vermont, the scene of his childhood, as the setting of his novels for a young audience. His first, *A Day No Pigs Would Die* (Knopf, 1973, $13.50; pap., Dell, $3.50; condensed in *More Juniorplots,* Bowker, 1977, pp. 16–19), has autobiographical overtones. It takes place in the late 1920s and tells the story of Rob Peck, age twelve, growing up in a Shaker atmosphere in Vermont. He has to assume a man's responsibilities when his loving father, the local hog butcher, dies suddenly of a heart attack. This setting and time frame are also used in the Soup series, which now numbers more than a dozen titles. Soup was Robert Peck's favorite friend as a child, and many of these stories are based loosely on childhood experiences. The first *Soup* (Knopf, 1974, $9.99; pap., Dell, $2.95) was published in 1974 and is an episodic account of the humorous, innocent mischief the two boys were capable of. In *Soup's Hoop,* in order to win the local basketball tournament, Rob and Soup must get the cooperation of seven-foot Piffle Shootensinker, an ace player who only functions on the court with an unusual musical accompaniment. A recent installment, *Soup in Love* (Delacorte, 1992, $14), tells what happens when Soup falls in love with a twin but can't tell his girlfriend from her sister. These good-natured stories are enjoyed by readers in grades 5 through 8.

Plot Summary

Rob and his friend Soup live in the basketball-crazed town of Learning, Vermont. They and the whole town are in big trouble. The big playoff game against their arch-rival, Pratt Falls, is coming up on Saturday. But the Learning Groundhogs' star center, Shorty Smith, has just sprained his ankle.

Shorty is true to his nickname. Also, he never scores more than about four points a game. Even so, Learning is lost without him because he is still the best player on the entire Learning team—all of the players have the nickname Shorty.

Desperate times call for desperate measures. Soup is never one to let an opportunity pass him by.

On their way to school, the two friends run into their all-time nemesis,

Janice Riker. It is an unfortunate encounter and the boys end up in a batch of sheep dip—an inauspicious beginning to the day. Janice is a force to be reckoned with.

At school, which consists of one room with twenty-eight students, the boys are shunted off by themselves because of their peculiar smell. Miss Kelly tells her students they must all go to the library and choose a book about a European country to study and report on.

Before Rob and Soup can get to the library, they run into the Braunschweiger brothers. That is, they meet up with the repair truck of the Braunschweiger brothers, which is being driven by someone they have never seen before. And he is seven feet tall!

His name is Piffle Shootensinker. He is a basketball star from the small European hamlet of Pretzelstein, and he has just moved to town. He is homesick. He is also the tallest living thing Rob and Soup have ever seen, and they watch in amazement as he swishes basketball after basketball right in the hoop.

Are the prayers of Learning, Vermont, answered? Not so fast. Unhappily, the boys soon discover that their new friend Piffle needs a musical instrument created in Pretzelstein in order to sink basketballs. It is called a spitzentootle. The boys have never seen one. Without the music of the spitzentootle, Piffle's concentration is off.

After some serious research in the library, Soup and Rob find a picture of a spitzentootle. They decide to use the town of Pretzelstein for their school assignment. They also learn that wool is the principal export of Pretzelstein and that there is some trouble from an ailment caused by wool, called sheepensneezer.

This, naturally, gives Soup an idea.

After chores one night, the boys go into the cellar of Soup's home, where they uncover a Melodeo, a kind of melodeon or small organ. The Melodeo sounds like a spitzentootle. They will learn to play it before Saturday's big game so that Piffle can shoot baskets and win the game for Learning.

It is not easy. And it doesn't work. A Melodeo is not a spitzentootle. That, however, is not their only problem. Besides missing his hometown and his spitzentootle, Piffle also misses his sheep and his sheepdog. What to do?

By Saturday night, as the big game is near, the boys are ready with Soup's latest outrageous plan. He has written a song called "Mein Pretzelsteiner Gal." And with Rob's help, he has actually built a spitzentootle. Well, sort of.

It takes some very adept maneuvering and sneaky tricks to get the spitzentootle to the gym.

The game proceeds. Halftime score is Pratt Falls 2, Learning 0. Intermission gives the boys a chance to plug in the spitzentootle and send an odor remarkably like sheep dip into the gym, whereupon Rob lets go with his rendition of "Mein Pretzelsteiner Gal."

It works!

Soon the score is tied at 2. But with one minute to go, Pratt Falls is up by 1.

Just when it seems that all is lost, Soup has one last surprise—the appearance at the gym door of a dog that looks remarkably like a genuine sheependag from Pretzelstein.

This obviously inspires Piffle. He shoots the basketball with one second left. It heads for the hoop—and the lights go out! Rob and Soup can't believe it. No one knows if the ball went in.

That is, until old Mr. McGillicuddy shuffles across the gym floor, takes out a ladder, climbs up, and calmly removes the ball from the netting where it stuck. Learning has won the big game.

Thematic Material

This is a zany, fast-paced, tongue-in-cheek, funny story about friendship, basketball, and small towns. Although there is nothing to be taken seriously, young readers will enjoy the silly antics and the fun and the friendship of the two boys as they try their darndest to get a win for old Learning.

Book Talk Material

Some of the zany scenes young readers will enjoy are: Rob and Soup in the sheep dip (pp. 5–9); the boys meet Piffle (pp. 24–28); getting the Melodeo (pp. 39–46); and Soup announces his three plans for victory (pp. 65–71).

Additional Selections

When thirteen-year-old Maizie joins her school's formerly all-male wrestling team, she faces all sorts of opposition and many humorous situations in *There's a Girl in My Hammerlock* (Simon & Schuster, 1991, $13) by Jerry Spinelli.

Fourteen-year-old Helen and her blind dog, Tuck, discover that the Korean boy the family has adopted is deaf in Theodore Taylor's *Tuck Triumphant* (Doubleday, 1991, $14.95). Tuck, the blind golden labrador retriever, was first introduced in *The Trouble with Tuck* (Doubleday, 1981, $10.95).

In Althena Lord's *Z.A.P., Zoe, and the Musketeers* (Macmillan, 1992, $13.-95), the four friends nicknamed Z.A.P., who are led by twelve-year-old Zach, share experiences in Albany, New York, during the summer of 1941. This multiethnic story of friendship is part of a series that includes *The Luck of Z.A.P. and Zoe.*

After many differences, Gopher, a likable kid, makes friends with Fletcher, the boy who has been bullying him and stealing his milk money, in Virginia Scribner's *Gopher Takes Heart* (Viking, 1993, $13.99).

The narrator, young Patrick O'Leary, retells humorous tales from Tickfaw, U.S.A., in Larry Callen's *Who Kidnapped the Sheriff? Or Tales from Tickfaw* (Little, Brown, 1985, $14.95).

For younger readers, Robert Newton Peck has produced a subseries about Little Soup. For example, in *Little Soup's Birthday* (pap., Dell, $2.99), Soup and Rob have to use a horse and sleigh to gather up the guests after a snowstorm, so that nine-and-a-half-year-old Little Soup can have the fine birthday party they planned for him.

About the Book

Booklist, April 15, 1990, p. 1637.
Horn Book Guide, January 1990, p. 247.
Kirkus Reviews, March 15, 1990, p. 429.
School Library Journal, April 1990, p. 122.
Wilson Library Bulletin, September 1990, p. 15.
See also *Book Review Index,* 1990, p. 634.

About the Author

Chevalier, Tracy, ed., *Twentieth-Century Children's Writers* (3rd ed.). St. James, 1989, pp. 769–770.
Commire, Anne, ed., *Something about the Author.* Gale, 1980, Vol. 21, pp. 113–114; 1990, Vol. 62, pp. 134–142.
Holtze, Sally Holmes, ed., *Fifth Book of Junior Authors and Illustrators.* Wilson, 1983, pp. 240–241.
Kirkpatrick, D. L., ed., *Twentieth-Century Children's Writers* (3rd ed.). St. Martin's, 1983, pp. 611–612.
Locher, Frances C., ed., *Contemporary Authors.* Gale, 1979, Vols. 81–84, pp. 442–443.
Sarkissian, Adele, ed., *Something about the Author: Autobiography Series.* Gale, 1986, Vol. 1, pp. 235–237.
Ward, Martha, ed., *Authors of Books for Young People* (3rd ed.). Scarecrow, 1990, p. 555.

Taylor, William. *Knitwits*
Scholastic, 1992, $13.95 (0-590-45778-0)

In 1991, the New Zealand writer William Taylor scored a huge hit with the American publication of *Agnes the Sheep* (Scholastic, 1991, $13.95), a humorous novel that immediately gained a place on many best book lists. It tells how two children, Belinda and Joe, inherit a stubborn, constipated sheep from an old lady and how they prevent the ungrateful animal from becoming somebody's blanket or Sunday dinner. In *Knitwits*, the narrator, Charlie Kenny, tells how his next-door neighbor, bossy, untruthful Alice Pepper, and he enter into a strange bet. This touching, often hilarious novel portrays a close, liberal family so progressive that they allow Charlie to witness the birth of his sibling. These novels are enjoyed by readers in grades 5 through 7.

Plot Summary

Charlie Kenny is not having a good day. It begins when Mr. Magoo dies, hit by a speeding truck. Mr. Magoo was one mean and ugly cat, but the Kennys had lived with him since Charlie was born. Charlie's father says he hates cats. If so, how come he keeps rubbing his eyes when they bury Mr. Magoo out in the backyard?

The next bad thing that happens is Charlie gets kicked off the school hockey team. His teacher, Ms. Mason-Dixon, who taught both his mother and father, is making him sit out a game because he used a swear word.

The third bad thing is that when he gets home, Charlie's mother tells him they are about to have a baby. This is the real kicker. Charlie is worried. How is a baby going to fit into this slightly crazy family? He confides this worry to the foul-mouthed girl next door, Alice Pepper. Alice Pepper is not sympathetic.

Why is Charlie worried about his family? His mother is a fashion model. Charlie can't understand why, because she certainly isn't beautiful. She runs around town in curlers and old jeans all day. His father is a carpenter and frequently out of work, and his grandmother is a feminist weight lifter. How can a little gray blob of a kid fit in here?

However, Charlie decides to get in the spirit of this pregnancy. He is going to make the baby a present, perhaps a sort of consolation prize for being born into such a strange group.

Charlie thinks the baby will be a boy, but Alice Pepper knows it will be a girl. She nags Charlie about the baby's gift until finally he blurts out that he is going to knit a sweater. He has no idea why he said that. He certainly doesn't know how to knit. But once Alice Pepper latches onto something, she will not let go. She bets Charlie that he can't knit the baby a sweater. She bets all her collections—and Alice Pepper is a big-time collector—against five dollars a week that Charlie will have to pay her for the rest of his life.

Just how is Charles Patrick Kenny going to learn how to knit? No one in his family knows how. The books in the library look as though they are written in a foreign language. Charlie has no recourse but Ms. Mason-Dixon, who, to say the least, is startled to hear this request. But, since she is anxious to get Charlie to learn *anything,* she agrees on knitting lessons at her home in exchange for some lawn mowing.

Frankly, even after a few lessons, it looks hopeless. Ms. Mason-Dixon despairs of this knitting project ever turning into a sweater. But Charlie is adamant. So, finally, armed with some last instructions, he is sent home to complete the sweater before the baby arrives. He is to return with the knitting in four pieces to be put together for the final garment.

Charlie feels he is finally getting the hang of this knitting business. The main trouble is finding the time and the place to knit, because, of course, he doesn't want to be discovered until the right time. Mostly, Charlie has to knit in the bathroom.

The baby is growing, and so is Charlie's sweater. In fact, he is quite startled at the length of it. It appears that the new baby will have to grow into a giant in order to wear it. By Charlie's reckoning, the blob, which is what Charlie figures the baby will be when born, will be about twenty times smaller than the sweater. But Charlie knits on. When the doctor says the baby will arrive sooner than expected, Charlie just knits faster.

There is some disagreement about the baby's name. Charlie's mother is voting for Alexandra if it's a girl; Charlie's father is currently calling the blob Jo, and Charlie opts for Munro. He just thinks it's a nice name.

Charlie finishes his knitting before the birth. When he takes the pieces to Ms. Mason-Dixon, her comment is "My my my." Not only is she astounded by the sheer size of the four pieces but by their many and varied colors. This is going to be some sweater!

The big day arrives. Charlie's mother has opted to deliver the baby at home, with Charlie and his father in attendance. It is a very exciting moment. At nineteen minutes past eight in the morning, Charlie's baby sister—not looking like a blob at all, but like a tiny, tiny person with wet black hair—is born. Charlie takes the day off school.

Charlie wraps up the wonderful sweater to be delivered as soon as the new baby is cleaned up. In the meantime, Grandma arrives with the smallest, ugliest kitten imaginable. She puts it outside the door and then exclaims, "Don't tell me . . . yes . . . you've gone and got yourself another cat . . . ." Charlie's father says, "Mr. Magoo Two . . . it's uncanny." Charlie can't believe his father can be so gullible sometimes!

It is time for Charlie's present. When it is opened, Grandma says, "Ye Gods and little fishes . . . what's that?" His mother bursts into tears. His father regards it as a wondrous work of art.

Alice Pepper has lost her collections, but she's pretty game about it, Charlie has to admit.

And now it's time for the baby's name. What will it be? Since his mother declares she has done most of the work in getting this child into the family, she gets to name it. They agree.

The new Kenny will be called Josephine Munro. How about that?

Charlie feels pretty good. Now it's time to feed Josephine Munro Kenny *and* Mr. Magoo Two.

Thematic Material

This is a wonderfully warm and funny story of a slightly askew family that shares a great sense of togetherness and love. Charlie is portrayed as a young boy with his feet firmly on the ground. He has a good knowledge of the ways of the world, including more correct facts about pregnancy and birth than are usually portrayed in books by American authors, and he takes in these occurrences with a child's wonderful curiosity and calm acceptance. His earnest wish to give his new sibling a gift shows a welcome sweetness rarely attributed to young boys in literature, a nice change and a delightful reading experience for this age group.

Book Talk Material

Several humorous incidents can serve as good introductions to the wonderfully wacky characters in this story. See: the demise of Mr. Magoo and the big announcement (pp. 2–6); the bet with Alice Pepper (pp. 12–16); Charlie learns to knit (pp. 19–25); the family discusses the baby's name (pp. 32–33); and Charlie has his troubles finding a place to knit (pp. 39–41).

Additional Selections

To improve her figure, Stacey earns money for a "Bust-er Sizer" by piercing her friends' ears in Nancy J. Hopper's *The Seven and One-Half Sins of Stacey Kendall* (Dutton, 1982, $9.95; pap., Dell, $2.75).

When nine-year-old Chelsea Martin begins to assert herself, such as by challenging some fifth-grade boys, she finds unexpected trouble in Becky Thomas Lindberg's *Speak Up, Chelsea Martin!* (Whitman, 1991, $11.95).

In Cheryl Zach's *Benny and the No-Good Teacher* (Macmillan, 1992, $12.95), Benny feels so out of place in this fourth-grade class with a strict new teacher that he will do anything to be transferred. This is a sequel to *Benny and the Crazy Contest* (Macmillan, 1991, $12.95).

In spite of everything, Rosy still can't play the violin after two years of lessons in Sheila Greenwald's *Give Us a Great Big Smile, Rosy Cole* (Little, Brown, 1981, $12.95; pap., Dell, $2.50).

Precocious Eton decides to take control of his sixth-grade teacher's mind for a science project in David A. Adler's *Eton Stanley and the Mind Control Experiment* (Dutton, 1985, $11.95).

About the Book

Booklist, November 1, 1992, p. 511.
Center for Children's Books Bulletin, January 1993, p. 158.
Kirkus Reviews, September 1, 1992, p. 1135.
School Library Journal, November 1992, p. 98.

About the Author

Chevalier, Tracy, ed., *Twentieth-Century Children's Writers* (3rd ed.). St. James, 1989, pp. 954–955.

3

Fantasy and Science Fiction

YOUNG imaginations are stretched by allowing them access to the magical worlds of fantasy and science fiction. In this section, there are twelve titles that do just that. They involve such situations as the plight of an obsolete robot, the problems faced by a young King Arthur, and the saving of their abbey home by a gallant band of mice. Each will arouse a sense of wonder in the reader as well as a voyage to a never-never-land.

Alcock, Vivien. *The Monster Garden*
Delacorte, 1988, $13.95 (0-440-50053-2); pap., Dell, $2.95 (0-440-40257-3)

This multitalented English writer has pursued a number of careers in her lifetime. From 1942 through 1946, during World War II, she was an ambulance driver in the British Army. Since then, she has worked as a secretary, a successful commercial artist, and from the 1980s on as a highly respected writer of children's books. In this area she has written suspenseful mysteries such as *The Cuckoo Sister* (Delacorte, 1986, $14.95), in which Kate, an eleven-year-old girl, tries to uncover a truth buried in the past after she is confronted by an older girl carrying a letter that states she is really Kate's sister who disappeared years before, and *The Mysterious Mr. Ross* (Delacorte, 1987, $14.95), the story of the strange events that occur after twelve-year-old Felicity rescues a young man from the ocean. Vivien Alcock also writes intriguing fantasies such as the present volume and *The Stonewalkers* (Delacorte, 1983, $12.95), in which a statue comes to life and begins recruiting stone figures from churchyards and gardens to fulfill a malevolent purpose. Although all her books have a distinctive English flavor, this rarely causes problems for readers, instead adding atmosphere and a sense of local color. Most of Vivien Alcock's books are intended for youngsters in grades 6 and up, but *The Monster Garden* can be read and enjoyed by readers in grades 4 through 6.

Plot Summary

If your name is Frances Stein, it seems natural that, like it or not, your nickname is going to be Frankenstein, particularly when your father is an important researcher in genetic engineering at the nearby VAG Laboratories where, classmates claim, monsters are being created. But this is not the only problem Frankie is facing. Although she is outgoing and has many friends, she wishes her family life would improve. Her mother died when she was born and her father, although always a good provider and never abusive, is so distant and absorbed in his work that he appears uncaring and remote. Frankie has three older brothers—Ben, her favorite, and Mike, both Cambridge students now touring in France; and David, a high-schooler, four years older than Frankie, who unfortunately regards her only as a pesky family appendage that he must tolerate. The household is completed by the reasonably competent housekeeper, Mrs. Drake, who also fails to supply the love and attention Frankie craves.

One day, after David returns from a visit to VAG with his father, Frankie notices he has a test tube partly full of a grayish matter that he obviously has taken from the laboratories. Frankie threatens to tell her father about the theft unless her brother shares some of it with her. Reluctantly, David complies. Frankie takes a bit only the size of a frog's egg with a nucleus-like spot in the center back to her room, where she places it on a white saucer on the windowsill. After pricking her finger so the goo is surrounded by blood similar to the blood agar her brother uses in his experiments, she settles down for the night. She is awakened by the sound of thunder and a flash of lightning so strong that at one point it seems to have hit the windowsill.

The following morning, she sees there is only a black smudge on the saucer, but cowering in the corner of the windowsill is a strange gelatinous creature about the size of a small mushroom with two small eyes staring at her. She also notices many of the leaves of her African violet have been eaten. At first she is repulsed and horrified by this creature, which begins slithering toward her in a gesture of friendship, but stifling her initial reaction—to flush it down the toilet—Frankie instead feeds it more of her blood and places it in an unused aquarium before leaving for school.

When she returns, she sees that the creature, although larger in size, is completely motionless. Frankie presumes, not without a feeling of relief, that it has died. She will bury it the next day, Saturday, in the garden beside her also-deceased goldfish. However, she is awakened in the morning by a gentle touch on her cheek. It is the monster, which has now grown primitive arms and legs and is lying on the pillow beside her. Frankie streaks out of bed with such violence that the poor monster scurries for safety under the rug, but later shyly emerges, anxious to play as any other baby would be. Suddenly Frankie feels a bond of affection and compassion for this helpless, misshapen creature.

Frankie feels she must tell someone her secret, if only to get help and advice. At first she thinks of her brother David, but after a conversation during which he admits there was no sign of life in his genetic material, she rejects this course of action, fearful he will tell their father. She also rejects telling her best friend, Hazel Brent, who also has a reputation for a loose tongue. Instead she chooses another classmate, the quiet Julia Hobson, who lives nearby. Both Julia and her slightly older brother, John, agree to help. After overcoming their initial fear and revulsion, they agree to help conceal the monster, which Frankie has named Monnie. But they counsel Frankie that she must tell her brother Ben when he returns from France in eight days. With the help of these two friends and Alf, the Steins' somewhat simple-minded part-time gardener, Frankie constructs a rabbit hutch hidden behind the hedge at the bottom of the Steins' garden. There Monnie, who is now the size of a healthy baby, is placed. However, in its new home it suffers terrible pangs of loneliness and whistles mournfully when Frankie isn't near. In the next two days, Monnie continues to develop at an alarming rate. It now has circular feet, one of which contains a mouth. On its head grow green tendrils that protect the gills through which it breathes. Because of its amazing affinity with water, Frankie realizes Monnie is really an amphibian.

In spite of Julia's protests, Frankie tells her close friend Hazel about Monnie. Now five people—Frankie, Julia, John, Alf, and Hazel—share the secret. Plans suddenly go awry when news comes that Ben plans to stay an extra week in France. In addition, Alf will soon be going away on vacation, and Frankie and Hazel are scheduled to start a seaside vacation the following week. A decision about Monnie must be made soon.

When brother David approaches the hedge looking for his sister, Frankie wraps Monnie in a blanket and flees to a garden plot owned by the Hobsons. Before she can decide on a further course of action, Hazel finds her and tells her that Julia has cracked under the tension and blurted out the truth to Dr. Stein. In desperation, Frankie, with Hazel's help, stows away with Monnie in the back of a gardener's van heading for Didon, a village situated on a wide creek close to the sea. There, toward sunset, she finds some rest in a public park. However, a group of young toughs find her and begin taunting Monnie, who, terrified, scurries to safety in the woods while Frankie single-handedly drives them off. Realizing Monnie must have gone into nearby Didon Creek, Frankie takes off her skirt and shoes and dives in, frantically calling out Monnie's name. She swims farther and farther into the creek until, exhausted, she realizes she hasn't the strength to get back to shore. Near drowning, she feels a strange sensation, a force pushing her toward the bank. When she awakens hours later, she is on a rock, and beside her head there is a tiny bunch of wildflowers—Monnie's final gift after saving her and beginning his natural life as a sea creature.

Dr. Stein locates Frankie and brings her home. With the help of a few lies from Frankie's other friends, Julia's story is discredited and Monnie's existence remains a secret. However, Frankie's brush with death, which Dr. Stein interprets as the suicide attempt of a lonely girl, produces a miraculous transformation in him. Suddenly he begins to shower her with the love and affection she has been denied all these years.

Frankie, however, still feels the loss of Monnie and longs to know his fate. One day she returns to Didon Creek and calls his name. Suddenly a beautiful sea creature appears, towering magnificently above her. Through gestures, it tells her that it has found its destiny and happiness within the wide sea. For an instant they hold hands, before it once again slips away, leaving Frankie alone.

Thematic Material

In many respects this novel resembles a cross between *E.T.* and *Beauty and the Beast.* Like these works, *The Monster Garden* contains serious themes beyond the usual elements of adventure and suspense associated with science fiction and fantasy. The nature of compassion, the meaning of beauty, and the bonds that unify all living creatures are explored in this novel. The effects of loneliness, father-daughter relationships, family life, and the universal need for love and acceptance are additional important themes. The challenges and dangers involved in genetic engineering are also examined. Frankie's innate integrity, her vulnerability, and her development of self-reliance and independence also add important subjects to this unusual fantasy.

Book Talk Material

After a brief discussion of genetic engineering, one of the following passages could be used to introduce this book: Frankie blackmails David into giving her a piece of the ectoplasm (pp. 3–7); the thunderstorm and its effects (pp. 9–13); Frankie thinks the monster is dead but gets a rude awakening (pp. 17–21); Frankie takes Julia and John into her confidence and introduces them to Monnie (pp. 29–33); Frankie persuades Alf to build the rabbit hutch (pp. 44–46); Monnie is taken to the hutch (pp. 55–61); and Frankie visits Monnie in the hutch at night (p. 63).

Additional Selections

Ten-year-old James meets a creature made of recycled garbage in an old dump in Peter Dickinson's *The Box of Nothing* (Delacorte, 1988, $14.95).

When Nate Twitchell's egg hatches, a dinosaur is born in Oliver Butterworth's *The Enormous Egg* (Little, Brown, 1956, $14.95; pap., Dell, $3.50; condensed in *Introducing Books,* Bowker, 1970, $3.50).

A bull seal from the Shetland Islands takes human form in Mollie Hunter's fantasy *A Stranger Came Ashore* (Harper, 1975, $13.89; pap., $3.50).

The Fossils, a mysterious group of older people, make Rachel realize how important her secret powers are in Margaret Buffie's *The Warnings* (Scholastic, 1992, $13.95).

Winnie must decide if she wants the gift of immortality in Natalie Babbitt's *Tuck Everlasting* (Farrar, 1975, $14.95; pap., $3.95; condensed in *Introducing More Books,* Bowker, 1978, pp. 194–197).

Mary and two friends, summering with parents who are looking for a loch monster in Scotland, accidentally discover the "beastie" themselves in Georgess McHargue's *Beastie* (Delacorte, 1992, $14).

Garet Atkins discovers a laundry chute is really a conduit through time that brings a visit from "Daisy," her twin from times past, in Anne Lindbergh's *Three Lives to Live* (Little, Brown, 1992, $14.95).

About the Book

Booklist, October 1, 1988, p. 263.
Center for Children's Books Bulletin, October 1988, p. 24.
Emergency Librarian, March 1989, p. 47.
Horn Book, November 1988, p. 781.
Kirkus Reviews, August 15, 1988, p. 1235.

School Library Journal, October 1988, p. 138.
VOYA, February 1989, p. 292.
See also *Book Review Digest,* 1989, p. 24; and *Book Review Index,* 1988, p. 13; 1989, p. 13.

About the Author

Chevalier, Tracy, ed., *Twentieth-Century Children's Writers* (3rd ed.). St. James, 1989, pp. 13–14.
Commire, Anne, ed., *Something about the Author.* Gale, 1986, Vol. 45, pp. 22–24.
Holtze, Sally Holmes, ed., *Sixth Book of Junior Authors and Illustrators.* Wilson, 1989, pp. 8–9.
Kirkpatrick, D. L., ed., *Twentieth-Century Children's Writers* (2nd ed.). St. Martin's, 1983, p. 20.
May, Hal, ed., *Contemporary Authors.* Gale, 1984, Vol. 110, p. 19.
Senick, Gerard J., ed., *Children's Literature Review.* Gale, 1992, Vol. 26, pp. 1–8.
Ward, Martha, ed., *Authors of Books for Young People* (3rd ed.). Scarecrow, 1990, p. 7.

Banks, Lynne Reid. *The Secret of the Indian*

Doubleday, 1989, $14.95 (0-385-26292-2); pap., Avon, $3.50 (0-380-71040-4)

Several years before the Disney studios produced *Honey, I Shrunk the Kids,* Lynne Reid Banks had already produced the first of her novels on the amazing marvel of miniaturization. Although English by birth, this author spent much of her childhood in Canada during World War II and ten years of her adult life in Israel. In addition to adult fiction, Ms. Banks has written a number of books for children and young adults. A recent example in the latter category is *Melusine* (Harper, 1989, $12.95; pap., $3.95; condensed in *Juniorplots 4,* Bowker, 1993, pp. 131–135), a fantasy involving a mysterious girl who is half woman and half snake. *The Secret of the Indian* is the third book in the Indian series. Although the events in the other two books are reviewed at the beginning of this novel (there is also a general summary below), readers will probably appreciate this concluding segment best if they have already read the previous installments or been told in advance the highlights of their plots. All three are set principally in present-day London and contain a few slang expressions like "dosh" for cash, but neither the setting nor the English expressions will deter better readers in grades 5 through 7 from enjoying these fantastic adventure stories.

Plot Summary

In the first book in this series, *The Indian in the Cupboard* (Doubleday, 1985, $15; pap., Avon, $3.50), nine-year-old Omri receives on his birthday an old tin medicine cabinet that had been found by his older brother, Gillon, and was once owned by their great-grandmother. With it comes a fancy little key attached to a red ribbon. Omri, who lives in London with his parents and two brothers, Adiel and Gillon, also receives a three-inch-high plastic American Indian from his best friend Patrick. After he accidentally places the Indian in the cupboard and locks the door, Omri discovers the cupboard has magical powers and can bring plastic figurines to life. The Indian, whose name is Little Bear, soon begins to dominate Omri's waking hours. He tells Omri he is the son of an Iroquois chief who lived in the Wild West almost two hundred years ago. To accommodate him properly, Omri constructs a tiny longhouse and, with the help of the cupboard's magic powers, supplies him with a horse to ride, appropriate weapons, animals to hunt, and eventually an Indian bride, Bright Stars.

Patrick eventually learns Omri's secret and insists that Omri bring to life a plastic Texan cowboy of one hundred years ago, who, because of his propensity for sobbing, is known as "Boo-Hoo" Boone. Although it takes some time for the cowboy and the Indian to drop their suspicious attitudes toward one another, all five soon become close friends. However, in time the boys realize they must return their newfound companions to their own times and cultures and through the transforming magic of the cupboard, Little Bear, Boone, and Bright Stars are replaced by their plastic counterparts.

In *The Return of the Indian* (Doubleday, 1986, $13.95; pap., Avon, $3.99), a year has passed and Omri has entered a short story contest with an entry entitled "The Plastic Indian" that retells in fictional format his adventures with Little Bear. When Omri finds he has won the first prize of £500, he is so elated he decides to share the news with Little Bear. However, when the Indian reappears with his pregnant wife, he is close to death from wounds received in a battle fighting the French and Algonquins during the French and Indian Wars. With Patrick's help, a small plastic nurse named Matron is located and brought to life to bring Little Bear back to health. Boone is also summoned. To help the Iroquois cause, Patrick and Omri collect a contingent of plastic Indians and send them via the cupboard, with some models of machine guns, to help in the ongoing battle. The boys discover that the magic key also fits the lock of a large seaman's chest that

Omri had recently bought. Using this, they can be transported in time and space to witness the battle firsthand. Unfortunately, miniaturization works for them in reverse, and they emerge only three inches tall. Although the Iroquois successfully repulse the attack, the cost in life is tremendous, partly because of disastrous misuse of the modern weapons. Patrick and Omri return to the present with Little Bear, Bright Stars, their new baby, Tall Bear, and the Iroquois soldiers, who now include eight dead and many wounded. Omri's parents are out for the evening, but before plans can be made to help the Indians, three skinheads try to burglarize the house. The boys bring to life a collection of Marines who successfully mount an artillery attack that frightens off the intruders. It is at this point that *The Secret of the Indian* begins.

After Omri's parents and brothers return and the police, who have been summoned to investigate the robbery, leave, quiet once again reigns and the boys are able to formulate plans. Patrick, who lives in the countryside, is staying with Omri while his mother is in London visiting Patrick's aunt and her twin children, cousins Emma and pesky Tamsin. He must return soon, so time is important. Matron is summoned to help nurse the wounded, but the situation is so bad that more professional medical personnel and hospital facilities are necessary. The boys know Tamsin owns some plastic models of doctors and hospital equipment, but they are also sure she is so mean that she won't lend them.

As a favor to his friend, Omri decides he will allow Patrick to time travel again. Patrick wants to visit Boone in the Wild West and, with the figurine of his friend in his pocket, climbs into the sea chest. There is a miscalculation, and, while Patrick appears miniaturized in Texas, Boone, although alive, is still in London, now suffering from the severe aftereffects of near-suffocation in Patrick's pocket.

While Omri is trying to cope with this situation, Patrick's cousin Emma accidentally wanders into his bedroom and discovers his colony of little people. Begrudgingly, he confesses to her the secret of the magical cupboard and manages to elicit her aid in bribing terrible Tamsin to relinquish her collection of medical figures, who, when brought to life, begin working on the wounded, including Boone. Although the cowboy is too sick to travel, Omri sends Patrick Boone's horse, hoping he will be of some help.

Patrick, now only three inches tall, finds he has been transported to a desolate Texan desert area next to the comatose body of Boone. While trying to find shelter from the intense heat, he suddenly sees Boone's horse appear. He attaches himself to one of the horse's legs and he is transported to the nearest town. There, at the local saloon, he is saved from some drunks who want to use him for target practice by one of the habitues, Ruby Lou, who happens to be Boone's girlfriend. With the help of Patrick, she and her friends find the still-unconscious Boone and transport him to her bedroom just before a killing cyclone hits the town.

Back in London, Omri's "doctors" and their makeshift hospital have saved the lives of both Boone and the wounded Indians; however, Omri's life becomes increasingly complicated when Mr. Johnson, the nosy school principal, seems close to discovering the secret of the cupboard. And, Patrick's mother is increasingly suspicious about her son's absence. Omri decides to return all the Indians, but as he is doing so, Emma secretly places one of her favorite models, a Western bargirl, in the cupboard. Patrick is also called back by Omri, but with the boy also comes the cyclone. It rips through Omri's house, destroying some furniture, including the sea chest, and leaving a path of destruction throughout southeastern England. Both boys are horrified at the consequences of their actions but are somewhat consoled when they learn that Emma's bargirl is really Ruby Lou, Boone's girlfriend. A gala wedding is planned, and Little Bear and his family return to be honored guests. After the festivities, Omri sends all his tiny friends back to their real homes, and, swearing Patrick and Emma to secrecy, he places a package containing the key and the cupboard in the family bank vault with instructions that it be opened only after his death.

Thematic Material

This novel is basically an exciting adventure that convincingly combines reality and magic. In addition to a fast-moving plot, the author has created sympathetic, believable characters, even though many of them are only three inches tall. A respect for other cultures is portrayed, and, more seriously, there is a strong antiwar and antiviolence message. The boys learn a lesson in responsibility and in the dangers of meddling in other people's lives when their thoughtless, albeit innocent, actions produce unfortunate and unexpected results. The boys' devotion and loyalty to their friends and to each other are important additional themes.

Book Talk Material

A brief introduction to the magical powers of the cupboard and its key should introduce the book effectively. The covers of any or all of the three books in the series will also draw interest (e.g., the cover of *The Secret of the Indian* shows a tiny Patrick staring into the face of an unconscious Boone). The plots of the previous two volumes are briefly retold in chapter 3 (pp. 16–21). Other important passages: Omri's parents arrive home and the police come (pp. 1–7); Patrick goes to the Old West and Emma discovers Omri's secret (pp. 35–39); Patrick in the wasteland (pp. 46–52); his ride on Boone's horse (pp. 69–76); and Ruby Lou saves him from the trigger-happy cowboys (pp. 77–85).

Additional Selections

Conrad's obsession with war leads him to believe he experienced action in a past war in *Conrad's War* (pap., Dell, 1986, $1.95) by Andrew Davies.

The Shrinking of Treehorn (Holiday, 1971, $11.95; pap., Dell, 95¢) by Florence Parry Heide is a delightful fantasy about a boy who can shrink in size.

Tia and Tony realize that they have special gifts for which they are being hunted in Alexander Key's *Escape to Witch Mountain* (Westminster, 1968, $10.85; pap., Simon & Schuster, $1.75).

Anthea, a newly orphaned girl, comes to live with her cousin Flora in a house haunted by the grandfather of the girls in Margaret Mahy's *Dangerous Spaces* (Viking, 1991, $12.95).

Patrick is transported to a parallel world while playing a computer game in a fast-paced, humorous adventure, *Finders Keepers* (Greenwillow, 1991, $12.95), by Emily Rodda.

Two girls enter the spirit world to save the life of a favorite rock musician in Nancy Springer's *The Friendship Song* (Macmillan, 1992, $12.95).

Noah uses a silver powder to shrink himself and his friend Nate to the size of his toys in *Back in Action* (Holiday, 1991, $13.95) by Elvira Woodruff. This is a delightful sequel to the equally exciting *Awfully Short for the Fourth Grade* (Holiday, 1989, $13.95).

About the Book

Booklist, September 15, 1989, p. 170.
Center for Children's Books Bulletin, January 1990, p. 104.
Horn Book, March 1990, p. 225.
Horn Book Guide, July 1989, p. 81.
Kirkus Reviews, September 15, 1989, p. 1398.
New York Times Book Review, January 21, 1990, p. 26.

School Library Journal, October 1989, p. 112.
VOYA, June 1990, p. 100.
See also *Book Review Digest,* 1990, pp. 1508–1509; and *Book Review Index* (under Reid Banks, Lynne), 1989, p. 684, 1990, p. 676.

About the Author

Chevalier, Tracy, ed., *Twentieth-Century Children's Writers* (3rd ed.). St. James, 1989, pp. 56–58.
Commire, Anne, ed., *Something about the Author.* Gale, 1981, Vol. 22, pp. 208–209.
Holtze, Sally Holmes, ed., *Sixth Book of Junior Authors and Illustrators.* Wilson, 1989, pp. 23–24.
Kirkpatrick, D. L., ed., *Twentieth-Century Children's Writers* (2nd ed.). St. Martin's, 1983, pp. 651–652 (under Reid).
Straub, Deborah A., ed., *Contemporary Authors* (New Revision Series). Gale, 1988, Vol. 22, pp. 381–382.
Ward, Martha, ed., *Authors of Books for Young People* (3rd ed.). Scarecrow, 1990, p. 36.

Brittain, Bill. *Dr. Dredd's Wagon of Wonders*

Harper, 1987, $11.50 (0-06-020713-2); pap., $3.50 (0-06-440289-4)

Bill Brittain spent most of his professional life as a classroom teacher in schools on Long Island, New York. Before turning to children's literature, he wrote prolifically in the mystery story genre and has had more than seventy stories printed in *Ellery Queen's Magazine.* His first juvenile novel was *All the Money in the World* (Harper, 1979, $12.89; pap., $3.50), a humorous fantasy in which having all the money in the world deposited in a young boy's backyard brings such results as a kidnapping and an interview with the president of the United States. In *Devil's Donkey* (Harper, 1981, $13.89; pap., $3.50), the author first used the setting of a rural town in New England called Coven Tree, a play on the name *Coventry* and the word for a band of witches. In this novel narrated by Stew Meat, the owner of the country store, young Dan'l Pitt offends a witch and is turned into a donkey. Stew and a farm girl succeed in reversing the transformation as well as winning a bet with the devil. These adventures are continued in the same setting with *The Wish Giver* (Harper, 1983, $12.95; pap., $3.50) and *Dr. Dredd's Wagon of Wonders.* The latter is again narrated by Stew Meat and tells about the terrible drought that hit Coven Tree and the sudden appearance in town of arch-villain Dr. Dredd and his two assistants. These books are enjoyed by readers in grades 3 through 6.

Plot Summary

It hasn't rained for ever so long in the small village of Coven Tree, tucked away in a remote corner of New England. The owner of the general store, Stew Meat, as he is affectionately known, recounts the story of that spring of the great drought and of the coming of Dr. Dredd and the awful fate that nearly destroyed his town.

An odd-looking stranger, known as Antaeus, World's Greatest Wrestler, appears in Coven Tree with posters proclaiming a free show in the clearing west of town on the following Saturday morning. Stew Meat is as curious as everyone else, and he shows up in the clearing along with fourteen-year-old Ellen McCabe and most of the townspeople.

There in the clearing stands a rather shabby wagon with a banner that announces "Dr. Dredd's Wagon of Wonders." Dr. Dredd himself is a sinister-appearing fellow who invites the townsfolk into the wagon to view, among other things, the armor of the mighty (so says Dr. Dredd) Black Knight of Etherium. But Stew Meat, Ellen, and the others are more interested in Bufu the Rainmaker, Miracle Boy of the East. Dr. Dredd assures them all that Bufu can indeed make rain.

Bufu turns out to be a rather skinny lad of about fifteen with blue eyes and a frightened glance. But, true to Dr. Dredd's word, he does make it rain right over the town clearing. The effort, however, seems to give him a terrible headache.

Dr. Dredd informs the impressed townspeople that Bufu is the doctor's servant and will only do his bidding. Perhaps, Dr. Dredd suggests, the town officials would like to meet with him to arrange for a little rainmaking. Stew Meat thinks there is something a bit fishy about Dr. Dredd, especially when the stranger refuses to name a price for the rainmaking service until after it is done.

That evening, Ellen and her mother are startled by a stranger hiding out in their barn. It is Bufu, who turns out to be Calvin Huckabee from Vermont. When the McCabes take him in, Calvin explains that he is running away from the cruel Dr. Dredd, who is his guardian and mistreats him dreadfully. It is true that Calvin has the strange ability to make rain—but even he can't explain how he does it. All he knows is that this gift brings on dreadful headaches. Calvin also tells Ellen and her mother that Dr. Dredd is an evil man who seeks power over everyone. He will destroy the town, Calvin declares.

Dr. Dredd comes to the McCabe house in search of Calvin, or Bufu, but Mrs. McCabe refuses to give him up. Soon the townspeople get to fighting about whether it is in their best interests to shelter Calvin, even though it is obvious that Dr. Dredd mistreats him, or whether they should surrender the lad and avoid Dr. Dredd's wrath.

Calvin explains that this is the way Dr. Dredd has ruined other towns. People forget about being decent to one another and start thinking only about what is good for themselves. Then the lying and cheating and fighting begin, and a good town is destroyed.

Stew Meat and Mrs. McCabe and Ellen are determined not to let that happen in Coven Tree. Calvin isn't so sure, and he wants to run away so Dr. Dredd will not destroy the town.

At first, Dr. Dredd tries to get his way by having Antaeus, the world's mightiest wrestler, fight the strongest man in town. That is Sven the blacksmith. Strong as he is, Sven cannot withstand the magical strength of Antaeus, until Calvin tells him the wrestler's power comes from the earth. He is strong only when his feet are on the ground. Sven is able to lift Antaeus in the air, and the blacksmith wins the fight.

But Dr. Dredd will not concede defeat. Now he puts his powers to work by reviving the Black Knight. Although the townspeople come together to stand firm against Dredd's evil, the power of the Black Knight is awesome. He can make the earth quake and bring down buildings or send them into flames.

Calvin fashions a pulley rope, and, with Ellen's help, catches the Black Knight and suspends him in the air by one leg. When they examine the armor, they find nothing inside. That's his secret power, Calvin explains. As soon as someone finds out there is nothing inside the armor, there is nothing to fear and the knight has no power.

But Dr. Dredd still has some power, and he cuts the small village off from all communication with the outside world. Then he tells the townspeople that if they had asked him to instruct Bufu to bring rain to their village, he would in return have planted a small seed in each person's heart, and its name would be Greed.

The townspeople still refuse to return Calvin to Dredd. Now the evil doctor unleashes a terrible dragon. Minute by minute the dragon grows larger. In time it will destroy the town.

Calvin cannot let harm come to these people who have helped him, and he runs off to Old Baldy, the highest of the mountain peaks that surround Coven Tree. He is followed by Ellen. Calvin begs her to go back, but she tells him she knows the mountain well and that without her he will run aimlessly until Dr. Dredd catches up with him.

Even with Ellen's help, Dr. Dredd finds them and, with the dragon's fire, captures Ellen. She tells Calvin to run, but he will not leave her. Instead, and despite the pain it brings him, he summons up the strongest and most terrible of storms. A great bolt of lightning arcs out of the clouds, striking the dragon. From the dragon, the bolt leaps to Dr. Dredd and destroys the evil man.

The town is saved, and Calvin stays in Coven Tree. He goes to school and supports himself by doing odd jobs. The one thing he won't do, he says, is make rain anymore. However, the people of Coven Tree notice that every once in a while, when the farmers are really in need of a little water for their crops, a shower or two always seems to come along at just the right time.

After that happens, you can always find Calvin at home. He has a headache.

Thematic Material

Dr. Dredd's Wagon of Wonders reads somewhat like an old-fashioned fantasy/fairy tale, where good and evil are laid out side by side for all to see and understand. Dr. Dredd is an evil figure; Calvin is pure of heart and strong of will. He stands up for the people of Coven Tree and for the fair damsel, Ellen McCabe. However, this damsel in distress has a touch of the nineties about her. She bosses Calvin around at every turn and is not against hopping into a fight herself instead of standing on the sidelines and letting someone else do it. This is a humorous, imaginative tale with a moral.

Book Talk Material

Young readers will like being introduced to the wonders of Dr. Dredd's wagon and to the powers of Bufu the Rainmaker. See: the townspeople see the wondrous wagon (pp. 12–18); Bufu makes it rain (pp. 27–29); Calvin talks about his strange power (pp. 47–50); and Calvin conjures up a "small rain" (pp. 75–79).

Additional Selections

Strange things happen in Coven Tree in Bill Brittain's *Professor Popkin's Prodigious Polish* (Harper, 1990, $13.95) when Luther Gilpin begins selling Professor Popkin's magical furniture polish.

Andrea orders wings from the back of her comic book, and their performance surprises her in *Mail-Order Wings* (Dutton, 1981, $12.95; pap., Avon, $2.95) by Beatrice Gormley.

A mischievous sprite is accidentally transported from Scotland to Canada, and his pranks cause serious problems for the Volnik family in Susan Cooper's *The Boggart* (McElderry, 1993, $14.95).

In Diana Wynne Jones's *The Ogre Downstairs* (Greenwillow, 1990, $12.95), two magic chemistry sets cause complications after two different families are united in marriage, bringing five children together.

With an older brother and a younger sister, Rianne finds that the opossum they have freed from a petting zoo not only can speak but also grant wishes in *Impossumble Summer* (Walker, 1992, $13.95) by B. W. Clough.

Tyler and Freckles discover a hidden room that contains an invention that transports them back in time in *The Disappearing Bike Shop* (Holiday, 1992, $13.95) by Elvira Woodruff.

In Diane Duane's *So You Want to Be a Wizard* (Delacorte, 1983, $14.95), Nita and friends embark on a journey to retrieve the *Book of Night and Moon.* A sequel is *Deep Wizardry* (Delacorte, 1985, $15.95; pap., Dell, $3.25).

About the Book

Booklist, July 1987, p. 1675.
Center for Children's Books Bulletin, June 1987, p. 182.
Horn Book, September 1987, p. 609.
Kirkus Reviews, June 15, 1987, p. 922.
School Library Journal, August 1987, p. 78.
See also *Book Review Digest,* 1988, p. 208; and *Book Review Index,* 1987, p. 97; 1988, p. 104.

About the Author

Chevalier, Tracy, ed., *Twentieth-Century Children's Writers* (3rd ed.). St. James, 1989, p. 135–136.
Commire, Anne, ed., *Something about the Author.* Gale, 1984, Vol. 36, pp. 36–39.
Holtze, Sally Holmes, ed., *Fifth Book of Junior Authors and Illustrators.* Wilson, 1983, pp. 50–51.
Lesniak, James G., ed., *Contemporary Authors* (New Revision Series). Gale, 1990, Vol. 30, p. 46.
Nakamura, Joyce, ed., *Something about the Author: Autobiography Series.* Gale, Vol. 7, pp. 17–30.

Conly, Jane Leslie. *Racso and the Rats of NIMH*
Illus. by Leonard Lubin. Harper, 1986, $13 (0-06-021361-2); pap., $3.95 (0-06-440245-2)

Jane Conly's father, Robert C. O'Brien, was awarded the 1972 Newbery Medal for his novel *Mrs. Frisby and the Rats of NIMH* (Macmillan, 1971, $14.95; pap., $3.95), a charming, exciting animal fantasy. It is the story of a gallant widowed mouse, Mrs. Frisby, who engages the help of a most unusual group of rats to move her sick son to safer quarters. The rats are unusual because of their extremely high intelligence, the result of experiments conducted in the NIMH laboratory, from which they have recently escaped.

When her father died, Jane Leslie Conly continued his writing career. In this sequel to *Mrs. Frisby,* the author focuses on the next generation. The story involves Timothy, Mrs. Frisby's son, and Racso, the son of the rebel rat Jenner, and their journey to a utopian valley slated for destruction. The characters of Mrs. Frisby, Jeremy, and Mr. Ages, all of whom are important in the first volume, are secondary in this book. A further sequel, *R-T, Margaret, and the Rats of NIMH* (Harper, 1990, $12.95; pap., $3.50), tells of Racso, his friends Christopher and Isabella, and their struggle to save their home after humans discover it. These novels are enjoyed by fantasy lovers in grades 4 through 8.

Plot Summary

After the highly intelligent rats escape from the NIMH lab, they establish a self-sufficient agricultural colony in a remote valley, where they hope to change the popular image of their species. As the story opens, Mrs. Frisby, a brown field mouse, is getting her son, Timothy, ready to go off to school a good distance away in a remote section of the state forest called Thorn Valley. The school is run by the superintelligent rats of NIMH. Timothy will be gone for nine months and Mrs. Frisby will miss him, but she knows Timothy will never be a physically strong mouse and so it is extremely important that he have a good education.

Jeremy the crow was to fly Timothy to school, but his mother broke her wing, and Jeremy must stay with her. So Timothy sets off on foot. During his journey he rescues a very small rat named Racso (Oscar spelled backwards), who is also headed for the school, where he wants to learn to read and write and become a hero. Although Racso is boastful and cheeky and Timothy is quiet and shy, the two become fast friends.

Timothy learns that Racso's father is Jenner, a tough, smart rat who everyone thought was dead. Jenner is an outcast from the rat colony. He had opposed the rats' escape from the lab and the move to Thorn Valley. When most of the rats followed their leader, Nicodemus, Jenner and a few others left the group and were presumed dead. Actually, Jenner had returned home, and Racso describes him as a sullen, beaten rat.

Timothy is injured on their journey to Thorn Valley, but Racso takes care of him. When they reach the school, Timothy receives the proper attention and will recover.

Racso, with his boastful ways, is not well received by the rats of NIMH at Thorn Valley. Although he lies to the others about his father, Nicodemus, the leader, knows the truth.

Actually, the rats have more important things to worry about than Racso. The water level is rising in Thorn Valley, and the rats figure the whole valley will be underwater by Christmas. Surveying parties are sent to seek the cause of this potential disaster. They learn the frightening truth—humans are building a dam at the northern end of Thorn Valley. When the dam is completed, all the rat homes will be flooded out. Although the human farmers in the area also oppose the dam, for their homes and farms will be destroyed, Representative Jones of the state legislature, whose cousin's construction company conveniently works at the dam site, has the power to push it through.

The rats hold meetings and decide to create a computer program that will knock out the dam and render it useless. This is a very difficult task, and everyone has a job to do. Racso is sent out with Isabella to map the south side of the creek. They are nearly discovered by some human reporters, and in fact a woman reporter finds a small basket that the rats were carrying. The rats are terrified the humans will realize the superintelligent rats of NIMH are in the area and will begin searching for them once again.

As the time for the dam to be completed approaches, the rats practice day and night, perfecting their plan. When the rats who will go on the mission are chosen, Racso is delighted to find his name on the list.

On the night before the dam is to open, the rats see a shadow crossing the dam. When they cannot find Brendan, they are afraid something terrible has happened to him. But Brendan turns up and says he was not up on the dam. Whom did they see?

Even with all their work, the rats cannot insert their program into the dam computer in time. All seems lost. The dam will open on schedule. Just then the lights go out. Power has been lost.

The power failure gives the rats time to get their program into the computer. The dam will never open. Thorn Valley will be saved. The humans report it was sabotage that caused the power failure. Someone—or something—chewed into the wires, knowing it would mean certain death. Who could have done that? It must have been the shadow the rats saw crossing the dam the night before it was to open. The rats discover a message left by the unknown hero. It reads: "My son is here. He cannot swim."

The hero is Racso's father, Jenner. He died to save his son and the other rats of Thorn Valley. He is a true hero and will be honored as such. Peace and tranquility return to the rats of NIMH and Timothy and Racso can go back to school.

Thematic Material

This is a delightful, imaginative fantasy filled with wit and tenderness. The reader is completely drawn into the world of the superintelligent rats of NIMH. The unbelievable is believable. The qualities, both good and bad, displayed by the rats point up the good and bad qualities that humans exhibit and understand. Racso is shown as a very small rat who tries to make up for his size by bravado and boastfulness, but who learns the values of trustworthiness and friendship and the true meaning of heroism.

Book Talk Material

Young readers will be interested in the personalities of the individual rats of NIMH and how they relate to one another. See: Mrs. Frisby calms a nervous Jeremy the crow (pp. 4–5); Timothy rescues Racso (pp. 16–19); Timothy and Racso discuss the marvelous item called candy (pp. 21–22); Timothy is injured (pp. 47–51); Racso is introduced to Thorn Valley (pp. 61–71); and Racso and Nicodemus talk about truth and Jenner (pp. 79–86).

Additional Selections

The squirrels and other animals of Central Park are so disgusted by the behavior of the humans who visit them that they decide to exclude them in *The Great Squirrel Uprising* (Orchard, 1992, $14.95) by Dan Elish.

In John Balaban's *The Hawk's Tale* (Harcourt, 1988, $14.95), a water snake, a toad, and deer mouse set out to find Mr. Trembly's niece Lilac.

Nine-year-old Eddie captures Sandy, the sandman, and is taken to Dreamland, where the evil wizard Mortimer tries to steal Eddie's imagination in the exciting title *Wide Awake in Dreamland* (Stargaze, 1992, $15.95) by John Duel.

Bilbo Baggins, a hobbit, sets out on a dangerous mission to the Lonely Mountain, where he hopes to recapture a treasure, in J. R. R. Tolkien's *The Hobbit* (Houghton, 1984, $24.45; pap., Ballantine, $4.95; condensed in *Juniorplots,* Bowker, 1967, pp. 197–199).

Twelve-year-old Jeremy Thatcher unknowingly buys a dragon's egg in Bruce Coville's *Jeremy Thatcher, Dragon Hatcher* (Harcourt, 1991, $16.95; pap., Pocket, $2.99), a book that cleverly mixes the real and the fantastic.

Matt and sister Kate have a dog, Toby, who suddenly begins to talk to alert them that a nearby laboratory is cruelly using animals in experiments in Anna Coates's *Dog Magic* (pap., Bantam, 1991, $2.99).

Mildred's first year at Miss Cackle's Academy for Witches is a disaster in Jill Murphy's *The Worst Witch* (Schocken, 1987, $7.95; pap., Puffin, $3.95). A sequel is *The Worst Witch Strikes Again* (Schocken, 1987, $7.95; pap., Puffin, $3.99).

About the Book

Booklist, June 1, 1986, p. 1458.
Center for Children's Books Bulletin, June 1986, p. 182.
Horn Book, September 1986, p. 588.
School Library Journal, April 1986, p. 85.
VOYA, June 1986, p. 86.
See also *Book Review Digest,* 1987, p. 371; and *Book Review Index,* 1986, p. 166.

About the Author

Ward, Martha, ed., *Authors of Books for Young People* (3rd ed.). Scarecrow, 1990, p. 144.

Hoover, H. M. *Orvis*

Viking, 1987, $12.95 (0-670-81117-3); pap., Puffin, $3.95 (0-14-032113-6)

H. M. Hoover says she especially enjoys juvenile literature that entertains while also appealing to the reader's imagination. Her own books certainly fulfill this combination. Since the 1970s, she has written about a dozen fine science fiction novels, beginning with such titles as *The Rains of Eridan* (o.p.) and *The Lost Star* (Viking, 1979, $11.95; pap., Puffin, $3.95). *Orvis,* the story of a journey to self-discovery made by three seemingly unwanted creatures, is read and enjoyed by youngsters in grades 5 through 8.

Plot Summary

Growing up in the twenty-sixth century has not been easy for twelve-year-old Toby, short for Tabitha, West. She is the only child of peripatetic filmmakers, who, with her grandmother Lillian, roam the solar system making movies for their very successful production company. Her childhood has been spent in various places, from a condominium on Mars and film locations in the ringworlds to different habitats on satellites. For the past two years she has led a fairly stable, although lonely, existence as a student at the Hillandale Academy in what was once Connecticut, now part of the reconstructed planet Earth. The Earth, once doomed by ecological mismanagement, has been partially saved by relocating most of its population to neighboring space colonies, imposing strict population controls, and restoring natural life to several highly organized urban centers. Although thousands of species have disappeared, there has been an attempt to recreate the environment of the Earth as it was several centuries earlier. However, between these rebuilt centers of civilization, there are still vast stretches of wasteland collectively known as The Empty.

Today, on a gray afternoon in April, sitting alone in a thicket in the spacious grounds around the school, Toby is despondent and discouraged. She has just received word from Lillian, the boss of the family, that at the end of the school term she will be transferred to a school on Mars, where she will begin studying communication arts in preparation for eventually joining her family in the film business. Although no one has visited her during her stay at Hillandale, she has become accustomed to the natural, albeit old-fashioned, Terran environment and has no desire to move again.

Her sorrowful thoughts are interrupted by a strange metallic cracking sound. It is an ancient robot slowly walking down the road. Toby has never seen one so old. With paint peeling, one of its six legs damaged, and obsolete design, it immediately arouses Toby's pity. She is soon joined in examining the robot by Thaddeus Hall, a ten-year-old fellow student, who like Toby has been all but abandoned by his space-traveling parents. And because of his unusual appearance, he is treated as a social outcast at the school. Together, the two youngsters begin questioning the robot. In spite of his decrepit appearance and strange, formalized speaking manner, he reveals an amazing array of abilities and a distinguished past—spanning more than four hundred years, many scientific expeditions, and a number of high-level posts. Now, instead of being rewarded for his accomplishments, he is considered obsolete and has been programmed to walk to the nearby Corona Landfill, known as The Dump, which will be his final resting place.

On her way back to school, Toby tries to think of ways to help the robot, who obviously is in distress at the thought of rusting away in a public garbage dump. The only person on Earth who perhaps could help is her great-grandmother, Mrs. Goldie Philips, a woman who lives on Fisher's Isle off the coast of Lake Erie. Toby has never met her great-grandmother, although she has seen her in family holograms. Life-extension drugs are now commonly used, and this, coupled with the plastic surgery available at youth clinics, means human beings live very long lives but look deceptively young. Toby's great-grandmother has refused cosmetic alterations and therefore looks her true age.

In the middle of the night, Toby is awakened by a tapping sound at the door of her dormitory room. Fearfully she opens it and finds the robot. He has been so frightened by the bears in the dump that he has followed her, by scent, to ask for temporary refuge. He introduces himself as Orvis. With a certain amount of trepidation, because she has heard that renegade robots can be dangerous, Toby hides Orvis in her closet.

In the morning, while Orvis is preening himself with Toby's lemon-scented bath oil, Toby has an interview with Dr. Ebert, her guidance counselor or Guardian, concerning her proposed transfer. Later that day, Dr. Ebert unexpectedly visits Toby's room and sees Orvis. She is so alarmed that she hastily summons the dean, Dr. Milhaus. He identifies Orvis as an acronym for a type of robot produced over four hundred years ago—Overland Reconnaissance Vehicle in Space. Fearful that during his lifetime the robot has been programmed with unhealthy and perhaps dangerous thoughts, he orders Orvis back to the dump.

For the next few days, both Toby and Thaddeus wonder about Orvis's fate. On the weekend, they decide to visit him in the landfill. After hours of searching and calling, they find him, buried under rubble by bulldozers. Extricating himself, Orvis modestly confesses that he would like to find a more hospitable place where he could still be productive in his retirement. Toby returns to the school and contacts her great-grandmother, who consents readily to a visit from Toby and friend Thaddeus during next week's spring break. She also agrees to supply her airtruck and chauffeur, Sanders, to transport the youngsters and the large gift that Toby mysteriously alludes to.

Toby finds an ill-smelling bin once used to transport cantaloupe, and the fastidious Orvis reluctantly agrees to be sealed inside it. The next day, Toby and Thaddeus enter the airtruck along with an oversized, odoriferous crate marked "Rock Samples."

Both youngsters fall asleep during the three-hour trip. Suddenly they are rudely awakened and ordered off the airtruck by two ruffians. Instead of Fisher's Isle, they have landed on a barren stretch of The Empty. The skyjackers unload the crate and, at gunpoint, force Sanders back into the plane to act as their guide. They take off, leaving Toby, Thaddeus, and the soon-to-be-unpacked Orvis in the middle of a wilderness about one hundred miles from their real destination. The robot says that during the trip he overheard Sanders respond to an SOS that had been faked to commandeer the plane.

Hoping to find help, the three set out along the broken remains of what had been a highway. Mustering their meager survival skills and Orvis's ability to locate for food and firewood, they spend several days walking through the wilderness. Suddenly, in the distance they see a walled village. They enter and are greeted by the inhabitants, about one hundred in number. Toby and Thaddeus learn from Mr. Milton, their leader, that the group tired many years ago of the overpowering dependence on technology and the synthetic civilization it produced and decided to move into the wilderness and create a society returning to life's basics. The guests are treated royally and showered with presents. But within a short time, they realize the inhabitants regard them as gifts from the stars who must stay in the village and eventually produce children. In spite of their hosts' many kindnesses, Toby and Thaddeus realize they must escape. One night, again with the help of Orvis, they creep out of the village. Although they ride all night on the robot's back, by morning they are overtaken by a van from the village. At the moment of capture, patrol planes appear. They have been scouring the skies for days searching for them. All three are whisked to safety.

After preliminary media appearances, they are flown to Fisher's Isle and a happy meeting with Goldie, who proves to be both a very wealthy woman and an ideal great-grandmother. She promises to intercede on Toby's behalf with Lillian and her parents so Toby can stay at Hillandale, and she also tells Thaddeus he should always consider Fisher's Isle his home. Orvis is offered a place in her household, but the robot decides he would be of greater value returning to the village and helping the struggling settlers. Each of the three weary travelers has found a measure of fulfillment and self-discovery.

Thematic Material

Besides being an exciting science fiction adventure, this novel is the story of three unwanted and unfulfilled creatures and their journey to self-worth and purpose in their lives. It is also the story of a girl's sympathy and compassion and her courageous attempts to save an unjustly discarded creature. The author portrays the results of a technology-dominated future by creating two contrasting cultures, one that is sterile and artificial and the other, although trying to return to a natural life, nevertheless is plagued with deprivation and superstition. Both pictures are filled with fascinating details that add realism and depth to this story. Friendship, the importance of family, survival, and bravery are additional important themes. The reader will also be moved by Orvis's attempts to understand human emotions like "love," "caring," and "independence" and his efforts to assimilate them into his programmed language.

Book Talk Material

There are a number of fine episodes that are excellent for reading or retelling. Some are: Toby meets Orvis and hears about his obsolescence problem (pp. 3–9); Toby's past (pp. 14–16); a description of life at Hillandale (pp. 29–31); Orvis visits Toby at night (pp. 33–35); Dr. Milhaus orders Orvis to the dump (pp. 56–58); and Toby calls Goldie and arranges the trip to Fisher's Isle (pp. 72–74).

Additional Selections

Rebecca, a novice detective, and her robot, Watson, share amusing adventures in Jane Yolen's *The Robot and Rebecca* (Knopf, 1980, $9.95). This is followed by *The Robot, Rebecca, and the Missing Owner* (pap., Knopf, $4.99).

In *My Robot Buddy* (Harper, 1975, $13.89; pap., $3.95) by Alfred Slote, Jack receives for his tenth birthday from his parents his very own Robot Buddy. There are several sequels, including *My Trip to Alpha 1* (Harper, 1983, $12.95; pap., $3.95).

Marilyn Z. Wilkes's *C.L.U.T.Z.* (Dial, 1982, $9.95; pap., Bantam, $2.50) tells how Rodney finds a friend in a Combined Level Unit/Type Z robot.

In Peni R. Griffin's *Hobkin* (McElderry, 1992, $14.95), two runaway youngsters move into an abandoned farmhouse that is haunted by a brownie who came to West Texas decades ago.

In the Act of Magic trilogy by Tom McGowen, a twelve-year-old boy, Lithim, and his father try to combat a prediction that aliens will destroy the earth. The first book is *The Magical Fellowship* (Dutton, 1991, $14.95).

In William Joyce's *George Shrinks* (Harper, 1985, $13.89; pap., $3.95), George wakes up to find he is small and must learn to cope with unusual situations.

Two schoolmates are plagued by the same nightmare about an endangered child in William Sleator's *Into the Dream* (Dutton, 1979, $13.95; pap., Knopf, $3.50).

About the Book

Book Report, January 1988, p. 33.
Booklist, June 15, 1987, p. 1602.
Center for Children's Books Bulletin, June 1987, p. 189.
Horn Book, September 1987, p. 617.
Kirkus Reviews, July 1, 1987, p. 993.
School Library Journal, June 1987, p. 96.
See also *Book Review Digest,* 1988, p. 821; and *Book Review Index,* 1987, p. 359; 1988, p. 380.

About the Author

Chevalier, Tracy, ed., *Twentieth-Century Children's Writers* (3rd ed.). St. James, 1989, pp. 465–466.
Commire, Anne, ed., *Something about the Author.* Gale, 1986, Vol. 44, pp. 89–92.
Holtze, Sally Holmes, ed., *Fifth Book of Junior Authors and Illustrators.* Wilson, 1983, pp. 154–155.
Lesniak, James, ed., *Contemporary Authors* (New Revision Series). Gale, 1992, Vol. 36, pp. 200–201.
Nakamura, Joyce, ed., *Something about the Author Autobiography Series.* Gale, 1989, Vol. 8, pp. 119–130.
Straub, Deborah A., ed., *Contemporary Authors* (New Revision Series). Gale, 1988, Vol. 22, p. 205.

Jacques, Brian. *Redwall*

Illus. by Gary Chalk. Philomel, 1987, $16.95 (0-399-21424-0); pap., Avon, $4.99 (0-380-70827-2)

Although *Redwall* was the first published in this fantasy series about a group of enterprising woodland creatures, chiefly mice, and their struggles against various forms of evil, it is actually third chronologically, with both *Mossflower* (Philomel, 1988, $16.95; pap., Avon, $4.99) and *Mariel of Redwall*

(Philomel, 1992, $17.95) preceding it in time. In *Mossflower,* the exploits of the gallant young warrior mouse, Martin, and the events leading up to the foundation of Redwall Abbey are recounted. In *Mariel of Redwall,* Mariel, the daughter of Joseph the bellmaker, gets help from Martin's spirit to fight the murderous Gobool the Wild, a pirate rat, and bring the giant Joseph Bell to the abbey. *Redwall* is followed by *Mattimeo* (Philomel, 1990, $16.95; pap., Avon, $4.99), the story of the exploits of the son of Matthias, the hero of *Redwall,* and his struggle against the wicked fox, Slagar. All four take place in a land similar to England at a time when knighthood—oops, micehood—was in flower. Their length (over 350 pages each) sometimes deters readers, but the chapters are short, often exciting cliffhangers, and the action is swift and constant. Booktalking these adventure-fantasies should attract readers in grades 5 through 8.

Plot Summary

Redwall Abbey is an ancient, beautiful edifice surrounded by outbuildings, extensive gardens, and a high wall on all four sides for protection. In front is a huge meadow and in the distance the ruins of St. Ninian's Church. On the other sides are the dense Mossflower Woods and a meandering river. This idyllic institution is directed by a beatific, gentle mouse, the elderly Abbot Mortimer. In addition to other mice who are members of the Order of Redwall—such as the ancient scribe and chronicler of Redwall, Methuselah, kindly Brother Alf, and the young eager novice, Matthias—there are many other woodland creatures like Constance the badger who also live and work in the abbey compound. Tonight is a special occasion, and a huge feast has been prepared, including a freshly caught grayling to celebrate Mortimer's Golden Jubilee as Father Abbot. Many guests arrive, including Ambrose Spike the hedgehog, the poor church mouse family—with twins Tim and Tess—and Mr. and Mrs. Fieldmouse, whose attractive daughter, Cornflower, immediately becomes a friend of Matthias. The banquet, held in the large Cavern Hole, is announced by the tolling of the abbey's large, sonorous bell, named Joseph Bell.

While these innocents are enjoying themselves, mischief is afoot outside. A gang of five hundred murderous, heavily armed bilge rats under the leadership of the arch-fiend one-eyed Cluny the Scourge are riding into town intent on pillage, death, and plunder. They set up headquarters in the ruined Church of St. Ninian and begin recruiting a motley crew of scurvy rats, ferrets, weasels, and stoats to augment their numbers.

News of the arrival of the rats spreads to the abbey, where many animals begin taking refuge and where preparations are begun in case of attack. Old Methuselah tells Matthias that in his youthful spirit and courage the young mouse resembles the legendary warrior Martin, who saved the abbey many generations ago and whose memory is immortalized in a tapestry depicting his exploits that hangs in the Great Hall. Soon a war council is formed at the abbey that includes Matthias, Constance the badger, the great digger Foremole, Ambrose Spike the hedgehog, and Winifred, an otter. Abbot Mortimer, a peace-loving mouse, continues to supervise the operation of the abbey.

The next day, Cluny the Scourge and his army march to the Great Gate of the abbey. He is a frightful figure with his bat-wing cloak, immense war helmet, and deadly thrashing tail, which he uses as a whip. He and his first lieutenant, Redtooth, are admitted into the Great Hall, where Cluny notices the Martin tapestry. They present to the War Council an ultimatum: surrender or be destroyed. Defiantly, the brave band of abbey residents refuses to surrender, and Cluny, swearing total destruction of Redwall, strides out. That night, he decides on a tactic that will shake the morale of his enemies. He summons Shadow, a rat known for his skill in climbing, and commands him to scale the abbey's walls that night and steal the part of the tapestry in which Martin appears brandishing his magical sword. Shadow succeeds but is discovered and, while trying to escape, falls from the parapet to his death still clutching the fragment of the tapestry, which Cluny victoriously places on his standard.

The following night, Matthias sets off to rescue the tapestry, but by the time he reaches Cluny's camp, the rat and much of his army have left to attack the abbey. Matthias and his newfound friend, a rabbit named Basil Stag Hare, succeed only in freeing a family of voles that Cluny had captured.

The first attack is successfully repulsed, but Cluny's ever-devious mind hatches another plan: a wooden plank will connect an elm tree growing outside the abbey walls and the parapet. Fortunately, Constance the badger sees this attempted invasion in time to tip the plank, sending Cluny and his henchmen tumbling to the earth below. Cluny suffers so many debilitating injuries that he is be unable to resume the attack for three weeks.

From a cryptic inscription found under the tapestry, Matthias and Methuselah discover that years ago Matthias was designated to lead his people to victory. To do this, he must recover Martin's magical sword, which, according to the inscription, is part of the weather vane on the abbey roof. Mrs. Squirrel, or Jess to her friends, obligingly climbs onto the roof, but the sword is not there. She is so violently attacked by a flock of vicious sparrows that mouse archers send a volley of arrows skyward. Jess is saved, and a ferocious wounded bird named Warbeak Sparra is captured. From the bird, Matthias learns that the sparrows were somehow able to dislodge the sword from the weather vane. With Warbeak, he climbs into the space under the roof where the sparrows live. He is captured and held by their insane leader, King Bull Sparra. In captivity, he learns that King Bull was responsible for allowing the sword to be captured by a giant poisonous viper, the adder Asmodeus, who now guards it in his quarry lair. During an escape attempt, Matthias and the mad king fall off the abbey roof. The king is killed, but Matthias miraculously survives. After returning briefly to the abbey, he bids a tender farewell to Cornflower and sets out to find Asmodeus.

During his absence, Cluny recovers and tries two new invasion tactics. The first is the construction of a siege tower on wheels. When it is secretly deployed, Cornflower accidentally discovers it. By pouring hot tea on the would-be invaders, she sets up an alarm that eventually leads to the burning of the tower. Cluny's second plan is to burrow under the abbey wall, but the ever-vigilant moles sense underground movements, and when the rats emerge on abbey ground, they are greeted by a dousing with boiling water. Cluny is further deterred when, in a daring raid, Jess Squirrel and Basil Stag Hare retrieve the stolen tapestry fragment. However, still undaunted, Cluny plans a third devilish scheme. He captures a family of dormice and with threats of death blackmails the father, Plumpen, into infiltrating a gang of mouse workers who are repairing the gate house. That night, inside the abbey grounds, the hapless mouse opens the bolts of the giant door. Cluny and his remaining warriors enter and, unopposed, capture Redwall Abbey.

In the meantime, with the help of a band of shrews, Matthias finds the way to Asmodeus's den. There he retrieves the sword, and in an amazing battle of both wits and strength, he kills the snake. When he learns Redwall has fallen, Matthias sets out accompanied on land by the shrew army, and above, by the sparrows, who are now led by Warbeak. Together they surprise Cluny, retake the abbey, kill the villainous rats and their allies, and free the inhabitants who were destined for execution. Cluny attempts to escape but is pursued by Matthias. It is a fight to the death. When Cluny traps Matthias in the bell tower and it appears that Matthias's end is near, the quick-thinking young mouse cuts the rope holding Joseph Bell, and the bell tumbles to the floor, crushing the hateful Cluny.

Shortly after the lifting of the siege, the ancient Abbot Mortimer feels death approaching. He tells Matthias that he must remain at the abbey not as a brother but as Matthias, the Warrior Mouse of Redwall. As the abbey's official protector, he should marry Cornflower and raise a family.

In a brief epilogue, we are told that is exactly what happens. Within a year of their marriage, Matthias and Cornflower have a young son, Mattimeo, who is destined to have his own thrilling adventures.

Thematic Material

This is a full-bodied, swashbuckling adventure story filled with amazing plot devices and scary cliff-hanging situations. Although peopled with animal characters, this story contains the ingredients of all standard epic fantasies, such as darkest evil versus purest good and a quest involving amazing adventures and hairbreadth escapes. Matthias embodies the qualities of the romantic knight: purity, a strong sense of honor, devotion to duty and a worthy cause, and unwavering courage. Refreshingly, many of the important and bravest characters in the novel (e.g., Winifred, Constance, and Warbeak) are female. The author's ability to create a convincing world where animals assume some human characteristics while retaining their natural innate traits is amazing.

Book Talk Material

This novel is filled with one exciting situation after another. A few are: Matthias and Abbot Mortimer are introduced (pp. 13–16); Cluny the Scourge and his rats travel toward Redwall (pp. 17–18; pp. 24–25); the inhabitants of the abbey hear about Cluny (pp. 33–38); Cluny and Redtooth enter the abbey with the ultimatum (pp. 49–55); Shadow steals part of the tapestry (pp. 70–76); Cluny marches on Redwall (pp. 81–83); and Matthias tries to recapture the tapestry fragment (pp. 85–92).

Additional Selections

The exploits of another legendary hero who helped the oppressed are retold in Howard Pyle's classic *The Merry Adventures of Robin Hood* (Peter Smith, 1989, $18.75).

A version of the Robin Hood story through twentieth-century eyes that involves both merry men and women is found in Robin McKinley's *The Outlaws of Sherwood* (Greenwillow, 1988, $12.95; pap., Ace, $3.95).

Four children travel in time to the days of Ivanhoe in Edward Eager's *Knight's Castle* (Peter Smith, 1989, $16.95; pap., Harcourt, $3.95). Another book in this series is *Half Magic* (Harcourt, 1954, $14.95; pap., $4.95).

In *Rabbit Hill* (Viking, 1944, $14; pap., Puffin, $3.99) by Robert Lawson, a group of animals wonder about the new tenants who are moving into the house on the hill. A sequel is *The Tough Winter* (Peter Smith, 1992, $16.50; pap., Puffin, $3.95).

Pongo and Missis must save a group of Dalmatian puppies captured by Cruella de Vil in Dodie Smith's *One Hundred and One Dalmatians* (Viking, 1989, $14.95; pap., Puffin, $3.95).

A huge wild cat moves from the marshes to a barn for warmth in the winter and encounters new dangers in Peter Parnall's *Marsh Cat* (Macmillan, 1991, $12.95).

After his family moves into an old English house, James is blamed when the resident ghost begins acting up in Penelope Lively's *The Ghost of Thomas Kempe* (Dutton, 1973, $14.95).

About the Book

Booklist, June 1, 1987, p. 1519.
Center for Children's Books, July 1987, p. 211.
Hornbook, January 1988, p. 71.
Kirkus Reviews, June 1, 1987, p. 858.
New York Times Book Review, August 23, 1987, p. 27.
School Library Journal, August 1987, p. 96.
See also *Book Review Digest,* 1988, pp. 875–876; and *Book Review Index,* 1987, p. 387; 1988, p. 409.

About the Author

Commire, Anne, ed., *Something about the Author.* Gale, 1990, Vol. 62, pp. 80–81.
de Montreville, Doris, and Hill, Donna, eds., *Third Book of Junior Authors.* Wilson, 1972, pp. 146–147.
Senick, Gerard J., ed., *Children's Literature Review.* Gale, 1990, Vol. 21, pp. 153–155.
Trosky, Susan M., ed., *Contemporary Authors.* Gale, 1989, Vol. 127, p. 220.

James, Mary. *Shoebag*

Scholastic, 1990, $12.95 (0-590-43029-7); pap., $2.95 (0-590-43030-0)

Mary James, an extremely versatile writer, uses a different pseudonym for each of the many genres in which she writes. To young adults, she is very well known as M. E. Kerr, the writer of such favorites as *Is That You,*

Miss Blue? (Harper, 1975, $12.89; pap., $2.95; condensed in *More Juniorplots,* Bowker, 1977, pp. 35–37) and *Dinky Hocker Shoots Smack!* (Harper, 1972, $12.89; pap., $2.95). Mary James is the name she has adopted for novels intended for the middle grades. *Shoebag,* the first of these, is a clever, amusing reversal of Franz Kafka's *Metamorphosis,* in which a human becomes an insect. In her novel, a cockroach named Shoebag is unwillingly transformed into a young boy. This book is popular with boys and girls in grades 4 through 6.

Plot Summary

All the cockroaches that live in the duplex apartment of the Biddles in the Beacon Hill section of Boston are named after the place where they were born. Thus our hero's name is Shoebag, and his parents, a caring, sacrificing mother and bad-tempered father, are known, respectively, as Drainboard and Under the Toaster. The colony's life is primarily nocturnal and relatively uneventful except for the raiding sorties of a renegade black jumping spider and occasional visits by his brown brother from next door. And on the first Monday of each month they all retreat to the apartment upstairs because it is fumigating day, and they must escape the deadly Zap fumes.

Mrs. Biddle, a hearty eater and somewhat untidy housekeeper, is an unwitting but convenient source of food. She cooks large, healthy meals for her husband and daughter, Eunice, and often leaves leftovers exposed overnight, much to the delight of her roach tenants.

Eunice, an unusually pretty child, is known to millions of television viewers as Pretty Soft because of her many appearances holding Mildred, the Persian cat owned by the neighbors upstairs, in immensely popular commercials advertising Pretty Soft toilet paper. In an effort to keep their Pretty Soft as innocent and beautiful in both mind and body as possible, the Biddles have sheltered her to the point of complete isolation from the outside world. They have hired as tutor-guardian Madam Grande de la Grande, a former show biz star, who is living proof of how fame vanishes after one's looks go. Pretty Soft is happy in her cocoon-like existence and spends hours gazing admiringly in a mirror or, equally admiringly, at reruns of her commercials. She leaves the apartment only to go to the TV station or to spend the first Monday of each month with Madam G de la G in the park, away from the unpleasant Zap odors.

One day Shoebag awakes in the middle of a dream and finds that a terrible thing has happened to him. His tail, known as a cenci, his three pairs of legs, his antennae, and his protective shell have all disappeared, and in their place is the naked body of a young, red-headed, freckle-faced boy. He is discovered in a clothes closet by Mr. Biddle, who at first thinks he is a thief. Hastily wrapped in a blanket, he is introduced to Mrs. Biddle and Pretty Soft. The three quickly decide to adopt this cute young boy as part of the family. Mr. Biddle renames him Stuart Bagg and tells him he must enter the Beacon Hill Elementary School as soon as suitable clothes can be purchased.

The night before he is scheduled to attend school, Shoebag creeps down to the kitchen to visit his roach family. His mother, Drainboard, understands her son's apprehensions and consents to accompany him to school inside his pencil box for moral support.

Because of an unforeseen snowfall, Shoebag is forced to wear a pair of Pretty Soft's pink-lined boots when he goes to school the next day. Even the jovial welcome from Mr. Doormatee, who continually emphasizes the last syllable of his princi*pal* title, and the comforting knowledge that his mother is close by can't protect Shoebag from the derisive taunts of his classmates, led by the school bully, Tuffy Buck, who, after seeing the boots, cruelly nicknames him Stuella. At lunch, Shoebag sits at a table with the other misfits and social outcasts, one of whom, a puny, unattractive girl nicknamed The Ghost, sees Drainboard moving from the pencil box into the lunch bag in search of food. Her screams bring Tuffy Buck to the table, but before he can cause Shoebag more trouble, a third boy intervenes. He is Gregor Samsa, who, because of his superior height and weight, is feared and respected by all, even Tuffy. He also has an air of mystery about him that is accentuated by his deep voice, dark reflecting glasses, unusual appearance, and habit of skipping school. Shoebag instantly feels he has an ally in this strange youngster.

In the next weeks, Shoebag, although he often visits the roaches secretly at night, gradually becomes an accepted member of his foster family. He is disturbed, however, that because Pretty Soft must be protected from anything unpleasant, including all negative influences, he is unable to tell the Biddles about Tuffy's ongoing bullying. He is also puzzled by the double standards humans have toward the animal kingdom: on the one hand, they mount campaigns to save the whales and seals, and on the other, they promote the mass murder of such industrious insects as ants and cockroaches.

One spring afternoon, coincidentally the first Monday of the month, Shoebag is enjoying himself in the park not too far from the bench where

Pretty Soft and Madam Grande de la Grande are seated awaiting the Zapping of the apartment. Suddenly, Shoebag is accosted by Tuffy, who is anxious to beat him up for a number of imagined affronts. Once more, Shoebag is saved by the mysterious Gregor Samsa. On meeting Pretty Soft, Gregor confesses a desire to pursue an acting career. Shoebag is amazed to see that in Gregor's reflecting glasses, Pretty Soft is completely featureless, whereas he is his true self, a cockroach. Later, when they are alone, Gregor explains to Shoebag that these are special glasses that allow people to see themselves as they really are. He also confides that he, too, is a transformed cockroach (real name: In Bed), but that, unlike Shoebag, he knows the secret spell that allows him to change easily from insect to human and back. Unfortunately, if he tells anyone the magic words, they cease to have power for him.

On the eve of a scheduled television appearance by Pretty Soft, Shoebag discovers that Drainboard has been captured by the jumping spider and is being held prisoner high up on the electric clock. Using the excuse that he needs the cockroach for science class, he elicits Pretty Soft's help in a rescue mission. Unfortunately, Pretty Soft loses her balance and falls off the ladder. The net result: Drainboard is saved, but Pretty Soft has a black eye. The next day she can't go to the studio, and the sponsor announces her career is finished. Surprisingly, the Biddles are relieved. Now their daughter can be ordinary Eunice once again, and there will be no more overprotection and deception. She will become, in Madam G de la G's words, "a civilian" and attend the regular elementary school with Shoebag.

Although Eunice's problems have been solved, Shoebag still longs to return to his natural state, particularly when he learns that Under the Toaster plans on moving the family to escape the onslaughts of the jumping spider. Hope of a transformation seems doomed, when Shoebag again encounters Gregor. Realizing that he wants to remain a human forever to pursue an acting career, Gregor reveals to a grateful Shoebag the words that will return him to roachdom. Before he utters them he writes separate farewell notes to Mr. and Mrs. Biddle and to Eunice. He becomes a cockroach again just in time to join his family in a carton containing a microwave being returned by the Biddles to a department store.

The next morning, the Biddles awake to a Shoebag-less home. They read their notes, and for the first time in her life, Eunice sheds a tear. In the meantime, the roaches begin settling into their new home in the appliance department. One day, Shoebag receives two pieces of excellent news. First, on the many television screens that surround their new home, he sees Gregor in a chewing gum commercial; and second, his father returns from a scouting expedition and happily announces that his family is only one floor away from the deli department!

Thematic Material

Although this is basically a witty entertainment, it supplies an interesting and telling roach's-eye view of the human condition. All sorts of human foibles and weaknesses are enumerated. For example, when Shoebag promises never to turn on his roach family, his father says, "He can't keep promises. He's a person." Conflicting attitudes toward nature, the cruelty often inflicted on others who are different or less fortunate, and the artificial world of television are three areas interestingly explored. It is also a story about the need to face reality and become one's own person without the use of mirrors and false images. Friendship, family solidarity, and the nature of alienation are secondary themes.

Book Talk Material

Children sometimes express the desire to assume the identity of a different type of animal, but perhaps they have never thought of the reverse situation. A brief discussion on this subject could lead to an introduction to Shoebag's problems and to Pretty Soft and the Biddle household. Specific passages are: Shoebag discovers he is a little boy (pp. 2–6); Shoebag settles into the human household (pp. 17–22); he revisits his roach family (pp. 34–35); and his first day at school (pp. 43–53).

Additional Selections

In the humorous science fiction novel *Stinker from Space* (Scribner, 1988, $12.95; pap., Fawcett, $3.99) by Pamela F. Service, a top agent from outer space assumes the body of a skunk when he crashes to earth.

In Mary Stolz's *Deputy Shep* (Harper, 1991, $12.95), a lazy police dog is required to investigate a series of burglaries in the quiet town of Canoville.

Mr. Fox outwits three rich, mean farmers in Roald Dahl's *Fantastic Mr. Fox* (Knopf, 1986, $14.95; pap., Puffin, $3.95).

Amos Mouse moves into Ben Franklin's hat and acts as his advisor in *Ben and Me* (Little, Brown, 1988, $14.95; pap., Dell, $2.75) by Robert Lawson.

Eve Titus's *Basil of Baker Street* (McGraw-Hill, 1958, $8.95; pap., Pocket, $2.50) is a mystery story about a mouse that moves into 221 Baker Street to be with his admired Sherlock Holmes.

The search for a lost heart takes three unusual people on a time travel adventure in the humorous tall tale, *Gregory, Maw, and the Mean One* (Houghton, 1992, $13.45) by David Gifaldi.

An amazing pig named Ace of Clubs is so clever he appears on television in Dick King-Smith's *Ace, the Very Important Pig* (Crown, 1990, $13.99; pap., Knopf, $3.99). This is a companion volume to the author's earlier *Babe, the Gallant Pig* (Crown, 1985, $11.95).

About the Book

Booklist, April 15, 1990, p. 1632.
Center for Children's Books Bulletin, March 1990, p. 164.
Horn Book Guide, January 1990, p. 255.
Kirkus Reviews, February 15, 1990, p. 264.
School Library Journal, June 1990, p. 124.
VOYA, October 1990, p. 219.
Wilson Library Bulletin, June 1990, p. 117.
See also *Book Review Digest,* 1990, p. 909; and *Book Review Index,* 1990, p. 408; 1991, p. 460.

About the Author

Chevalier, Tracy, ed., *Twentieth-Century Children's Writers* (3rd ed.). St. James, 1989, pp. 523–525 (under Marijane Meaker).
Commire, Anne, ed., *Something about the Author.* Gale, 1980, Vol. 10, pp. 124–126 (under Marijane Meaker); 1990, Vol. 61, pp. 117–127 (under Marijane Meaker).
de Montreville, Doris, and Crawford, Elizabeth D., eds., *Fourth Book of Junior Authors and Illustrators.* Wilson, 1978, pp. 210–212 (under M. E. Kerr).
Garrett, Agnes, and McCue, Helga P., eds., *Authors and Artists for Young Adults.* Gale, 1989, Vol. 2, pp. 123–138 (under M. E. Kerr).
Kerr, M. E., *Me Me Me Me Me.* Harper, 1983, pap., NAL.
Kirkpatrick, D. L., ed., *Twentieth-Century Children's Writers* (2nd ed.). St. Martin's, 1983, pp. 428–429 (under M. E. Kerr).
May, Hal, ed., *Contemporary Authors.* Gale, 1983, Vol. 107, pp. 332–336 (under Marijane Meaker).
Nilsen, Alleen Pace, *Presenting M. E. Kerr.* Twayne, 1986.
Roginski, Jim, *Behind the Covers, Vol. II.* Libraries Unlimited, 1989, pp. 161–176 (under M. E. Kerr).
Sarkissian, Adele, ed., *Something about the Author: Autobiography Series.* Gale, 1986, Vol. 1, pp. 141–154 (under M. E. Kerr).
Ward, Martha, ed., *Authors of Books for Young People* (3rd ed.). Scarecrow, 1990, p. 392 (under Marijane Meaker).

Jansson, Tove. *Comet in Moominland*
Illus. by the author. Farrar, 1990, $13.95 (0-374-31526-4); pap., $3.95 (0-374-41331-2)

Tove Jansson was born in 1914 in Helsinki to two artistic Swedish parents. These facts explain why, when she began her Moomintroll saga, she wrote in Swedish and illustrated the tales herself. *Comet in Moominland,* first published in 1946, is generally considered to be the first in this eleven-volume series, although the author had previously written a short story introducing the chief characters and locales. Although Henry Z. Walck published English translations of several of these titles during the 1950s, they remained out of print until recently when Farrar, Straus and Giroux rescued them from oblivion, embarking in 1990 on a project to reprint the series. The Moomintroll books are extremely popular both in Continental Europe and in Britain where they have been favorably compared to both the Pooh and Oz series. In *Comet,* the reader meets the most important characters in the series. The hero is Moomintroll, a trusting, good-natured youngster who looks like a white miniature hippopotamus, although he walks about on two legs. His parents are the loving, ever-dependable Moominmamma and the somewhat distant Moominpapa, who is forever engaged in keeping his memoirs up to date. Moomintroll's friends are Sniff, a self-centered, immature creature who resembles a tiny kangaroo with a long mouselike tail, and the philosopher Muskrat, who feigns a total disdain for earthly pleasures while secretly enjoying them immensely. Other characters introduced in this volume include Snufkin, a friendly little wanderer who wears a large green hat and plays the mouth organ; the Hemulen, a male creature who wears a long, ballooning dress; the Hattifatteners, tubelike beings who can neither speak nor hear; and the very helpful silk monkey. Snorks look like Moomintrolls but, like chameleons, can change the color of their skin. During his travels, Moomintroll meets two of them, Snork and his sister, the attractive, feather-brained Snork Maiden, whose most distinguishing physical characteristic is her beautiful bangs. All these characters live in Moomin Valley in Moominland, "where everyone does what they like and seldom worries about tomorrow." This series is enjoyed by better readers in grades 3 through 6.

Plot Summary

One day Moomintroll and his live-in friend, Sniff, decide to explore the Mysterious Path they recently discovered in Moomin Valley. They soon encounter the silk monkey, who leads them through the junglelike vegetation to the sea. While Moomintroll dives for pearls, Sniff continues his exploration and discovers a cave where, with the help of the silk monkey, the two friends hide the beautiful pearls Moomintroll has collected. That night in the Moomin family's blue home, sounds of a terrible storm and a knocking at the door are heard. It is the Muskrat, who, although claiming worldly comforts are meaningless to him, welcomes an invitation to come inside, drink a glass of wine, and become part of the family. Ominously, he states that he has seen forebodings of evil days to come.

The next day, after gathering pears with the help of the silk monkey, Moomintroll and Sniff take a picnic to their cave, where they discover the pearls have mysteriously been arranged in a pattern resembling a star with a tail. Later, they see sea gulls, ants, and Momma's jam jars grouped in the same way. Muskrat claims these are portents involving a comet. Moomintroll is so disturbed that he decides he must travel to the huge Observatory of the Lonely Mountains to ask the Professors what these omens signify.

The next day, ever-attentive Moominmamma packs rucksacks full of food, clothes, and other provisions for Moomintroll and Sniff, and the two set off by raft on their quest. At first the voyage on the river is uneventful, but toward evening, the tiny raft is surrounded by savage, hungry crocodiles. Ingeniously, Moomintroll distracts them by tossing his wooly trousers overboard, and the two escape. They travel under strange gray skies that seem to indicate the presence of a foreign body in the sky. One day, intrigued by the sound of distant music, they pull into shore. Beside his yellow tent, they discover a tramp named Snufkin playing a mouth organ. Always game for adventure, he decides to join the travelers, but before he does, Snufkin shows them a crevice leading to a cave filled with glowing garnets. Sniff foolishly goes in to gather some jewels and is attacked by a giant lizard who jealously guards his treasure. Sniff barely manages to scamper to safety.

While Snufkin regales Sniff and Moomintroll with stories of his adventures, the three continue their journey by raft. Suddenly the river becomes turbulent and filled with rapids. Without warning, they are cast underground and are thrown onto a cavelike shore lit only by a small crack that reveals a glimpse of sky. Fortunately, a passing Hemulen searching for insects for his collection casts his butterfly net into the cave, and the three clamber to safety above ground.

They must now begin their climb into the Lonely Mountains. As they approach the observatory, they repulse an attack by a marauding eagle, and Moomintroll recovers a lovely gold bracelet. He wonders if could belong to the Snork Maiden, a beautiful creature Snufkin had mentioned meeting on one of his adventures. At the observatory, their worse fears are confirmed: A giant comet is approaching and will crash to earth in five days on October 7 at 8:42 P.M., or four seconds later. The sky is now turning a hot, red color and the land is becoming parched.

Moomintroll realizes he must get back to Moomin Valley as soon as possible to warn his parents. Before long, they encounter a terror-struck Snork, who begs them to help save his sister, who is being devoured by a poisonous bush. After a life-endangering battle, Moomintroll is able to rescue the lovely girl, who identifies herself as Snork Maiden. As he had thought, she is also the owner of the lost bracelet. At once, the two are attracted to each other. The Snorks decide to join the band and seek safety in Moomin Valley.

The grim, arduous journey is enlivened by a visit to the Village Stores, where Moomintroll buys Snork Maiden a looking glass, and she gives him a medal for saving her life. Later that night, they enjoy a village dance party in the forest.

The sea has dried up because of the incredible heat caused by the approaching comet. So the five courageous travelers must cross the mud and shallow ponds on stilts. When Moomintroll is attacked by an octopus, the quick-thinking Snork Maiden saves his life by shining the sun's reflection from her looking glass into the beast's eyes, temporarily blinding him. On another occasion, they use the billowing skirt of a passing Hemulen to serve as an air balloon when they encounter a horrible tornado.

Late on the morning of October 7, they finally arrive at Moominhouse, where there is a joyful reunion. It is decided that all should seek refuge from the comet in the cave that Sniff found. So Moomintroll, his parents, the Snork, Snork Maiden, the Hemulen, Sniff, and Snufkin begin the journey down the Mysterious Path to the cave. At first philosopher Muskrat derides trying to survive in a world without meaning, but, as expected, he too joins them. A few minutes before the expected cataclysm, Moomintroll is able to locate the silk monkey and bring her into the cave. There is suddenly a dreadful hissing sound, but the comet misses the earth and miraculously veers off into outer space. One by one the survivors leave the cave to begin life anew.

Thematic Material

This story uses the classic elements of the fantasy-quest: a journey to save civilization, a guileless hero, a blushing maiden, and faithful friends.

It is also the story of small creatures who, like children, are extremely vulnerable. The book portrays a model family with an affectionate, understanding, and forgiving mother at its center. Readers will identify with Moomintroll's innocence, courage, and devotion to family and friends. Although the characters come in many strange shapes and forms, each reveals human characteristics that young readers can easily recognize. The breakneck speed of the plot and the fantastic adventures add a great deal to the book's appeal, and, for the perceptive reader, there is also a subtle, mischievous humor throughout.

Book Talk Material

If possible, it is ideal to introduce this fantasy by showing some of the illustrations and identifying the chief characters. There is also a wealth of self-contained incidents useful for retelling or reading. Some are: Moomintroll and Sniff walk along the Mysterious Path and discover the cave (pp. 9–26); Muskrat arrives at Moomintroll's home (pp. 27–33); the picnic in the cave and discovery of the cometlike patterns (pp. 37–40); Moomintroll talks with Muskrat and decides to go to the observatory (pp. 41–45); the encounter with the crocodiles (pp. 48–51); Snufkin is introduced (pp. 52–58); Sniff and the giant lizard (pp. 59–63) and the adventure in the rapids and rescue by a Hemulen (pp. 68–73).

Additional Selections

Milo enters a magic land in which wordplays on the English language are everywhere in Norton Juster's *The Phantom Tollbooth* (Random, 1961, $15.95; pap., Knopf, $3.95; condensed in *Juniorplots,* Bowker, 1967, pp. 184–188).

Four children travel through time in the seven-volume series Chronicles of Narnia by C. S. Lewis, which begins with *The Lion, the Witch and the Wardrobe* (Macmillan, 1988, $12.95; pap., $5.95).

In Philippa Pearce's *Tom's Midnight Garden* (Harper, 1958, $13.89; pap., $4.95; condensed in *Introducing Books,* Bowker, 1970, pp. 252–256), Tom finds he can travel through time and visit the former occupants of an old house.

Using a setting of New York City at the turn of the century, Nancy Willard creates an amazingly original variation on an old story in *Beauty and the Beast* (Harcourt, 1992, $19.95).

Patricia Wrightson's *The Nargun and the Stars* (Macmillan, 1986, $13.95;

What, indeed, is going on?

At first skeptical, David starts to believe Luke when he claims he has been in some kind of prison and that these strange people want to return him to that dark underworld. What kind of prison? For what crime? David soon takes up a strange challenge from Mr. Wedding. He must discover something—he does not know what or where—by a certain designated time. If he does, his friend Luke will be free forever.

With the aid of Luke and, surprisingly enough, Cousin Astrid, who is not really so uncaring after all, and with his own ingenuity, David tries to discover the key to Luke's freedom.

After many strange twists and turns and with Luke holding back a hill of fire, David finds a tomblike structure upon which rests a woman warrior. The heavy object across her chest looks like an odd pickax. Although it is almost too heavy to carry, David takes the weapon and returns through the burning hill to Luke. He has found the object that will free his friend.

All the mysterious happenings are solved. David learns that Luke and the others are Norse gods, whom his errant curses brought back. Luke is Loki, god of fire and mischief, put in prison for the killing of the god Baldur. Mr. Wedding is Woden, chief of the gods; the Frys are Frey and Freya, gods of sex and fertility; and so on. It is said that on the day of the Final Battle, Woden and Loki will be on opposite sides, the gods will be killed, and the world will be destroyed.

In the meantime, David will return to his own world, but it will be a different one now. He learns that his great-aunt, great-uncle, and cousin have been stealing money that rightfully belonged to him. Fearful that the Frys were actually on their trail, they have run away. David is left in the care of Astrid, and they look forward to forming a bond of love and friendship.

Thematic Material

This is two stories in one: a straightforward tale of an ordinary but likable English schoolboy in a family of uncaring relatives, and a fantasy that concerns Norse gods and ravens that talk and huge snakes that pop up from the ground. There is an interesting contrast between the very real and cold world of David's family life, and the fantastic happenings that occur once Luke has been freed from his underground prison by David's curses. Young readers will sympathize with David's feelings as he tries to deal with his family's cold ways and will cheer his heroics as he defends his friend Luke.

Book Talk Material

The contrast between David's unhappy home life and his fantastic adventures with Luke will serve as good introductions to this tale of fantasy and adventure. See: David's family unhappily greets his unexpected arrival (pp. 3–11); the decision is made to send David off to study math for the holidays (pp. 16–18); David first meets Luke and they battle the snakes (pp. 21–27); Luke sets a building afire (pp. 43–46); David meets the mysterious Mr. Wedding (pp. 65–74).

Additional Selections

The Norse legend of how Balder, god of light and joy, fought evil Loki is retold by Edna Barth in *Balder and the Mistletoe* (Houghton, 1979, $10.95).

The stories of Norse sagas and of Odin, the Wanderer, are included in Padraic Colum's classic 1920 book *The Children of Odin* (Macmillan, 1984, $15.95; pap., $8.95).

Characters from mythology and folklore like Siegfried and Baba Yaga come alive and take Mandy and friend Owen into space to combat Earth invaders in Pamela F. Service's *Weirdos of the Universe, Unite!* (Macmillan, 1992, $13.95).

In the first of the Hed fantasies by Patricia A. McKillip, *The Riddle-Master of Hed* (Macmillan, 1976, $14.95), Morgon, prince of Hed, accompanied by the harpist Deth, sets out to answer the riddle of the three stars on his forehead.

The Book of Three (Holt, 1964, $16.95; pap., Dell, $3.50) by Lloyd Alexander is the first of a five-volume fantasy known as the Prydain Cycle about the pigkeeper Taran and his struggle against evil. The second is *The Black Cauldron* (Holt, 1965, $15.95; pap., Dell, $3.50).

Gom, son of Stig, a woodcutter, knows the language of animals and is one with nature in Grace Chetwin's *Gom on Windy Mountain* (Lothrop, 1986, $12.75; pap., Dell, $3.50). A sequel is *The Riddle and the Rune* (Macmillan, 1987, $15.95; pap., Dell, $3.50).

In Beatrice Gormley's *Paul's Volcano* (Houghton, 1987, $12.95; pap., Avon, $2.50), Adam and the new kid in school tangle over a science fair volcano model that seems to have a mind of its own.

About the Book

Book Report, November 1988, p. 35.
Booklist, October 1, 1988, p. 320.
Center for Children's Books Bulletin, September 1988, p. 11.

Horn Book, November 1988, p. 789.
Kirkus Reviews, July 15, 1988, p. 1061.
School Library Journal, September 1988, p. 184.
VOYA, February 1989, p. 295.
See also *Book Review Digest,* 1989, p. 845; and *Book Review Index,* 1988, p. 420; 1989, p. 424.

About the Author

Chevalier, Tracy, ed., *Twentieth-Century Children's Writers* (3rd ed.). St. James, 1989, pp. 300–306.
Commire, Anne, ed., *Something about the Author.* Gale, 1976, Vol. 9, pp. 116–118.
Evory, Ann, ed., *Contemporary Authors* (New Revision Series). Gale, 1981, Vol. 4, pp. 336–337.
Holtze, Sally Holmes, ed., *Fifth Book of Junior Authors and Illustrators.* Wilson, 1983, pp. 166–167.
May, Hal, and Lesniak, James G., eds., *Contemporary Authors.* Gale, 1989, Vol. 26, pp. 184–186.
Nakamura, Joyce, *Something about the Author: Autobiography Series.* Gale, 1989, Vol. 7, pp. 155–170.
Olendorf, Donna, and Telgen, Diane, eds., *Something about the Author.* Gale, 1993, Vol. 70, pp. 115–118.
Senick, Gerard J., ed., *Children's Literature Review.* Gale, 1991, Vol. 23, pp. 177–198.

King-Smith, Dick. *Martin's Mice*

Illus. by Jez Alborough. Crown, 1988, $13 (0-517-57113-7); pap., Dell, $3.25 (0-440-40380-4)

The English writer Dick King-Smith is known on both sides of the Atlantic for his delightful farmyard fantasies such as *Martin's Mice,* in which anthropomorphic animals face problems and dangers that actually give insights into the human condition. Two other excellent examples are *The Fox Busters* (Delacorte, 1988, $13.95; pap., Dell, $2.95), in which three courageous pullets with unusual flight-and-fight abilities are able to withstand the deadly attack of four marauding foxes; and *Babe: The Gallant Pig* (Crown, 1988, $11.95; pap., Dell, $3.25), the story of Fly, a sheepdog, who teaches his friend Babe, a motherless piglet, the skills of shepherding so Babe will escape Farmer Hogget's plans to have him grace someone's dinner table in the near future. All three are enriched by the author's humorous word plays, in which puns, double entendres, and reworked cliches are used to create an animal's-eye view of the world. They are suitable for readers in grades 3 through 6 or younger for read-aloud purposes.

Plot Summary

Dulcie Maude, a farmyard cat and mother of three young kittens, Robin, Lark, and Martin, soon discovers to her disappointment that Martin is different from the other kittens. While they enjoy play fights and rough-and-tumble games, Martin is peace loving and dislikes violence. Furthermore, he cannot abide the taste of mouse and is appalled at the thought of killing one. Instead, he is happy to eat the canned Happipuss provided daily by the farmer, his wife, or sometimes their daughter. As a result, his brother and sister tease him continually and call him "scaredy-cat" and "wimp." Dulcie Maude begins to despair that her son will never grow to be a normal, red-blooded, mouse-catching cat.

However, one day Martin inadvertently does catch a mouse. Although he tells the little creature that he means no harm, the mouse begs for mercy, telling him she is pregnant. Martin, who knows little of the ways of life, thinks this is her name until she introduces herself as Drusilla. Martin is so enchanted with this feisty little rodent that he decides to adopt her as a pet, like the three rabbits that are kept in pens by the farmer's daughter. He places Drusilla in an unused bathtub in the barn loft and begins to care for her, bringing her food, supplying materials for a nest, removing the plug so she can have toilet facilities, and, hardest of all for him, wetting his paws in the pond so he can bring her tiny droplets of water. Drusilla, although endearing in many ways, is inclined to be somewhat bossy and thankless, particularly after she has a litter of eight children to care for. With nine mouths to feed and the additional burden of keeping the existence of his pets a secret from his mother and siblings, Martin has his paws full.

As they mature, Drusilla's children, whom she names numerically, One to Eight, long for freedom and the world outside the bathtub. Martin seeks advice from the other farm animals. When the highly respected but very pompous boar tells him they should be released, Martin gives each mouse a lecture on the dangers mice face every day and sets them free.

Drusilla, now alone, craves a little male companionship. After receiving a minilecture on the facts of life, Martin sets out to find her a husband. When he returns and deposits a big, handsome mouse in the tub for Drusilla, he is horrified to discover she is in the clutches of a big tomcat, a tabby with markings like Martin's. The old battle-scarred cat introduces himself as Pug. After exchanging details of their lives, Pug realizes Martin is really his son. Although he disagrees with Martin's fondness for mice, he respects his son's beliefs and courage so much that he returns Drusilla to the bathtub and an expectant Cuthbert, her new beau.

In the weeks that follow, Pug and Martin become close friends, although Pug is independent and rarely stays in one place long. Drusilla now shows the unmistakable signs of another pregnancy. One day, Martin hears the sound of the farmer's footsteps approaching the loft. Hastily, he lifts Drusilla out of the tub, but during the second rescue, Cuthbert faints in Martin's mouth. The farmer leaves after congratulating Martin on his brilliant mousekeeping, but Drusilla, thinking Cuthbert is dead, accuses Martin of murder and waddles off into the darkness.

When Cuthbert regains consciousness, he too leaves. Martin is inconsolable and misses Drusilla terribly. From Eight, the last of the first litter, he learns that Drusilla has had twelve more children, whom she has named after each of the months. Luckily, there were only three girls: April, May, and June. Martin also learns that Drusilla will not see him again because she is afraid that he will put her back in captivity.

Martin does not understand Drusilla's attitude, but soon learns first-hand what the loss of personal freedom means. Visitors to the farm who are looking for a pet take Martin back to their city apartment. Although well fed and doted upon, Martin longs fiercely for his farmyard home. One day, when the cleaning woman leaves a window open, he escapes and wanders, totally lost, into the grounds of a large estate. There he meets Alex Smart, a cunning red fox. After hearing about Martin's home and the existence of three caged mouth-watering rabbits, Alex promises to explore the surrounding area to determine the exact location of Martin's farm.

He finds it, but before he can harm the rabbits he is driven off by Pug and Dulcie Maude. Returning to the estate, a somewhat chagrined Mr. Smart gives the necessary directions to Martin, who gleefully sets off.

Back home, he is greeted by a family that now respects and accepts him. He also has an emotional reunion with Drusilla, who is once again pregnant. They renew their friendship—this time on Drusilla's terms.

Thematic Material

On the surface this is a humorous animal fantasy, but in the spirit of Aesop. From the mouths and the actions of Martin and his friends come many insights into human behavior and an exploration of the meaning of freedom, friendship, and the use and misuse of pets. Martin, a feline

Candide, triumphs in spite of (and partly because of) his inexperience and innocence. It is also a story where the outsider and underdog (or cat) gains the love and respect of others through courage and perseverance. The need for tolerance and understanding in dealing with others is stressed, as is the importance of family relationships.

Book Talk Material

The delightful illustrations of Jez Alborough could be used to introduce the principal characters in this novel. For example, the dust jacket of the hardcover edition shows Martin being confronted by bossy Drusilla (foot on bathtub stopper) and surrounded by her first eight cubs. Specific passages are: Martin learns about mice and pets (pp. 1–6); Martin catches Drusilla (pp. 6–11); Martin gets food for Drusilla and she has her first litter (pp. 11–22); he supplies her with toilet facilities (pp. 25–29) and decides to set the youngsters free (pp. 40–45); and Martin brings home a mate for Drusilla and meets Pug (pp. 50–65).

Additional Selections

Freddy the Pig and his farm animals become sleuths in *Freddy the Detective* (Knopf, 1989, $9.99; pap., $4.95) by Walter R. Brooks. Also use sequels such as *Freddy Goes Camping* (Knopf, 1986, $9.99; pap., $4.95).

Ralph, an adventurous mouse, has a motorcycle that he rides inside the hotel where his parents live in Beverly Cleary's *The Mouse and the Motorcycle* (Morrow, 1965, $13.95; pap., Avon, $3.50). This is followed by *Runaway Ralph* (Morrow, 1970, $14.95; pap., Avon, $3.50).

A clever white mouse and her friend Bernard of the Mouse Prisoners' Society are the principal characters in *Miss Bianca* (pap., Dell, $2.50) by Margery Sharp. There are many sequels.

Little Tricker, the squirrel, finally gets even with Big Double the bear who has been bullying all the forest animals in Ken Kesey's *Little Tricker, the Squirrel* (Viking, 1990, $14.95).

Huey, a basset hound, and his friend Taxi, part Siamese-part neurotic, encounter Boots, a beautiful young cat, in Gen LeRoy's *Taxi Cat and Huey* (Harper, 1992, $14).

In *Spider Kane and the Mystery Under the May Apple* (Knopf, 1992, $13; pap., $3.50) by Mary Pope Osborne, butterfly Mimi is kidnapped by Emperor Moth and boyfriend Leon calls in Spider Kane to help.

Marvin, a mouse, and two friends leave their home in Macy's and travel in a gift box to a summer camp in Vermont in Jean Van Leeuwen's *The Great Summer Camp Catastrophe* (Dial, 1992, $13).

About the Book

Booklist, February 1, 1989, p. 939.
Horn Book, January 1989, p. 71.
Kirkus Reviews, December 1, 1989, p. 71.
School Library Journal, January 1989, p. 78.
See also *Book Review Digest,* 1989, p. 901; and *Book Review Index,* 1988, p. 450; 1989, p. 450.

About the Author

Chevalier, Tracy, ed., *Twentieth-Century Children's Writers* (3rd edition). St. James, 1989, pp. 527–528.
Commire, Anne, ed., *Something about the Author.* Gale, 1987, Vol. 47, pp. 139–140.
Holtze, Sally Holmes, ed., *Sixth Book of Junior Authors and Illustrators.* Wilson, 1989, pp. 156–157.
Kirkpatrick, D. L., ed., *Twentieth-Century Children's Writers* (2nd ed.). St. Martin's, 1983, pp. 431–432.
Locher, Frances C., ed., *Contemporary Authors.* Gale, 1982, Vol. 105, pp. 258–259.
Straub, Deborah A., ed., *Contemporary Authors* (New Revision Series). Gale, 1988, Vol. 22, p. 247.
Ward, Martha M., ed., *Authors of Books for Young People* (3rd ed.). Scarecrow, 1990, p. 394.

Stolz, Mary. *The Cuckoo Clock*

Illus. by Pamela Johnson. Godine, 1987, $13.95 (0-87923-653-1)

This author's name has become synonymous with quality literature since her first book was published more than forty years ago. She began with what were once called "problem" novels for young adults. *To Tell Your Love* (o.p.), appeared in 1950 and was hailed for its depth of characterization and its honesty in depicting the problems of adolescents. Others such as *The Organdy Cupcakes* (o.p., condensed in *Juniorplots,* 1967, pp. 121–123), the story of three student nurses, followed. In the 1960s, Mary Stolz began writing for a younger audience with such successes as *A Dog on Barkham Street* (Harper, 1960, $14.89; pap., $3.50), in which Edward Frost, a fifth-grader, tries to avoid the bully who lives next door while trying to persuade his parents he is mature enough to own a dog. The same events are retold from a different point of view in *The Bully of Barkham Street* (Harper, 1963, $14.89; pap., $3.95). In *The Cuckoo Clock,* fantasy and reality mix in the story of a foundling, his friendship with an old clock maker, and the wooden cuckoo that comes to life. It is enjoyed by readers in grades 4 through 6.

Plot Summary

In a time long ago, Erich, a foundling boy, lives in the home of Herr and Frau Goddhart in a little village near Germany's Black Forest. Herr Goddhart is a kindly man of whom the boy is fond. Everyone in the village believes Frau Goddhart to be a saintly woman. But young Erich knows otherwise and feels little affection for her at all. In front of the townspeople, she pretends to be kind, generous, and warmhearted. At home she is a tyrant, giving little in the way of love and generosity to her husband and six children. The townspeople think it wonderful that Frau Goddhart took Erich in "as one of her own" when he was found on the Goddharts' doorstep. In truth, Frau Goddhart took him in only to put on a "good face," because the entire town was witness to the fact that the baby had been left at her home. Behind closed doors, she treats the boy as one of the lowest of her servants.

Erich has never known love or happiness until the day he visits Old Ula, the town's wondrous clock maker, and his old dog, Brangi. Ula and Erich become friends, and Ula is able to persuade Frau Goddhart to let the boy come to his shop for a few hours each day as an apprentice. Erich does learn some of the skills of the old master, but he also gains much wisdom as Ula sets aside time to school the boy in reading and mathematics and other subjects he has not been allowed to learn at the Goddhart home.

One day Baron Balloon, who fancies himself the most important citizen of the village, comes to the shop to demand that Ula make him the finest of all clocks as a Christmas present for the baron's daughter, Britt, who, despite the meanness and pomposity of her father, is a lovely and sweet child. Ula explains that such fine craftsmanship takes time. He cannot possibly deliver such a clock so quickly. Ula advises the baron to go to Fritz, the young clock maker at the other end of the village. No amount of cajoling will change Ula's mind.

When the baron stalks off much insulted, Ula tells Erich of his newfound decision. The old man is going to make the finest clock he has ever created. Erich is going to help him, and it will be Ula's greatest, and last, work.

Through the next months, the old clock maker and his young assistant toil endless hours on this masterpiece. Out of the wood springs the finest cuckoo clock in all the land. Ula even leaves a small side of the clock uncarved so young Erich may add his contribution. Erich fashions a miniature dog to honor Brangi.

When the clock itself is finished, the clock maker carves the cuckoo and puts it inside its new home. Now, the old man and the young boy discover they have created a magic clock, for the bird sings a beautiful and magical song— in fact, all the 36 songs of the birds of the Black Forest.

True to Old Ula's prediction, this magical clock is his last work, and he dies soon after. But before his death, in front of Herr and Frau Goddhart, he leaves his finest tools and his fiddle to Erich, for he predicts the boy will one day be a great artist. Frau Goddhart is not happy with the gift, reasoning that her own children should have such fine things.

Much is made of the funeral of Old Ula, which is attended by his great-nephew, who has inherited the old man's few possessions. After the funeral, Baron Balloon arrives, and with reluctant aid from Erich, convinces the nephew that the masterpiece of a clock is really his—a present to his daughter, Britt. The baron buys the clock from the great-nephew, but Erich notices that the cuckoo has disappeared.

Soon after Erich, along with Brangi, returns to the Goddhart home, he realizes that he can no longer stay there. Fearful for the dog's well-being and aware that Frau Goddhart aims to relieve him of the tools and fiddle that were his gift from Ula, Erich takes the dog and leaves. When he does so, he discovers that Brangi has been holding the cuckoo, unharmed, in his mouth.

Erich hides Brangi in a thicket and goes to Baron Balloon's castle to deliver the cuckoo to Britt. When the bird is returned to the wonderful clock, it sings again, and Britt is enchanted. Erich realizes, however, that only he and Old Ula could hear its magic song. He leaves to travel, with Brangi, out into the world to make his fortune.

But all this happened many years ago. The village near the Black Forest is now a city, and on the wall of an elegant apartment hangs Old Ula's magical cuckoo clock. Each day the man and woman who own the clock sit down to watch the marvelous bird emerge from the double doors and flute his woodsy call. When the bird goes back inside, he sings all day long, all 36 songs of the birds of the Black Forest. But all its listeners hear is "Cuckoo . . . cuckoo . . . cuckoo."

Thematic Material

In this "once-upon-a-time" fantasy of Old World charm, the characters are good and bad, love and warmth and goodness are rewarded in kind, and a young reader can truly believe that behind those beautiful doors a wooden bird has come to life to sing its magic song.

Book Talk Material

The goodness of Old Ula and the bond of love between him and young Erich are main themes in this fantasy fairy tale. See: Baron Balloon demands a clock from Old Ula (pp. 9–13); Erich first feels the bonds of friendship with the old clock maker (pp. 23–25); Erich and Ula talk of the dream about the wondrous clock (pp. 34–36); the magic bird sings (pp. 41–44); and Old Ula gives Erich his tools and his fiddle (pp. 47–48).

Additional Selections

Caitlin's new doll comes alive but proves to have a very disagreeable disposition in Helen V. Griffith's *Caitlin's Holiday* (Greenwillow, 1990, $12.95).

In *Amy's Eyes* by Richard Kennedy (Harper, 1985, $15; pap., $6.95), Amy's doll, Captain, comes alive and takes Amy, who has now become a doll, off on a rousing adventure on the high seas.

In Elisabet McHugh's *Wiggie Wins the West* (Macmillan, 1989, $12.95; pap., Dell, $3.25), Wiggie the cat sees himself as the Carter family's fearless protector on a journey from Virginia to Idaho.

Two ghost children encounter a young mortal, eleven-year-old Jerry, and explore contemporary life together in Sarah Sargent's *Jerry's Ghosts* (Macmillan, 1992, $13.95).

Over Sea, Under Stone (Harcourt, 1966, $14.95; pap., $3.50) by Susan Cooper is the first of a prize-winning, five-part fantasy of children involved in a classic good-versus-evil struggle set principally in Cornwall and Wales. The fourth in this series, *The Grey King* (Macmillan, 1975, $14.95; pap., $3.50) won the 1976 Newbery Medal.

A little boy sets out to rescue a dragon in Ruth Stiles Gannett's *My Father's Dragon* (Random, 1986, $14.95; pap., Knopf, $4.95), a Newbery Honor book. A sequel is *Elmer and the Dragon* (pap., Knopf, $3.99).

Little people no bigger than a pencil live in an old house and borrow from the inhabitants in Mary Norton's *The Borrowers* (Harcourt, 1953, $13.95; pap., $3.95). One of the many sequels is *The Borrowers Afloat* (Harcourt, 1959, $12.95; pap., $3.95).

About the Book

Booklist, December 15, 1986, p. 652.
Center for Children's Books Bulletin, May 1987, p. 179.
Kirkus Reviews, March 1, 1987, p. 376.
School Library Journal, April 1987, p. 105.

About the Author

Chevalier, Tracy, ed., *Twentieth-Century Children's Writers* (3rd ed.). St. James, 1989, pp. 921–923.

Commire, Anne, ed., *Something about the Author.* Gale, 1976, Vol. 10, pp. 165–167.

Fuller, Muriel, ed., *More Junior Authors.* Wilson, 1963, pp. 195–197.

Harte, Barbara, and Riley, Carolyn, eds., *Contemporary Authors* (First Revision Series). Gale, 1969, Vols. 5–8, pp. 1104–1105.

Kirkpatrick, D. L., ed., *Twentieth-Century Children's Writers* (2nd ed.). St. Martin's, 1983, pp. 728–729.

Metzger, Linda, ed., *Contemporary Authors* (New Revision Series). Gale, 1984, Vol. 13, pp. 477–479.

Sarkissian, Adele, ed., *Something about the Author: Autobiography Series.* Gale, 1987, Vol. 3, pp. 281–292.

Telgen, Diane, ed., *Something about the Author.* Gale, 1993, Vol. 71, pp. 189–194.

Ward, Martha, ed., *Authors of Books for Young People* (3rd ed.). Scarecrow, 1990, p. 677.

Yolen, Jane. *The Dragon's Boy*

Harper, 1990, $14 (0-06-026789-5)

Jane Yolen is one of the most prolific writers of books for the young, with nearly one hundred titles suitable for children of all ages. For readers in grades 2 to 4, two of her important books are *Sleeping Ugly* (pap., Putnam, 1981, $6.95), a variation on the Sleeping Beauty story; and *The Seeing Stick* (Crowell, 1977, $14.89), the story of a blind Chinese princess who learns to "see" with her fingers when she feels a cane that an old woodworker has carved with many adventures. For middle grades, *The Devil's Arithmetic* (Viking, 1988, $12.95; pap., Puffin, $3.95) is a time travel story that takes a twelve-year-old Jewish girl from a Passover Seder in America to Poland in 1942, where she becomes Chaya on her way to a concentration camp. *The Dragon's Boy* is a complete change of pace. Using clever name changes, it retells the boyhood of King Arthur, who becomes Artos in this account. The young lad discovers that the wisdom he thought came from an old dragon actually comes from a figure who is an alias of Merlinnus. This suspenseful, often humorous tale of courage and the search for justice is suitable for readers in grades 4 through 7.

Plot Summary

Artos is the youngest and smallest of the boys of Beau Regarde castle. Since he was a baby, he has been cared for by kindly Sir Ector and Lady

Marion. They have raised him as one of their own, along with their son, Cai, and cousins Bedvere and Lancot. Although Sir Ector and Lady Marion are kind to him, Artos never feels that he truly belongs. The older boys sometimes tolerate him, and sometimes taunt him. Mostly they ignore him, never asking him to join their games.

One day Sir Ector's prize hound, Boadie, escapes the castle grounds. It is Artos's job to watch out for the hound, so he sets out after her into the boggy wastelands north of the castle. He does not find Boadie, who returns to the castle safe and sound. But he does stumble upon an entrance to a cave. Frightened but curious and intrigued, Artos steps inside the dark interior to explore. He is immediately nearly paralyzed with fear by a booming voice that commands him to "Stay!"

The voice, it turns out, belongs to a dragon. At least that is what the voice says. Artos can't exactly see the dragon, because it is very dark in the cave. However, he certainly can hear the dragon's fierce breathing and very loud voice. Although the dragon sounds very frightening, he doesn't really act that way. As it turns out, the dragon hasn't had any visitors for a very long time. He invites Artos to sit a spell and tells the boy that he will pay him for this visit.

"How would you like to be paid?" asks the dragon. "In gold, in jewels, or in wisdom?"

Artos, never having had a conversation with a dragon before, friendly or not, is not at all convinced the creature doesn't intend to eat him. Trying not to antagonize the dragon, he replies that he would like to be paid in wisdom. He figures that is the most prudent reply.

The dragon is pleased with his answer. "Return tomorrow and bring me some stew with meat in it," the dragon says. "Then I will begin to give you wisdom." But when Artos leaves the cave, the dragon also gives him a large red jewel.

Artos returns to the castle with his jewel and with no intention of ever returning to the cave. However, now that he has what certainly must be a valuable jewel, he reasons that he can have the castle smithy make him a sword. With a sword, he might gain some respect and notice from the other boys.

Artos finds the sword maker in the midst of an argument with Old Linn, Sir Ector's apothecary. Old Linn resembles a tortoise, but as a storyteller he has no equal and Artos has no chance to interrupt to ask the sword maker for a sword in exchange for the red jewel.

Although he has told himself he will not go back to the cave, Artos feels drawn to return to the dragon the following day. But how will he get the stew with meat he was ordered to bring? His only recourse is to bribe the scullery maid, Mag, who is very fond of Artos. In exchange for the stew with meat, Artos is obliged to reward Mag with a kiss on the cheek. He feels this is a very high price to pay.

The dragon is pleased with the stew and with the boy's return. Many visits to the cave follow. Young Artos learns wisdom from the old dragon—he learns from books and from stories. The dragon teaches him to play a game with cups that delights and mystifies the other boys. But the dragon cautions him that true wisdom comes from *inter linea*—from reading between the lines. That goes for people as well, the dragon says. Curiously, the dragon calls him "Artos Pendragon, Arthur son of the dragon."

Artos takes his jewel to the smithy again and this time is promised a fine sword. The smithy produces a number of swords, all rejected by Artos for one reason or another. Finally, the smithy makes a sword with a pattern on the blade that resembles a dragon's mouth. Artos accepts this one.

Pleased with his fine possession, Artos takes it to show to the dragon, but the cave is dark. The dragon has gone off somewhere, Artos reasons, and he vows to return the next day. But life has become a happier place for the young boy, and many days go by with barely a thought of the dragon. Artos is treated with more respect by his companions. His new sword, plus the wisdom gained from the dragon, have brought him friendship. Even Lady Marion seems to look at him with new interest.

Artos is included on a trip with Lady Marion to the market fair in Shapwick that will take a few days. He has never been so far from the castle, nor has he ever seen so many people in one place. It is a great experience for him. Yet, during these exciting days, Artos begins to see the shallowness of Cai and his cousins, their casual cruelty, their foolishness, their thoughtless treatment of the feelings of others.

Upon his return to the castle, Artos can barely wait to visit the cave once more. He fears it will be dark again. And indeed, at first there is only silence when he enters. Then he hears a moan. The dragon is back. Although the dragon tries to keep Artos from coming closer, the boy will not be kept away, and he finally sees what he was not meant to see. The cave is not occupied by a dragon at all, but by a man. An old man. It is Old Linn the apothecary. It is Old Linn, not the dragon, who has been imparting wisdom to Artos!

Artos is angry about this deception, and he refuses to believe it when

Old Linn says that he, Artos, is the dragon's son. Then Old Linn explains what he means. Years before, he had borne Artos away from his mother, before his birth father ever saw him. He carried the baby to Sir Ector's castle and has been watching over him ever since. He swore he would keep the boy's name and lineage a secret until Artos proved himself worthy.

"Look through that door," Old Linn tells him, pointing outside the cave. "Through that door, Pendragon, are the men you must learn to lead."

But young Artos knows he does not yet have the wisdom. I cannot do it alone, he tells Old Linn. Together the boy and the old man leave the cave.

I think I'm beginning to understand wisdom, Artos tells Old Linn as they walk toward the castle.

"You may not look like a dragon . . . but you are a dragon indeed. And," Artos adds, "I am the Dragon's Boy."

Thematic Material

This tale of the future King Arthur is a coming-of-age story set in medieval times as the young Artos slowly learns to "look between the lines" of books and people to find wisdom and to prepare himself for his destiny. A nicely told fantasy capturing the flavor and spell of the Arthurian legends. Subthemes are those of bravery and justice.

Book Talk Material

Several incidents make a fine introduction to this story of a young boy gaining wisdom. See: Artos first meets the dragon (pp. 12–19); Artos decides he must have a sword (pp. 29–34); Artos brings the dragon stew (pp. 39–45); the dragon teaches him the game with cups (pp. 63–67); and Artos gets his sword (pp.71–73).

Additional Selections

One of the best retellings of the exploits of the grown King Arthur is Howard Pyle's *The Story of King Arthur and His Knights* (Peter Smith, 1987, $17.95).

T. H. White has also written about the childhood of King Arthur, whom he calls Wart, a corruption of Art, in *The Sword in the Stone* (Putnam, 1938, $11.95; pap., Dell, $3.50; condensed in *Juniorplots,* Bowker, 1967, pp. 202–204).

Prince Jen, a pampered, clever young man, has a series of adventures while seeking knowledge from a neighboring king in Lloyd Alexander's *The Remarkable Journey of Prince Jen* (Dutton, 1991, $14.95; condensed in *Juniorplots 4,* Bowker, 1993, pp. 183–188).

A poor lad woos his lady love in an exciting story of Arthurian romance, Margaret Hodges's *The Kitchen Knight* (Holiday, 1990, $14.95).

A spirited princess volunteers to become a dragon's servant and companion in Patricia Wrede's *Dealing with Dragons* (Harcourt, 1990, $15.95).

In Andre Norton's time-warp fantasy *Red Hart Magic* (Harper, 1976, $14.90), two misfits see their counterparts at three different periods in English history.

After he is trapped under a rock, Merlin, the Arthurian magician, spins eight tales of medieval adventure in Peter Dickinson's *Merlin Dreams* (Delacorte, 1988, $19.95).

About the Book

Booklist, September 15, 1990, p. 165.
Center for Children's Books Bulletin, January 1991, p. 134.
Horn Book, January 1991, p. 72.
Kirkus Reviews, August 15, 1990, p. 1175.
School Library Journal, October 1990, p. 122.
See also *Book Review Digest,* 1991, p. 2048; and *Book Review Index,* 1990, p. 894; 1991, p. 994.

About the Author

Chevalier, Tracy, ed., *Twentieth-Century Children's Writers* (3rd ed.). St. James, 1989, pp. 1075–1079.

Commire, Anne, ed., *Something about the Author.* Gale, 1973, pp. 237–239; 1985, Vol. 40, pp. 217–230.

de Montreville, Doris, and Crawford, Elizabeth D., eds., *Fourth Book of Junior Authors and Illustrators.* Wilson, 1978, pp. 356–358.

Estes, Glenn E., ed., *American Writers for Children since 1960: Fiction* (Dictionary of Literary Biography: Vol. 52). Gale, 1986, pp. 398–405.

Evory, Ann, ed., *Contemporary Authors* (New Revision Series). Gale, 1984, Vol. 11, pp. 542–545.

Kinsman, Clare D., ed., *Contemporary Authors* (First Revision).Gale, 1975, p. 888.

Kirkpatrick, D. L., ed., *Twentieth-Century Children's Writers* (2nd ed.). St. Martin's, 1983, pp. 850–853.

May, Hal, and Straub, Deborah, eds., *Contemporary Authors* (New Revision Series). Gale, 1990, Vol. 29, pp. 463–469.

Sarkissian, Adele, ed., *Something about the Author: Autobiography Series.* Gale, 1986, pp. 327–346.

Senick, Gerard J., ed., *Children's Literature Review.* Gale, 1982, pp. 255–269.

Ward, Martha, ed., *Authors of Books for Young People* (3rd ed.). Scarecrow, 1990, pp. 772–773.

4

School and Friendship Stories

YOUNG people like to read about situations and problems with which they are familiar. These include getting along at school and making and keeping friends. The nine books in this section explore various locales and variations on these topics. Some are humorous and light-hearted, while others explore the deeper, more serious aspects of these subjects. In each, however, the reader is exposed to worthwhile, quality writing while exploring different aspects of the process of growing up.

Auch, Mary Jane. *Kidnapping Kevin Kowalski*
Holiday, 1990, $13.95 (0-8234-0815-0)

Mary Jane Auch, although a relative newcomer to the field of children's literature, has written a number of fast, funny, and popular novels for middle-grade readers. Among them is *Seven Long Years Until College* (Holiday, 1991, $13.95), in which Natalie finds there are four things disturbing her life: she is entering sixth grade, her mother is about to remarry, her sister is leaving for college, and her best friend is moving away. This story tells how she accommodates to these changes, including adjusting to the new stepfather and having a chance to visit her sister in her new surroundings. Another popular novel in a similar vein is *Mom Is Dating Weird Wayne* (pap., Bantam, $2.99). In 1992 this author wrote and illustrated her first picture book, *The Easter Egg Farm* (Holiday, 1992, $14.95). In *Kidnapping Kevin Kowalski,* Ryan and Mooch hope to prepare friend Kevin for summer camp by kidnapping the partially disabled boy for an overnight camping trip. The hopes, fears, and concerns of these three friends are revealed in this novel as well as a glimpse at three different patterns of family life. It is enjoyed by readers in grades 4 through 6.

Plot Summary

Ryan and Mooch and Kevin, who are about to enter the seventh grade, have been best friends practically forever. A few months ago, while biking with Ryan, Kevin was hit by a car. He suffered a severe head injury and was in a rehab center for two months. Now he is back home, but he has not called his friends.

Ryan and Mooch decide to visit Kevin even though they are afraid of what they may find. Will he be the same old Kevin? The same old crazy Kevin who could always find something nutty for them to do?

The boys quickly discover that Kevin is in many ways himself, but in many ways different. He kids with them in the same old ways, but he often looks and acts listless and bored. His left arm seems impaired, and he does not walk well. Yet he is obviously happy to see his friends.

After a few visits with Kevin, the boys realize his mother is treating him like an invalid, or a baby. Ryan is convinced that Kevin could do more on his own if only he had the confidence. Mooch isn't so sure.

The boys talk to Kevin about the upcoming Boy Scout camp they usually attend in the summer. Mrs. Kowalski rejects the idea, although Mr. Kowalski wants Kevin to go. His mother is afraid Kevin will hurt himself.

Ryan, who feels guilty that he did not do enough to help his friend after the bike accident, even though help arrived almost immediately, concocts an elaborate plan to "kidnap" Kevin and spend a night in the woods behind the boys' homes. They will show Kevin he really is capable of doing more things than he believes he can. Mooch is convinced that the FBI will soon be on their trail, but he reluctantly agrees to go along with the scheme. They also enlist the aid of Kevin's sister, Emily, who will try to keep Kevin's mother occupied and out of the way.

The boys tell the Kowalskis that Kevin is staying the night with Ryan; Ryan tells his family he will be at Mooch's; and since Mooch's mother never seems to care where he is anyway, no one tells her anything.

Mooch borrows his older brother's all-terrain vehicle to transport the boys and their belongings into the woods, where they have stored a tent and supplies. Kevin is surprised and apprehensive at first when he realizes they will be spending the night in the woods, but he begins to relax and enjoy himself.

As the day and night pass, Ryan begins to understand that, although it is true that Kevin can do much more than his mother allows him, his friend does have some handicaps. His left hand is awkward and sometimes useless. He cannot walk far without tiring, and on occasion he is mentally confused. He cannot, for instance, remember a string of numbers, which is why he never called Ryan or Mooch on the phone. He tries to explain to Ryan that these are things he must live with forever.

All in all, however, Ryan thinks his idea was a good one and that Kevin has more confidence in himself. The next morning the boys decide to go swimming in the old ore bed. Kevin used to outswim them all. He still does, but Mooch, who never really learned to swim, very nearly drowns. Despite his disabilities, Kevin saves his friend.

The boys agree they will not mention the swim in the ore bed to their parents, but that they will tell the Kowalskis—and the other parents—about their overnight camping trip to prove that Kevin is capable of going to camp with them.

They return from their adventure to find a distraught Mrs. Kowalski—the boys' absence has been discovered. She calms down a bit when all is explained and when Kevin tells her he really does want to go to camp and that she must stop treating him like a baby. She promises that she will think about it, and says he must prove to her over the next few days that he really can take care of himself.

Ryan is sure his plan has worked and that the three friends will be going off to camp as usual. Just like always. But he also realizes that it will never be "just like always" again. Kevin will always be Kevin, but a different Kevin, not quite the boy he knew. Kevin realizes that and can live with it. So can Ryan. For one thing is the same and always will be, they are really and truly friends.

Thematic Material

This is a touching, warm story with a tinge of sadness. It deals with the real-life tragedy of an accident that leaves permanent and lasting disability; with the heartbreak and fear of an overprotective parent afraid to lose her child again; with the struggle to learn to live with a disability and the realization that there are some things that will never be the same again. But most of all, it is a story of friendship, friendship that can endure even while it must change.

Book Talk Material

Many incidents in this book will give insight into the treatment and feelings of those who have become disabled. See: Ryan and Mooch first

Emergency Whistle Ring, and his speech and actions are reenactments of the thrilling installments he heard the night before. He is especially fond of Chet Barker, ruthless, clear-eyed Master Spy, and his sidekick, the faithful but brilliant Skipper O'Malley. These two roughly echo the relationship between himself and his best friend, Mario Calvino. The homes of these classmates in Brooklyn are so close together that they can use a plank between their bedroom windows to visit each other or exchange homework, the latter being a one-way transaction because Frankie is too absorbed with the radio to bother with mundane school assignments. Mario, a hard-working, thoughtful youngster, lives alone with his working mother. His father was killed in the war. Frankie lives with his mother and father and, since his brother Tom went to war, a roomer, the quiet Mr. Swerdlow, a conscientious medical student who wants only to be left alone to study. In Frankie's dream world, however, Mr. Swerdlow is really a mad scientist intent on destroying the war effort, if not the world.

Frankie's hyperactive imagination continually gets him into trouble. Playing the part of the investigative Chet Barker, Frankie sneaks into Mr. Swerdlow's room to show Mario the student's skull-less skeleton in the closet. Unfortunately, he is caught by Mr. Swerdlow and reported to his parents. Frankie also has trouble at school, where the patience of his teacher, the beautiful Miss Gomez, has reached breaking point because of his poor grades and his disruptive comments about his favorite radio shows. (Through some sleuthing, Frankie has also found that Miss Gomez's boyfriend has been killed in the war.)

Frankie's brother, Tom, is sent home from the war because of a severe leg wound. Instead of the conquering hero Frankie had imagined, his brother has become a sullen, bitter man who is still in pain and wants to be left alone. He takes over Frankie's room and the young boy is banished to the basement where, alas, there is no radio! Something must be done. In the basement, Frankie discovers a transmitting device belonging to his Uncle Charlie. Suddenly he imagines this long-absent relative is an important secret agent, probably this very minute engaged in an operation that could mean the end of the war.

One night, Frankie, with a mask under his eyeglasses and wearing his father's hat and overcoat, decides to trace the movements of Mr. Swerdlow with the help of sidekick Mario. They lose the scent quickly, but instead spot Miss Gomez crying on a park bench. In his disguise, Frankie appears before her and assures her that things will soon be all right. Inwardly, Frankie believes the perfect solution would be to evict Mr.

Swerdlow and have Miss Gomez and Tom marry and move into the vacant room so that he can have his old perch back.

When Mr. Swerdlow brings home a wrapped package from the post office, Frankie is convinced it is either a bomb or secret plans. Defying Frankie's parents' ban, Frankie and Mario secretly enter Mr. Swerdlow's room and find a newly unwrapped skull. Frankie decides to hide a speaker under the bed and frighten the student with moans and groans, that supposedly come from the mouth of the skull. Unfortunately, Mr. Swerdlow is not that easily intimidated. He traces the wires to the basement, confronts Frankie, and announces to Mr. and Mrs. Wattleson that he is moving immediately. Although Frankie is punished by being grounded completely, Phase One of his plan has been achieved.

One day when his parents are both out, Frankie sneaks out for some air and encounters a stranger who is examining the house. Frankie introduces himself as Chet Barker, and the man tells him that he is Mrs. Wattleson's older brother, Charlie. Frankie questions the man, but instead of being the spy the boy imagined, his uncle confesses to being a small-time crook, a bookie, who has just been released from prison after serving a nine-year sentence. He begs for some food and swears Frankie, alias Chet, to secrecy before moving on and leaving Frankie with another fantasy exploded.

Events at school are reaching a climax. Miss Gomez is tired of keeping Frankie after school every day and decides she must see his parents to discuss his abysmal school record. She sends a note home with the boy who, using a tip from his *Sky King Junior Spy Manual,* steams the envelope open and learns that Miss Gomez will visit his parents at seven o'clock on Thursday night. Frankie, in turn, tells his parents they must attend a very important parent-teacher meeting at school on Thursday evening at seven o'clock. Frankie's father will be working, but his mother agrees to go. Phase Two is in operation: Tom and Miss Gomez are to meet alone.

After his mother has left for the school on Thursday evening, Frankie goes to talk to Tom. Before mentioning Miss Gomez, he again questions his brother about being a war hero and asks about the glory of fighting in battles. Tom, with a violence Frankie has never seen before, tells him what war is really like—about the carnage, filth, blood, and fear. Shaken, Frankie changes the subject and tells Tom that his teacher is coming and he wants Tom to meet her. When she arrives, Tom panics at the thought of meeting a stranger and, with Frankie's help, uses the plank to crawl over to Mario's house. He slips and dangles in midair, holding onto the window sill. Mario calls the police and fire department for help. Miss Gomez and Frankie rescue Tom and drag him inside just as the police cars and fire engines arrive, along with a very irate Mrs. Wattleson. Pandemonium results.

Six months later, the war is over and Miss Gomez and Tom are getting married. Frankie, as Chet Barker, plans The Wedding Night Caper. He places his radio transmitter under their bed and hears Miss Gomez, now Mrs. Wattleson, tell Tom of how she received comfort and a promise of better times from a strange-looking boy in the park. To this day, she wonders who that masked kid was, anyway.

Thematic Material

Avi recreates the innocence of childhood fifty years ago. The effervescent humor and the authentic touches of homefront living during World War II give added dimensions to the story. The problems of separating reality from fantasy and the true nature of heroism are important themes. Above all, the reader will remember the irrepressible, well-meaning, but exasperating Frankie Wattleson, a.k.a. Chet Barker, Master Spy.

Book Talk Material

Some of the excerpts from the radio scripts would make for good reading-aloud. Some samples: *Captain Midnight* (pp. 1–3); *The Shadow* (pp. 8–9); *The Iceman* (pp. 23–26); and *The Lone Ranger* (pp. 32–42). Some other interesting passages of dialogue are: Frankie and Mario talk about school and Miss Gomez (pp. 4–8); Frankie and Mario visit Mr. Swerdlow's room and get caught (pp. 10–20); Frankie is found reading *Radio Digest* by Miss Gomez (pp. 28–31); Miss Gomez and Frankie have a heart-to-heart talk (pp. 31–34); and news comes that Tom is coming home and Frankie is moving to the basement (pp. 44–46).

Additional Suggestions

Stage fright comes to Reesa along with the honor of reading her essay before five hundred people in Susan Beth Pfeffer's *What Do You Do When Your Mouth Won't Open?* (Delacorte, 1981, $8.95; pap., Dell, $2.95).

In Thomas Tryon's *The Adventures of Opal and Cupid* (Viking, 1992, $14), Opal May Thigpen, age thirteen, leaves her small town with her performing elephant, Cupid, to hit the big time in New York City.

Pinch, whose father is a trainer of hunting pigs, has a prize pig named Homer who is so admired that he is stolen in Larry Callen's *Pinch* (Little, Brown, 1975, $14.95).

Steve and Max find a time machine that sends to medieval England them for three days in the humorous *Max and Me and the Time Machine*

(Harcourt, 1983, $13.95; pap., Harper, $3.95) by Gery Greer and Bob Ruddick.

Germy needs money and gerbil-raising seems to be the answer in Rebecca C. Jones's *Germy Blew It—Again* (Holt, 1988, $13.95; pap., Knopf, $3.50), a sequel to *Germy Blew It* (Dutton, 1987, $12.95; pap., Troll, $2.95).

Dinky, a lonely compulsive eater living in Brooklyn, tries many ways to gain her parents' attention in *Dinky Hocker Shoots Smack!* by M. E. Kerr (Harper, 1972, $12.89; pap., $2.95).

A group of English boys must face the realities of war when one of their friends is killed in an air raid during World War II in Susan Cooper's *Dawn of Fear* (Harcourt, 1970, $14.95; pap., Macmillan, $3.95).

About the Book

Booklist, August 1992, p. 2012.
Center for Children's Books Bulletin, October 1992, p. 35.
Kirkus Reviews, August 1, 1992, p. 986.
School Library Journal, October 1992, p. 112.
See also *Book Review Index,* 1992, p. 41.

About the Author

Bowden, Jane, ed., *Contemporary Authors.* Gale, 1978, Vols. 69–72, pp. 621–622.
Chevalier, Tracy, ed., *Twentieth-Century Children's Writers* (3rd ed.). St. James, 1989, pp. 45–46.
Commire, Anne, ed., *Something about the Author.* Gale, 1978. vol. 14, pp. 269–270.
Holtze, Sally Holmes, ed., *Fifth Book of Junior Authors and Illustrators.* Wilson, 1983, pp. 15–16.
Metzger, Linda, ed., *Contemporary Authors* (New Revision Series). Gale, 1984, Vol. 12, pp. 517–518 (under Wortis, Avi).
Roginski, Jim, ed., *Behind the Covers.* Libraries Unlimited, 1985, pp. 33–42.
Senick, Gerard J., ed., *Children's Literature Review.* Gale, 1991, Vol. 24, pp. 1–15.

Christopher, Matt. *The Hit-Away Kid*

Illus. by George Ulrich. Little, Brown, 1988, $9.95 (0-316-13995-5); pap., $3.95 (0-316-14007-4)

Matt Christopher has always had an avid interest in many kinds of sports, and it shows in his writing. Since his first novel for middle-grade readers, *The Lucky Baseball Bat* (pap., Little, Brown, 1993, $3.95), appeared in 1954, he has written dozens of exciting sports stories for this age group. Two are *Red-Hot Hightops* (Little, Brown, 1987, $14.95; pap., $3.95) in which a girl who is too shy to show off her basketball skills or speak to a boy she likes experiences a change in her life after she finds a pair of red sneakers in her locker; and *Tackle Without a Team* (Little, Brown, 1989, $13.95), the story of a young football player who is dismissed from his team because marijuana is found in his duffle bag and sets out to find the person who planted it there. In addition to plenty of fast sports action, Christopher's books usually explore social or personal problems. In *Hit-Away Kid,* Barry, the central character, learns the true meaning of sportsmanship when he bends the rules to win at baseball. This simple novel is intended for youngsters in grades 2 through 4. The others noted above are for slightly older readers.

Plot Summary

If there is one thing Barry McGee, left fielder for the Peach Street Mudders, loves more than baseball, it is being the hero of the team—the hit-away kid. Well, perhaps there is one thing Barry loves even more than baseball and being a hero, and that's winning. Nothing beats winning.

During a game in which the Mudders are losing to the Belk's Junk Shop, Barry discovers just how much winning means to him. A ball is smacked out to left. If it's a hit, the Junk Shop will score. If Barry catches the ball, the inning is over. Barry makes a great catch, getting his glove under the ball just before it hits the ground. But then the ball rolls off the glove onto the grass. No one sees. "I got it!" Barry yells, quickly scooping the ball back into his glove. "Out!" shouts the umpire.

Some of the fans call "Nice catch!" as Barry runs in from the field. Then he hears his sister's voice. "You dropped it," Susan of the big mouth tells him. "I saw you."

Barry tells her to keep quiet, but the Mudders lose anyway. On the way home Susan accuses her brother of cheating in other games, too, just because he likes to win. Barry cuts her off with, "Maybe I do cheat sometimes, but not all the time. And I don't do it to hurt anybody."

Susan isn't buying that, and Barry feels just a little guilty.

At supper that night, Barry's dad asks about the game. Barry says he got two hits even though they lost. His father thinks that's great. Then Barry surprises everyone, especially Susan, by admitting that he dropped the ball and he didn't tell anyone. No one thinks that's great. But Barry promises it won't happen again, and the incident is over. He feels better, too.

The next day Barry and his friend Jose go skateboarding, with Susan tagging along. They run into Smart-Alec Frost and his buddies, all members of the High Street Bunkers baseball team. Alec is the star pitcher and a bully.

Alec steals a figurine that Susan had been carrying in her pocket. It belongs to their younger brother, Tommy. Alec says he won't give it back unless Barry—the big-deal hit-away kid—gets two home runs off him at their upcoming game. If Alec can strike Barry out twice, the figurine is his.

On game day, Barry wishes he could play sick. He's never hit two home runs in his life. His first time at bat, Barry strikes out. But the second time he gets a home run. One to go.

With the score Bunkers 5, Mudders 2, Barry hits a drive to deep left center. As he rounds second base, he misses the bag, but no one notices. Barry wrestles with his conscience, then steps off the base and lets himself get picked off. When the coach screams at him, Barry admits he was out anyway because he missed the base.

Barry's last time at bat, he pops out. The game is over. The Mudders lose. So does Barry.

As he walks off the field, he hears the voice of Smart-Alec. He holds out the figurine. "You won it fair and square," he says. "I have to hand it to you for telling the coach you missed second base."

"I guess a person can change, if he does the right thing," Barry says to Susan.

Susan winks at him and agrees.

Thematic Material

This is a simple friendship and sports story with an important message about personal honesty. Barry is portrayed as a young boy who understandably glories in the attention given to him for his prowess on the ball field. But he quickly learns that the way dishonesty makes him feel isn't worth the glory. Young readers will get the point.

Book Talk Material

Barry's feelings about his actions on the ball field can spark a discussion about winning at all costs. See: Barry drops the ball and hears his sister's accusing voice (pp. 7–10); Barry lies to his teammate (pp. 11–12); a conversation about cheating with Susan (pp. 21–23); Barry tells his family that he cheated (pp. 24–27).

Additional Selections

Fifth-grader Warren is smart in school but awful in sports in *My Horrible Secret* (Delacorte, 1983, $10.95; pap., Dell, $3.25) by Stephen Roos.

Ezra's father wants the boy to take an interest in chess, but Ezra has been smitten by *Baseball Fever* (Morrow, 1981, $12.95; pap., Dell, $2.95), a novel by Johanna Hurwitz.

Three problems for the hero of E. L. Konigsburg's *About the B'nai Bagels* (Macmillan, 1971, $14.95; pap., Dell, $3.50) are coping with Bar Mitzvah studies, losing a best friend, and adjusting to a mother who manages your Little League.

Eleven-year-old Jason believes the school custodian is really Buck McHenry, a famous pitcher from the old Negro League, in Alfred Slote's *Finding Buck McHenry* (Harper, 1991, $13.89; pap., $3.95).

In Robert Kimmel Smith's *Bobby Baseball* (Delacorte, 1989, $13.95; pap., Dell, $3.50), Bobby, a ten-year-old, plans for baseball stardom, but events turn out otherwise.

Lensey Namioka's *Yang the Youngest and His Terrible Ear* (Little, Brown, 1992, $13.95) mixes music and baseball in a story of friendship between a tone-deaf Chinese-American boy and his white counterpart, Matthew, who loves his violin more than sports.

In *The Macmillan Book of Baseball Stories* (Macmillan, 1993, $14.95), by Terry Egan et al., there are nineteen true stories about people at all levels of importance who have influenced the sport.

About the Book

Booklist, April 1, 1986, p. 1340.
Center for Children's Books Bulletin, May 1988, p. 174.
School Library Journal, May 1988, p. 96.
See also *Book Review Index,* 1988, p. 152.

About the Author

Commire, Anne, ed., *Something about the Author.* Gale, 1971, Vol. 2, pp. 58–59; 1987, Vol. 47, pp. 54–57.

Holtze, Sally Holmes, ed., *Fifth Book of Junior Authors and Illustrators.* Wilson, 1983, 1982, pp. 68–69.

Nakamura, Joyce, ed., *Something about the Author: Autobiography Series.* Gale, 1990, Vol. 9, pp. 69–87.

Ward, Martha, ed., *Authors of Books for Young People* (3rd ed.). Scarecrow, 1990, p. 127.

Greene, Constance C. *Just Plain Al*

Viking, 1986, $12.95 (0-670-81250-1); pap., Dell, $2.95 (0-440-40073-2)

Although Constance Greene is most closely associated with lighthearted stories involving preadolescent heroines, some of her novels touch on more serious subjects. For example, in *Beat the Turtle Drum* (Peter Smith, 1992, $16.25; pap., Dell, $3.25; condensed in *Introducing More Books,* Bowker, 1978, pp. 7–9), thirteen-year-old Kate is stunned when her younger sister falls from an apple tree and is killed. When her mother retreats into drugs and her father to alcohol, Kate is left to make her own adjustment to this terrible loss. In a light vein, Greene has written about a hyperactive fifth-grader in the Isabelle books. The first, *Isabelle the Itch* (pap., Puffin, 1992, $3.99), describes how Isabelle channels her energy into both winning the fifty-yard dash at school and assuming the responsibilities of her brother's paper route. Al (short for Alexandra) first appeared in *A Girl Called Al* (Viking, 1969, $12.95; pap., Puffin, $3.95) and tells how Al and her friend in the seventh grade learn a great deal from the assistant superintendent in their apartment building. The friend is the unnamed narrator of the series. *Just Plain Al,* the fifth in the series, continues to exude New York City ambience in a story of Al's identity crisis when she reaches her fourteenth birthday. A further installment is *Al's Blind Date* (Viking, 1989, $12.95; pap., Puffin, $3.95). These books are enjoyed by readers in grades 5 through 8.

Plot Summary

Next week, Al will hit the big one-four—fourteen years old. She thinks this calls for a name change. Her best friend, the narrator, isn't so sure, but perhaps that is because she is only hitting the small one-three. Al—for Alexandra—thinks that perhaps Alex or Zandra or Zandi might carry a little more pizzazz. And she isn't going to stop there. Al has other improvements in mind for the upcoming new age. She's too uptight, for instance; perhaps she should become more of a free spirit.

To her friend the narrator, Al is already a fairly free spirit. She wears cloggy red shoes and a T-shirt that says "Alexandra the Great" and she likes a boy in Ohio named Brian. He lives near Al's father and her stepmother. Al lives with her mother, who is a pretty free spirit herself, just down the hall from her friend the narrator in a New York City apartment.

While Al is contemplating her new name, the two girls are invited to dinner at the Rainbow Room—a fancy dancy place atop the RCA building in Rockefeller Center. Their host will be Al's mother's latest beau, Stan. Because it's Al's birthday, he's going to take them all to dinner.

This invitation means a trip to Bloomingdale's for new duds. When they come out of the store, the narrator gives some money to a bag lady. For a long time afterward, she can't forget the look in the woman's eye.

Just when both girls are outfitted for the splendid dinner, the whole deal falls through. Stan has to go off somewhere on business. No Rainbow Room. No celebration. *Nada.*

But the narrator's mother saves the day. She suggests giving a birthday party for Al. They'll have a rib roast—an occasion indeed. They'll invite Al's mother and the narrator's friend Polly, and they'll also invite the narrator's grandfather. He likes Al.

Al adores the idea of a birthday party. Her mother even agrees to come and says, according to Al, she will bring the horses doovries. As Al explains, it has something to do with pineapple and cream cheese and curry powder.

The big night arrives. So does Al, looking very grown up and glamorous, and her mother, looking the same. Before the night is over, it's plain to see that Grandfather is enchanted with Al's mother. Both girls think that's droll.

Al isn't quite so sure how droll it is a few days later when she is told that her friend's grandfather is going to take her mother to the ballet. A date, for heaven's sake, and he's about sixty-five! The imagined romance causes a short rift between the two girls.

On the day before school is to begin, the girls, along with Polly, decide to have one last blast in the city. However, they can't agree what they want to do, and when the subject of Grandfather and Al's mother comes up again, the whole day goes sour.

But Al, now at the advanced age of fourteen, bounces right back when school begins. Mr. Keogh, a teacher of whom the girls are quite fond, soon asks them for a favor. He wants them to accompany him and some other teens to a nursing home to visit his father and some of the other residents. Mr. Keogh thinks they can do some cheering up and entertaining.

The girls are not at all sure, but they say yes. Everyone is pretty nervous when they arrive at the nursing home on Saturday. But before long, there is Al, the center of attention again. Everyone seems to enjoy the young people, and the visit is declared a great success.

On Sunday the girls go to visit friend Polly. Usually Al spends with her mother. But this week she is free because Stan is back and Mother has a snazzy new dress to go to some big affair at the Plaza. So much for Grandfather in the scheme of things. Order is restored.

On the bus trip to Polly's, Al confesses that she has finally figured it out. It doesn't matter what your name is as long as you've got it all together, as long as you're doing the best you can. The two friends get to laughing so much that the bus driver has to tell them to get off, it's the end of the line.

"Oh, no, sir," replies Al. "It's only the beginning. Only the beginning."

"Don't get fresh with me," says the bus driver.

Thematic Material

With warmth and a certain amount of wackiness, the author presents a humorous, light picture of young teens in New York City—a little savvy and street smart, but young and naive and wonderfully vulnerable underneath the veneer. Al is irrepressible, forever dreaming of new horizons, forever off on another tangent concerning the mysteries of life. Young teens will find her antics familiar, real, and amusing.

Book Talk Material

Scenes of the girls' life in the city make a good introduction to this story of young teenagers in an urban setting. See: the two girls discuss the upcoming dinner at the Rainbow Room (pp. 10–11); the shopping trip to Bloomingdale's and meeting the bag lady (pp. 16–21); they visit Polly's apartment for chicken cacciatore (pp. 28–34); they look for their friend Rudy, who plays the violin on street corners (pp. 42–45); the party (pp. 70–83).

Additional Selections

In *All but Alice* (Macmillan, 1992, $13.95) by Phyllis Reynolds Naylor, Alice's trials in the seventh grade include a talent show, an earring club, and Dad's new date.

Anxious to make friends in her middle school, sixth-grader Dinah runs for class president in Claudia Mills's *Dinah for President* (Macmillan, 1992, $14.95), a sequel to *Dynamite Dinah* (Macmillan, 1990, $12.95).

Alex and her friend Jenny explore Madame Van Dam's mysterious trunk with unexpected results in *The Fortuneteller in 5B* (Holt, 1991, $14.95) by Jane Breskin Zalben.

When Pam moves into Jo's apartment building, Jo is thrilled at the thought of making a new friend in Ann Reit's *Promise You Won't Tell* (pap., Dell, 1992, $2.50).

Miranda tries a variety of summer jobs, hoping she will make enough money to buy contact lenses in Johnniece Wilson's *Poor Girl, Rich Girl* (Scholastic, 1992, $13.95).

Sixth-grader Cassie adjusts to living with an aunt and uncle in rural Vermont while her mother completes college in Cynthia Stowe's *Dear Mom, in Ohio for a Year* (Scholastic, 1992, $13.95).

In her sequel to *Freaky Friday* (Harper, 1972, $14; pap., $3.95; condensed in *More Juniorplots,* Bowker, 1977, pp. 19–21), Mary Rodgers tells what happens when a father and son exchange bodies in *Summer Switch* (Harper, 1982, $14; pap., $3.50).

About the Book

Book Report, May 1987, p. 31.
Booklist, September 15, 1986, p. 132.
Center for Children's Books Bulletin, February 1987, p. 107.
Kirkus Reviews, October 1, 1986, p. 1509.
School Library Journal, October 1986, p. 175.
Wilson Library Bulletin, February 1987, p. 48.
See also *Book Review Digest,* 1986, p. 299; 1987, p. 305.

About the Author

Chevalier, Tracy, ed., *Twentieth-Century Children's Writers* (3rd ed.). St. James, 1989, pp. 403–404.
Commire, Anne, ed., *Something about the Author.* Gale, 1977, pp. 121–122.
de Montreville, Doris, and Crawford, Elizabeth D., eds., *Fourth Book of Junior Authors and Illustrators.* Wilson, 1978, pp. 158–159.
Evory, Ann, and Metzger, Linda, eds., *Contemporary Authors* (New Revision Series). Gale, 1983, Vol. 8, p. 205.
Fadool, Cynthia R., *Contemporary Authors.* Gale, 1976, Vols. 61–64, p. 224.
Nakamura, Joyce, ed., *Something about the Author: Autobiography Series.* Gale, 1991, Vol. 11, pp. 129–147.

Hurwitz, Johanna. *Roz and Ozzie*
Illus. by Eileen McKeating. Morrow, 1992, $13 (0-688-10945-4)

Johanna Hurwitz has written a number of very popular series for readers in the middle grades. They are characterized by realistic situations, good humor, and believable characters. *The Adventures of Ali Baba Bernstein* (Morrow, 1985, $12.95; pap., Scholastic, $2.50) is the first book about David Bernstein, who tires of his everyday name and, after deciding on a new one, finds that all the David Bernsteins he meets at a namesake birthday party are really different individuals. In *Busybody Nora* (Morrow, 1990, $12.95), the heroine of another series decides she wants to get to know all of the 200 residents of her large apartment building in New York City. In *Roz and Ozzie,* nine-year-old Roz finds that she is unfortunately always attached to Ozzie Sims, age seven, because they live in the same two-family house and Ozzie happens to be her uncle! Her attempts to shake this constant companion produce many funny and good-natured episodes. This story is enjoyed by readers from grades 2 through 4.

Plot Summary

Almost-nine-year-old Rosalind Sasser—Roz—is trying to fit in. She's in a new school in a new fourth grade, and she's looking for a new best friend. Perhaps she has found one in Brie Morgan, who for the first time is riding home with her on the school bus and will spend the afternoon at Roz's house. Brie has pierced ears, and Roz hopes to persuade her mother to let her have her ears pierced too.

Just when it seems everything is going as Roz has planned, Ozzie starts acting up again, with his stupid riddles and his dumb penny collection that he drops all over the floor. Ozzie Sims, the tagalong from the second grade, lives right next door to Roz and follows her everywhere. Actually, Brie thinks Ozzie is kind of amusing, but of course she doesn't have to put up with him every minute. *She* doesn't have a second-grader for an uncle!

Roz explains to a surprised Brie that young Ozzie is the half brother of Roz's mother. Ozzie's mother is Roz's grandmother, who remarried just about the time Roz's mother married Roz's father. It's all very confusing.

Actually, Roz's whole family is a little confusing. Her mother is working on her doctor of literature degree; her father teaches high school English. Since her mother is at school a lot, Roz and her father often eat TV dinners when they aren't next door at Ozzie's, or Grandma's.

That very night Roz and her father do go to Grandma's for her chicken vegetable soup. Roz discovers, to her amazement, that Ozzie made the soup. Roz can't believe it; all she ever thought Ozzie made was bad jokes. And he never stops explaining about his stupid penny collection, how he's always on the lookout for a penny with two pieces of wheat on the back because the government has stopped making them and they're valuable. All this is fuss over nothing, as far as Roz is concerned.

Roz's mother OKs the pierced ears, but she doesn't have time to take her to have it done. Roz's father says he'll go, which is OK except that Ozzie tags along too. It's scary at first, but having someone there, even Ozzie, helps. A few days later Roz and Ozzie go to Bargain World, where she mistakenly thinks he is stealing something. She is embarrassed to find he is only trying to hide the enameled earrings he is buying for her newly pierced ears.

Now it is time for Roz's birthday. She and her father bake cupcakes to take to school for her party. Her mother offers to drop them off at party time, but she somehow locks the car with the motor running and the cupcakes inside. After many tries to unlock the doors, calls to Roz's father, a cupcake order to the bakery, and the involvement of the police, Roz ends up with 72 cupcakes and a truly memorable party.

A few days later there is a school fire drill. The students are not supposed to talk during the drill, but wouldn't you know Ozzie would cause a fuss by dropping his dumb penny collection again? He is dragged off to the principal, and Roz realizes he is in trouble. She decides to help him, even if he is a pest.

Roz explains the importance of Ozzie's collection to the principal. Apparently the principal is impressed, because he tells Ozzie he's lucky to have someone care about him that much.

Can that be true? Roz just blushes at the principal's words. Later, when she is standing in line at the school cafeteria, she counts her change and realizes she has been given a wheat penny!

Maybe, just maybe, if she pays attention, she can collect a whole roll of wheat pennies. Wouldn't that be a splendid birthday gift for Ozzie?

Thematic Material

This is a warm and funny story of love, friendship, and family. Ozzie is a typical second-grader who just doesn't seem to get the message that he's not wanted. And Roz finds out even a pest can be a friend.

Book Talk Material

The relationship between Roz and her "uncle" Ozzie forms the basic structure of this story of love and friendship. See: Ozzie drops his penny collection on the bus (pp. 4–7); Ozzie and his endless jokes (pp. 10–13); Ozzie scares Brie (pp. 18–21); Ozzie makes chicken vegetable soup (pp. 28–30); and Ozzie tags along for the ear piercing (pp. 45–54).

Additional Selections

Oscar develops eight steps to get rid of his creepy younger brother for the summer in Barbara Park's *Operation: Dump the Chump* (Knopf, 1982, $8.95; pap., Avon, $2.75).

In the humorous tale *Itchy Richard* (Houghton, 1991, $12.95) by Jamie Gilson, a class of second-graders and their teacher combat an epidemic of head lice.

Black fourth-grader Mary has a low opinion of herself, but an assignment in connection with a celebration of black history helps in Eleanora E. Tate's *Thank You, Dr. Martin Luther King, Jr.* (Watts, 1990, $13.90; pap., Bantam, $3.99). This is a companion volume to *The Secret of Gumbo Grove* (Watts, 1987, $12.90; pap., Bantam, $2.95), in which Raisin stirs up trouble in her black community by investigating some local history.

Third-grader Juliet tries to be perfect in every way until Jonah Twist and friends teach her to relax and be part of the gang in *Juliet Fisher and the Foolproof Plan* (Macmillan, 1992, $12.95) by Natalie Honeycutt. This is part of the Jonah Twist series.

Molly Lottmann starts fifth grade and has pangs of loneliness that lead to learning independence in Susan Shreve's *Wait for Me* (Morrow, 1992, $13).

In *Leprechauns Don't Play Baseball* (pap., Scholastic, 1992, $2.75) by Debbie Dadey and Marcia Jones, some third-grade students at Bailey Elementary School are convinced their substitute gym teacher is really a leprechaun from Ireland.

Sibling rivalry gets out of hand when sixth-grader Jill becomes jealous of all the attention her younger sister gets from their single-parent mother in Constance Hiser's *Sixth-Grade Star* (Holiday, 1992, $13.95).

About the Book

Booklist, February 15, 1992, p. 1104.
Center for Children's Books Bulletin, May 1992, p. 240.
Kirkus Reviews, April 15, 1992, p. 538.

School Library Journal, May 1992, p. 92.
See also *Book Review Index,* 1992, p. 435.

About the Author

Chevalier, Tracy, ed., *Twentieth-Century Children's Writers* (3rd ed.). St. James, 1989, pp. 487–488.
Commire, Anne, ed., *Something about the Author.* Gale, 1980, Vol. 20, pp. 88–90.
Evory, Ann, and Metzger, Linda, eds., *Contemporary Authors* (New Revision Series). Gale, 1983, Vol. 10, pp. 236–237.
Holtze, Sally Holmes, ed., *Sixth Book of Junior Authors and Illustrators.* Wilson, 1989, pp. 144–146.
May, Hal, and Straub, Deborah A., eds., *Contemporary Authors* (New Revision Series. Gale, 1989, Vol. 25, p. 225.
Telgen, Diane, ed., *Something about the Author.* Gale, 1993, Vol. 71, pp. 99–101.
Ward, Martha, ed., *Authors of Books for Young People* (3rd ed.). Scarecrow, 1990, p. 358.

Lisle, Janet Taylor. *Afternoon of the Elves*

Orchard, 1989, $12.95 (0-531-05837-9); pap., Scholastic, $2.75 (0-590-43944-8)

A favorite theme in Janet Taylor Lisle's fiction is the nature of reality and the hidden magic that exists in everyday living. In all her works, the writing is deceptively simple, disguising the fact that there are serious underlying themes. For example, in *The Great Dimpole Oak* (Orchard, 1987, $11.25), she writes about a majestic oak tree and how everyday people relate to it. In *The Dancing Cats of Applesap* (Macmillan, 1984, $12.95; pap., Bantam, $2.50), Melba discovers that the cats in Jigg's Drug Store possess special talents. In *Afternoon of the Elves,* nine-year-old Hillary befriends an unpopular girl, Sara-Kate, who tends a tiny village in a weed-infested garden where she claims the elves live. The open ending leaves one wondering how Sara-Kate will survive separation from her mother and if the girl is herself a kind of elf or merely a disturbed child. These novels are read by youngsters in grades 4 through 6.

Plot Summary

Nine-year-old Hillary is amazed when Sara-Kate speaks to her. Sara-Kate is eleven, and even though they live in neighboring properties, the girls have had no contact at all until the afternoon Hillary sees the elf village in Sara-Kate's backyard. Hillary isn't convinced at first that it really is an elf village; she thinks it could possibly be mice. But Sara-Kate is positive. "Mice," she says with authority, "don't make villages in people's backyards."

Hillary is indeed impressed by the elf village, the roofs of whose houses are made of maple leaves attached to sticks at jaunty angles. In fact, she is in awe of Sara-Kate's entire backyard. It is a mess—full of tangled junk like old tires and rusty engine parts, broken glass, and pieces of rope. It is, if one understands the true nature of elves, a perfect place for an elf village, so different from Hillary's own manicured backyard, where her father carefully tends the grass and shrubs.

Hillary's mother isn't actually very pleased about her daughter's budding friendship with Sara-Kate, a strange, birdlike, secretive child who wears an odd assortment of clothes and men's working boots to school. Hillary's best friends, Jane Webster and Alison Mancini, think Sara-Kate is weird too; they warn Hillary not to pay too much attention to Sara-Kate Connolly.

Yet there is something fascinating about Sara-Kate. Hillary finds herself drawn more and more to the tangled backyard as she and Sara-Kate discover obvious evidence of elves at work and play, like the elf Ferris wheel made out of old bicycle tires. Never once does Sara-Kate invite Hillary inside the house, however, nor does Hillary ever see Sara-Kate's mother. Other things are strange about Sara-Kate too. She eats mint leaves and berries and refuses to discuss anything about her family with her new friend. But despite this strangeness, Hillary falls under the magical spell of the older girl's imagination as the mysterious world of elves becomes real for them both.

When Sara-Kate is missing from school for a few days, Hillary gets up the courage to knock on the Connolly back door. There is no answer, but the door opens and Hillary steps into one of the strangest houses she has ever seen. Everything seems to have been changed into something else—like a large white stove with no door in the center of the room near a bureau with no drawers. When Hillary's curiosity takes her upstairs, she comes upon Sara-Kate rocking a figure in her arms—her mother? Sara-Kate screams at Hillary, who flees the house.

But after a heavy snowstorm Sara-Kate allows Hillary back into the yard so they can uncover the village, which they do. And finally, Sara-Kate talks about her mother, who she admits is sick. She asks Hillary if she has any money to get groceries. Hillary takes some money from her mother's wallet and goes to the store for her friend.

When she returns with the groceries, she is invited inside Sara-Kate's home for lunch. Hillary now realizes Sara-Kate runs the entire household for her sick mother. Sara-Kate admits to stealing if the checks from her father don't arrive on time, and she admits that sometimes her mother's mind doesn't work just right.

Both girls are startled when Hillary's mother arrives at the Connolly home looking for her daughter. Before they can stop her, she enters the weird household. Despite Sara-Kate's protests, she goes upstairs and discovers the sick Mrs. Connolly.

Things happen quickly after that. Mrs. Connolly is taken away for treatment, and Sara-Kate is sent off to relatives without even saying goodbye. The strange house is cleaned and tidied for new tenants. Hillary worries that the workmen will trample the elf village.

Hillary's mother and friends think she has been used by Sara-Kate. Perhaps Hillary was just someone useful to have around. Could that be true? Hillary thinks about the older girl's secretiveness and unexplained disappearances. Hillary is very sad during the dark winter days that follow. She misses her friend's crisp manner and her quickness. The magic seems to have gone out of her days.

Then Hillary begins to look at Sara-Kate in a new way. Perhaps she left the elf village behind on purpose. Perhaps it was a message telling Hillary she was all right. Perhaps the elf village was Sara-Kate's way of saying she was still there.

Hillary decides she must move the elf village into her own backyard, an idea not favored by her mother. But Hillary is adamant. "A place like that shouldn't be allowed to fall apart," she says.

Reluctantly, her mother agrees that perhaps a spot behind their garage, full of rocks and briars, might do.

Hillary agrees and goes out into the darkening afternoon to rescue the elf village.

Thematic Material

This sensitive story walks a line between the real world of mental illness and poverty and the loneliness of children and the wonderful world of imagination and fantasy. Hillary is an impressionable young girl who gathers the inner strength to defend her strange friend from the unkindness of others and finds her life enriched by the older girl's imaginings. Sara-Kate is wise beyond her years because she has to be, a child who must act as an adult for a parent who cannot, whose clever, inventive mind fashions a world of elves who lead a life quite different from the problems brought on by sickness and poverty. A thoughtful story, especially for the imaginative reader.

Book Talk Material

Descriptions of the elf village and of Sara-Kate will serve as a good introduction to this fine story. See: at first Hillary is skeptical about the village (pp. 1–4); the elves build a Ferris wheel (pp. 17–21); Hillary and Sara-Kate discuss elf life (pp. 25–29); the two girls construct a highway network for the village (pp. 33–34); and they discuss elf language and collecting starlight (pp. 36–39).

Additional Selections

Nealy Compton keeps a collection of her important possessions under a neighbor's house until one night the house burns in Doris Buchanan Smith's *Best Girl* (Viking, 1993, $13.99).

In Ann Warren Turner's *Rosemary's Witch* (Harper, 1991, $13.95), after a move to an old house, nine-year-old Rosemary meets a 150-year-old witch who wants the house back.

In Constance C. Greene's *Beat the Turtle Drum* (Viking, 1976, $13.95; pap., Dell, $3.25), Kate's young sister, Jess, rents a horse for a glorious week, but death changes their family life.

In Virginia Hamilton's *Sweet Whispers, Brother Rush* (Putnam, 1982, $15.95; condensed in *Juniorplots 3,* Bowker, 1987, pp. 166–170), fourteen-year-old Tree meets a handsome young stranger called Brother Rush, but is he real or a ghost?

Sylvia Peck's *Kelsey's Raven* (Morrow, 1992, $14) is a tale of romance, coming of age, and friendship involving Dustin, a chimney sweep, a girl named Kelsey, and a raven rescued from a fireplace.

In order to join the most important clique at school, Tracy must drop her friend, unpopular Kelly, in Patricia Hermes's *Friends Are Like That* (Harcourt, 1984, $12.95; pap., Scholastic, $2.50).

In Louann Gaeddert's *Your Former Friend, Matthew* (Dutton, 1984, $11.95), Gail finds that Matthew suddenly is no longer interested in their friendship.

About the Book

Booklist, August 1989, p. 1979.
Center for Children's Books Bulletin, October 1989, p. 37.
Emergency Librarian, January 1990, p. 48.

Horn Book, September 1989, p. 622.
Horn Book Guide, June 1, 1989, p. 69.
Kirkus Reviews, April 1, 1989, p. 1161.
New York Times Book Review, November 12, 1989, p. 28.
School Library Journal, September 1989, p. 254.
Wilson Library Bulletin, March 1990, p. 3.
See also *Book Review Digest,* 1990, p. 1104; and *Book Review Index,* 1989, p. 500; 1990, p. 495.

About the Author

Commire, Anne, ed., *Something about the Author.* Gale, 1990, pp. 112–113.
Nakamura, Joyce, ed., *Something about the Author: Autobiography Series.* Gale, 1992, Vol. 14, pp. 157–166.

Snyder, Zilpha Keatley. *Libby on Wednesday*

Doubleday, 1990, $14.95 (0-385-29979-6); pap., Dell, $3.50 (0-440-40498-3)

Zilpha Snyder has had a distinguished career as a writer of books for middle and junior high school readers. One of her earliest works, *The Egypt Game* (Macmillan, 1967, $14.95; pap., Dell, $3.99; condensed in *Introducing Books,* Bowker, 1970, pp. 43–46), was a runner-up for the 1968 Newbery Medal. It tells of an interracial friendship between two impressionable eleven-year-old girls, April and Melanie, and their obsessive interest in ancient Egypt. With four others, they copy ancient rites, build a mud statue to the god Set, and engage in rituals known as the "Egypt game." Eventually, this leads to the capture of a deranged murderer and April's working through her personal problems. The author has also written several stories about the Stanley family. In one of them, *The Headless Cupid* (Macmillan, 1971, $14.95; pap., Dell, $3.25), Newbery Honor book, a young girl escapes her problems through an interest in the occult but gradually learns to accept reality. In *Libby on Wednesday,* an eleven-year-old girl discovers when she enrolls in a regular school that her special abilities are derided by her classmates. This novel, which explores the problems of creativity and insecurity, is enjoyed by readers in grades 5 through 7.

Plot Summary

Libby's unconventional—even for California—family is rather shocked when she tells them she has decided to quit school *again.* Actually, her mother isn't shocked, but that's because her mother isn't there to hear her decision. Libby's mother is off in New York City, where she usually is, being an actress. But the rest of the family is alarmed. There is Libby's father, Christopher, a poet and somewhat vague about everything; Gillian, Libby's grandmother, and her sister, Cordelia, who are forever fighting, over issues such as who is better looking—Robert Redford or Charlton Heston; and Elliott, a friend of the family who a long time ago just dropped in and stayed (thank heavens, because he is a wonderful cook).

Anyway, Libby, at eleven, wants to quit the Morrison, California, Middle School. She had quit once before, after one day of kindergarten. At that time the family agreed that Libby, very smart for her age, should be educated at home. And educated she was, so that now, at age eleven, the subjects taught to other kids her age just bore her. However, her actress mother, on one of her infrequent visits, decided Libby was not "socialized" enough, and so off to school she went.

That was bad enough, because even though Libby is educationally very advanced, she is also very shy and uneasy with kids her own age. But the really bad thing is that she has won a writing contest at school, and the top five winners have been put into a writing workshop—meeting every Wednesday.

Libby does not want to go. But her unconventional family doesn't bend this time. And so she attends the writing club meetings.

An unlikely group it is, too. There is nasty Gary Greene, who makes smart remarks about everybody. There is twitchy Alex Lockwood, who has a wonderful sense of humor along with cerebral palsy. The other workshop members are Tierney Laurent of the punk hairdo and Wendy Davis, who looks just like you're supposed to look at age eleven, the all-American preteenager.

Despite herself, Libby begins to enjoy the workshop although she doesn't enjoy her fellow students. She is certain they all don't like her—mostly because they make fun of her small stature—especially Gary Greene. But as the school year goes on and the meetings continue, Libby begins to form tentative friendships, first with Alex and then with Tierney and Wendy. It's impossible, they all agree, to form a friendship with Gary.

Just when things are beginning to brighten up for Libby, Miss O, who leads the workshop, is involved in a serious auto accident. For a while it looks as though the workshop group will be terminated because there is no teacher to lead it. But the group members don't want to break up. Libby's family agrees they should continue meeting on Wednesdays, in the strange, wonderful old tree house in Libby's backyard.

One Wednesday, when Gary doesn't show up for the workshop, Libby gets a strange telephone call. She is sure it's Gary's voice, and he is whispering something about not being able to get there. Then suddenly, Libby hears yelling and Gary's voice shouting, "No. Don't. I wasn't calling them." And the line goes dead.

They decide to go to Gary's house and see what's going on. When they arrive, no one seems to be home, but the front door opens at Libby's push. Inside they find Gary's father—dead drunk. Upstairs, they find Gary, unconscious, with blood streaming down his face.

The children call for help. It turns out that Gary's father is an alcoholic, and has abused Gary many times before. Gary is sent to live with relatives in another city. The workshop members do not expect to see him again, but they begin to understand some of the reasons for his nasty behavior.

The workshop—now reduced to four—continues to meet and to write. Then, one Wednesday, to their complete surprise, in walks Gary. He has returned to live with his father, who is out of the clinic. Gary thinks he'll be all right now. He won't drink anymore.

At first, Gary is quiet and rather nice, but pretty soon reverts to his old self. When Gary leaves, the others agree it isn't going to be easy getting along with him. But they understand that underneath that bluff exterior, Gary Greene is just plain scared. They hope his father is going to be OK. They hope Gary is going to be OK too.

Thematic Material

A story to be enjoyed by good readers, *Libby on Wednesday* presents somewhat above-average and talented children who nonetheless have the same childish fears as others their own age facing an adult and often unpleasant world. Each of the five in the writing workshop has his or her own demons to overcome—Libby's shyness, Alex's affliction, Tierney, the punk-looking kid, living in the shadow of a beautiful family. Their interaction is realistically presented, and Libby's offbeat family adds a touch of humor.

Book Talk Material

Libby's unconventional family life should serve as a good introduction to this story of an unusually educated young girl and her efforts to cope with the more conventional world. See: Libby tells the family she is going to quit school *again* (pp. 6–10); Libby talks about the writing contest (pp. 12–20); Libby finds refuge in her Treehouse (pp. 25–27); the journal entries (pp. 29–35).

Additional Selections

For eleven-year-old Lena Rosen, the only Jewish girl in the neighborhood, the ordinariness of Moose Street is more complex than others perceive in Anne Mazer's *Moose Street* (Knopf, 1992, $13.95).

With the help of a reclusive writer, three young loners who are entirely different become friends in J. Clarke's *Riffraff* (Holt, 1992, $14.95).

A Seattle widower opens his house to a divorcee and her son in *Second Family* (Scribner, 1992, $12.95) by Diane Johnston Hamm, a novel that explores loneliness and the meaning of loss.

Fifth-grader Edith Gold encounters an anti-Semitic bully when she enters a new school in Los Angeles in Leda Siskind's *The Hopscotch Tree* (Bantam, 1992, $15), a story set in the 1960s.

Living during the poverty of the 1930s in England, Mary hopes to earn some prize money by entering her pigeon, Speedwell, in a race in France in Ann Turnbull's *Speedwell* (Candlewick, 1992, $14.95).

Ruth White's *Weeping Willow* (Farrar, 1992, $16) is set in a West Virginia town in the 1950s and tells of a girl who escapes the horror of an abusive father by trusting friends around her.

Addie, living in a close-knit pioneer farm family, is disappointed when a visit by two cousins proves to be a mixed blessing in Laurie Lawlor's *Addie's Long Summer* (Whitman, 1992, $11.95), part of the Addie series that includes *Addie Across the Prairie* (Whitman, 1986, $10.50).

About the Book

Booklist, February 1, 1990, p. 1095.
Horn Book, May 1990, p. 336.
Horn Book Guide, January 1990, p. 241.
Kirkus Reviews, February 1, 1990, p. 185.
School Library Journal, April 1990, p. 124.
VOYA, February 1991, p. 358.
Wilson Library Bulletin, June 1990, p. 117.
See also *Book Review Digest,* 1990, p. 1721; and *Book Review Index,* 1990, p. 761; 1991, p. 849.

About the Author

Chevalier, Tracy, ed., *Twentieth-Century Children's Writers* (3rd ed.). St. James, 1989, pp. 903–905.
Commire, Anne, ed., *Something about the Author.* Gale, 1971, Vol. 1, pp. 202–203; 1982, Vol. 28, pp. 192–194.
de Montreville, Doris, and Hill, Donna, eds., *Third Book of Junior Authors.* Wilson, 1972, pp. 270–271.
Kinsman, Clare D., and Tennenhouse, Mary Ann, eds., *Contemporary Authors.* Gale, 1974, Vols. 9–12, p. 851.

Kirkpatrick, D. L., ed., *Twentieth-Century Children's Writers* (3rd ed.). St. Martin's, 1983, pp. 714–716.

Sarkissian, Adele, ed., *Something about the Author: Autobiography Series*. Gale, 1986, Vol. 2, pp. 215–216.

Ward, Martha, ed., *Authors of Books for Young People* (3rd ed.). Scarecrow, 1990, pp. 660–661.

Vail, Rachel. *Wonder*

Orchard, 1991, $13.95 (0-531-05964-2); pap., Puffin, $3.99 (0-14-036167-7)

This is Rachel Vail's first novel for young readers. It has been highly praised by critics and appeared on many of the best-book lists for 1991. *Wonder* tells the story of Jessica, who gets her nickname because she wears a dress with large polka dots—looking suspiciously like a Wonder Bread wrapper—when she goes to school for her first day in the seventh grade. It is a novel of friendship, first boyfriends, and a journey to greater self-confidence. Whitman Levy, who has a small role in *Wonder,* becomes the central character in Vail's second novel, *Do-Over* (Orchard, 1992, $14.95). In this story, Whitman always wants a do-over, a second chance to change something that has just happened, whether it is an unfortunate basketball decision or a confrontation with his parents. Both novels are characterized by refreshing honesty and humor. They are enjoyed by readers in grades 5 through 8.

Plot Summary

Jessica can't believe how her life has changed since she left the sixth grade. In her opinion, "Seventh grade sucks." In the sixth grade she was reasonably popular, and her best friend was Sheila. Now Jessica isn't popular anymore, and Sheila went to camp this past summer, which only proves how camp can change a person, because she certainly isn't Jessica's best friend now.

Things go from bad to worse the very first day of seventh grade. Sheila shows up with her new SCANTA buddies—SCANTA stands for Sheila-Cathy-Andi-Nancy-Tracy-Amy, the dumbest girls ever to live. They are all wearing red sweatpants and white Izods. Of course, no one told Jessica about this and there she is in a brand-new sweatshirt dress with colored dots. It had seemed so neat in the dress shop, but when she got to school and ran into SCANTA, Tracy said, "Nice dress," and then, "Looks like a Wonder Bread explosion."

So they all took to calling Jessica "Wonder," and things just generally went downhill from there.

As if that weren't enough, Jessica's dad is having trouble with his business, and she's afraid they'll all go to the poorhouse; her younger brother, Benjamin, is more trouble than usual; and she can't even talk to her mother about anything anymore. Life is really a drag.

There is one bright spot—Conor O'Malley—her Orange Crush. He is practically the most terrific, to say nothing of the cutest, boy in the entire class. Jessica can't believe it when he calls her one day and asks for help with his math homework. She knows Conor is a brain, so she hangs up on him! Sometimes Jessica wonders why she acts so dumb.

Another miracle happens and Conor calls back and they talk a little, the way they used to when they were in the sixth grade and not so self-conscious about each other. He wants to know why she isn't friends with Sheila anymore. What can she tell him? She really doesn't know either, so she just says "We drifted apart" to sound cool.

Jessica and Conor begin "hanging out" together, and she wonders if she should regard him as her "boyfriend." It's hard to know.

Sheila has a party. Of course, Jessica isn't invited, but Conor is. Later, Jessica finds out they played Run-Catch-Kiss at the party, and Conor caught Sheila, so that means he kissed her. Life is a real bummer again. Jessica tells Conor the only thing possible: "I never want to see you again, you little geek!"

To save Jessica from being a total jerk, Conor's friend Jordy tells her Conor doesn't really care about Sheila and wants Jessica to be his girlfriend. He also says Conor is right that minute sitting down by the "crick" by himself. So Jessica just happens to stroll down to the crick, and she and Conor talk. They even kiss—her first, outside of games, which don't count anyway.

Jessica finds out that her dad's business trouble stems from the fact that his business partner, her Uncle Tommy, has been taking money out of the company. It's even possible they'll go bankrupt. Jessica decides to start saving money to help out.

Maybe it's just because she is going out with Conor, but Jessica begins to notice the SCANTA group is being a little more friendly. They still call her "Wonder," but it doesn't have such a mean ring to it. In fact, she is even invited to Tracy's party. At first, she gets mad at Conor again because she thinks he asked Tracy to invite her, but that turns out not to be true.

Tracy's party is a costume affair, and Jessica has the most wonderful idea. She goes as a loaf of Wonder Bread! And she gets the best-costume award. Now she'll have the whole class calling her Wonder, she figures.

After the party, Jessica is suddenly "in" with the SCANTA girls. It's wonderful. That is, until Tracy suddenly starts talking about Sheila, Jessica's "former" best friend. Sheila said, according to Tracy, that Conor is a good kisser and she should have gone out with him while she had the chance. Jessica thinks back to the party when they were playing kissing games and Sheila and Conor got paired off . . . she can't decide which of them she hates more.

Jessica is on top of the world. Her brand new friends don't seem to think Sheila is so wonderful. SCANTA is dead, too. Everything is wonderful. So how come she goes home and cries?

A few days later, when Jessica is out with her new friends, they run into Sheila. Tracy says some pretty mean things to her. "Lighten up," Jessica says to Tracy, and then can't believe she actually said such a thing. "You just remember who your friends are," Tracy tells her.

Jessica thinks about those words later that night when Sheila calls her. Sheila says Jessica was the only true friend she'd ever had and she was sorry she screwed it up. She warns Jessica she can't trust her new friends. She also tells her that when she and Conor were paired off at the party, all he did was talk about Jessica.

That night, Jessica has a long talk with her mother, something she hasn't done since she was just a "kid."

"No matter who you're friends with," her mother tells her, "no matter what you do, *that's* who you'll have to face every day for the rest of your life. Decide what you need to do to make *that* person proud."

The world is a difficult place when you're in the seventh grade. Conor waits for Jessica in the hall one day. Maybe they'll get to be friends again. Jessica thinks about calling Sheila to go to the mall this weekend. Maybe not yet. It might take a little time to heal that friendship.

Maybe things will get better when my hormones settle down, Jessica decides.

Thematic Material

In the Judy Blume tradition, this is a realistic look at the ups and downs, the terrors—real and imagined—of growing up. Jessica is a seventh-grader at loose ends, caught between the little-girl world she has almost, but not quite, left, and the problems of an early teenager faced with kissing a boy and trying to understand what it takes to have and be a friend. The ambivalence of Jessica's world is clearly expressed, and young readers should identify with the joys and torments.

Book Talk Material

The crises that Jessica confronts will be understood and enjoyed by young readers and will serve as an excellent introduction to this story of a young girl on the verge of growing up. See: the "Wonder Bread" dress (pp. 4–6); Conor telephones Jessica (pp. 31–36); Jessica calls Conor a geek in front of everybody (pp. 48–49); Jessica can't believe it when her dad cries (pp. 61–65); Jessica and Conor fight about the party and Jessica talks to Tracy (pp. 82–84).

Additional Selections

Dorrie is dismayed when the Conger boys move next door but, in time, true friendship develops in Ellen Conford's *Me and the Terrible Two* (Little, Brown, 1974, $14.95).

In *The Long Way Home* (Lothrop, 1990, $13.95) by Barbara Cohen, young Sally's problems involving her mother's cancer and separation from her twin sister are helped by a relationship with an elderly bus driver.

After his parents divorce, Mark moves to a new neighborhood and encounters problems in adjusting in Robert Kimmel Smith's *The Squeaky Wheel* (Delacorte, 1990, $13.95).

Jessy, her father, and a new stepfamily settle into a home in San Antonio, where Jessy is able to piece together clues from a talking parrot and find a treasure, in *The Treasure Bird* (McElderry, 1992, $12.95) by Peni R. Griffin.

A number of exciting and humorous advents chronicle the growing friendship between two boys in *Tac's Island* (pap., Troll, $2.95) by Ruth Yaffe Radin. A sequel is *Tac's Turn* (pap., Troll, $2.95).

In Barthe DeClements's *Five-Finger Discount* (Delacorte, 1989, $13.95; pap., Dell, $3.25), Jerry is afraid the school bully knows Jerry's father is in prison for stealing.

Alex Frankovitch is lousy at baseball, but he hates T. J. Stoner to remind him of it continually in Barbara Park's *Skinnybones* (Knopf, 1982, $9.95; pap., $2.95).

About the Book

Booklist, September 1, 1991, p. 54.

Center for Children's Books Bulletin, September 1991, p. 24.

Horn Book Guide, Spring 1992, p. 74.
Kirkus Reviews, August 15, 1991, p. 1095.
School Library Journal, August 1991, p. 196.
VOYA, October 1991, p. 234.
Wilson Library Bulletin, February 1991, p. 84.
See also *Book Review Digest,* 1992 (n.p.); and *Book Review Index,* 1991, p. 924; 1992 (n.p.).

Wells, Rosemary. *Through the Hidden Door*
Dial, 1987, $14.95 (0-8037-0276-0); pap., Scholastic, $2.75 (0-590-41786-X)

Rosemary Wells writes for a wide range of ages and interests. Preschool and primary grade youngsters know her as the creator of such characters as the young rabbit named Max who has many adventures in such books as *Max's Bath* (Dial, 1985, $3.95). Older readers associate her name with several taut, suspenseful adventure stories such as *When No One Was Looking* (Dial, 1980, $14.95; pap., Scholastic, $2.95; condensed in *Juniorplots 3,* Bowker, 1987, pp. 253–257), the Edgar Allan Poe Award winner that combines fast tennis action and the investigation of a possible murder; and the equally exciting *The Man in the Woods* (Dial, 1984, $12.95; pap., Scholastic, $2.95), in which a young girl's attempts to help a boy unjustly accused of causing an accident lead to a mystery involving drug smuggling. The present novel is also a well-crafted page-turner. Because it combines a school story involving corruption and deceit with the exploration of an ancient archeological site, one reviewer called it a cross between Robert Cormier's *The Chocolate War* and an Indiana Jones thriller. It is a first-person narrative told by its hero, Barney Pennimen, and takes place during a single school year. Students from grade 5 through the junior high grades enjoy this novel.

Plot Summary

To avoid ridicule because of his lisp and escape the constant bullying, when he entered the prestigious Winchester Boys' Academy in Massachusetts, Barney Pennimen reluctantly allied himself with a gang of five vicious, power-hungry jocks who were both star players on all the school's sports teams and amateur terrorists who maintained their power through threats and destructive pranks. That was two years ago. Barney is now thirteen, beginning the eighth and last grade at Winchester and looking forward to graduation and acceptance at a top prep school. Except when he's excited, he has his speech problem under control. However, he is still in the thrall of the same gang members, known by other students as the "untouchables:" Danny Damascus, Brett MacRea, Matthew Hines, Shawn Swoboda, and their unscrupulous leader, Rudy Sader. Barney's participation has ranged from aiding in the dirty tricks department to supplying crib notes that abet wholesale cheating on exams. Barney is disgusted with himself but feels he lacks the courage to extricate himself from the situation.

One day two unrelated but portentous events occur that change forever the life of Barney Pennimen. The first is a minor earthquake that is scarcely noticed at the time. The second involves Bonnie, the pet collie of the headmaster, Mr. Finney, and his wife, known as Dr. Dorothy because she is involved in scientific research and the raising of laboratory animals. Barney and the untouchables spot the dog, who seems to be in pain and bleeding at the mouth. Seeing an opportunity to revenge themselves on their hated headmaster, Rudy and the rest begin throwing stones at the helpless animal. Distraught at this senseless act of cruelty, Barney, now lisping, begs the boys to stop. Snowy Cobb, an extremely nearsighted sixth-grader, intervenes and leads the dog to safety. Barney is convinced Snowy will tell Mr. Finney about the incident and all six will be expelled, but Snowy, because of his vision problem, is unable to identify any of the assailants. He does tell Mr. Finney that the only boy trying to stop the attack had a lisp.

Under harsh questioning by Mr. Finney and Mr. Silks, one of the senior teachers, Barney cracks and tells the truth. As punishment, Barney loses all privileges and is given an essay writing assignment. The five other boys are expelled. However, within a few days, following a board of trustees meeting during which Danny Damascus's father, a prominent trustee, bribes the school administration with the promise of a new swimming pool and other members voice dismay at the loss of the school's best athletes, there is a complete reversal of the decision. The boys are reinstated, Mr. Finney resigns, and power-hungry Mr. Silks becomes the new headmaster. Although Barney's punishment stands, the others are reinstated without any disciplinary action.

Barney now is the school pariah and so fearful of reprisal by the gang that he welcomes spending after-school hours in the library researching his essay topics. There he slowly gets to know another school outcast, Snowy, the withdrawn, suspicious, and secretive young boy who saved the dog. This nonathletic, myopic youngster with strange white-blond hair is in the library researching the origin of the unusual bone that had somehow become lodged in the dog's teeth, causing the bleeding on the day of the stoning.

During Thanksgiving break, Barney goes home to visit his father in rural Colorado. Mr. Pennimen, whose wife died several years before, is a successful, globe-trotting antiques dealer. He is so anxious about his son's well-being that after failing to persuade him to leave Winchester, he gives Barney a tiny pistol for protection. Back at school, Barney hides the pistol in a deserted stable. Snowy follows him and secretly pockets the gun.

Slowly, Snowy begins to confide in Barney. His parents are separated. His mother lives in Europe, and his father, a Marine officer, is missing in action and presumed dead. Snowy has moved off campus to town, where he lives with the Finneys, who have relocated close to Dr. Dorothy's laboratory. One day Snowy reveals that he is exploring a cave, the opening to which was exposed after the earthquake. Bonnie had found the entrance and led him inside. It was there that she found the mysterious bone Snowy has been investigating. Blindfolded, Barney is led through the opening and down a mud tunnel. In the first chamber, Snowy removes the blindfold, and the two walk along a narrow ledge surrounded by stalactites above and stalagmites below into a gigantic cavern that seems to stretch forever. Here, Snowy has started to excavate the sandy floor and has already uncovered strange miniature steps. Like Snowy, Barney becomes intrigued with the mystery of the hidden cave. Every day after school and all during the Christmas vacation, a blindfolded Barney accompanies Snowy into the cave where, in spite of freezing cold and with only flashlights and kerosene lamps to pierce the darkness, they begin moving the sand using garden tools. Soon, fantastic sites are revealed: roadways, an amphitheater, and a many-tiered temple decorated with images of snakes. Gradually an incredulous Barney begins to believe, like Snowy, that they are uncovering a city where a race of people only six inches high lived about one hundred thousand years ago. Unfortunately, Barney accidentally pricks his finger on a snake fang that guards one of the tombs. He almost dies from the poison, but does recover and the two boys continue excavating. The whereabouts of the cave remain a secret even to Barney, who is still blindfolded before entering and leaving.

The infamous five are caught cheating, and they blame an innocent Barney. When Barney is ambushed in Rudy's room and is about to be beaten up, Snowy manages to help him escape by diverting the attention of the gang. Now both are marked for revenge.

One day while working in the cave, the two are surprised by a noise behind them. They have been followed by the untouchables who, believing the site is a model the boys are building, begin destroying it. An enraged Snowy pulls out the pistol. Barney grabs it from him and shoots out the lights. Somehow, in the blackness, Snowy blindfolds Barney and leads him out of the cave, leaving the five intruders trapped below.

Snowy is so hurt by the destruction of the excavations that he runs away from the Finneys, leaving Barney to cope with the problem of the five trapped boys. Finally Barney's conscience prevails. Using Bonnie as a guide, he is able to find the entrance to the cave and free the thankless culprits.

In an epilogue written the following fall, Barney, who is now a freshman at the prestigious Exeter Academy where Mr. Finney has become headmaster, receives a letter from Peter Mellor, a friend still at Winchester. He is now Snowy's roommate. Between the news items Peter writes, "Every afternoon he blindfolds me and takes me to a place I have promised never to tell about."

Thematic Material

In addition to being an exciting mystery-adventure, this novel explores complex questions of morality and the meanings of good and evil. Barney realizes the price one pays for abandoning one's moral convictions and yielding to peer-pressure. The gradual development of his self-confidence, independence, and responsible behavior is well portrayed. The actions of the untouchables and Mr. Silks illustrate how power and authority can corrupt and be misused. Peer-group dynamics and complex adult-juvenile relationships are explored. A positive, trusting bond between father and son is depicted, and the friendship between Barney and Snowy reveals themes of loyalty, devotion, perseverance, and trust. The excitement of archaeological digs is also well portrayed.

Book Talk Material

Some interesting passages that could be used to introduce this book are: the attack on Bonnie (pp. 3–7); Barney describes his career at Winchester (pp. 7–10); he worries about Bonnie's well-being and the consequences of the stoning (pp. 12–19); the interrogation by Mr. Finney (pp. 20–29); the untouchables are expelled, then reinstated (pp. 30–34); Snowy and Barney in the library (pp. 34–39); the bone is dated (pp. 42–44); and Barney's first visit to the cave (pp. 61–72).

Additional Selections

A mysterious stranger takes a lonely boy through a whirlpool and into a different world in Janet Taylor Lisle's *The Lampfish of Twill* (Orchard, 1991, $15.95).

A group of animals call on the peculiar Keeting to help them save part of the Australian forests from developers in Patricia Wrightson's *Moon-Dark* (McElderry, 1987, $13.95).

In Marion Dane Bauer's *On My Honor* (Houghton, 1986, $12.95; pap., Dell, $3.25), Joel is devastated with grief and guilt when his friend dies in a river where they were forbidden to swim.

The manor house Maggi's father is repairing is found to be haunted in Robert Westall's *Ghost Abbey* (Scholastic, 1989, $12.95; pap., $2.95).

In *The Runaways* (Harper, 1989, $13.95; pap., $3.95) by Ruth Thomas, Nathan and Julia don't like each other, but they stay together when they find money and run away.

Mourning the death of her father, Kate is changed by an ancient Indian charm stone in Pamela Service's *Vision Quest* (Macmillan, 1989, $12.95).

Five fifteen-year-old orphans become involved in a bizarre mind-bending experiment in William Sleator's *House of Stairs* (Dutton, 1974, $14.95; pap., Puffin, $3.95; condensed in *More Juniorplots,* Bowker, 1977, pp. 43–46).

About the Book

Booklist, April 15, 1987, p. 1296.
Center for Children's Books Bulletin, July 1987, p. 220.
Horn Book, July 1987, p. 474.
Kirkus Reviews, May 1, 1987, p. 728.
New York Times Book Review, July 19, 1987, p. 18.
School Library Journal, April 1987, p. 114.
Wilson Library Bulletin, September 1987, p. 68.
VOYA, February 1988, p. 284.
See also *Book Review Digest,* 1988, p. 1826; and *Book Review Index,* 1987, p. 808; 1988, p. 858.

About the Author

Chevalier, Tracy, ed., *Twentieth-Century Children's Writers* (3rd ed.). St. James, 1989, pp. 1024–1025.
Commire, Anne, ed., *Something about the Author.* Gale, 1980, Vol. 18, pp. 296–298.

de Montreville, Doris, and Crawford, Elizabeth D., eds., *Fourth Book of Junior Authors and Illustrators.* Wilson, 1978, pp. 343–345.

Kirkpatrick, D. L., ed., *Twentieth-Century Children's Writers* (2nd ed.). St. Martin's, 1983, pp. 810–811.

Locher, Frances C., ed., *Contemporary Authors.* Gale, 1980, Vols. 85–88, pp. 624–625.

Olendorf, Donna, ed., *Something about the Author.* 1992, Vol. 69, pp. 214–217.

Sarkissian, Adele, ed., *Something about the Author: Autobiography Series.* Gale, 1986, Vol. 1, pp. 279–291.

Senick, Gerard J., ed., *Children's Literature Review.* Gale, 1989, Vol. 16, pp. 199–214.

5

Personal and Social Problems

During the middle grades, young readers are increasingly able to step outside their own immediate experiences and identify vicariously with the problems that children their age face in locales and times far different from their own. The twelve books in this section give these readers opportunities for such experiences. Some involve personal problems, such as having to live with strange relatives and adjusting to the death of a loved one; others, on a larger canvas, explore such social problems as poverty, the homeless, and racial prejudice.

Buss, Fran Leeper. *Journey of the Sparrows*
Lodestar, 1991, $15 (0-525-67362-8); pap., Dell, $3.50 (0-440-40785-0)

Using a documentary style, Fran Leeper Buss tells, through the eyes of Maria, the terrible plight of illegal aliens in the United States. This courageous girl, originally from El Salvador, makes a perilous journey to save her older sister, Julia, and young brother, Oscar. In this novel, today's newspaper headlines come alive as we read about a family being broken apart by the bonds of poverty and deprivation. It is read by students in grades 5 through 8.

Plot Summary

For fifteen-year-old Maria, the journey to the United States from her home in El Salvador is long and terrifying. She knew it would be difficult, but Maria was not prepared for the reality. During most of the journey, she, along with her sickly six-year-old brother, Oscar, and her pregnant older sister, Julia, are enclosed in a crate. Far greater than this discomfort is the fear they will be discovered. Maria and her family are illegal aliens. They cannot enter the United States under the legal quota from El Salvador and are trying to enter illegally to escape the dreaded Guardias in their own country. Maria will never forget the Guardias. They killed their father and Julia's husband and attacked Julia herself.

Added to her worry about their own journey is Maria's fear for her mother's safety and that of another young child, Teresa. They are now in hiding in Mexico, but they hope to be able to join the rest of the family later in Chicago.

Making the treacherous journey with Maria and the others is Tomas, a friend who is about her age.

After what seems an eternity of fear and misery, they arrive safely in Chicago. Here, another worry takes over. Will they be caught? What will be done to them? How can they live in this strange land? What if Julia needs to go to a hospital when the baby comes? Will she be deported?

The family has journeyed to Chicago to join other illegal refugees from El Salvador. They crowd into a small apartment shared by many who have escaped the brutal life in their own country. The thought of what they left behind gives them the strength to go on in this new land. And despite the hardship, fear, and despair that surrounds them, they find friendship and caring, especially in a kindly midwife and a priest.

Maria feels she is lucky to find work in a sweatshop, even though it is reminiscent of the terrible working conditions of the early 1900s. Her hours are long and the work hard, but she is able to earn a little money to help feed her family. In her spare time, her friend Tomas begins to teach her English.

Maria worries constantly about the continuing poor health of her young brother, as well as Julia's impending delivery. As though these worries are not enough, Maria suddenly has to leave her job. She certainly doesn't want to, but she knows she will eventually be forced to submit to the sexual demands of the man who is her boss. And that she will not do.

To help ease the pain of her family's fear and misery, Maria begins to tell stories of the little sparrow who brings the rainbow. She also draws pictures. In time, this new talent blossoms and she is able to sell a few pictures.

When Julia's time comes, a baby girl is born. Although this brings much happiness, it also means there is yet another mouth to feed.

Day after day, Maria and her family wait for word of their mother and Teresa. Finally, news reaches them, but it is bad. The authorities have stopped their mother as she tried to escape north with the child. She has been sent back to El Salvador. However, Teresa is still being hidden in Mexico.

Someone will have to go on a dangerous journey south to rescue the little girl.

Maria knows Julia is in no condition to make such a trip. So, exhibiting more bravado than she feels, she sets off by herself. With the help of friends, she takes a bus south to Texas and then into Mexico, where she succeeds in finding her infant sister amid other starving children.

Maria uses what little money she has to help the children. Then, with Teresa, she begins the perilous journey back to Chicago. Until they can live legally in the United States, Maria knows they are going to have a difficult life. But at least she feels there is promise and a reason to believe the future will be better for them all.

Thematic Material

This story was written with the assistance of Daisy Cubias, an activist who left El Salvador as a young woman to work in the United States. Her brother, sister, and brother-in-law were murdered in El Salvador. This is a stark, realistic story that pulls no punches in details of the terrible hardships endured by people who must escape the persecution of their homeland only to live in fear and poverty as illegal aliens in the United States. Not a pretty story, it nonetheless gives the promise of hope and the strength and dignity of the human spirit.

Book Talk Material

The details of what these young escapees must endure, both en route to the United States and in daily life, will make a powerful introduction to this story. See: Maria and the others endure the perilous journey in the crate (pp. 6–9); they arrive in Chicago (pp. 17–20); life in the crowded apartment (pp. 25–30); Maria goes to work in a sweatshop (pp. 34–39); and the immigration raid (pp. 68–71).

Additional Selections

A Puerto Rican family moves to a neighborhood where Spanish isn't spoken in Nicholasa Mohr's *Felita* (Dial, 1979, $12.89).

In Winifred Madison's *Maria Louisa* (Harper, 1971, $9.89), a young girl encounters prejudice against Chicanos when she and her younger brother move to San Francisco to live with an aunt.

A young girl learns self-reliance when she must keep her orphaned family together in rural North Carolina in Vera Cleaver and Bill Cleaver's *Where the Lilies Bloom* (Harper, 1991, $14.89; condensed in *More Juniorplots,* Bowker, 1977, pp. 128–131). A sequel is *Trial Valley* (Harper, 1987, $12.89; pap., $3.50; condensed in *Introducing More Books,* Bowker, 1978, pp. 201–204).

In marginal notes written in a book, Rifka describes her incredibly harrowing journey from Russia to America in 1918 in *Letters from Rifka* (Holt, 1992, $14.95) by Karen Hesse.

In Gaye Hicyilmaz's *Against the Storm* (Little, Brown, 1992, $14.95), twelve-year-old Mehmet and his family endure impossible hardships when they must leave their Turkish village and relocate in Ankara.

Because their baby sister is dying, Naledi and her brother leave their South African village to find their mother, who works for a white in Johannesburg, in Beverley Naidoo's *Journey to Jo'burg* (Harper, 1986, $14).

In 1980, twelve-year-old Dara becomes separated from her family when she joins a refugee camp in war-torn Cambodia in Minfong Ho's *The Clay Marble* (Farrar, 1991, $13.95).

About the Book

Booklist, October 1, 1991, p. 317.
Center for Children's Books Bulletin, January 1992, p. 120.
Horn Book, November 1991, p. 742.
Kirkus Reviews, September 15, 1991, p. 1220.
School Library Journal, October 1991, p. 120.
VOYA, December 1991, p. 306.
See also *Book Review Digest,* 1992; and *Book Review Index,* 1991, p. 134; 1992 cum.

Cassedy, Sylvia. *Lucie Babbidge's House*

Harper, 1989, $13.89 (0-690-04798-3); pap., Avon, $3.99 (0-380-71812-X)

Although Sylvia Cassedy (1930–1989) wrote some fine picture books, such as *The Best Cat Suit of All* (Dial, 1991, $10.95), she is best known for her ambitious, disturbing novels that often deal with reality and fantasy. For example, in *Behind the Attic Wall* (Harper, 1983, $14.89; pap., Avon, $3.99), Maggie, a hostile, rebellious child who has been expelled from all her boarding schools, reluctantly stays with two great-aunts. There, behind the attic wall, she relates to two articulate dolls who draw her into their secret world. *M.E. and Morton* (Harper, 1987, $13.89; pap., $3.95), tells of eleven-year-old Mary Ella, who is ashamed of having an older mentally disabled brother, and how she learns the meaning of compassion and acceptance through her friendship with a strange girl named Polly. In *Lucie Babbidge's House,* a young orphan, who is an outcast at school, takes refuge in creating a family with the dolls who live in a forgotten dollhouse she finds in the orphanage. Elements of the supernatural enter gradually, as Lucie discovers the dolls are gaining control over her pen pal's family. This complex, highly original novel is enjoyed by better readers in grades 4 through 7.

Plot Summary

At Norwood Hall, an orphanage, eleven-year-old Lucie Babbidge is an outcast, an oddball. Her teacher, Miss Pimm, regards her as impertinent and obstinate. Her classmates ridicule her and call her Goosey-Loosey. She is a sad-looking child, her hair in knots, her voice a kind of croaking whisper, her hand-me-down clothes messy and often dirty.

Lucie often seems oblivious to the taunts and meanness of her schoolmates and teacher. She has a secret life, a life she lives to the fullest, about which no one else knows. In this wonderful life, at Lucie Babbidge's house, everything is different. Dada and Mumma are wonderful and loving; Olive, the maid, is suitably droll; and her five-year-old brother, Emmett, is funny and pesty, just as a brother should be. Their life together in the Babbidge household is perfect, especially when Mumma announces the coming of a new member of the family.

When Miss Pimm instructs the girls in the art of letter writing and insists they compose a letter to some "personage," Lucie obeys by writing to Delia Hornsby. When Miss Pimm asks the identity of this person, Lucie tells her that she once owned the Babbidge house.

When classes are over each day and the other little girls have run off to their play, Lucie runs under a dark stair to a small storeroom that she had discovered two years before. In it she found a dollhouse. She straightened the house and its furnishings and named the four little figures, except for the girl doll's name; she could think of nothing right for her.

Lucie spends hours in her private world. When she returns to the classroom, she cannot explain her absences. Her classmates tease her and tell the teacher she is lying about where she has been. But they don't know, of course. Even when Lucie is not in her private room under the stair, she is often "not there."

In Lucie Babbidge's house, the baby is born, a newcomer to the family. The infant is a girl. Lucie names her Maud.

In Lucie Babbidge's other world, she begins receiving responses from the original letter she wrote to Delia Hornsby. Funny, Delia's household has a new baby too. She implores Lucie to write to her again.

The other little girls eventually discover Lucie's dollhouse. They invade Lucie's other world, and they take the dolls and run.

For the next three weeks, Lucie is ill in bed, her teeth chattering, her face like clay. When she awakes, she finds a pile of letters from Delia. Strangely enough, Delia's problems mirror her own. Delia tells Lucie that she and her family have been abducted. She implores Lucie's help. But what can Lucie do?

Not long afterward, one of the little girls' rooms is found torn apart. Miss Pimm is very disturbed and feels that Lucie's behavior has taken a violent turn. Lucie, as usual, says little. In time, she realizes where the stolen dolls are and retrieves them from one of the other girls' desks.

Now she can help Delia. Before long, Delia writes that her whole family has been rescued.

This time, when Miss Pimm tells her for the thousandth time to "pick your head up," Lucie answers out loud. "How can I, Miss Pimm," she says, "when it never fell off in the first place?"

The other little girls stop what they are doing in all corners of the room and stare in surprise.

Thematic Material

This is a strange, haunting, and offbeat story of a little girl in emotional and mental pain who has retreated far from reality into a world she can tolerate, a world that gives her the love she finds nowhere else. It is richly woven and compelling, and it points out the power of imagination, a power so strong it can change one's existence. The story may not be for every young reader, but good readers who can let themselves be carried away into Lucie's emotional state will find the experience rewarding.

Book Talk Material

The stark contrast between life in the classroom and life in Lucie Babbidge's house, between Lucie's real and other worlds, will serve as an excellent introduction to story of a lonely, tormented child. See: the botany lesson (pp. 3–11); at home with the Babbidges (pp. 12–17); Lucie writes her first letter to Delia Hornsby (pp. 22–25); Mumma and Dada are invited to the ball (pp. 39–41); Delia writes to Lucie (pp. 45–46); under the stairs with the dollhouse (pp. 81–88).

Additional Selections

Marjorie Filley Stover's *When the Dolls Woke* (Whitman, 1985, $10.95; pap., Scholastic, $2.50) tells of the intertwining lives of a human, a doll family, and a dollhouse that Gail received from Great-Great-Aunt Abigail.

A girl is befriended by spirits that live in the cemetery where her parents are caretakers in Colby Rodowsky's *The Gathering Room* (Farrar, 1991, $11.95; pap., $3.45).

Gilly Ground tries to escape from his horrifying foster home in Julia Cunningham's *Dorp Dead* (Pantheon, 1965, $6.99; pap., Knopf, $2.95).

Eleanor Estes's *The Moffats* (Harcourt, 1941, $14.95; pap., Dell, $3.25) tells the story of a poor but loving family with four children growing up in Connecticut. One of its sequels is *The Middle Moffat* (Harcourt, 1983, $10.95; pap., Dell, $3.25).

The minds and bodies of eight special children who have either mental or physical handicaps are explored in Rachel Anderson's *The Bus People* (Holt, 1992, $13.95).

A candid family story about two very different girls who are cousins reveals layers of understanding love in Virginia Hamilton's *Cousins* (Putnam, 1990, $14.95; pap., Scholastic, $2.95).

When Mary Belle and her siblings are abandoned, she must take charge in a haunting novel of shattered dreams, *Mama, Let's Dance* (Little, Brown, 1991, $14.95), by Patricia Hermes.

About the Book

Center for Children's Books Bulletin, September 1989, p. 5.
Horn Book, November 1989, p. 768.
Horn Book Guide, July 1989, p. 69.
Kirkus Reviews, September 15, 1989, p. 1401.
School Library Journal, September 1989, p. 272.
See also *Book Review Digest,* 1990, pp. 303–304; and *Book Review Index,* 1989, p. 139; 1990, p. 136.

About the Author

Commire, Anne, ed., *Something about the Author.* Gale, 1982, Vol. 27, pp. 39–40.
Holtze, Sally Holmes, ed., *Sixth Book of Junior Authors and Illustrators.* Wilson, 1989, pp. 49–50.

Locher, Francis C., ed., *Contemporary Authors.* Gale, 1982, Vol. 105, p. 107.
Senick, Gerard J., ed., *Children's Literature Review.* Gale, 1992, Vol. 26, pp. 9–16.
Straub, Deborah A., ed., *Contemporary Authors* (New Revision Series). Gale, 1988, Vol. 22, p. 73.
Ward, Martha, ed., *Authors of Books for Young Readers* (3rd ed.). Scarecrow, 1990, pp. 116–117.

Cleary, Beverly. *Dear Mr. Henshaw*

Morrow, 1983, $12.95 (0-688-02405-X); pap., Dell, $3.99 (0-440-41794-5)

During her many years writing children's books, Beverly Cleary has created such memorable characters as Beezus and Ramona Quimby, Henry Huggins and his dog Ribsy, the marvelous mouse, Ralph, and an unusual cat named Socks. She has also written teenage novels such as *Jean and Johnny* (Morrow, 1959, $12.95; pap., Dell, $2.95) and an unusually frank and candid memoir of her childhood and youth, *A Girl from Yamhill* (Morrow, 1988, $15.95; pap., Dell, $3.95; condensed in *Juniorplots 4,* Bowker, 1993, pp. 308–313). In 1984, she received the Newbery Medal for *Dear Mr. Henshaw,* in which, through journal entries and a series of letters to her protagonist's favorite author, Boyd Henshaw, Cleary takes Leigh Botts from the second to the sixth grade, during which time he begins to accept his parents' separation and the fact that his father, although absent, still loves him. In its sequel, *Strider* (Morrow, 1991, $13.95; pap., Avon, $3.99), Leigh is fourteen and continues to keep his journal/diary. Although he is still troubled by his parents' divorce, his attention is now taken up with an abandoned dog that he and his friend Barry Brinkerhoff find. Together they share the responsibility for caring for the animal. Because of his track-team record, Leigh also gains personal satisfaction and confidence plus acceptance by his peers. In short, he is making a successful transition into adolescence. The sequel is intended for a slightly older reader than *Dear Mr. Henshaw,* which is loved by those in grades 4 through 6.

Plot Summary

Dear Mr. Henshaw is a series of letters written by Leigh Botts from his home in California to his favorite author, Boyd Henshaw. When the letters begin, Leigh is in the second grade and is apt to make spelling mistakes, such as *freind* for *friend*. By the end of the book, he is a sixth-grader who writes rather well-composed letters and might also become a writer when he grows up.

Leigh occasionally gets replies from Mr. Henshaw, who encourages him to write (hence the diary). The letters reveal the often lonely life of a sensitive boy who misses his father and has trouble making friends.

Leigh's father is a trucker, gone for long stretches of time on the highway. Leigh's mother says that was part of the reason why she and his father divorced; her husband, she tells Leigh, is in love with his truck, not his family. Leigh doesn't want to believe that, of course, and he lives for the times when his father calls or sends postcards. They are few and far between.

Since the divorce, Leigh and his mother have lived in a small ramshackle house and his mother often works at night to support them, especially when his father is late sending the checks. On those evenings Leigh amuses himself by putting down his feelings in his diary, still in the form of letters to Mr. Henshaw.

Leigh also misses his dog, Bandit, who went off with his father. The boy understands that his father must get lonely too out on the road by himself, but he wishes Bandit were at home with him.

Besides loneliness, Leigh's other big problem is that someone keeps stealing things out of his lunchbag. His mother works for a catering business, so his lunches often contain very tasty and unusual items. But more often than not, they are missing by lunchtime. When Leigh complains about this to his one friend at school, Mr. Fridley, the school custodian, Mr. Fridley suggests a burglar alarm. It sounds like a good idea, except how do you put an alarm in a lunchbag?

Now in the sixth grade, Leigh is sure his father will show up at Christmastime. Instead, on Christmas Eve a stranger arrives at their door. He is a trucker who was passing through, and Leigh's father asked him to drop off a present. It is a jacket for Leigh.

In January, his father phones from Oregon, where he is waiting for a load of potatoes. He promises to call Leigh in about a week, but the call never comes. Finally, out of loneliness, Leigh calls his father at his trailer over in Bakersfield. To his surprise, his father answers. He isn't off on the highway somewhere, and he didn't even call! His father says he was just about to call him. Then he tells him the bad news that Bandit ran off when his father left the truck cab door open.

For a while after that, lonely and bitter, Leigh hates his father. He talks to his mother about him. His mother says his father is not a bad man; he will just never grow up.

In February, an envelope arrives from Albuquerque, New Mexico. His father writes on a paper napkin that he is sorry about Bandit and encloses $20. Leigh spends some of the money for a lunchbox of the type truckers carry and equipment to rig a burglar alarm. With some advice from the hardware dealer, Leigh fashions a workable alarm. It actually goes off, and although he never does catch the lunch burglar, the thefts stop, and Leigh is much admired in his class for his cleverness. In fact, classmate Barry asks Leigh over to his house to help rig up an alarm for his bedroom to keep his pesty sisters out. At last, he has a friend.

One day in March, as Leigh is returning from mailing a letter to Mr. Henshaw, he sees a big rig in front of his house. There stands his father—and Bandit! His father had heard on his CB that another trucker had picked Bandit up, so now he is returning him to Leigh. His mother comes home from work while they are talking and asks his father inside for a cup of coffee.

Much to Leigh's embarrassment, his father asks his mother if there is any chance they can get back together. "No," his mother replies, "there isn't a chance."

When his father leaves, he promises to write more often. "Sure, Dad," Leigh says, but he knows now that it isn't always possible to count on his father. However, before he leaves, Leigh tells him to take Bandit with him. His father needs Bandit a whole lot more than Leigh does.

Thematic Material

This is a sensitive, insightful story of a young boy growing up, often lonely without his father and with few friends, finding refuge and solace in words and expressing himself. Funny and wise in its observations, it shows the gradual changes that bring a young boy to his own niche in the world and help him to look at his parents with love, achieving a growing understanding of their failings as well as their positive attributes. It is a compassionate, warm story.

Book Talk Material

Some of the letters to Mr. Henshaw point up how Leigh matures and can serve as a good introduction to this sensitive story. See: third-grader Leigh writes to Mr. Henshaw and talks about Bandit (p. 2); as a sixth-grader, he sends Mr. Henshaw a list of questions to answer (pp. 7–8); Leigh begins to reply to some of Mr. Henshaw's questions (pp. 14–17); the diary entries begin (pp. 39–53); Leigh builds the lunchbox alarm (pp. 93–98).

Additional Selections

Sarah confides her problems to her diary, causing a catharsis that allows for personal growth in Hila Colman's *Diary of a Frantic Kid Sister* (pap., Archway, 1985, $2.50).

An old diary helps a young girl trace some of her aunt's lost friends in Doris Orgel's *A Certain Magic* (Dial, 1976, $7.95).

An eleven-year-old boy copes with the loneliness of rural mountain life and finally develops a friendship with a neighbor boy in Robbie Branscum's *The Adventures of Johnny May* (Harper, 1984, $11.89).

Sam Mott, a sixth-grader, thinks he is dumb until his learning disability is diagnosed in Jamie Gilson's *Do Bananas Chew Gum?* (Lothrop, 1980, $12.95; pap., Pocket, $1.95).

Twelve-year-old Henry writes to his pen pal, Lesley, about his overly enthusiastic mother and the two friends begin promoting a marriage for her in Janice Marriott's hilarious *Letters to Lesley* (Knopf, 1991, $7.99).

The Turbulent Term of Tyke Tiler by Gene Kemp (Faber, 1990, $10.95) is the humorous story of Tyke's friendship with Danny, a boy with a speech impediment.

About the Book

Booklist, September 1, 1983, p. 80.
Center for Children's Books Bulletin, October 1983, p. 24.
Horn Book, October 1983, p. 570.
Kirkus Reviews, September 1, 1988, p. 160.
New York Times Book Review, October 23, 1983, p. 34.
School Library Journal, September 1983, p.120.
See also *Book Review Digest,* 1984, p. 288; and *Book Review Index,* 1983, p. 112; 1984, p. 149.

About the Author

Chevalier, Tracy, ed., *Twentieth-Century Children's Writers* (3rd ed.). St. James, 1989, pp. 209–210.
Commire, Anne, ed., *Something about the Author.* Gale, 1986, Vol. 43, pp. 53–61.
Estes, Glenn E., ed., *American Writers for Children since 1960: Fiction* (Dictionary of Literary Biography: Vol. 52). Gale, 1986, pp. 85–91.
Fuller, Muriel, ed., *More Junior Authors.* Wilson, 1963, pp. 49–50.

Kirkpatrick, D. L., ed., *Twentieth-Century Children's Writers* (2nd ed.). St. Martin's, 1983, pp. 182–184.
Metzger, Linda, ed., *Contemporary Authors* (New Revision Series). Gale, 1985, Vol. 8, pp. 34–62.
Riley, Carolyn, ed., *Children's Literature Review*. Gale, 1976, Vol. 2, pp. 44–51.
Senick, Gerard J., ed., *Children's Literature Review*. Gale, 1985, Vol. 8, pp. 34–62.
Ward, Martha, ed., *Authors of Books for Young People* (3rd ed.). Scarecrow, 1990, p. 132.

Ellis, Sarah. *Pick-Up Sticks*
Macmillan, 1992, $13.95 (0-689-50550-7)

Sarah Ellis, the young Canadian writer, has brought refreshing honesty, humor, and pathos into each of her novels. In the first, *A Family Project* (Macmillan, 1988, $13.95; pap., Dell, $3.25), she writes about the Robertsons' excitement at the prospect of a new addition to the family group. Jessica, age eleven, is so eager that she studies babies and their care as a volunteer class project at school. When Lucie arrives, the family's happiness is complete until, without warning, she dies of crib death. The adjustment to this tragedy and the painful process of grieving make for a moving reading experience. *Next-Door Neighbors* (Macmillan, 1990, $12.95; pap., Dell, $3.25) is the story of Peggy, a minister's daughter, and her personal problems when her family moves to a new home in Western Canada. By trying too hard to make friends, she only creates problems for herself. But eventually, with the help of George, the son of a refugee janitor, and Sing Lee, the gardener of her malevolent, wealthy next-door neighbor, she overcomes her shyness and learns to understand the many faces and layers of friendship. Sarah Ellis's third novel, *Pick-Up Sticks,* also deals with the trauma of moving but from a different point of view. It takes place chiefly in the suburban area around the city of Vancouver, British Columbia. All three of these novels are recommended for readers in grades 5 through 8.

Plot Summary

Thirteen-year-old Polly is not the product of a conventional family. She is the only child of a single parent, Mum, who wanted a child without the encumbrances of marriage. Mum is a loving, caring mother, and their relationship has been very close. But their finances are always tight because her mother, an independent stained-glass designer, brings in little money and must pay for the upkeep of a studio. Also, Polly is in the stage of adolescence when conformity and security are of great importance. Mum's unorthodox life-style, effervescent, sometimes indelicate behavior, and liberal attitudes are an increasing source of embarrassment and anxiety.

After completing her volunteer work at the public library, where she hopes to work as a page when she becomes fourteen, Polly walks home. Polly and her mother have always lived in the same place, a small apartment in a house that was originally built as a single-family dwelling. In the front hallway she visits with Ernie, the retarded son of their elderly neighbor, Mrs. Protheroe. Ernie, although an adult, has the mind of a child, and Polly and he share a special, loving friendship.

Mum has some disturbing news for Polly. Their building is slated for demolition, and they have been given a two months' eviction notice. Both realize finding an apartment within Mum's limited budget will be difficult. As always, when times become stressful, Polly retreats to the bathroom to practice on her French horn.

At school the next day, Polly and her dear friend Vanessa discuss Vanessa's favorite topic, their English teacher, Mr. Taylor. Vanessa's crush on him has reached the proportions of an obsession. Now, through intricate detective work, she has learned his address and telephone number. Tomorrow after school, with Polly's moral support, she plans to call him.

The implications of moving and the possibility of having to change schools trouble Polly. During her last period, she asks Miss Anicott, a guidance counselor, for advice. Polly is somewhat relieved to hear that exceptions can be made and a change is not always mandatory.

Vanessa's telephone call to Mr. Taylor yields only an answering machine message, saying Jim and Rusty are not available. Ever the optimist, Vanessa is certain Rusty is only Mr. Taylor's faithful dog but vows over the weekend, again with Polly's help, to invade his territory and find out in person. This foray also proves fruitless. Vanessa, face covered with a ski mask, becomes so nervous when she sees Mr. Taylor's house that she begs to go home.

Reading the "For rent" ads in the local newspaper becomes a daily ritual for Polly and Mum. At the dentist, the nurse tells them about a reasonably priced apartment that will be available soon. On visiting it, Mum wants to reject it because of its insipid decor and the rigid management policy. Polly is appalled by her mother's attitude and forces her to investigate further. However, the rental involves an under-the-table payment that makes it unacceptable both financially and morally for Mum.

They visit more places but nothing suitable within their limited price range. Mum doesn't seem unduly distressed by these disappointments; if necessary she and Polly can move to her one-room studio temporarily. However, Polly's resentment and panic grow daily until she is on the verge of suggesting her mother get a decent-paying steady job instead of living the precarious life of an artist.

Matters reach a climax when Mum's brother, successful yuppie businessman Uncle Roger, and his equally successful wife, Aunt Barbie, visit and offer Mum the opportunity to become the resident manager of an apartment building that a friend owns. In exchange for being available full-time and doing cleaning and housekeeping, she would receive a free apartment and a modest salary. Mum, however, rebels both at the thought of restrictions on her own work and at her brother's implication that this building does not rent to nonwhites. She politely but firmly refuses the offer. Before Roger and Barbie leave, they invite Polly to live with them and their daughter, Stephanie, until permanent housing can be found.

Polly is furious with her mother's high-handed manner and the implication that she really doesn't care about her own daughter's welfare. After a confrontational scene during which she accuses her mother of neglect, Polly accepts her uncle's offer and moves out. At the same time, Polly's growing impatience with Vanessa's crush on Mr. Taylor provokes a quarrel, and the two end their friendship.

At first, life with Mum's relatives is exotic and seemingly ideal. Polly has her own huge bedroom, television, and private bath, and both Roger and Barbie seem genuinely fond of her, although they are often away on business. Daughter Stephanie, a spoiled, snobbish older teenager, is sometimes a pain but can be avoided. All this material wealth doesn't satisfy Polly completely, however, and in spite of seeing her mother regularly, she gradually realizes how much she misses their closeness and affection.

Mum has joined a citizen's group that is petitioning City Hall to convert an abandoned building into condominiums. Polly attends one of their meetings with her mother and feels guilty afterward when she tells Roger and Barbie about the people at the meeting in a derisive and condescending way. She realizes that these people, whom Roger calls waifs and misfits, are her mother's friends.

In order to use one of the family's cars one Friday evening, Stephanie is forced to take Polly along with her. Instead of going to the movies, as she has told her parents she was going to do, Stephanie is joined by pal Chelsea and two boys for an evening of "gross busting," that is, vandalizing the property of people with the bad taste to own outdoor ornaments like garden gnomes and plastic statues. When they shoplift such supplies as toilet paper and glue, Polly demands to be let out. Nauseated and frightened, she is left in a deserted part of town. Surrounded by darkened warehouses and wet from rain, she decides she must find Mum's studio.

The next day, Polly gathers up her things and moves in with her mother. After writing a conciliatory card to Vanessa, Polly and Mum visit Ernie and Mrs. Protheroe, who are now living in a comfortable condominium. Perhaps one day soon they too will have a new home.

Thematic Material

The uncertainties of adolescents, their conflicting values, and their need for security and acceptance are realistically portrayed in the mixed emotions Polly has for her mother and herself. Polly's growth to self-realization is realistically depicted, as are Mum's difficulties in being a single parent and answering Polly's question, "Why did you choose to be a mother if you can't do it right?" The concept that love involves accepting both strengths and weaknesses in people is stressed. Using as a metaphor the game of pick-up sticks, the author shows how life involves the intertwining of many elements and how disturbing one can effect the whole. Other subjects dealt with are conservatism and conformity versus liberalism and freedom, friendship, acceptance of handicaps, and student-teacher relations.

Book Talk Material

Some passages that would interest readers are: Polly helps in the library (pp. 1–4); Mum tells her they must move (pp. 6–8); Polly visits the guidance counselor about changing schools (pp. 19–22); Vanessa tracks down information about Mr. Taylor (pp. 14–16); the phone call (pp. 24–25); Mum rejects the "insipid" apartment (pp. 29–36); and Polly, with Vanessa in a ski mask, visit Mr. Taylor's neighborhood (pp. 38–41).

Additional Selections

The story of the tender relationship between a daughter, her single-parent mother, and the mother's boyfriend is told in Norma Klein's *Mom, the Wolf Man and Me* (Pantheon, 1972, $9.99; pap., Avon, $3.50; condensed in *More Juniorplots,* Bowker, 1977, pp. 10–13).

Mama will even steal to give her sons what they want in *Mama* (Simon & Schuster, 1992, $13; pap., Dell, $2.50) by Lee Bennett Hopkins.

In *You Shouldn't Have to Say Goodbye* (Harcourt, 1982, $12.95; pap., Scholastic, $2.50) by Patricia Hermes, a thirteen-year-old girl must adjust to her mother's death from cancer.

When her family moves to Hawaii, Sara keeps her friends back home in touch through her audiotapes in Jan Slepian's *The Broccoli Tapes* (Putnam, 1989, $13.95).

A preadolescent grows into a self-confident teen during the few years that her young brother is a member of the family in Elizabeth Laird's *Loving Ben* (Delacorte, 1989, $14.95).

A lonely young girl is befriended by a young couple who move into a nearby trailer in *Looking On* (Knopf, 1976, $10.99; pap., $3.25) by Betty Miles.

Betty Levin's *The Trouble with Gramary* (Greenwillow, 1988, $13.95) tells about Merkka's love for a grandmother who the town's children think is weird.

About the Book

Booklist, January 1, 1992, p. 931.
Center for Children's Books Bulletin, February 1992, p. 154.
Horn Book, March 1992, p. 208.
Kirkus Reviews, January 1, 1992, p. 51.
School Library Journal, March 1992, p. 237.
See also *Book Review Digest,* 1992, p. 576; and *Book Review Index,* 1992, p. 264.

About the Author

Olendorf, Donna, ed., *Something about the Author.* Gale, 1992, Vol. 68, pp. 68–70.

Fleischman, Sid. *Jim Ugly*

Illus. by Marcia Sewall. Greenwillow, 1992, $14 (0-688-10886-5); pap., Dell, $3.50 (0-440-40803-2)

Sid Fleischman originally made his mark as a writer of tall tales for young people that artfully combined history, adventure, and humor. His first book for young readers was *Mr. Mysterious and Company* (Little, Brown, 1962, $14.95; pap., $4.95), the story of a traveling magic show that toured the West in the 1880s and involved an entire family, including Pa, who was Mr. Mysterious in performance. *The Whipping Boy* (Greenwillow, 1986, $13.95; pap., Troll, $2.95), which won the 1987 Newbery Medal, uses a change of setting and tells of royal derring-do in the adventures of Prince Roland, a.k.a. Prince Brat, and Jemmy, the boy who has been hired to receive the whippings intended for Brat. Perhaps Fleischman's most enduring character is McBroom, the New England farmer who, in a typical adventure, *McBroom Tells the Truth* (Little, Brown, 1981, $12.45), acquires land so rich that it produces four crops per day. *Jim Ugly* returns to the Old West. It is narrated by Jake, who runs away after his father's burial to find out if he is really dead. There follows a series of wild and woolly adventures and a twisting plot that is both clever and amusing. It is enjoyed by readers in grades 4 through 6.

Plot Summary

This is a boy-dog story with a difference. Jim Ugly, whose real dog name is Amigo, is part short-eared timber wolf and parts of other things. He is also proud, aloof, and a one-man dog. His man is Sam Bannock, an actor in the frontier West. But Sam has disappeared.

Sam and his son, Jake, had been staying with Cousin Aurora and her husband, Axie, on their homestead in Blowfly, Nevada, where Aurora raises about a million chickens. Jake has never understood why his father insisted they come to Blowfly but it has to do with missing diamonds and a $2,500 bounty on his father's head in San Francisco. Jake's father said he had no diamonds, but that he did run into some trouble in San Francisco that resulted in a bullet in the shoulder. So he figured they'd better lay low for a while.

So they had been living in Blowfly until Sam disappeared about a week ago. Aurora and Axie told Jake his father was killed over in Smoketree Junction and the three of them attended his closed-casket funeral. But Jake doesn't believe his father is dead. Part of the reason is Jim Ugly. He is one smart dog, and Jim Ugly just doesn't act as though Sam Bannock is dead. Jake can't explain it but Jim Ugly thinks Sam is alive. So Jake thinks so too.

Jake decides he will go to Smoketree Junction to find out the truth.

He gives Jim Ugly an old shirt of his father's to smell, and the two set off in an uneasy alliance. When they get to Smoketree Junction, a scattering of buildings on the railroad line, Jim Ugly throws himself down in front of the Indian Princess Hotel as though he'd been there all his life. Inside, Jake finds a doctor who says he removed the bullet from his father's shoulder. The doctor gives Jake the bullet and also tells him of a bounty hunter in town named Skeats.

Jake lets Jim Ugly smell the bullet. The dog sets off toward Truckee with Jake close behind. In Truckee they find not Jake's father, but Skeats, the bounty hunter. Jake figures the doctor must have given Jake the wrong bullet. This must be the bullet he removed from Skeats and that's why Jim Ugly was following the wrong man.

Skeats wants Jake to do some spying for him, but the boy refuses. Skeats does tell Jake, however, that he is looking for a Wilhelmina Marlybone-Jenkins. Jake goes to the Magnolia Theater in search of his father and there he finds the lady in question, as well as Mr. Cornelius and the Arizona Girl. He learns that Miss Wilhelmina is also looking for his father—to horsewhip him, she says. To Jake, it looks like romance. Jake tells his three new acquaintances about the bounty hunter who is after Wilhelmina.

The boy who plays the part of William Tell's son in the current production falls ill, and Jake is talked into substituting for him. He learns that Mr. Cornelius is also looking for his father. Mr. Cornelius says Sam has thirty or forty pounds of diamonds that belong to him. Jake defends his father and says he would never steal them.

Jake soon runs into Skeats again, who lifts him off the ground with one arm trying to get information from him. But Jim Ugly is right there to the rescue. For the first time, Jake thinks maybe Jim Ugly might be more than a one-man dog.

Jake and Jim Ugly travel west with the theater troupe, but Mr. Cornelius stays in Truckee. In Sacramento, Jake is surprised to run into Cousin Aurora. She gives him a letter that came the day after he and Jim Ugly left for Smoketree Junction. The letter is from his father, saying that it would be best if his whereabouts remain unknown.

When the troupe gets to San Francisco, Jake once again plays the part of William Tell's son. One night he is amazed to recognize the man playing the part of a soldier right on stage with him—it is his father!

Later, Jake, his father, and Jim Ugly are reunited. Seeing the dog with his father, Jake fears Jim Ugly will remain his father's dog—the bond between them seems so strong. But Jake puts that out of his mind in his joy at seeing his father again. Sam Bannock explains that Cousin Axie pretended to bury him to put the bounty hunter off his father's trail. But, Sam admits, Axie should have told Jake the truth.

When Jake, Sam, and Jim Ugly return to Blowfly, Jake at last learns the whole truth. Some time before, Jake's father had discovered Mr. Cornelius and Skeats at an abandoned mine. They were "salting" the mine with diamonds, scattering real diamonds around so they could convince investors the mine was valuable. They planned to sell shares and make millions of dollars in the swindle. But Axie and Jake's father had later returned and picked about thirty pounds of diamonds out of the junk in the mine. That was why Cornelius and the bounty hunter were after Jake's father and why Axie staged the fake funeral.

Where were the diamonds now? Jake's father had mixed them with the chicken mash and fed them to the chickens at the homestead in Blowfly. That herd of chickens is a diamond mine with legs!

Back in San Francisco, Jake and his father visit Wilhelmina, and Jake decides he likes the idea of his father marrying her. He also likes the idea that Jim Ugly is now *his* dog, whom he calls by his real name—Amigo.

Thematic Material

This is a fast-paced, light mystery-adventure with comic overtones. The uneasy relationship between boy and dog is nicely drawn; the world of the stage in the frontier West creates a fun-filled atmosphere of another time and place. The characters are not deeply etched, but they are likable and move the story along in a believable manner.

Book Talk Material

Several incidents can serve as a good introduction to this comic mystery. See: Jake and Jim Ugly set off for Smoketree Junction (pp. 11–13); Jim Ugly leads Jake to the doctor (pp. 25–31); they meet the bounty hunter (pp. 47–53); Jake meets the theater troupe (pp. 56–62); and Jim Ugly saves Jake (pp. 78–82).

Additional Selections

After Uncle Ugly is gunned down and his treasure map stolen by Catfish Grimes, fifteen-year-old Artemis Bonner takes off, intent on revenge, in Walter Dean Myers's action-filled comic novel, *The Righteous Revenge of Artemis Bonner* (Harper, 1992, $14).

Set in Wisconsin during 1918, *Rascal* (Dutton, 1984, $13.95; pap., Puffin, $3.95; condensed in *Juniorplots,* Bowker, 1967, pp. 45–47) by Sterling North is the true story of a young boy and his pet raccoon.

A mutt named Mutt is featured in Farley Mowat's reminiscences of a Canadian boyhood, *The Dog Who Wouldn't Be* (Little, Brown, 1957, $18.95; pap., Bantam, $3.99).

Thirteen-year-old Michael, who is fearful of being branded a coward, conquers his fears during a trip to see his father in Colorado in *Face to Face* (Houghton, 1991, $13.95; pap., Dell, $3.50) by Marion Dane Bauer.

Luke, a "boomer" in the oilfields, is continually moving his family from job to job until they rebel in Ruby C. Tolliver's *Boomer's Kids* (Hendrick-Long, 1992, $14.95).

In Lynn Hall's *Windsong* (Scribner, 1992, $11.95), Marty wants a dog more than anything, and she gets her chance when working with Orland, a local greyhound breeder.

Alvin Schwartz's *Whoppers* (Harper, 1975, $12.95) is an amusing anthology subtitled *Tall Tales and Other Lies Collected from American Folklore.*

About the Book

Booklist, May 15, 1992, p. 1680.
Center for Children's Books Bulletin, March 1992, p. 179.
Horn Book, May/June 1992, p. 340.
Kirkus Reviews, April 1, 1992, p. 463.
School Library Journal, April 1992, p. 113.
See also *Book Review Digest,* 1992, p. 651; *Book Review Index,* 1992, p. 294.

About the Author

Chevalier, Tracy, ed., *Twentieth-Century Children's Writers* (3rd ed.). St. James, 1989, pp. 350–351.
Commire, Anne, ed., *Something about the Author.* Gale, 1976, Vol. 8, pp. 61–63; 1990, Vol. 59, pp. 89–95.
de Montreville, Doris, and Hill, Donna, eds., *Third Book of Junior Authors.* Wilson, 1972, pp. 86–87.
Evory, Ann, ed., *Contemporary Authors* (First Revision Series). Gale, 1992, Vol. 5, pp. 191–192.
Lesniak, James G., ed., *Contemporary Authors* (New Revision Series). Gale, 1992, Vol. 37, pp. 187–190.
Kirkpatrick, D. L., ed., *Twentieth-Century Children's Writers* (2nd ed.). St. Martin's, 1983, pp. 194–195.
Senick, Gerard J., ed., *Children's Literature Review.* Gale, 1988, Vol. 15, pp. 101–113.

Fox, Paula. *The Village by the Sea*
Orchard, 1988, $13.99 (0-531-08388-8); pap., Dell, $3.50 (0-440-40299-9)

Like other great writers of juvenile fiction, Paula Fox has the uncanny ability to create a world based entirely on the perceptions and feelings of her young heroes and heroines. Although many of her novels, like *The Village by the Sea,* deal with complex human emotions and tangled relationships, her plots evolve quietly, logically, and without melodrama and usually involve the gaining of emotional maturity through an intensely moving experience.

She is the recipient of all the major literary awards in the field, including the Hans Christian Andersen Medal for her collective works and the 1974 Newbery Medal for *The Slave Dancer* (Macmillan, 1982, $14.95; pap., Dell, $3.50; condensed in *More Juniorplots,* Bowker, 1977, pp. 82–86). Other recommended titles by this author found in the Bowker plots series are: *How Many Miles to Babylon?* (Macmillan, 1982, $12.95; condensed in *Introducing Books,* Bowker, 1970, pp. 11–14), *One-Eyed Cat* (Macmillan, 1984, $14.95; pap., Dell, $3.50; condensed in *Juniorplots 3,* Bowker, 1987, pp. 214–218) and for a slightly older audience, *The Moonlight Man* (Macmillan, 1986, $14.95; pap., Dell, $3.50; condensed in *Seniorplots,* Bowker, 1989, pp. 65–69). Although told in the third person, *The Village by the Sea* is seen through the eyes of ten-year-old Emma. It is enjoyed by readers in grades 4 through 8.

Plot Summary

Ten-year-old Emma's safe and secure world is suddenly threatened when she learns her adored and adoring father must undergo bypass surgery for his worsening heart condition and she must spend two weeks with her Aunt Bea and Uncle Crispin while her mother looks after her father. Emma's father teaches music in the private school she attends in New York City. She is a quiet, sensitive girl who has grown up with two loving parents, and now she is fearful about both her father's illness and about her stay with relatives she barely knows.

Aunt Bea is her father's half-sister. Their father, Emma's grandfather, remarried after the death of Bea's mother, his first wife. Bea is almost twenty years older than Emma's father, and even he, a kindly, soft-spoken man, admits Bea has grown into something of a terror, still bitter because of her supposed rejection after the second marriage. To Emma, all this is remote, ancient history, because she never knew her grandparents.

Emma's aunt and uncle live close to the eastern end of Long Island in a many-roomed log structure overlooking Peconic Bay, a saltwater inlet that separates the island into two forks. During the drive out with Uncle Crispin, Emma is impressed with the knowledge, gentleness, and somewhat eccentric behavior of this man who, she learns, continues to teach violin lessons to supplement their meager income. Although the journey is only two hours, Emma enters a totally new world—one of sand dunes, scrub pines, potato fields, small towns, and shopping malls.

Emma is not prepared for her reception by Aunt Bea. She is slovenly, dressed in a tattered sweater, long black skirt, and beaded moccasins. She is sitting at a table covered with dirty dishes, chiefly half-empty teacups. Uncle Crispin tries to ease the situation, but Bea is cold and sarcastic.

After showing Emma to her room overlooking the beach, Uncle Crispin returns downstairs to clean up and prepare lunch. Alone, Emma begins the diary that she promised her father she would keep. She writes: "I'm here. Uncle Crispin is really nice although a little peculiar. The bay and beach are great. Aunt Bea is . . . ." Here she stops, unable to sum up her initial feelings for the strange, hostile woman.

After a walk on the beach with Uncle Crispin, Emma decides to wash up. On the floor of the bathroom, embedded in a dirtball, she finds a tiny plastic deer, the kind found on a bottle of brandy. After dinner—a rather sad affair cooked by Uncle Crispin while his wife watches television—she shows the ornament to Uncle Crispin who becomes visibly agitated. Later that night, Emma hears from her room an argument between Bea and Crispin during which Bea insists that the deer must be an old one, because she has given up drinking. Emma draws a two-week calendar on her scratchpad and thankfully crosses off day one.

The next day, Emma's mother calls with news that the operation was successful and that her father is now in intensive care. Uncle Crispin suggests an outing to Montauk Point, some thirty miles away, to celebrate. Bea reluctantly agrees to join them, but only a few miles from home, she demands that Crispin pull in at a thrift shop. Much later she emerges with armloads of secondhand clothing and bedding. Exhausted by her spree, she now commands Crispin to take her home. So much for Emma's celebration!

Aunt Bea's erratic, selfish behavior both repels and frightens Emma who, unable to understand this bitter, unhappy woman, takes every opportunity to avoid contact without being rude. Fortunately, later that day she meets an outgoing girl her age on the beach, who introduces herself as Alberta—Bertie for short. As usual, she is spending the summer with her grandmother, a neighbor of Aunt Bea whom Bertie calls Lady Bonkers. The two become instant friends. On the third day after their meeting, they begin to use flotsam and jetsam found on the beach—sea shells, bits of driftwood, seaweed, glass, starfish, bottles, and stones—to build a miniature village.

As the days pass and her father's recuperation progresses, Emma continues an uneasy truce with her aunt by losing herself in her friendship with Bertie and in the construction of the village by the sea. Aunt Bea seems vaguely annoyed that her niece is paying little attention to her, but Uncle Crispin is happy that Emma has an interest to fill her days.

The day before Emma is to leave, the village is complete, and Bertie takes pictures of their masterpiece. Emma invites Bea and Crispin to inspect their handiwork. Bea refuses, making a lame excuse, but Crispin visits and later enthusiastically reports his visit to a seemingly unimpressed Bea.

In the middle of the night, Emma is awakened by a strange sound. She is so excited at the prospect of being reunited with her mother and father that she can't get back to sleep. She decides to visit the village by moonlight. When she reaches the beach, she finds a vandal has completely destroyed each of the tiny structures. On the sand, she sees tiny beads that match those on Aunt Bea's moccasins. Shattered, she returns home, where Uncle Crispin awaits her in the kitchen. Through her tears, she tells him what happened, and Crispin tries to explain Aunt Bea's behavior, quoting the adage, "Envy's a coal hissing hot from hell."

The following morning, Aunt Bea stays in her room, and Emma tells Bertie the sad news. Surprisingly, Bertie takes it much more philosophically than Emma. At least, she reminds Emma, there are photographs of their project. Aunt Bea doesn't come out of her room to say goodbye, and Emma knows Uncle Crispin has confronted her with her act of vandalism.

Back with her parents, Emma, still filled with hatred toward her aunt, is reluctant to discuss her stay on Long Island until, one day, she opens her diary and finds that the sentence "Aunt Bea is . . ." has been completed with the words "a sad, bad old woman." It is in her aunt's handwriting. Suddenly Emma's hatred dissolves into feelings of sadness and understanding.

Thematic Material

Emma's journey to her relatives is also a journey to new wisdom and emotional maturity. The destructive effects of envy and hatred are shatteringly depicted, as are the healing powers of compassion and understanding. The novel depicts complicated human relationships and studies two contrasting marriages effectively. The setting and atmosphere of eastern Long Island are also well created. Some additional themes involve friendship, good parent-daughter relations, and the need for self-esteem.

Book Talk Material

A general introduction to Emma and her family problems should interest readers. Some specific passages of importance are: Emma asks her father and mother about Aunt Bea (pp. 3–9); the ride to Long Island with Uncle Crispin (pp. 19–23); meeting Aunt Bea (pp. 25–29); from supper to bedtime on the first day (pp. 51–59); the thrift shop episode (pp. 77–83); and building the village (pp. 97–99).

Additional Selections

An egocentric girl learns about life during a summer working for her English teacher in *A Summer's Lease* (Dutton, 1979, $13.95), by Marilyn Sachs.

In Madeleine L'Engle's first novel about the Austin family, *Meet the Austins* (pap., Dell, 1981, $3.50; condensed in *Introducing Books,* Bowker, 1970, pp. 14–17), Maggie, a spoiled orphan, comes to live with the Austins.

Freddie spends a summer with two eccentric great-aunts on an island off the Maine coast and learns about himself in Irwin Hadley's *The Original Freddie Ackerman* (McElderry, 1992, $14.95).

When her mother enters an alcohol rehabilitation center, twelve-year-old Birdie moves in with an aunt and uncle but is fearful of becoming too attached to them in *Two of a Kind* (pap., Avon, 1992, $3.50) by Ann Gabhart.

Opie, a volunteer in a home for the elderly, becomes involved in a resident's fight to purchase a house in Eth Clifford's *The Rocking Chair Rebellion* (Houghton, 1978, $13.95).

In Vicki Grove's *Goodbye, My Wishing Star* (Putnam, 1988, $12.95; pap., Scholastic, $2.75), twelve-year-old Jeno finds her life is falling apart when her family is forced to sell their farm and move to the city.

Poverty and its effects on family life feature in Janni Howker's *Isaac*

Campion (Greenwillow, 1986, $10.25; pap., Dell, $2.95), a reminiscence of a ninety-six-year-old man about the sad death of his brother in 1901.

About the Book

Booklist, December 1, 1988, p. 75.
Center for Children's Books Bulletin, July 1988, p. 227.
Emergency Librarian, January 1989, p. 48.
Horn Book, September 1988, p. 625.
New York Times Book Review, February 5, 1989, p. 37.
School Library Journal, August 1988, p. 93.
VOYA, October 1988, p. 181.
Wilson Library Bulletin, April 1989, p. 94.
See also *Book Review Digest,* 1989, p. 547; and *Book Review Index,* 1988, p. 276; 1989, p. 278.

About the Author

Chevalier, Tracy, ed., *Twentieth-Century Children's Writers* (3rd ed.). St. James, 1989, pp. 357–358.
Block, Ann, and Riley, Carolyn, eds., *Children's Literature Review.* Gale, 1976, Vol. 1, pp. 59–65.
Commire, Anne, ed., *Something about the Author.* Gale, 1979, Vol. 17, pp. 59–60.
Commire, Anne, ed., *Something about the Author.* Gale, 1990, Vol. 60, pp. 29–38.
de Montreville, Doris, and Crawford, Elizabeth D., eds., *Fourth Book of Junior Authors and Illustrators.* Wilson, 1978, pp. 135–136.
Estes, Glenn E., ed., *American Writers for Children since 1960: Fiction* (Dictionary of Literary Biography: Vol. 52). Gale, 1986, pp. 143–156.
Lesniak, James G., ed., *Contemporary Authors* (New Revision Series). Gale, 1992, Vol. 36, pp. 140–144.
Locher, Frances C., ed., *Contemporary Authors.* Gale, 1978, Vols. 73–76, pp. 214–215.
Ward, Martha, ed., *Authors of Books for Young People* (3rd ed.). Scarecrow, 1990, p. 242.

Holman, Felice. *Secret City, U.S.A.*
Scribner, 1990, $14.95 (0-684-19168-7)

This writer, with only a few published books, has made a unique and lasting contribution to literature for young people. Her *Slake's Limbo* (Macmillan, 1974, $13.95; pap., $3.95) broke ground with its honest depiction of the poverty, depravity, and violence that exist only slightly below the surface of life in parts of New York City. In this story, Artemis Slake flees from an oppressive home situation and a stifling school environment and takes refuge underground in the subway system of New York. In *The Wild*

Children (Macmillan, 1983, $12.95; pap., Puffin, $4.95), she tells of lonely Alex, who joins a group of homeless children after the Russian Revolution of 1917. In *Secret City, U.S.A.*, some youngsters led by the enterprising Benno escape the squalor and poverty of the big city in a house they find under the inner-city rubble. The characters speak in a street-talk jargon that adds to the realism. These novels are enjoyed by readers in grades 6 through 10.

Plot Summary

The place is the slums of a big city. Thirteen-year-old Benno wanders the streets of the barrio grieving for his grandfather, JoJo, who has just died. JoJo's death leaves a room empty in the overcrowded apartment where his family lives, but it does not mean more space for Benno, nor does it ease the ache in his heart. Sometimes Benno goes to the top of his tenement building in the barrio; there is more space there and life seems more free.

With his friend Moon, the child of deaf parents, Benno one day wanders into an area not too far from the barrio that seems a wasteland. It is totally deserted; no one lives there anymore; not a thing moves. The city-owned buildings are abandoned.

"We're like explorers," Benno says to Moon. "We're the *discoverers* of this place," Moon agrees. "We're the discoverers of this country," Benno declares.

The two boys return to the area because it gives them a sense of space, of another world, where they find peace and quiet and a strange security. They find a way into one of the buildings and discover that it is in good condition, but filthy, filled with debris. They decide to keep the place a secret—in fact, they name it Secret City, U.S.A.—and begin to clean it up. They intend to keep it as their space, their own little corner of the world away from the poverty and overcrowding, the smells and the danger of the barrio, and the threat from the evil Poison gang.

Before long, Benno and Moon realize they cannot do all the work of cleaning up their building by themselves. First, they take young Willie, who is homeless, into their confidence. Willie not only helps with the cleanup enthusiastically but often stays overnight in Secret City, U.S.A., as a kind of patrolman. Next, Moon's two young cousins, Juan and Paco, join the group. They are all sworn to secrecy.

In time, the inhabitants of Secret City grow to eight young boys, ages six to thirteen. With true pioneer spirit, they fashion bath facilities and clean and scrub the old building until it becomes more livable than the homes most of them know; they even plant a garden out back.

There are always dangers, of course. One of the eight boys, Louie, has had some contact with the Poison gang, running errands for them. They want him back. The boys are very careful not to be followed when they go to the Secret City. There is also danger from the packs of hungry wild dogs that roam the area. And Benno must, of course, keep his whereabouts secret from his family.

The happiness the boys find in this private space is still not enough for Benno, and he begins to envisage Secret City as a refuge for the homeless. Moon isn't so sure. There are so many of them, and many of them need more than just a place to stay. But Benno holds on to his dream.

The months pass, and summer comes. The boys keep working to improve their Secret City. There are close calls—near-miss run-ins with the gang members, the always-dangerous dogs, and a fearful moment when Moon's uncle, Tio Chico, uncovers their secret. But the space remains theirs, and the boys have something very special together.

Naturally, it has to end someday. The time comes when one of the gang members follows Louie, despite his caution, to the Secret City. The gang member, in turn, is followed by the police. One of them discovers the garden behind the house and realizes someone must be living on the property. It looks like Secret City, U.S.A., will be lost.

But luck turns up in the person of their friend Marie Lorry, a social counselor, and her friend Pete, a reporter. Suddenly, Benno and his friends are front-page news. Newspaper articles tell the story of eight young boys trying to make a better world for themselves in a deserted, devastated part of the city. The articles call them pioneers. Benno is delighted.

The boys cannot stay in their private space. They must return to their families. Homeless Willie will not return to the streets, however. Louie is going south with his mother, and Willie will become part of their family.

Marie Lorry tells them a private commission has been set up. The whole Secret City area is going to be rebuilt. The city-owned derelict buildings will be restored for low-income families like Benno's. It looks as though, in the near future, Benno is going to have that private space he so desperately wants.

Marie says the new commission needs a name. Because Benno and

Moon discovered the area, they should get to name it. Since it isn't a secret anymore, they can't call it Secret City, U.S.A.

Benno and Moon agree: It will be called "JoJo's Space."

Thematic Material

This is a compassionate story of a sensitive young boy and his friends growing up in the harsh world of the barrio. They are tough and street smart, but their yearnings for security and a sense of home are real and ring true. The outcome may seem improbable in the harsh reality of today's cities, but young readers will understand the pride and love Benno and Moon feel for the private space they have created. Their Secret City, U.S.A., will be cheered by every youngster who has ever yearned for a room or a space of his or her own.

Book Talk Material

The discovery of the deserted area and the boys' attempt to make it into a home will serve as good introductions to this warm story of hope in the barrio. See: Benno and Moon wander into the wasteland and become pioneers (pp. 17–20); they enter the house (pp. 29–34); Willie joins the group (p. 53); Juan digs a garden (pp. 65–67); and Benno wonders about letting Louie in on the secret (pp. 68–73).

Additional Selections

A group of black teenagers in New York City become the owners of a rundown slum building in Walter Dean Myers's *The Young Landlords* (pap., Puffin, 1989, $4.99).

A lonely middle-aged man living in a hotel for men in New York City finds a restaurant that gives him promise of having his dreams come true in Cynthia Rylant's *An Angel for Solomon Singer* (Orchard, 1992, $14.95).

A novice magician overcomes an alcoholic father and a taunting classmate in Bjarne Reuter's *Buster's World* (Dutton, 1989, $12.95).

Eleven-year-old Clay is forced to live on the streets of New York after his mother disappears from their hotel room in Paula Fox's *Monkey Island* (Orchard, 1991, $14.95).

Twelve-year-old Louise finds out her friend Bean shoplifts, but she realizes this is partly due to the pressures of poverty, in Elizabeth Wild's *Along Came a Blackbird* (Harper, 1988, $10.89).

The Diary of LaToya Hunter: My First Year in Junior High (Crown, 1992,

$16), by LaToya Hunter, is the actual diary of a twelve-year-old girl growing up in the Bronx, New York, and facing the problems of inner-city life.

The loss of the father's job forces a family to move to a smaller apartment and puts ten-year-old Callie in charge of her six-year-old brother in Susan Terris's *The Latchkey Kids* (Farrar, 1986, $15).

About the Book

Book Report, November 1990, p. 44.
Booklist, May 1, 1990, p. 1704.
Horn Book, May 1990, p. 335.
Horn Book Guide, January 1990, p. 249.
Kirkus Reviews, April 15, 1990, p. 577.
School Library Journal, April 1990, p. 140.
VOYA, June 1990, p. 104.
Wilson Library Bulletin, March 1991, p. 13.
See also *Book Review Digest,* 1990, p. 841; and *Book Review Index,* 1990, p. 377; 1991, p. 424.

About the Author

Chevalier, Tracy, ed., *Twentieth-Century Children's Writers* (3rd ed.). St. James, 1989, pp. 464–465.
Commire, Anne, ed., *Something about the Author.* Gale, 1975, pp. 131–132.
de Montreville, Doris, and Crawford, Elizabeth D., eds., *Fourth Book of Junior Authors and Illustrators.* Wilson, 1978, pp. 182–183.
Evory, Ann, ed., *Contemporary Authors* (First Revision Series). Gale, 1981, Vol. 3, pp. 280–281.
Kirkpatrick, D. L., ed., *Twentieth-Century Children's Writers* (3rd ed.). St. Martin's, 1983, p. 386.
Metzger, Linda, and Straub, Deborah A., eds., *Contemporary Authors* (New Revision Series). Gale, 1986, Vol. 18, pp. 231–232.
Ward, Martha, ed., *Authors of Books for Young People* (3rd ed.). Scarecrow, 1990, p. 344.

Hughes, Dean. *Honestly, Myron*
Macmillan, 1982, o.p.

Dean Hughes is perhaps best known in the area of children's literature for his many books featuring Nutty Nutshell. In *Nutty for President* (pap., Bantam, 1986, $2.50), a wheeler-dealer named William Bilks takes charge of the fifth-grade election in which Nutty is involved, and in *Nutty Knows*

All (Macmillan, 1988, $13.95; pap., $3.95), Nutty gets caught up in an amazing science experiment that results in his head glowing in the dark. On the more serious side, *Family Pose* (Macmillan, 1989, $14.95) is a novel set in Seattle that tells of a runaway, eleven-year-old David, who is discovered sleeping in the hall of a hotel and is helped by a reformed alcoholic who is also the night bellboy. *Honestly, Myron* returns to the more lighthearted mood of most of this author's works. In it, Myron and his teacher, Mr. McEnelly, express such shock at the way Lustre Bright tells lies that Myron takes a vow to tell the truth at all times and at all costs. This, in turn, causes great havoc and hilarity. It is a novel enjoyed by readers in grades 4 through 7.

Plot Summary

Eleven-year-old Myron Singleton can't understand why someone doesn't do something about Lustre Bright in his fifth-grade class. The girl is simply a liar; she tells the most outrageous stories. Surely anyone can see that, even the teacher, Mr. McEnelly, who is only a year or two out of college and doesn't seem to know how to handle much of anything.

One day, Lustre finally goes too far and actually embarrasses Mr. McEnelly in front of the whole class. His reaction is to go see the school principal, Mrs. Kendall, and he asks Myron to go along to prove his point about Lustre's stories. Myron is terrified of Mrs. Kendall, and she, it turns out, is not thrilled with having Myron brought into her office to talk about the tall stories told by one Lustre Bright. Mrs. Kendall tends to think Lustre is just imaginative. Myron knows better.

Mr. McEnelly doesn't get far with Mrs. Kendall, but he seems determined to cure Lustre of her tall stories. Lincoln's birthday is coming up, and this seems a perfect time to make a dramatic presentation to the class, pointing out the qualities of Honest Abe. Mr. McEnelly is hoping to impress Lustre, but instead impresses Myron. He impresses him so much that Myron, as though determined to make up for a lifetime of fibs and fabrications, vows that he will never again tell a lie. He will be as great a man as Honest Abe. Maybe he, Myron Singleton, will even grow up to be president.

Even with such noble intentions, Myron runs into trouble right away, at the dinner table that night with his father and mother. His parents agree that he should always be truthful, but they aren't thrilled when Myron reports that his father sometimes tells Myron not to mention certain things to his mother. And his mother isn't pleased when Myron tells his father the truth about his mother running over the bike with the car . . . and on it goes.

Myron isn't exactly satisfied with his first encounter with the whole truth, but he vows to continue his honesty quest at school the next day. That doesn't go so well either. When he tells Marilyn Barber that most kids don't like her because she's too sarcastic she plops him right down on the wet ground.

Then Myron gets in hot water with none other than Mr. McEnelly, who started this whole honesty business in the first place. Mr. McEnelly seems to feel Myron doesn't know the difference between honesty and unkindness. So, there's another visit to the school principal. Mrs. Kendall doesn't mince words. She tells Myron he needs to learn to keep his mouth shut and just say nothing sometimes.

Myron isn't convinced.

All in all, despite some setbacks, Myron still feels pretty good about his honesty kick. That night in his room, he listens to a local radio station, and is amazed to hear Mrs. Kendall and others talking about a coming bond issue to build a new elementary school. Mrs. Kendall says how crowded the classrooms are and she warns that if the bond issue isn't passed by the voters, the school will be in crisis.

Well, Myron is shocked. Sure, a couple of the classrooms are crowded, but not all of them, and there's not the crisis that Mrs. Kendall is painting. Myron knows how to straighten this out. He calls the radio station, announces himself, and tells them Mrs. Kendall is wrong. He also tells the station that although someone said the Riv-u-let Rivet Company will be coming to town and opening up lots of new jobs, thereby causing the school population to grow, Myron heard from his own father, who does business with Riv-u-let, that the company isn't coming to town at all.

Things certainly get into a turmoil after that. Not only is everyone now on Myron's case—including the principal, who doesn't relish being called a liar; and his own father, who is, to say the least, furious—but the local television station invites him to be their guest.

A big meeting is called with Myron, his parents, and the principal. They try to make Myron understand that, perhaps, honesty has to be used with a little discretion. Myron doesn't see it their way. Mrs. Kendall tells him that when he goes on television—because, of course, they have to let him go on—he's to use a little discretion. He doesn't have to lie, just use some discretion. Myron says he understands.

Myron does try to be discreet, at the same time telling the truth. It isn't easy. Somehow, he tells the television interviewer how his parents and the principal told him to think before he speaks and that it would have been better if he had shut up in the first place because the bond issue just had to be passed and even Mrs. Kendall said that Abraham Lincoln probably stretched the truth sometimes . . . .

The upshot is that Mrs. Kendall has to make a speech defending the honesty of Abraham Lincoln—she never, as Myron seemed to indicate, said the president was a habitual liar.

Myron even gets on the national news. The school bond issue doesn't pass, and Myron knows he's to blame. It seems being honest is just a whole lot more complicated than he had thought.

But Myron feels better after the local newspaper editor writes an editorial about how Myron's statements had made the voters mad and caused them to reject the bond issue. However, the editor sees valid reasons for supporting the bond. He tells the voters that if they all look at the issue with an unbiased eye, as Myron did, perhaps they'll vote for it next time.

Wouldn't you know Lustre Bright would have the last word in class, though? She tells everybody she always knew Myron would be a hero because one day he saved her life when a great big black car pulled up in front of the playground and two guys got out and you could see bulges under their coats where their guns were strapped . . . . Myron just gazes out of the window.

Thematic Material

This is a humorous look at how children can sometimes take an adult's words in a most literal way. Myron is perhaps more stubborn and headstrong than most in his decision to plunge ahead with his honesty at all costs. But the story does illustrate the sometimes bewildering mixed messages that grownups can convey to children by the incongruities of their words and actions.

Book Talk Material

Is it always a good thing to tell the whole truth? The following incidents showing how Myron reacted to certain situations with total honesty can stimulate answers to that question. See: Myron confronts his parents with true tales at the dinner table (pp. 34–43); Myron tells Marilyn what her classmates think of her (pp. 44–48); Myron and Mr. McEnelly get into an honesty debate (pp. 52–56); Myron calls the radio show (pp. 73–80); and Myron goes on television (pp. 125–129).

Additional Selections

Felicia, the brash, tactless heroine of Ellen Conford's *Felicia the Critic* (Little, Brown, 1973, $14.95; pap., $4.95; condensed in *Introducing More Books,* Bowker, 1978, pp. 4–7), gets into trouble both at home and at school because she doesn't know when the truth can hurt.

When Harriet's secret notebook is discovered with her candid remarks on her friends, problems about honesty are raised in Louise Fitzhugh's *Harriet the Spy* (Harper, 1964, $14.95; pap., Dell, $3.50). A sequel is *The Long Secret* (Harper, 1965, $13.95; pap., Dell, $3.50).

Hobie Hanson's fourth-grade class goes on a camping trip for three days in a story of how youngsters learn to live together, *4B Goes Wild* (Lothrop, 1983, $12.95; pap., Pocket, $2.95) by Jamie Gilson. There are several other Hobie Hanson books available, including *Sticks and Stones and Skeleton Bones* (Lothrop, 1991, $12.95), where Hobie, now in the fifth grade, has a fight with his best friend.

Ivy decides to save the twenty-seven-pound lobster that her father, who owns a fish market, plans to raffle off in Nancy Buss's *The Lobster and Ivy Higgins* (St. Martin's, 1992, $13.95).

Fourth-grader Sam can't control his big dog, Wally, who has just been tossed out of obedience school in Alison Cragin Herzig's *The Big Deal* (Viking, 1992, $13.50).

Herbie helps Raymond conquer his fear of reading in front of an audience in exchange for Raymond helping Herbie with his fear of sleeping in a cobwebby attic in Suzy Kline's *Herbie Jones and the Dark Attic* (Putnam, 1992, $14.95).

In part of a popular series by Carolyn Haywood, lovable Eddie gets a job in a pet shop in *Eddie's Menagerie* (Morrow, 1978, $12.88).

About the Book

Booklist, June 1, 1982, p. 1312.
Kirkus Reviews, April 15, 1982, p. 489.
School Library Journal, August 1982, p. 117.
See also *Book Review Index,* 1982, p. 254.

About the Author

Commire, Anne., ed., *Something about the Author.* Gale, 1983, Vol. 33, pp. 99–100.
Holtze, Sally Holmes, ed., *Sixth Book of Junior Authors and Illustrators.* Wilson, 1989, pp. 139–140.
Locher, Frances C., *Contemporary Authors.* Gale, 1982, Vol. 106, pp. 257–258.

Straub, Deborah A., ed., *Contemporary Authors* (New Revision Series). Gale, 1988, Vol. 22, pp. 212–213.
Ward, Martha, ed., *Authors of Books for Young Readers* (3rd ed.). Scarecrow, 1990, p. 353.

Little, Jean. *Different Dragons*

Viking, 1987, $14.95 (0-670-80836-9); pap., Puffin, $3.95 (0-14-031998-0)

Canadian writer Jean Little has produced a number of excellent books for middle-grade readers, many dealing with children who must adjust to physical handicaps. The author herself has limited vision but even as a youngster refused to be treated as blind and, instead, chose to enroll in regular schools. Her first novel, *Mine for Keeps* (pap., Little, Brown, 1962, $4.95), tells of the fears of Sally Copeland, a victim of cerebral palsy, who must leave the sheltered environment of a special school and return home to live where she will attend a public school. In *From Anna* (Harper, 1972, $14.89; pap., $3.95), a young girl moves with her family from oppression in her native Germany to Canada, where it is discovered that a vision problem is causing her awkwardness and inability to perform many tasks. This story is continued in *Listen for the Singing* (Harper, 1991, $14.89; pap., $3.95). *Different Dragons* tells about a young boy—probably age seven or eight—and his attempts to conquer such fears as facing a large dog and leaving home for a weekend. Although most of Jean Little's novels are for readers in grades 4 through 7, this one is suitable for a slightly younger audience, grades 3 through 5.

Plot Summary

Benjamin Tucker hates to admit it, but he is afraid of things—lots of things, like thunderstorms, and animals, and strange people and places. That's why he is so upset about this coming weekend. His father is driving him to Aunt Rose's from their home in Vancouver. His parents are going to a weekend conference, and his older brother, Jimmy, is going to visit a friend. So Ben has to stay with Aunt Rose, all the way from Friday until Sunday, when the family will come for him. He doesn't think he can last that long. He doesn't even know Aunt Rose. Jimmy says she is terrible.

On the drive to Aunt Rose's house, Ben tries to tell his father how he feels, but he just starts to cry, and his father tells him to grow up.

When they get to the house, Ben has to admit that Aunt Rose doesn't really seem so bad. She acts kind of friendly, in fact. She even asks what he'd like for supper that night. They have Ben's favorite food—spaghetti. And he is going to sleep in a bunk bed. Things are looking up.

That is, until Aunt Rose pulls out her surprise. It arrives at 7:30 that evening. Ben can't believe his eyes when a great big enormous gigantic cream-colored Labrador retriever puppy with floppy ears comes bounding into the house. His name is Gully—short for Gulliver Gallivant—and Ben thinks he is the biggest thing he's ever seen.

Aunt Rose apologizes for not telling him about the surprise. She hadn't realized he was that frightened of dogs. She puts Gully in the kitchen, figuring Ben will get used to the friendly dog in a little while. But Ben knows he won't. Not ever.

Ben can't imagine he will ever get to sleep that night, but he does. When he wakes up, he thinks, "It's Saturday morning and tomorrow Mom and Dad will come for me." Then he hears a whack-whack-whack and opens his eyes. Gully is right beside his bed! Ben just freezes in terror.

Aunt Rose rescues him and then takes him on a tour of the house, where she and his father grew up. There is a trapdoor attic, which intrigues Ben. It kind of frightens him to think about the darkness and cobwebs up there, but maybe there is hidden treasure too!

The weekend seems longer than ever when Ben discovers his aunt doesn't own a television. He can't believe it. What will he do all day? Aunt Rose seems to think he might make friends with the girl next door, even though she is a little older than Ben. Her name is Hana Uchida, and her family is from Japan. She turns out to be not only older but taller than Ben, and besides that, she loves dogs and is very self-assured about everything.

Ben finally has to admit to Hana that he doesn't like dogs; he doesn't tell her he's afraid of them. She tells him he's in for trouble, because Gully is supposed to be a birthday present.

Aunt Rose is understanding about that too. She did plan to give Gully to Ben as a birthday present, but if he is really afraid of dogs, then perhaps his brother, Jimmy, will like him.

Just to make things worse, a thunderstorm blows in. Ben is really afraid of thunderstorms. He gets under his bunk to hide from his fright, only to discover he has company. Gully is afraid too.

It takes some bravery on his part, but Ben begins to understand that Gully really is frightened, and he tries to reassure the quivering animal. By the time the storm is over, Gully is Ben's devoted slave. But Ben isn't changing his mind—never!

When Aunt Rose has to go out for a while that afternoon, Ben decides to tackle the mystery of the trapdoor. After a few games of fetch with Gully just to keep the dog away, Ben gets the ladder for the attic. Just as he's about to embark on his adventure, who comes in but Hana!

Ben is angry that she is intruding on his adventure, and the two have an argument. Hana accuses him of being a big sucky baby because he is afraid of Gully, no matter what he says.

Well, I'll show her, Ben decides. And he leads her to the trapdoor and tells her what he is going to do. That's when he realizes even people like Hana—who seems so confident about everything—have fears of their own. Hana is terrified of climbing the ladder into the attic.

But with Ben's coaching, she agrees to try. He goes up first and opens the trapdoor, then urges Hana to climb the ladder. As she does, a rung breaks. Ben catches her and drags her into the attic. They are both safe—but now they are both stuck in the dark attic. Hana starts to cry, and Ben tells her not to be such a big baby.

It's a long afternoon until Aunt Rose comes home, and no one hears the children screaming for help. But when Aunt Rose enters the house, Gully leads her to the trapdoor.

Ben and Hana are rescued, and Gully seems pretty proud of himself.

The next day when Ben's parents come for him, they find a strange sight. Ben and Gully are playing ball together. His father can't believe it.

"Looks like you've slain a dragon," Ben's father says.

Ben just decides to play it cool. "He's not a dragon," Ben tells his father. "He's my birthday present."

Thematic Material

A gentle, thoughtful story that realistically portrays the real and imagined fears of childhood. Although Ben seems young for his age, his terrors are frighteningly real to him, and bit by bit he strives to overcome them, which he does in believable fashion. The story develops a nice lesson in understanding that different people have different fears, and a friendly hand can always help overcome them.

Book Talk Material

The things Ben fears can spark a discussion of childhood fears that many young readers may share. See: Ben worries about the upcoming weekend with an aunt he doesn't know (pp. 3–8); Ben meets Gully and hides behind his aunt (pp. 23–25); the thunderstorm (pp. 55–63); Ben discovers Hana's fear (pp. 95–102).

Additional Selections

Dana tries to prove to everyone that she is not a coward in Susan Beth Pfeffer's *Courage, Dana* (pap., Dell, 1984, $2.75).

Eight-year-old Sophie has a best friend who is manipulated by the class bully into telling Sophie's secrets in *Tell Me Your Best Thing* (Dutton, 1991, $13.95) by Anna Grossnickle Hines.

When her best friend moves to California, nine-year-old Polly's life in rural Vermont goes wrong in Mary Stolz's *Ferris Wheel* (Harper, 1977, $12.89).

Sophie is saving all her money to buy a stuffed hedgehog until she sees a homeless beggar in the streets in *Sophie and the Sidewalk Man* (Four Winds, 1992, $12.95) by Stephanie S. Tolan.

Sydney Taylor's *All-of-a-Kind Family* (Taylor, 1951, $11.95; pap., Dell, $3.50) and its many sequels take an affectionate look at a loving Jewish family on Manhattan's Lower East Side early in the century.

Just Like Jenny (Delacorte, 1982, $12.95; pap., Dell, $2.50) by Sandy Asher is the story of two girls, their friendship, and their ballet training.

Through their friendship with a lonely old neighbor, Otis and Will learn that their mother really cares about them in Lisa Fosburgh's *Mrs. Abercorn and the Bunce Boys* (Macmillan, 1986, $12.95; pap., Dell, $2.75).

About the Book

Booklist, June 1, 1987, p. 1523.
Center for Children's Books Bulletin, July 1987, p. 214.
Emergency Librarian, March 1987, p. 28.
Kirkus Reviews, April 15, 1987, p. 642.
School Library Journal, June 1987, p. 98.
See also *Book Review Digest,* 1987, p. 1139; and *Book Review Index,* 1987, p. 469.

About the Author

Chevalier, Tracy, ed., *Twentieth-Century Children's Writers* (3rd ed.). St. James, 1989, pp. 598–600.
Commire, Anne, ed., *Something about the Author.* Gale, 1971, Vol. 2, pp. 178–179.
de Montreville, Doris, and Crawford, Elizabeth A., eds., *Fourth Book of Junior Authors and Illustrators.* Wilson, 1978, pp. 228–229.
Kirkpatrick, D. L., ed., *Twentieth-Century Children's Writers* (3rd ed.). St. Martin's, 1983, pp. 487–488.
Nasso, Christine, ed., *Contemporary Authors* (New Revision Series). Gale, 1977, Vols. 21–24, pp. 541–542.
Olendorf, Donna, ed., *Something about the Author.* Gale, 1992, Vol. 68, pp. 139–143.
Senick, Gerard J., ed., *Children's Literature Review.* Gale, 1982, Vol. 4, pp. 146–154.
Ward, Martha, ed., *Authors of Books for Young People* (3rd ed.). Scarecrow, 1990, p. 443.

Petersen, P. J. *Liars*
Simon & Schuster, 1992, $14 (0-671-75035-6)

P. J. Petersen's first book for young readers was *Would You Settle for Improbable?* (Delacorte, 1981, $8.95; pap., Dell, $3.25; condensed in *Juniorplots 3,* Bowker, 1987, pp. 94–98). In a junior-high setting, it tells how a substitute teacher asks Michael Parker and his two best friends to help her rehabilitate a known delinquent. When one of the boys says it is an impossible task, she counters with, "Would you settle for improbable?" It is followed by a sequel, *Here's to the Sophomores* (Delacorte, 1984, $13.95; pap., Dell, $2.50). In these books, as in *Liars,* the author uses northern California, where he lives, as a background setting. *Liars* tells the story of fourteen-year-old Sam who, along with discovering he has the ability to dowse—that is, locate underground water—he finds he knows when someone is not telling the truth. This amazing aptitude, plus a baffling mystery set in a remote area, are two elements that lead to an exciting plot, which also contains an interesting comment on family relationships. These books are enjoyed by readers in grades 5 through 9.

Plot Summary

Sam's friend Marty describes their hometown of Alder Creek in northern California as SOT and MOTSOT (Same Old Thing and More of the Same Old Thing). Even Sam admits Alder Creek is pretty much off the beaten path. It's about a two-hour drive from the nearest town, the school has one room, and Sam and Marty constitute the entire eighth grade. Even so, they have a bigger class than another friend of Sam's—Carmen *is* the seventh grade.

Things liven up a little for Sam and Marty and Carmen when the whole school goes on a field trip. They head out to Uncle Gene Gaither's place to do a little dowsing, which Uncle Gene refers to as water witching. Out in the pasture, Uncle Gene urges the kids to try to find water with his forked stick. None of them can until Sam tries. Right away the stick starts bobbing up and down like it has a mind of its own. Uncle Gene says Sam has the "gift."

Dr. Vincent snorts at the "gift" and tells Sam dowsing has no basis in scientific fact. But Dr. Vincent *would* say that. He has a degree in biology, wears walking shorts, and is the closest thing to a medical doctor in Alder

Creek. He is also chairman of the school board and head of the volunteer fire department. He would have been mayor if Alder Creek had a mayor.

Sam doesn't know if dowsing is for real or if he has the "gift," but he does know he gets a kind of tingling sensation up and down his arms whenever anyone lies to him. That's annoying enough, but what's worse, Sam finds out that everyone lies! He keeps getting the tingling sensations when almost anyone talks to him. Everyone in their tiny town is a liar; they lie about the smallest things. Sam can't believe it. Worse than that, Sam discovers that even his own father lies to him!

Sam and his father have lived alone since Sam's mother died in a car accident two years before. It has been hard to adjust to her death, made more difficult by the fact that Sam and his father never talk about it. Not at all.

Sometime later, the boys meet Uncle Gene again. The old man tells them he is about to get one hundred dollars, which he will use for a real hunt for the Barkley Mine. No one in town but Uncle Gene believes that old tale of the Barkley Mine, supposedly filled with gold. But where is the hundred dollars coming from? He confides in the boys that he has run across a patch of marijuana planted illegally out by Fisher Peak, taken Polaroid pictures of it, and reported it to the authorities. The reward is one hundred dollars. Uncle Gene expects the sheriff to be out to check it the next day. Then he'll get his money and be off to find the gold mine.

Sam and Marty just smile.

Over the next few days, Sam's "gift" continues to bug him. He keeps getting little surges: Mr. Lopez isn't telling the truth about his mother-in-law; Jenny Cavalo lies about her horse doing tricks. Sam begins to wonder if there is such a thing as an honest person. Uncle Gene wonders when he is going to get his money. The authorities keep saying they have to investigate. In the meantime, he mysteriously "wins" fifty dollars from some company to go off on a free trip to Reno. Uncle Gene doesn't want to go; he thinks the whole thing sounds fishy. Sam agrees.

Things become even more suspicious when Sam and Marty go fishing and discover two flat tires on the brush buggy—deliberately flattened. Next, someone burglarizes Uncle Gene's cabin and finally sets fire to it. What's going on in Alder Creek?

Sam talks to his father about Uncle Gene and asks who would want to hurt him. Are they after the maps of the Barkley Mine that Uncle Gene keeps talking about? Sam says Uncle Gene told Dr. Vincent about the maps and that he has a secret partner who is paying him for a share of what he finds in the mine. Sam's father just shrugs and says everyone has to have a dream. During the conversation, Sam gets the old familiar tingling in his arms; his father is lying about something.

After the fire the townspeople get together and move an abandoned trailer to Uncle Gene's land for his new home. When the boys go to the trailer to check on Uncle Gene he is not there. After some searching, they find him tied up in an old mine shaft. Someone is out to get him.

Sam runs for help. When he returns with his father and others, they find Marty has been tied up too, but is unhurt. He didn't see the man who did it.

Uncle Gene turns up at Sam's house later and asks to stay the night because he is sure someone is watching his trailer. He brings an envelope with him. Later, Sam discovers the envelope contains old maps and photocopies that he has seen a dozen times before.

A mysterious phone caller tells Sam that Carmen has been kidnapped and that he had better bring the envelope he is hiding for Uncle Gene right away. Even though Sam knows his father has been lying to him, he tells him what has happened. With his father's help, Sam delivers the envelope and discovers that the kidnapping threat is a hoax and the mysterious voice belongs to none other than Dr. Vincent!

In the end the mystery is unraveled. In the envelope with Uncle Gene's famous maps are the Polaroid pictures he took of the illegal marijuana field. The pictures also show a stainless steel walking stick—Dr. Vincent's! He is the one who planted the marijuana and the one behind the mysterious mishaps at Uncle Gene's cabin. Dr. Vincent wanted to scare the old man and recover the evidence against himself. Instead, he's off to the county jail.

Another mystery is unraveled when Sam discovers Uncle Gene's silent partner is none other than his own father, and that's what his father has been "telling lies" about. He didn't want anyone to know he has been giving Uncle Gene money to live under the guise of being a partner in the dream gold mine.

Life settles down in Alder Creek. Sam still ponders the little white lies people tell and mostly he just tries to ignore the tingling sensation when it happens. And he and his father finally get out pictures of his mother and talk about missing her. Uncle Gene goes off hunting for the mine. Sam hopes he finds it after all. Maybe that way he and Marty can get a trip out of SOT and MOTSOT.

Thematic Material

This is a nice picture of life in a very rural community. Sam, Marty, and Carmen are typical youngsters who love their country home, although they realize its shortcomings and even dream one day of seeing other worlds. Sam's dilemma about people telling "white lies" is well drawn. As Marty says, "Everybody lies about fish." Sam begins to realize that perhaps there are good lies and bad lies, and if his "gift" doesn't allow him to know which is which, what good is it? Marty has his own answer; he says he believes everybody, even liars. This story is also a pleasing look into people helping each other in times of need.

Book Talk Material

Sam's confusion over his "gift" and his reactions to people's lies will serve as a good introduction to this light mystery. See: Sam tries water witching (pp. 6–9); Sam can tell that the stranger in town is lying (pp. 20–21); Sam realizes even Carmen has lied to him (pp. 27–28); Sam and Marty discuss the "gift" (pp. 35–39); Sam can't believe his own father is telling a lie (pp. 60–61).

Additional Selections

In Alfred Slote's emotional story about family relationships, *The Trading Game* (Harper, 1990, $14.89; pap. $3.95), Andy Harris, a baseball card collector, wants a card that shows his grandfather.

Four youngsters build a boat to use at Coney Island, New York, in *The Alfred Summer* (Macmillan, 1980, $13.95; pap., Scholastic, $2.50) by Jan Slepian.

Set in a remote part of Alaska, Walt Morey's *Gentle Ben* (Dutton, 1965, $12.95; pap., Avon, $2.95; condensed in *More Juniorplots*, Bowker, 1977, pp. 220–223) tells the story of the friendship between a boy and an outcast bear.

In Ivan Southall's *Rachel* (Farrar, 1986, $14), Rachel and Eddie get lost in a deserted mining area in rural Australia.

David faces danger when he tries to find his younger brother who has wandered off in search of a phantom dog in *Blair's Nightmare* (Macmillan, 1984, $12.95; pap., Dell, $3.25) by Zilpha Keatley Snyder.

In Eva-Lis Wuorio's *Detour to Danger* (Delacorte, 1984, $12.95; pap., Dell, $2.95), Nando and his friend uncover a terrorist plot while on a trip to Spain.

About the Book

Booklist, June 1, 1992, p. 1754.
Kirkus Reviews, July 1, 1992, p. 852.
School Library Journal, April 1992, p. 119.
VOYA, October 1992, p. 228.

About the Author

Commire, Anne, ed., *Something about the Author.* Gale, 1986, Vol. 43, p. 186; Vol. 48, pp. 179–181.
Holtze, Sally Holmes, ed., *Sixth Book of Junior Authors and Illustrators.* Wilson, 1989, pp. 221–222.
May, Hal, ed., *Contemporary Authors.* Gale, 1985, Vol. 112, p. 395.

Rylant, Cynthia. *Missing May*

Orchard, 1992, $12.99 (0-531-08596-1)

In the few years she has been writing books for young people, Cynthia Rylant has scored an amazing success at various reading levels. For the primary ages, she has written several prize-winning texts for picture books, including two Caldecott Honor books and a charming series of Henry and Mudge books about a boy named Henry, his dog, Mudge, and their many adventures in everyday situations. For middle-grade readers, she has two excellent collections of short stories. The first, *Children of Christmas* (1987, Watts, $11.99), consists of six quiet but poignant stories about emotions evoked during Christmas time. The second, *Every Living Thing* (Macmillan, 1985, $12.95; pap. $3.50), contains twelve sentimental stories about people whose lives have changed because of their association with animals. Her books of poetry include *Waiting to Waltz: A Childhood* (Macmillan, 1984, $12.95), a collection of thirty poems about growing up in a small town in Appalachia. Among her novels are *A Blue-Eyed Daisy* (Macmillan, 1985, $11.95; pap., Dell, $3.25), about the sad and troubled world of Ellie, age eleven, and simple but important episodes that take place during the year in which she approaches adolescence. Peter, the thirteen-year-old hero of *A Fine White Dust* (Macmillan, 1986, $13.95; pap., Dell, $3.50; condensed in *Introducing Bookplots 3,* Bowker, 1990, pp. 230–234), is a deeply religious boy who faces a personal crisis when the traveling Preacher Man first mesmerizes him with his evangelical powers and then cruelly rejects him. The title refers to a crumbling ceramic cross with white dust that Peter owns. *Missing May,* winner of the 1993 Newbery Medal, although a brief novel, contains a deep emotional message in its ninety pages. It is narrated by its central character, a twelve-year-old girl named Summer. All three of these novels are suitable for readers in grades 5 through 8.

Plot Summary

Summer's mother died when she was just a baby, and her life has been a succession of stays with different relatives around the state of Ohio until one day, when she is six, she meets elderly Aunt May and Uncle Ob, who are visiting from West Virginia. They offer to adopt Summer and take her back with them to their home in Deep Water. For the next six years, Summer's life is filled with a love and affection she never knew existed.

May and Ob are poor. They live in a rusty old trailer perched on a mountainside, surrounded by a garden that May cultivates religiously. Ob, a tall scarecrow of a man, is a disabled war veteran who spends his time building whirligigs, actually pieces of delicate sculpture with names like Fire and Love. They are stored on shelves inside the trailer, and when the overhead fan is turned on, the trailer becomes magically alive with a maze of beautiful spinning objects. May and Ob love one another so wholly and completely that Summer thinks it is a miracle that they still have enough left over for her. But they do. May, who is best at articulating their feelings, tells Summer over and over again that they regard her as a gift from above to brighten their declining years and that, like all precious gifts, she must be cherished and cared for with both devotion and love. For Summer, May becomes the symbol of all that is good, unselfish, and kind in this world.

When Summer is twelve and in the seventh grade, the impossible occurs. While working in her garden, May suddenly dies. Somehow, neither Summer nor Ob can accept the fact that their loving May is gone. After the funeral, when all the relatives have returned home, the two are left alone in the quiet of their lonely trailer. Ob begins living a trancelike existence, too numb to grieve, and Summer, herself hurting from her loss, is alarmed at this decline but powerless to help.

The arrival of Cletus Underwood in their lives about three months after May's death provides an unusual diversion. Cletus is a classmate of Summer's who everyone considers to be odd bordering on eccentric. His passion for collecting objects started with potato chip bags, passed through stages involving spoons and buttons, and is now focused on pictures he retrieves chiefly from old magazines and newspapers and saves in a battered suitcase. One day, Ob sees him in their old car searching for newspapers, and, much to Summer's distress, invites him into the house. Ob finds Cletus and his pictures fascinating, but to Summer he is a kook to be tolerated only because he diverts Ob's mind from thoughts of May. Cletus begins visiting fairly regularly.

One day when Ob and Summer are in the garden, Ob straightens up suddenly, claiming he has felt May's presence. He is so puzzled and excited by this mystical experience that he talks of getting a spiritual adviser to help him communicate with her. When Cletus tells how he once had an amazing out-of-body experience and saw dead relatives when he was on the verge of drowning, Ob elicits his help. The three stand out one cold February afternoon, and while Ob tells stories of May's many wonderful qualities, all pray for some sign of her presence. Time passes and nothing happens. Finally, Ob slouches back to the trailer.

Ob's depression and lethargy increase to the point where he oversleeps and roams about the trailer during the day in his pajamas. The amazing Cletus comes up with another idea. He produces a clipping from a six-month-old newspaper announcing the services of the Reverend Miriam B. Conklin, who calls herself a Small Medium at Large, at the Spiritualist Church in Glen Meadows, a town some three hours away by car, and suggests they visit her for help. Ob becomes excited at the prospect of reaching May via the Reverend Conklin, and plans are made to drive to Glen Meadows, spend the night at a motel, and return by way of the state capital, Charleston, where they will tour the public buildings that Cletus, in particular, is anxious to visit. Ob and Summer visit Cletus's parents to ask their permission to take the boy with them. Summer has become increasing fond of the strange youngster and his unusual insights into human feelings, and when she meets his loving parents and sees how proud they are of their son and his unusual gifts, her affection for him grows.

When they reach Glen Meadow, a further disappointment awaits them. They are told at the church that the Reverend died some months before and that there is no one who can help them. Crushed and dejected, Ob decides to return immediately to Deep Water. Minutes seem like hours as they drive in silence. After they pass the exit to Charleston, suddenly Ob turns the car around and happily announces they will tour the capital after all. In that miraculous moment, through his love for Summer, he has finally accepted May's death and the necessity of continuing his life.

When they return to the trailer after a wonderful visit in Charleston, Summer now feels free to grieve for May. She sobs uncontrollably while Ob holds her close to him. Finally the morning arrives, bringing with it consolation, release, and hope. Together, Ob and Summer take Ob's whirligigs out of the trailer and into May's garden, where they fill it with movement and the spirit of life.

Thematic Material

This is a novel not only about accepting death and about the process of grieving but also about the need to care for people, because they are all that is important in this world. This sense of caring proves to be the salvation of both Ob and Summer. In its simple style, sly humor, and depth of perception, this multilayered novel speaks forcefully about values, the nature of love and friendship, families, and the power of love to overcome loss.

Book Talk Material

Some important passages that could be used in a booktalk are: Summer's first night in the trailer (pp. 5–8); Ob feels May's presence (pp. 11–14); introducing Cletus (pp. 17–18); Cletus shows Summer one of his newest acquisitions (pp. 25–27); Cletus tells of his near-death experience (pp. 28–32); Ob, Cletus, and Summer try to reach May's spirit (pp. 33–37); and Ob and Summer visit Cletus's parents (pp. 60–66).

Additional Selections

Ten-year-old Jesse must adjust to the death of his friend, Leslie, in Katherine Paterson's touching *Bridge to Terabithia* (Harper, 1987, $13.89; pap., $3.50; condensed in *Introducing More Books,* Bowker, 1978, pp. 38–40).

In Barbara Garland Polikoff's *Life's a Funny Proposition, Horatio* (Holt, 1992, $13.95), a twelve-year-old boy tries to understand the meaning of life while recovering from the death of his father.

A young loner meets a couple who change her life in Vera Cleaver and Bill Cleaver's *Hazel Rye* (pap., Harper, 1985, $3.95).

In Carole S. Adler's *Split Sisters* (Macmillan, 1986, $10.95; pap., $3.95), Mother leaves Manhattan, taking one daughter with her and leaving the other to stay with her stepfather.

A family is brought together with a new sense of love and unity after the death of their baby in *A Family Project* (Macmillan, 1988, $13.95; pap., Dell, $3.25) by Sarah Ellis.

After her grandmother dies, the life of Flora, a twelve-year-old girl, is further disrupted when a family of distant relatives move in, in Emily Rhoads Johnson's *A House Full of Strangers* (Dutton, 1992, $14).

Seriously troubled following his brother's death, Andrew goes to the family's castle in Scotland, where he encounters the ghost of an ancestor, in Eleanor Cameron's *Beyond Silence* (Dutton, 1980, $9.95).

About the Book

Booklist, February 15, 1992, p. 1105.
Center for Children's Books Bulletin, March 1992, p. 192.
Horn Book, March 1992, p. 206
Kirkus Reviews, January 15, 1992.
School Library Journal, March 1992, p. 241.
VOYA, April 1992, p. 34.
See also *Book Review Index,* 1992, p. 787.

About the Author

Chevalier, Tracy, ed., *Twentieth-Century Children's Writers* (3rd ed.). St. James, 1989, pp. 903–905.
Commire, Anne, ed., *Something about the Author.* Gale, 1988, Vol. 50, pp. 182–188.
Holtze, Sally Holmes, ed., *Sixth Book of Junior Authors and Illustrators.* Wilson, 1989, pp. 255–256.
Nakamura, Joyce, ed., *Something about the Author: Autobiography Series.* Gale, 1992, Vol. 13, pp. 155–163.
Senick, Gerard J., ed., *Children's Literature Review.* Gale, 1988, Vol. 50, pp. 167–174.
Trosky, Susan M., *Contemporary Authors.* Gale, 1992, Vol. 136, pp. 357–360.
Ward, Martha, ed., *Authors of Books for Young People* (3rd ed.). Scarecrow, 1990, p. 616.

Taylor, Mildred D. *The Gold Cadillac*

Illus. by Michael Hays. Dial, 1987, $12.89 (0-8037-0343-0)

Mildred Taylor is best known in children's literature for her continuing series about the Logans, a strong, proud black family and their struggle for survival in a segregated South. In *Roll of Thunder, Hear My Cry* (Dial, 1976, $15; pap., Bantam, $3.50; condensed in *More Juniorplots,* Bowker, 1977, pp. 72–74), the 1977 Newbery Medal winner, the narrator, young Cassie, tries to maintain her identity and feeling of self-worth in a white-dominated society while her parents struggle to keep the parcel of land they own. In one of the many continuations, *Let the Circle Be Unbroken* (Dial, 1981, $15.95; pap., Puffin, $3.99; condensed in *Juniorplots 3,* Bowker,

1987, pp. 226–230), Cassie's family suffers such extreme economic problems that both her father and brother must leave home to find work, and Cassie witnesses a miscarriage of justice when a young black boy is wrongfully convicted of murder. *The Gold Cadillac* is a short book of only 43 pages, including some expressive full-page sepia paintings by Michael Hays. In it, a young black girl, 'lois, tells of the prejudice encountered during a trip to the South during the 1950s in the family's new gold Cadillac. This story, based on an experience of the author, is read by youngsters in grades 3 through 5.

Plot Summary

It is a Saturday morning in Toledo, Ohio, vintage 1950s. 'lois and her older sister, Wilma, are stunned and excited when their father drives up in front of their house in a brand new gold Coupe De Ville Cadillac. And what is even more surprising, it's theirs! Her father says he saw it on the showroom floor and couldn't resist it, so he traded in their year-old Mercury for this amazing car.

Before dashing off to tell everyone, 'lois and Wilma look inside the new car. It has gold everything—leather seats, carpeting, dashboard. It looks, 'lois decides, like a car for rich folks.

What with the girls shouting and neighbors looking out their windows, a crowd quickly gathers around the shining new car. Mr. Pondexter and Mr. LeRoy and Mr. Courtland down the street admire the vehicle as their father stands proudly showing off this outstanding family possession.

Relatives and neighbors alike are impressed and thrilled with the gold Cadillac. However, one very important person is not thrilled at all. Mother-dear is anything but happy. 'lois can tell that immediately by the look on her face. In fact, she is downright angry. She is angry because their Mercury was a perfectly good car and because they are supposed to be saving for a better house in a better neighborhood, not for a showy gold Cadillac.

Mother is so angry she refuses to ride in the new car, so the girls and other relatives and Father take off on a tour of Toledo. The tour is too short, so they go right on to Detroit and visit relatives there. Everyone is pleased with the new car, and they think it's pretty funny Mother won't ride in it.

Sunday comes, and 'lois figures her mother will give in and ride to church in the new car. But she doesn't. What's more, she won't let the girls ride to church in the new car either. That evening their father and mother go out to dinner at the corner cafe, but 'lois can tell that things still aren't right.

Everyone on the block knows Mother won't ride in the Cadillac, so they kid Father about it a lot. Everyone thinks it's a pretty big joke, until their father declares he has decided to drive the new car south to visit the girls' grandparents in Mississippi.

One of the uncles warns him not to go. "Wilbert," he says, "it's like putting a loaded gun to your head."

"I paid for the car," says Father, "and I'll drive it where I please."

"But those folks down south don't want to see a northern Negro driving a fine car," Mr. Pondexter tells him.

Another uncle warns him about a possible lynch mob.

The girls don't know what *lynch* means, but they don't like the sound of it.

But their father is determined to go. When their mother realizes this, she says, "Then the girls and I'll be going too."

As it turns out, the family, plus assorted uncles, aunts, and cousins, set off for the South in a procession consisting of the gold Cadillac, a Ford, a Buick, and a Chevrolet, and lots of food packed in picnic hampers.

Once in the South, 'lois begins to understand why her mother insisted on packing so much food. Signs begin to appear that say "White Only" and "Colored Not Allowed." The girls have never seen them before, and Father sadly explains what they signify.

In Mississippi, they run into something worse than signs. Two white policeman stop them and accuse Father of stealing the fine gold car. It takes some hours before he is released, and 'lois spends a terrified night while her father gets some sleep in the car.

The next day Father drives back to Memphis, where he leaves the gold car with a cousin, and the family continues on to visit the grandparents in Cousin Halton's four-year-old Chevy.

During the week the family spends in Mississippi, 'lois asks her father many questions, including what the "White Only" signs mean. Her father tells her what it means to be black in the United States in the 1950s.

Sometime after their return to Toledo, the gold Cadillac disappears. Father has turned it in, and they drive around in an old Model A Ford while they wait for the car he ordered—another Mercury.

Father tells 'lois that now they have more money toward a better house. 'lois understands that, but she remembers the thrill of the gold Cadillac. She also remembers the terrifying trip South, something she may never forget.

Thematic Material

This is a sensitive story that, even though it may seem somewhat dated to young readers who have grown up since the Civil Rights movements of the 1960s and 1970s, forcefully portrays the horrors of bigotry and racism. 'lois and her sister are rather naive, protected young girls in a closely knit family, and young readers will be able to understand why the trip South will leave a strong mark on their memories of childhood.

Book Talk Material

The fun of Father proudly bringing home the gold Cadillac and the emerging signs of bigotry on the trip South can stimulate discussions of how segregation and racism profoundly affect the lives of adults and young people. See: 'lois first sees the new car (pp. 11–12); Mother reacts to the car (pp. 13–16); neighbors admire the Cadillac (p. 21); the first signs of segregation appear on the trip South (pp. 29–30); they are stopped by policemen in Mississippi (pp. 30–33); 'lois asks her father about segregation (pp. 36–37).

Additional Selections

Ludell (Harper, 1975, $14.89) by Brenda Wilkinson is the tender story of a girl's year in the fifth grade in a southern segregated school during the mid-1950s.

A conservative California town reacts unfavorably when a white minister and his family adopt a black child in John Neufeld's *Edgar Allan* (Phillips, 1968, $18.95; pap., Dutton, $2.95; condensed in *Introducing Books,* Bowker, 1970, pp. 17–20).

A poor sharecropper, his family, and a faithful dog play important roles in *Sounder,* the 1970 Newbery Medal winner by William Armstrong (Harper, 1969, $13.95; pap., $3.95; condensed in *More Juniorplots,* Bowker, 1977, pp. 1–4). A sequel is *Sour Land* (Harper, 1991, $13.89; pap., $3.50).

An eleven-year-old black girl named Beth has many adventures, including saving an injured Philip Hall, in Bette Greene's *Philip Hall Likes Me, I Reckon, Maybe* (Dial, 1974, $15.95; pap., Dell, $3.50; condensed in *Introducing More Books,* Bowker, 1978, pp. 26–29), a story about growing up in rural Arkansas.

In *Go Fish* (Harper, 1991, $12.89) by Mary Stolz, a black boy, eight-year-old Thomas, spends a day fishing with his grandfather on the Gulf of Mexico.

Apartheid in South Africa is explored in Sheila Gordon's *The Middle of*

Somewhere (Orchard, 1990, $13.95), the story of nine-year-old Rebecca, whose family must move to make room for housing for whites.

Three friends—a white and two black boys—try to thwart an attack on some Irish gypsies by Klan members in *Circle of Fire* (Macmillan, 1982, $12.95) by William H. Hooks.

About the Book

Booklist, August 1987, p. 1759.

Horn Book, September 1987, p. 606.

New York Times Book Review, November 15, 1987, p. 37.

School Library Journal, September 1987, p. 171.

See also *Book Review Digest,* 1988, pp. 1704–1705; and *Book Review Index,* 1987, p. 751; 1988, p. 799.

About the Author

Chevalier, Tracy, ed., *Twentieth-Century Children's Writers* (3rd ed.). St. James, 1989, pp. 951–952.

Commire, Anne, ed., *Something about the Author.* Gale, 1979, Vol. 15, pp. 275–277.

Estes, Glenn E., ed., *American Writers for Children since 1960: Fiction* (Dictionary of Literary Biography: Vol. 52). Gale, 1986, pp. 364–368.

Holtze, Sally Holmes, ed., *Fifth Book of Junior Authors and Illustrators.* Wilson, 1983, pp. 307–309.

Kirkpatrick, D. L., ed., *Twentieth-Century Children's Writers* (2nd ed.). St. Martin's, 1983, pp. 754–755.

Locher, Frances C., ed., *Contemporary Authors.* Gale, 1980, Vols. 85–88, p. 579.

May, Hal, and Straub, Deborah A., eds., *Contemporary Authors* (New Revision Series). Gale, 1989, Vol. 25, pp. 440–441.

Olendorf, Donna, and Telgen, Diane, eds., *Something about the Author.* Gale, 1993, Vol. 70, pp. 222–226.

Sarkissian, Adele, ed., *Something about the Author: Autobiography Series.* Gale, 1988, Vol. 5, pp. 267–286.

Senick, Gerard J., ed., *Children's Literature Review.* Gale, 1985, Vol. 9, pp. 223–229.

Ward, Martha, ed., *Authors of Books for Young People* (3rd ed.). Scarecrow, 1990, pp. 1091–1092.

6

Family Life

FAMILIES come in all sizes and shapes. Each is unique in nature and composition. The ten novels in this section explore many of these variations and include voyages of self-discovery by each of the protagonists within a family setting.

Bawden, Nina. *Humbug*

Houghton, 1992, $13.45 (0-395-62149-6)

The first children's books by the English writer Nina Bawden appeared in the early 1960s. She began with exciting adventure stories like the recently reissued *The White Horse Gang* (Houghton, 1992, $13.95). *Squib* (Lothrop, 1982, $12.95; pap., Dell, $3.50), which was first published in 1971, was a transitional work ushering in a period dealing with more serious themes. In *Squib*, a twelve-year-old girl sees a shy younger boy at her playground and at first hopes it is her long-lost younger brother. Instead she uncovers a sad tale of child abuse and maltreatment. In *Carrie's War* (Lippincott, 1973, $13.89; pap., Dell, $4.95), a novel based on the author's own experiences, Carrie and her younger brother are evacuated from World War II London to a small town in Wales. Because the head of the house, Mr. Evans, is so penny-pinching and the new environment so strange, Carrie finds she is waging her own private war. Another excellent novel from this period is *The Peppermint Pig* (Lippincott, 1975, $13.89; pap., Dell, $4.95), set in turn-of-the-century England. When Poll's father leaves to find his fortune in America, she, along with her mother and three siblings, must leave their comfortable London home and move to the relative poverty of life in a Norfolk market town. The title comes from the peppermint pig, the runt of the litter, that Mama buys to divert them during these difficult times.

Humbug is set in contemporary England. There are a few expressions that might be unfamiliar to American readers, but the conflict is universal, and all youngsters will empathize with Cora and her problems. This novel is suitable for readers in grades 4 through 6.

Plot Summary

When Father has an opportunity to study Japanese banking for six months and take Mother with him, the two decide their three children should stay with their grandparents, whom they adore. The youngsters are twelve-year-old Alice, ten-year-old William, and Cora, who is eight. Their grandparents live in a small English town in one of the twin semiattached houses at the end of a charming road. When the youngsters arrive, however, the situation is not quite as they expected. Overactive Granny has fallen out of an apple tree and broken her hip. She is bedridden and, when the children arrive, is being visited by the new next-door neighbor, a fussy, overly solicitous woman named Sunday Dearheart, or Aunt Sunday, as she says she would like to be known.

Sunday has a daughter, Angelica, who is Cora's age, and it has been decided that Cora will stay next door until Granny is more mobile. Cora is a bright, outspoken girl who wants to remain with her family. She complains bitterly to Alice and William but is powerless to change the decision.

As expected from her name, Angelica is a pretty, blond girl, whom Cora instinctively dislikes. After only a few minutes in the Dearheart household, Cora realizes Angelica is a mean-spirited youngster who has been spoiled rotten by her saccharine-sweet mother. Cora hopes she will have her own bedroom, at least, but is told she will have the bottom bunk in Angelica's room because the box room, where she sleeps in her grandparents' identical house, is occupied by Old Ma Potter. Cora wonders who this could be and is finally told she is Sunday's mother, a retired former schoolteacher and headmistress who has been forced by old age to leave her own home, Underhill, and come to live with her daughter and granddaughter. The identity and absence of Mr. Dearheart are never explained.

At dinner on her first night at the Dearhearts', Cora meets Ma Potter, a crumpled, withdrawn, silent woman who, to Cora's dismay, is either ignored or treated with scorn by both Sunday and Angelica. As these two prattle on about how they love each other and would never be parted as Cora has been from her parents, Cora hears Ma Potter mumble "humbug," under her breath. She realizes Ma Potter is neither as deaf nor as senile as she would like others to believe.

That evening, Grandpa comes over to check on his Cora and is assured by Aunt Sunday that Cora and Angelica have become close friends. "Not so," Cora would like to add. After dinner, Cora visits Ma Potter in her tiny, book-filled room. After talking about books and lending a copy of *The Jungle Book* to Cora, the old lady indicates that it is difficult to live in a household so filled with pretense and deception. She has found two words that help: the first, *I.G.N.O.R.E.*, and the second, a more powerful one, *humbug*. She advises Cora to use both when necessary.

When she enters their bedroom, Cora finds Angelica holding a glass tumbler against the wall between the two houses. She is listening to William and Alice. Claiming she can't divulge details, Angelica nevertheless tells Cora they have been discussing their young sister, how difficult and unlovable she is, how their parents many times wanted to put her up for adoption, and that the three children were not taken to Japan is because Cora is too unmanageable. She wonders if any of this could be true, and if it is, why anyone would be so spiteful and cruel to repeat it.

Cora's reprieve from this terrible situation is delayed further when her grandmother goes back to the hospital for additional operations. Whenever she tries to tell Grandpa, Alice, or William about her unhappiness, either Aunt Sunday or Angelica is present, and her complaints are ascribed to childish petulance. Cora's only escape is in visiting Ma Potter, who reads to her and tries to help her accept the situation.

One day Aunt Sunday allows Angelica to show Cora Sunday's jewel box. Cora is amazed at the contents. When Angelica leaves the room for a few minutes, she admires a large diamond ring and replaces it carefully in the box before Angelica returns.

The next morning Angelica has a dental appointment, and Ma Potter suggests Cora accompany her to the library. They are picked up by a cab driven by Mr. Hughes, a dear friend of Ma Potter's who was once the janitor at her school. Instead of going to the library, they drive to Underhill, the old lady's former home, now boarded up and on sale. Ma Potter is particularly anxious for Cora to see the folly, a charming smallish outbuilding that could serve as a summer house. As they approach the building, Ma gives the key to Cora, who, after entering the lovely hideaway, absentmindedly puts the key in her pocket. They spend a pleasant day talking and touring the grounds. Ma Potter explains that in spite of Angelica's often-repeated claim that her father is away on secret government business, he is a washing machine salesman who uses every opportunity to escape his wife and child.

Cora's brief happiness ends abruptly when they return to their shared prison. Aunt Sunday's diamond ring is missing, and she accuses Cora of the theft. Cora denies it, but when her belongings are searched, the ring is found. Cora is outraged and hurt at this injustice, but she can't find anyone to believe her innocence. She is convinced Angelica was responsible but has no proof. When Grandpa does not support her and tries to explain Cora's actions as a prank, Cora feels completely betrayed. In shame and confusion, she remains that night at the Dearhearts in spite of her grandfather's offer to take her back to his house.

The next morning, Aunt Sunday's behavior convinces Cora that she knows her daughter is guilty, but the woman is preoccupied with a command appearance she must make that day at Angelica's private school, where the girl has been accused of fomenting trouble. When the two girls are alone, Angelica again accuses Cora of the theft. Cora is so enraged she grabs Angelica around the throat. Suddenly Angelica becomes motionless. Cora is convinced she has strangled her. In a panic, she calls for Ma Potter, then takes her backpack and rushes from the house.

Cora finds the key to Underhill in her pocket. After buying some provisions with her spending money, she finds her way there by bus. At Underhill, she discovers she is not alone. A stray, harmless drifter is also using the premises as home. He is friendly, and after making a fire, the two share a dinner from Cora's canned goods. Afterward, an exhausted Cora falls asleep. She is awakened during the night by footsteps. The stranger has disappeared, but Ma Potter, who has guessed where she is hiding, and Mr. Hughes are standing over her ready to take her home.

Back at Grandpa's, all are relieved and overjoyed at Cora's reappearance. She realizes she is really wanted and loved by her family. A special welcome comes from Granny, who was released that day from the hospital. When Ma Potter goes with Mr. Hughes to spend the night with his family, Cora notices the Dearheart home is in darkness, and no mention has been made of Angelica. A curious but apprehensive Cora decides not to ask questions until someone volunteers information.

The next morning, Cora sees a stranger mowing the Dearhearts' grass. It is the long-absent Mr. Dearheart, who explains that the family is giving up the house because Angelica has been expelled from her school for misbehavior. She and her mother have moved temporarily into his flat in London while searching for a new school.

Relieved and vindicated, Cora returns to her family. She is joined by Ma Potter who announces that, with the help of the Hughes family, she is going to move back to Underhill. The phone rings. It is long distance from Japan. When Cora speaks to her parents, they ask her about her visit. Not to worry them, she says she has had a nice time with the people next door but that they have now gone, and she is back with her grandparents. In the distance, she hears Ma Potter murmur, "Humbug."

Thematic Material

The dictionary defines *humbug* as rubbish, nonsense, or something intended to deceive. Cora learns to distinguish between its various forms and the consequences of each. Cora also discovers that wickedness and heartlessness really exist and are often masked by a facade of benevolence. She also discovers grownups can be dishonest and life can sometimes be unfair and unjust. In this lesson in growing up, she also learns the value of honesty and of accepting people not on the basis of appearances, but for their true nature.

Book Talk Material

Some interesting passages are: the children arrive at their grandparents' home, and Cora is told she will be staying with the Dearhearts (pp. 3–6); Cora meets Angelica (pp. 9–13); the first meal with the Dearhearts and Ma Potter (pp. 14–20); Cora visits Ma Potter (pp. 27–30); Angelica tells Cora what she has heard from next door (pp. 32–37); and Cora, Angelica, and the jewel box (pp. 51–54).

Additional Selections

Maggie and her grandmother run away when the old lady is threatened with being committed to a nursing home in Eleanor Clymer's *The Get-Away Car* (Dutton, 1978, $8.95).

During an airplane trip across country in her grandfathers' old Piper Cub, Birch learns about the family in *Coast to Coast* (Delacorte, 1992, $14) by Betsy Byars.

A friendship between two girls of different backgrounds is disrupted when one becomes brain damaged in *Bringing Nettie Back* (Macmillan, 1992, $13.95) by Nancy Hope Wilson.

An annoying new boy forces Jonathan to view his life differently in Doris Buchanan Smith's *The Pennywhistle Tree* (Putnam, 1991, $14.95).

Lexie reluctantly agrees to have a joint party with an unpopular classmate to celebrate their birthdays in Lisa Eisenberg's *Happy Birthday, Lexie* (Viking, 1991, $12.95). This is a sequel to *Leave It to Lexie* (Viking, 1989, $11.95).

Dorothy faces the problems of moving to a new house and attending a new school in a beginning chapter book, *Starring Dorothy Kane* (Greenwillow, 1992, $14) by Judith Caseley.

In Kristi D. Holl's *No Strings Attached* (Macmillan, 1988, $12.95), June finds it difficult when she and her mother move in with crabby old Franklin Cooper.

About the Book

Booklist, October 1, 1992, p. 329.
Center for Children's Books Bulletin, November 1992, p. 68.
Kirkus Reviews, July 15, 1992, p. 918.
School Library Journal, October 1992, p. 112.
See also *Book Review Index,* 1992, p. 62.

About the Author

Chevalier, Tracy, ed., *Twentieth-Century Children's Writers* (3rd ed.). St. James, 1989, pp. 56–58.
Commire, Anne, ed., *Something about the Author.* Gale, 1973, Vol. 4, pp. 132–133 (under Kark, Nina).
de Montreville, Doris, and Crawford, Elizabeth D., eds., *Fourth Book of Junior Authors and Illustrators.* Wilson, 1978, pp. 29–31.
Evory, Ann, and Metzger, Linda, eds., *Contemporary Authors* (New Revision Series). Gale, 1983, Vol. 8, p. 285 (under Kark, Nina).
Kirkpatrick, D. L., ed., *Twentieth-Century Children's Writers* (2nd ed.). St. Martins, 1983, pp. 67–69.
May, Hal, and Lesniak, James G., eds., *Contemporary Authors* (New Revision Series). Gale, 1990, Vol. 29, pp. 40–41.
Riley, Carolyn, ed., *Children's Literature Review,* Gale, 1976, Vol. 2, pp. 8–15.
Ward, Martha, ed., *Authors of Books for Young People* (3rd ed.). Scarecrow, 1990, p. 45.

Brooks, Bruce. *Everywhere*

Harper, 1990, $12.89 (0-06-020729-9); pap., $3.95 (0-06-440433-1)

Bruce Brooks's previous novels were written primarily for a young adult audience. The first, *The Moves Make the Man* (Harper, 1984, $14.89; pap., $3.95), which is read and enjoyed by many middle school as well as junior high students, tells about the friendship cemented on the basketball court between a hip, cheeky, black student, Jerome Foxworthy, and a white boy, Bix, whose family is undergoing severe emotional problems. In his second,

Midnight Hour Encores (Harper, 1986, $13.89; pap., $3.95), we meet a musically talented but bossy girl who travels across-country to attend an audition and find the mother who deserted her at birth. In *Everywhere,* Brooks evokes some of the great Southern writers of the past, such as Carson McCullers and Flannery O'Connor, in this tale of a boy who tries to save his grandfather's life by joining friend Dooley in a ritual called soul switching. This story of faith and loneliness explores the nature of life and death in a brief text of only seventy pages. It is set in the South of the not-too-distant past and is enjoyed by better readers in grades 4 and up.

Plot Summary

He is ten years old, and he is about to lose what he loves most in the world—his grandfather. His beloved grandfather, of Richmond, Virginia, has suffered a heart attack. Right now his grandfather is in the upstairs bedroom with his grandmother watching over him, waiting to see if he will pull through. The boy thinks back to a night some time ago when he felt himself part of the entire night sky and said to his grandfather, "I am everywhere." And his grandfather had replied, "I'm there with you."

Now he is alone. That is, he is alone until Lucy, the local nurse, arrives with her nephew, an eleven-year-old black boy named Dooley who has an active imagination and knowledge of a mysterious ritual known as "soul switching." As Dooley explains it, the idea is to give up an animal's life to save the human in question. The boy isn't so sure about this, but Dooley sounds very positive.

First, Dooley wants to know what animal his grandfather resembles. The boy thinks perhaps a lion, but there are no lions handy, so they settle on a turtle. And they do find a turtle down by Dooley's favorite spot on the creek.

Much as he wants his grandfather to live, the boy feels more and more guilty about the impending death of the turtle. But Dooley is just so positive.

Next, the boy must bring Dooley something of his grandfather's that he likes to wear. That would be a bow tie. The boy steals upstairs and comes down with a magnificent bow tie of polished indigo silk specked with tiny, pale-orange triangles outlined by single threads of luminous aqua. It is splendid.

Dooley also requests two kinds of nail polish, which the boy finds in his grandmother's things.

Now it is time for the switch. Dooley tells him to climb on the porch roof and peer into his grandfather's room so he will be able to give Dooley the signal when the time for the switch is right. Then Dooley will take the turtle into his grandfather's work shed, put his grandfather's initials—EDB—on it, and then do the awful deed that will save his grandfather's life.

With great reservations, the boy does as instructed. But when he peers into his grandfather's window from the porch roof, he sees his grandfather making jerking motions on the bed and his grandmother and Lucy looking much alarmed. At the same time, the boy realizes Dooley has gone into the shed to kill the turtle. "No," he yells, "don't do it!"

His grandmother hears him and pulls him into the bedroom. Suddenly his grandfather is still. His eyes blink and open and look at his grandson. "Don't go everywhere," the boy says.

"Okay. Sure. I won't," replies his grandfather.

It takes time, but by the end of the summer when the boy is ready to leave his grandparents to go home, his grandfather is well on the way to recovery from his heart attack. Before the boy goes, his grandfather decides they should make something together in the work shed. They will make a pencil box for school.

In the shed, his grandfather discovers a live turtle with the initials ED on its back. It must have got trapped in the shed, says his grandfather. But the boy knows, and when he finds some old chicken bones, he also knows what really happened at the "soul switching."

The boy just has to see Dooley before he returns to school. He didn't even thank him, and he doesn't really know what to say now that he knows Dooley's secret. But he goes down into the hollow where Dooley lives and finds him in church with his family. As the boy watches through the church window, he wonders what he can give Dooley in return. His new pencil box perhaps?

Then Dooley's father says something to him, and Dooley turns his head. The boy sees around his neck a flash of indigo silk specked with orange triangles trimmed in aqua. It is a fine bow tie, a splendid bow tie . . . and it is Dooley's.

Thematic Material

This is a warm, spellbinding story of the power of love and how children can cope with the pain of impending loss. The boy is torn between his love for his grandfather and his feelings of helplessness and concern over killing even a turtle. Dooley is a delightful character, an eleven-year-old filled with confidence and wisdom beyond his years. The warmth of the relationship between the boy and his grandfather is lovingly portrayed. Young readers should enjoy this sensitive story.

Book Talk Material

The details of the "soul switching" will interest readers. See: Dooley brings up the idea (pp. 11–12); the boys discuss the animal his grandfather resembles (pp. 13–15); they look for turtles at the creek (pp. 20–28); the boy finds the right tie (pp. 44–49); the moment of the switch (pp. 53–56).

Additional Selections

A young woman brings happiness to four motherless children in Robert Burch's *Ida Early Comes Over the Mountain* (Viking, 1980, $13.95; pap., Puffin, $3.95).

Delrita, age thirteen, is ashamed of her Uncle Punky, who has Down's syndrome, but everything changes when they go to live with an aunt and uncle in June Rae Wood's *The Man Who Loved Clowns* (Putnam, 1992, $14.95).

In Martin Waddell's *Little Obie and the Flood* (Candlewick, 1992, $13.95), Obie and his grandparents lose everything in a flood but still have enough charity to take in orphaned Marty.

Eleven-year-old Brady, who lives with her grandfather, tries to arrange a reunion with her long-lost father in Patricia Hermes's *Take Care of My Girl* (Little, Brown, 1992, $14.95).

In Rosa Guy's *The Ups and Downs of Carl Davis III* (Delacorte, 1989, $13.95), a young black boy feels out of place in the South Carolina town where he is sent to straighten out.

Two outsiders, a boy and a girl, are marooned on an island by vindictive fellow camp mates in Brock Cole's *The Goats* (Farrar, 1987, $15; pap., $3.95; condensed in *Juniorplots 4,* Bowker, 1993, pp. 14–18).

In Cristina Salat's *Living in Secret* (Bantam, 1993, $15), Amelia's mom, a lesbian, and partner, Janey, want to kidnap Amelia from her dad so they can live happily in California.

About the Book

Booklist, October 15, 1990, p. 441.
Center for Children's Books Bulletin, October 1990, p. 23.
Horn Book, January 1991, p. 72.
Horn Book Guide, July 1990, p. 83.

New York Times Book Review, September 8, 1991, p. 40.
School Library Journal, September 1990, p. 224.
Wilson Library Bulletin, October 1990, p. 123.
See also *Book Review Digest,* 1991, pp. 247–248; and *Book Review Index,* 1990, p. 105; 1991, p. 118.

About the Author

Commire, Anne, ed., *Something about the Author.* Gale, 1988, Vol. 53, p. 7.
Holtze, Sally Holmes, ed., *Sixth Book of Junior Authors and Illustrators.* Wilson, 1989, pp. 43–44.
Senick, Gerard J., ed., *Children's Literature Review.* Gale, 1991, Vol. 25, pp. 16–26.

Bunting, Eve. *Our Sixth-Grade Sugar Babies*

Harper, 1990, $12.89 (0-397-32452-9); pap., $3.95 (0-06-440390-4)

Eve Bunting has written more than 100 books for young people in a variety of genres and for many different audiences. In addition to *Sugar Babies,* she has written many humorous stories for preteens about the problems of growing up, such as *Karen Kepplewhite Is the World's Best Kisser* (Houghton, 1983, $13.45). She is also very well known for a series of exciting mystery stories, among them *Someone Is Hiding on Alcatraz Island* (Houghton, 1984, $13.45; pap., Berkeley, $3.50). *Sugar Babies* takes place over a few days in Pasadena where the author currently lives with her family. The central character and narrator is young Vicki Charlip. This novel is particularly suited to girls in grades 4 to 6.

Plot Summary

The placid, everyday life of eleven-year-old Vicki Charlip and her friend Ellie is unexpectedly enlivened by two occurrences. The first is an unusual assignment from Mrs. Oda, their popular and well-liked sixth-grade teacher in Tilman Elementary School. For one week, each student must carry and care for a five-pound bag of sugar as if it were a baby. It is hoped that this exercise in simulated parenthood will teach both responsibility and an understanding of the sacrifices necessary to raise a family. The second incident is the arrival of the Shub family, new across-the-street neighbors for Vicki. What makes this event important is that, in addition to the parents and young son, there is also a dimpled dreamboat of about thirteen who "is to die for." He is somewhat out of reach because he attends seventh grade at the junior high, but nevertheless the girls are paralyzed with infatuation. Ellie immediately names him Terrific Hunk, or Thunk for short.

Vicki lives on a pleasant tree-lined street in a residential part of Pasadena. Her mother, who was divorced when Vicki was only two, is a certified accountant who works from an office in their home. Vicki's father now lives in Waterloo, Iowa, and has a new wife, Moshi, and a four-year-old daughter, Keiko. Last summer, Vicki spent a few very happy days visiting them. Recently, her father has asked that she come again for two weeks to take care of Keiko during the day while he and his wife take courses. Her mother says Vicki is much too young to shoulder such responsibilities, but Vicki secretly hopes that if she excels at the sugar baby assignment and proves she is responsible, her mother will change her mind.

Vicki knows all her neighbors on the street, including Mr. Ambrose, once a successful businessman who has been sinking into a benign senility. He stands outside his house for hours waving at passing motorists and making innocuous comments about the weather. Vicki often visits him, although she realizes he hears but no longer comprehends her remarks. He is perfectly harmless, but his daughter, Ophelia, is so concerned for his well-being that she has given up a nursing career to care for him.

On the first day of the sugar baby assignment, all the students except Horrible Harry Hogan, the pesky, interfering kid who sits directly behind Vicki, bring their sugar babies to school. Mrs. Oda tells Vicki her child is a girl. She names her Babe; Ellie, who has a boy, calls him Sweet Sam.

On her way home from school, Vicki stops to visit Mr. Ambrose, who, as usual, is greeting each passerby with a wave and a vacant smile. To make conversation, Vicki tells him about Babe and also about Thunk and how he got his name. Suddenly she realizes with horror that Thunk's young brother is eavesdropping on their conversation.

Back home, Vicki and Ellie see Thunk in front of his house talking with cute Cynthia Sanders, another seventh-grader. Vicki invents a flimsy excuse to join the conversation. She finds out that Thunk's real name is Sam and that he is as charming as he is beautiful. Unfortunately, his young brother appears and reports on the conversation he overheard. An embarrassed and humiliated Vicki beats a hasty retreat.

At school the next day, everyone arrives with their charges, now transformed into doll-like creatures. Vicki has painted a cherubic face on her sugar package and dressed Babe in clothes from a Cabbage Patch doll.

Characteristically, Horrible Harry has drawn a Dracula-like face on his and outfitted it accordingly. Much to Vicki's disgust, Dracula appears to have designs on Babe's neck.

Vicki is chatting with Mr. Ambrose again when Thunk rides by on his bicycle. He asks Vicki if she will show him the way to the public library. Hastily, she hides Babe behind a palm tree, asks Mr. Ambrose to take care of it, and races home to get her bike. At the library, she finds that Cynthia and Harry Hogan are there. Thunk and Cynthia pair off to do some schoolwork, and Vicki and Harry talk briefly. Amazingly, in this new environment, he doesn't seem nearly as obnoxious as in the classroom.

On the way home, Vicki stops at the Ambrose home and finds to her horror that Babe has disappeared! She searches frantically, but there is no sugar baby. In her frustration and shame, she lashes out angrily at poor bewildered Mr. Ambrose, accusing him of causing her baby's disappearance. Confused and desperate, Vicki takes some money from her savings box and furtively buys another five-pound bag of sugar in the local general store. With mounting guilt, she hastily paints on a duplicate face and dresses it in other doll clothes, so expertly that even her mother cannot tell the difference.

Later that evening, a distraught Ophelia calls on Vicki and her mother. Her father has disappeared, and she is becoming frantic with worry. A neighborhood search is quickly organized, and the police are called in. The hours tick by, and there is still no word. Increasingly, Vicki feels responsible for his disappearance. Even though she knows that telling the truth will ruin her chances of going to Iowa, she tells her mother and Ophelia about her missing sugar baby, how she replaced it, and how she had told Mr. Ambrose he was to blame. Suddenly, Ophelia knows where her father is. Years before, when she was a small child, Ophelia wandered off while she and her father were shopping in Bleshnell's, a large local department store. It took hours to find her, and her father had always felt a burden of guilt about the incident. The three race to Bleshnell's. With only a few moments before closing, Vicki finds Mr. Ambrose in the doll department. When he sees the second Babe in Vicki's arms, his face brightens with a smile of relief.

Back home, Vicki's mother calls her former husband and works out a compromise concerning the baby-sitting problem. Keiko will come to Pasadena for a two-week visit, and both Vicki and her mother will take care of her. Vicki is pleased about this and even happier when her mother finds the original Babe hidden under a rubber tree by their driveway. In his own way, Mr. Ambrose had taken care of Vicki's baby as she had asked.

The next day at school, Vicki summons the courage to tell Mrs. Oda and the class about her carelessness and failure as a surrogate mother. The effects are not as disastrous as expected. Mrs. Oda generously compliments Vicki on her honesty and courage. Vicki even receives a note from Dracula inviting Babe to the movies on Friday night—provided, of course, that a certain Vicki Charlip and Harry Hogan can accompany them as chaperones.

Thematic Material

Although this is essentially a lighthearted story featuring a likable, vulnerable heroine, it also focuses on some of the anxieties and insecurities of the preteen age, particularly those involving social relationships. Hidden within the story are valuable lessons concerning honesty and responsibility. The author has accurately captured the speech and expressions of sixth-graders as well as their misgivings and preoccupation with an emerging interest in the opposite sex. There is an affectionate and realistic portrait of a single-parent family plus important secondary themes involving friendship, self-acceptance, respect for elders, and the need to understand and help the infirm.

Book Talk Material

Explaining the title and displaying the dust jacket should arouse interest in this story. Some interesting passages are: Mrs. Oda reviews the assignment (pp. 13–20); Ellie and Vicki exchange plans on how to meet Thunk (pp. 38–42); Vicki's talk with Thunk and Cynthia is interrupted by Thunk's young brother (pp. 43–51); and class members introduce their sugar babies (pp. 68–72).

Additional Selections

Katie, a sixth-grader, becomes involved in a censorship case in Betty Miles's *Maudie and Me and the Dirty Book* (pap., Knopf, 1988, $2.95).

When Robin and Veronica, the leaders of the sixth grade, quarrel, Robin learns the meaning of being an outsider in Ilene Cooper's *Queen of the Sixth Grade* (Morrow, 1988, $12.95; pap., Puffin, $3.99).

Dinah, age twelve, is overweight and no one lets her forget it in *Dinah and the Green Fat Kingdom* (pap., Dell, $1.75) by Isabelle Holland.

In Lois Lowry's *Taking Care of Terrific* (Houghton, 1982, $13.95; pap., Dell, $3.25), young baby-sitter Edna is accused of kidnapping her charge.

In Barthe DeClements's *Sixth Grade Can Really Kill You* (Viking, 1985, $12.95; pap., Scholastic, $2.50), "bad Helen" acts up to cover her embarrassment about her reading problem.

A young boy named Mousi incurs the wrath of the school bully and awaits his inevitable punishment in Betsy Byars's *The 18th Emergency* (Viking, 1973, $12.95; pap., Puffin, $3.95).

Fifth-grader Amanda Pinkerton is too successful in promoting the acceptance of her unpopular classmate Walter Brinkman in *Valentine Frankenstein* (Macmillan, 1992, $12.95) by Maggie Twohill.

About the Book

Booklist, October 15, 1990, p. 441.
Center for Children's Books Bulletin, November 1990, p. 55.
Horn Book Guide, July 1990, p. 73.
Kirkus Reviews, November 1, 1990, p. 1529.
School Library Journal, October 1990, p. 113.
See also *Book Review Digest,* 1991, p. 267; *Book Review Index,* 1990, p. 115; 1991, p. 129.

About the Author

Chevalier, Tracy, ed., *Twentieth-Century Children's Writers* (3rd ed.). St. James, 1989, pp. 152–154.
Commire, Anne, ed., *Something about the Author.* Gale, 1980, Vol. 18, pp. 38–39 (under Anne Evelyn Bunting); 1991, pp. 60–69.
Evory, Ann, ed., *Contemporary Authors* (New Revision Series). Gale, 1982, Vol. 5, p. 85; 1987, Vol. 19, pp. 97–99.
Holtze, Sally Holmes, ed., *Fifth Book of Junior Authors and Illustrators.* Wilson, 1983, pp. 60–61.
Kinsman, Clare D., ed., *Contemporary Authors.* Gale, 1975, Vols. 53–56, pp. 75–76.
Kirkpatrick, D. L., ed., *Twentieth-Century Children's Writers* (2nd ed.). St. Martin's, 1983, pp. 136–137.
Senick, Gerard J., ed., *Children's Literature Review.* Gale, 1992, Vol. 28, pp. 41–67.
Ward, Martha, ed., *Writers of Books for Young People* (3rd ed.). Scarecrow, 1990, p. 77.

Byars, Betsy. *Wanted . . . Mud Blossom*

Delacorte, 1991, $14 (0-385-30428-5); pap., Dell, $3.50 (0-440-40761-3)

Betsy Byars is one of the most honored and enjoyed writers of children's books. She tells of her childhood, including encounters with snakes, in the amusing *The Moon and I* (Simon & Schuster, 1992, $14.98). She began writing while her husband worked on his Ph.D. Her first book was panned, but her second, *The Midnight Fox* (Viking, 1968, $13.95; pap., Puffin, $3.99), was an immediate success. It tells the story of the great bond that grows between a boy who is spending a summer on his aunt's farm and a wild fox he watches for two months until it steals some chickens and must be hunted. Perhaps her best-known work is the 1971 Newbery Medal winner, *The Summer of the Swans* (Viking, 1970, $14; pap., Puffin, $3.99; condensed in *More Juniorplots,* Bowker, 1977, pp. 106–109). In it, a self-conscious fourteen-year-old girl reaches unexpected maturity when Charlie, who is retarded and unable to speak, wanders away and can't be found. The Blossom family first appeared in *The Not-Just-Anybody Family* (Delacorte, 1986, $13.95; pap., Dell, $3.50). Here we meet eleven-year-old Vern, who breaks into jail to visit Grandpa. Grandpa is in prison for shooting at some teenagers who deliberately drove over his collection of cans. We also meet young Maggie, the mainstay of the family, and seven-year-old Junior, whose legs get broken in an attempt to fly from the barn roof. Another member is Mud, the family dog, who takes the spotlight in this sequel, one of many tales about this poor but funny clan. It is enjoyed by readers in grades 5 through 8.

Plot Summary

Slightly wacky, a little flaky, a small bit off center: such phrases may catch the gist of the unusual people who make up the Blossom family, but they just don't say it all. Take this weekend, for instance.

Junior is nearly mad with anticipation. He's been driving everyone crazy with his "surprise" and annoying his mother because she has told him not to dig holes and he has been digging a hole, except that he swears it isn't a hole, and she really hasn't got time to fuss with this because her mind is on buying a new pants suit in case she gets to go out this weekend—for a change.

It turns out that Junior's surprise is that he has been given the class hamster—Scooty—to take home for the weekend. It's supposed to be an exercise in responsibility, but to Junior it's just fun, and he has been digging for days—not a hole, but an apartment for the hamster with lots of rooms and tunnels, covered with boards. Junior gets off the school bus and puts Scooty in his new apartment. Then he runs into the house to see if his grandfather, Pap Blossom, has any news about Mad Mary. She is just about Junior's best friend in the entire world. She lives in a cave, she looks like a wild woman, and Pap is afraid she is missing, so he is calling the police to check on her.

No news on Mad Mary. But by the time Junior gets back to the hamster apartment, it is empty, and the boards have been shoved aside. Worse than that, Pap's dog, Mud, has pine needles and dirt on his nose.

Junior practically goes berserk! Mud has eaten the school's hamster—so much for getting an A in responsibility. Junior wants to murder Mud right on the spot, but Pap won't hear of it.

Calmer heads prevail, and Mud is put on trial for murder. This is at the suggestion of Junior's sister, Maggie, who will be the prosecutor. In Mud's defense stands Ralphie, who adores Maggie and is the only kid in the whole school who has an artificial leg, the result of an accident with a power mower a few years ago. Pap will be the judge, and the jury will be composed of Junior's brother, Vern, and his friend Michael, who both seem to find the whole affair hilarious.

Junior thinks the trial idea is dumb because Mud is guilty and that's all there is to it. Mud himself is bored with the whole to-do and goes under the porch to sleep, so he has to be tried in absentia.

While all this is going on, Mad Mary wakes up to find herself in the hospital. Seems she had passed out on the road from malnutrition and some people found her and took her to the hospital. When the hospital staff asks her for the name of someone to call, the only friend she can think of is Pap Blossom.

The trial gets under way after some spirited dispute about such matters as whether there should be other dogs on the jury so Mud can be tried by a panel of his peers.

When the trial is concluded, but before Vern and Michael can deliver their verdict, Ralphie is struck by a brilliant idea. The reason why Vern and Michael have found the whole trial so hilarious is that Scooty the hamster isn't dead at all, just stolen away by the two boys and hidden in Vern's room. Maggie doesn't think Ralphie is so brilliant, however, and she's mad at him for waiting so long to uncover the secret.

Junior is relieved about Scooty, but now he wants to kill Vern. Pap proposes a small fistfight instead.

Ralphie goes home but decides to phone Maggie to make up. As soon as she answers, he blurts out, "I love you." Which would be OK except that it isn't Maggie who answers the phone, but her mother.

Mad Mary comes out of the hospital, and Pap persuades her to spend a night with the Blossoms before returning to her cave. Junior says she can sleep in his room. But when Junior sees Mad Mary, he can't believe it. Her hair is combed and her clothes are new—is this really his friend? She doesn't even smell the same. But she sounds the same. She's still Mad Mary, Junior's best friend.

The trial is over, Mad Mary is OK, no one's angry at Mud anymore, and Ralphie even ends up with a kiss from Maggie. As for Junior, well, come Monday morning, there he is on the school bus with Scooty, right as rain in his cage. Junior has decided he will be cautious about taking on responsibility in the future. It's a lot of work. Yet, there's something to be said for it. Rebecca, who's never bothered with Junior at all and certainly never sat with him on the school bus, sits right down next to him. Of course, maybe she only wants to admire Scooty; however, maybe not . . . .

Thematic Material

This is a funny, warm story of delightful characters in a slightly wacky family. In this, the fifth book about the Blossom family, the members march to their own drummers, but their love and caring shine through even in life's most impossible moments. The author shows a special skill at depicting the concerns and earnest preoccupations of young children, not to mention a very real dog.

Book Talk Material

A number of amusing episodes can serve as an introduction to this thoroughly likable family and their friends. See: Junior and his mother discuss whether or not he is digging a hole (pp. 2–3); Ralphie and Maggie meet a turtle on the road (pp. 8–14); Mud loses the battle over going to the basement (pp. 36–37); and Mud's a murderer (pp. 64–68).

Additional Selections

In Mark Geller's *Who's on First?* (Harper, 1992, $14), fourteen-year-old Alex tries to find a suitable escort for Carol, his older sister, when she is invited to their cousin's ritzy wedding.

A thirteen-year-old boy, his three younger brothers, and a nurse are left in charge when Mom gets sick in Joan Carris's *When the Boys Ran the House* (Harper, 1982, $12.95).

When a crazed character named Brighteyes steals from an eccentric theatrical family, the group sets out on a series of one-night stands to find the culprit in the action-filled comedy *The Merry Muldoons and the Brighteyes Affair* (Orchard, 1992, $14.95) by Brooks McNamara.

Mattie and twin sister Pru solve a number of everyday problems, such as Mattie's search for a date for the eighth-grade Sadie Hawkins Day dance, in Mary E. Ryan's *Me, My Sister, and I* (Simon & Schuster, 1992, $15), a sequel to *My Sister Is Driving Me Crazy* (Simon & Schuster, 1991, $15; pap., $3.95).

In *The Secret Life of Dilly McBean* (Macmillan, 1986, $14.95; pap., Scholastic, $2.50) by Dorothy Haas, a rich orphan who has the secret power of magnetism is kidnapped and then rescued by a cast of very unusual characters.

When three children learn that a local animal shelter is closing, they try to find homes for its stray dogs, cats, and other animals in *A Home Is to Share—and Share—and Share* (Macmillan, 1984, $12.95) by Judie Angell.

In *Moonkid and Liberty* (Little, Brown, 1990, $13.95) by Paul Kropp, Libby and Ian are living with their nonconformist father when their mother reappears and wants them to come live with her.

About the Book

Booklist, September 15, 1991, p. 148.
Center for Children's Books Bulletin, October 1991, p. 32.
Horn Book, July 15, 1991, p. 595.
Kirkus Reviews, July 15, 1991, p. 928.
New York Times Book Review, December 15, 1991, p. 29.
School Library Journal, July 1991, p. 72.
VOYA, August 1991, p. 168.
See also *Book Review Digest,* 1992; and *Book Review Index,* 1991, p. 136; 1992.

About the Author

Block, Ann, and Riley, Carolyn, eds., *Children's Literature Review.* Gale, 1976, Vol. 1, pp. 35–38.
Chevalier, Tracy, ed., *Twentieth-Century Children's Writers* (3rd ed.). St. James, 1989, pp. 166–168.
Commire, Anne, ed., *Something about the Author.* Gale, 1987, Vol. 46, pp. 36–47.
de Montreville, Doris, and Hill, Donna, eds., *Third Book of Junior Authors.* Wilson, 1972, p. 55.
Estes, Glenn E., ed., *American Writers for Children since 1960: Fiction* (Dictionary of Literary Biography, Vol. 52). Gale, 1986, pp. 52–66.
Kirkpatrick, D. L., ed., *Twentieth-Century Children's Writers* (3rd ed.). St. Martin's, 1983, pp. 148–149.
Lesniak, James G., ed., *Contemporary Authors* (New Revision Series). Gale, 1992, Vol. 36, pp. 68–70.
Sarkissian, Adele, ed., *Something about the Author: Autobiography Series.* Gale, 1986, Vol. 1, pp. 53–68.
Senick, Gerard J., ed., *Children's Literature Review.* Gale, 1986, Vol. 16, pp. 41–66.
Ward, Martha, ed., *Authors of Books for Young People* (3rd ed.). Scarecrow, 1990, pp. 104–105.

Hamilton, Virginia. *Drylongso*
Illus. by Jerry Pinkney. Harcourt, 1992, $18.95 (0-15-224241-4)

Virginia Hamilton is one of the most honored and respected contemporary writers of juvenile fiction. She deals with the black experience as seen through the eyes of young characters who, in addition to exploring their racial identity, are facing the problems associated with growing up. Several of her titles have already been analyzed in other volumes of the Bowker Plots series, including the 1975 Newbery Medal winner, *M.C. Higgins the Great* (Macmillan, 1974, $15.95; pap., $3.95; condensed in *More Juniorplots,* 1977, pp. 195–199), a story set in a rural mining area close to the Ohio River where a thirteen-year-old black boy is growing up in a house threatened by imminent destruction from encroaching slag heaps. In *The People Could Fly* (Knopf, 1985, $18.99; condensed in *Introducing Bookplots 3,* Bowker, 1990, pp. 223–226), the author brilliantly retells twenty-four American black folktales with the help of forty striking illustrations by Leo and Diane Dillon. *Drylongso* has the same air of the folktale. With amazing simplicity and the quality of a myth, this brief story tells of a strange boy's visit to a drought-ridden farm in 1975 and of the magical results. Watercolors by Jerry Pinkney enhance the text. The book is read by youngsters in grades 3 through 5.

Plot Summary

The title comes from a word handed down by early generations of the African-American community during the Plantation Era. Drought came so often and was so regular that the word *drylongso* came to mean ordinary.

This particular *drylongso* story takes place somewhere west of the Mississippi River in 1975, during another time of long drought. In fact, little Lindy doesn't remember a time when there was plenty of water, when everything and everyone on her family's small farm weren't covered with dust, when it was not a near-impossible struggle to make anything grow. Her dad and her Mamalou remember such a time, of course, but they don't look for it to happen again soon.

Despite the drought and the constant dust, Lindy is a cheerful child. She talks to the sunflowers as she wipes the dust from their leaves, and she talks to her father as she helps him plant the spindly tomato seedlings and sprinkles them with a few precious drops of water. Her dad calls it "pouring on the gravy." That makes Lindy laugh.

One afternoon when Lindy is helping her dad with the planting, she looks up to see what appears to be a brown, high wall on the horizon, and coming right at them. "Dad, it's . . . it's coming!" she screams.

Lindy's father looks up and his mouth falls open. But he stays calm, taking her hand and saying, "Come." Together they head for the farmhouse where Mamalou is at her chores. Before they go inside, Lindy back looks at the onrushing wall and sees what looks like a stick running in front of it.

Once inside, Mamalou wets cloths to cover their faces. For what is coming is, indeed, a wall, a wall of dust, a dreaded plains dust storm.

Just before the dust storm hits, the running stick turns out to be a young boy. Lindy's dad pulls him into the house, where he collapses coughing on the floor.

Suddenly, the day turns dark as night as the storm completely envelops them. Dust sifts in through the wallboards, covering them, covering everything. Lindy can hardly breathe.

Her dad tells her to breathe through the wet cloth. She does and feels better.

When the young boy can speak, he tells them his name is Drylongso. Lindy laughs at that, but Drylongso explains that he was born during a time like this, a time of no rain—it was "dry so long." His mother said that after he came into the world life would be better.

Drylongso says he was separated from his family in a planting field when the dust storm hit. He seems to know a good deal about times of drought. He tells Lindy that droughts in the United States usually appear every twenty years or so. Lindy's dad agrees.

Through the day and night, the dust storm rages. In the morning Lindy wakes to a dull sunlight. Every single thing in the farmhouse is covered in dust. But outside is even more amazing. It looks like an ocean of dust; it is piled everywhere in big waves.

Pretty soon Drylongso is walking around the farm with a strange-looking forked branch in his hand. He explains to Lindy that it is a dowser, or divining rod. It helps find water, if you have the gift. Drylongso says he has the gift.

After much walking about the land, Drylongso tells Lindy's dad where he should plant his seeds, in a place he has not planted before.

Lindy's dad is skeptical. Should he put in all that work on the word of a boy? He decides to trust him.

The whole family works with Drylongso to build trenches and plant seeds. As the day wears on, Lindy says she feels cool earth between her toes.

"Cool means there is faint moisture," says her dad.

It takes a good three days to finish the planting.

"Do we water them now?" Lindy asks.

Drylongso takes up a pick and breaks into a high bank near their plantings. Out comes water, a trickle at first, but steady like a pump.

"Water's been there all the time," her dad says.

"You just have to know how to find it," says Drylongso.

The next day, while Lindy is dreaming of all the tomatoes and vegetables they are going to eat, all the water to drink, and all the things that will grow, her dad and Drylongso go to town. But her dad returns without the boy. He has gone to find his own family, and he thought it would be easier to leave Lindy without saying goodbye. Lindy is crushed. She knows she will miss him. In a short time, he has become her brother.

Lindy finds Drylongso's dowsing rod. He left it for her. She picks it up, but she doesn't have the gift. She points the dowser to the sky. Nothing happens. "I made rain someplace," she tells Mamalou. "I made rain in California!"

Someday, Lindy thinks, I'll use this dowsing rod to find Drylongso again. But that night when she goes to bed, she suddenly figures out why Drylongso didn't say goodbye.

"He's coming back," she says out loud. "He'll come back when it's cool again."

Thematic Material

This is a quiet, thoughtful story of a loving black family in hard times. Drylongso is a gentle although somewhat mysterious boy, who "has the gift." The story brings a message of hope for the future in the midst of bad times. An easy, enjoyable read for this age group.

Book Talk Material

The description of the oncoming dust storm will serve as a good introduction to this book; see pp. 10–18. See also: Drylongso explains about his name (pp. 22–23); the aftermath of the storm (pp. 29–32); Drylongso uses the dowser (pp. 33–40); and Drylongso finds water (pp. 44–46).

Additional Selections

Laura welcomes the Cates family's move to a farm, but her fourteen-year-old brother resents the change, causing serious problems in Ruth Wallace-Brodeur's *The Godmother Tree* (Harper, 1992, $13).

In Laurence Yep's *Dragonwings* (Harper, 1975, $14.89; pap., $3.95), a father and son in San Francisco at the time of the Wright Brothers build and fly an airplane.

In spite of her family's objections, Tibby is drawn to a fundamentalist sect called "the Believers" in Rebecca C. Jones's *The Believers* (Arcade, 1989, $13.95; pap., Knopf, $3.95).

Amanda, age twelve, visits her grandmother in Memphis during the Great Depression and discovers new family ties in George Ella Lyon's *Borrowed Children* (Orchard, 1988, $12.95; pap., Bantam, $2.95).

Breaker (Houghton, 1988, $13.45) by N. A. Perez is the story of a fourteen-year-old slate picker in a Pennsylvania coal-mining town.

Race relations are explored when a black family moves to an all-white community during the Reconstruction era in Ouida Sebestyen's *Words by Heart* (Little, Brown, 1979, $14.95; pap., Bantam, $3.99).

Spooky ghost stories are included in the ten tales based on African-American history and culture that span the period from the days of slavery to the 1940s in Patricia C. McKissack's *The Dark-Thirty: Southern Tales of the Supernatural* (Knopf, 1992, $15).

About the Book

Booklist, July 1972, p. 1938.
Center for Children's Books Bulletin, October 1992, p. 43.
Kirkus Reviews, October 1, 1992, p. 1255.
School Library Journal, January 1993, p. 98.

About the Author

Block, Ann, and Riley, Carolyn, eds., *Children's Literature Review.* Gale, 1976, Vol. 1, pp. 103–107.

Chevalier, Tracy, ed., *Twentieth-Century Children's Writers* (3rd ed.). St. James, 1989, pp. 442–444.

Commire, Anne, ed., *Something about the Author.* Gale, 1973, Vol. 4, pp. 97–99; updated 1989, Vol. 56, pp. 60–70.

de Montreville, Doris, and Crawford, Elizabeth D., eds., *Fourth Book of Junior Authors and Illustrators.* Wilson, 1978, pp. 162–164.

Estes, Glenn E., ed., *American Writers for Children since 1960: Fiction* (Dictionary of Literary Biography: Vol. 52). Gale, 1986, pp. 174–184.

Garrett, Agnes, and McCue, Helga P., eds., *Authors and Artists for Young Adults.* Gale, 1989, Vol. 2, pp. 53–64.

Kirkpatrick, D. L., ed., *Twentieth-Century Children's Writers* (2nd ed.). St. Martin's, 1983, pp. 353–354.
Metzger, Linda, and Straub, Deborah A., eds., *Contemporary Authors* (New Revision Series). Gale, 1987, Vol. 20, pp. 207–212.
Nasso, Christine, ed., *Contemporary Authors* (First Revision). Gale, 1977, Vols. 25–28, p. 299.
Senick, Gerard J., ed., *Children's Literature Review*. Gale, 1986, Vol. 11, pp. 94–95.
Ward, Martha, ed., *Authors of Books for Young People* (3rd ed.). Scarecrow, 1990, p. 527.

Haseley, Dennis. *Shadows*

Illus. by Leslie Bowman. Farrar, 1991, $12.95 (0-374-36761-2); pap., $3.95 (0-374-46611-4)

Dennis Haseley is primarily known as the writer of the text of several fine picture books. His first, *The Scared Dog* (o.p.), appeared in 1983 and tells the story of a Native American boy who finds a miraculous bird and, through this experience, also finds his own identity and place in the world. *The Old Banjo* (pap., Macmillan, 1990, $3.95) is another unusual book for very young readers. It tells of a farm full of instruments that no one plays anymore. In its short, tightly written text, *Shadows* combines realism and imagination when a lonely boy's life is changed by his grandpa teaching him to make shadow pictures. This story of self-discovery and familial love is simple enough to attract reluctant readers. It is read by students in grades 3 through 5.

Plot Summary

While his mother is up in Connecticut looking for work, Jamie is spending the summer with his Aunt Elena and Uncle Edward. They live in rural West Virginia, where they own an odds-and-ends store. Jamie helps them but it is a lonely life for him. However, Grandpa starts to visit and things get better.

Grandpa shows Jamie the magic of using his hands to make shadows come to life on the wall. Suddenly, there appears a bobcat, or a hawk, or even a dog named Tobias. Grandpa offers to teach him the wonderful mysteries of this talent. Jamie doesn't quite get the hang of it at first, but Grandpa assures him that with time and practice, he will become a great shadow maker, just like another little boy did some years before.

The other little boy is, as Jamie knows, his own father, Grandpa's son and Aunt Elena's brother. Jamie's father was killed in an accident at his factory, which is why his mother is now looking for teaching work up in Connecticut.

Grandpa comes by every now and again to teach Jamie shadows and to tell him stories about the wonderful, daring exploits of his father. Jamie begins to realize that Aunt Elena does not approve of Grandpa's visits. She doesn't exactly say why. Jamie is also aware that Aunt Elena keeps a very close watch on his own behavior, almost as though she is looking for something wrong to sprout up.

One day Aunt Elena and Uncle Edward must attend an all-day antiques show. It is quite far from home and not something that Jamie would enjoy anyway so they decide to leave him at home alone.

After his aunt and uncle leave, Jamie faces a long day by himself. But even before he has a chance to get lonely, Grandpa arrives. To Jamie's delight, they are going to spend the day together. They end up having supper at Grandpa's rundown cabin. It is a glorious time for Jamie.

When they return to the house, however, his aunt and uncle are back from the show. Aunt Elena is furious with her father for taking Jamie away without letting anyone know where he was. In dismay, Jamie overhears his aunt tell his grandfather that perhaps he should not come to see the boy anymore. Elena feels her father is a bad influence on the boy. For one thing, he is constantly making up heroic stories about Jamie's father. Jamie learns that the stories aren't true. According to Aunt Elena, Jamie's father was much more reckless than adventuresome. In fact, it was his own recklessness that just might have caused his accidental death.

After that night, Jamie doesn't want to stay with his aunt and uncle any longer. He is relieved when word comes from his mother that she has found a job in Connecticut. She will soon be coming down to West Virginia to pick him up. Jamie will be glad to go—somehow the magic has gone out of shadows on the wall. Jamie just can't make them dance anymore.

One night as Jamie lies sleepless, the shadows return and beckon to him. He follows them out into the night. They lead him all the way to Grandpa's cabin, where he finds the old man nearly overcome by smoke from a backed-up stove flue. Jamie and his shadows save the old man.

Later, Jamie tells Grandpa what he overheard about his father. He knows what Aunt Elena said, but just maybe, Jamie tells Grandpa, his dad really was all the things Grandpa said—in a way. Just as those shadows really did come and lead Jamie to the cabin. Grandpa just hugs him.

Grandpa and Aunt Elena and Uncle Edward see Jamie and his mother off at the station for their new life in Connecticut. He sheds some tears, but he's not really sad to go. He's got his shadows to take with him, all the way north.

Thematic Material

This is a sensitive story of dreams and imagination set against the realities of life. Grandpa sees the adventuresome spirit of his dead son in the person of his grandson Jamie, but Aunt Elena sees only the heartache and disaster caused by what she views as her brother's recklessness. Jamie is portrayed as a sensitive, thoughtful young boy who is aware of the conflicts in his family but still imaginative enough to dream.

Book Talk Material

Grandpa's instructions for making shadows serve as an excellent introduction to this short story of family love. See: Grandpa and Jamie meet (pp. 5–10); Jamie tries to make a hawk fly (p. 14); Jamie meets Robert the bobcat (pp. 24–27); and Jamie learns the story of Tobias, mascot of a whole regiment of soldiers (pp. 30–35).

Additional Selections

A misfit boy fights to keep his grandfather from a retirement home in Stella Pevsner's *Keep Stomping Till the Music Stops* (Houghton, 1979, $13.50).

World War I Pittsburgh is the setting of Gloria Skurzynski's *Good-Bye, Billy Radish* (Macmillan, 1992, $14.95), the story of a friendship between a young American boy and the son of Ukrainian immigrants and of its tragic end.

While spending a summer in the country, two young girls conquer their grief and loneliness in Kevin Henkes's *Words of Stone* (Greenwillow, 1992, $13).

Lisa is overprotective of her younger brother, who has special needs, in a tender novel about growing up, *Commander Coatrack Returns* (Houghton, 1989, $13.95; pap., Dell, $3.25) by Joseph McNair.

Tony must assume family responsibilities when his father leaves home and his mother sinks into alcoholism in *Safe at Home!* (Macmillan, 1992, $12.95) by Peggy King Anderson.

Ten-year-old Lottie wants to become a prima ballerina, but her pet dog produces conflicts, in Rumer Godden's *Listen to the Nightingale* (Viking, 1992, $15).

Charlie faces the usual problems of an eleven-year-old, but they are minor compared to those of his sister, Annie, who has Down's syndrome, in *My Sister Annie* (Boyds Mills, 1993, $14.95) by Bill Dodds.

About the Book

Booklist, July 1991, p. 2045.
Center for Children's Books Bulletin, July 1991, p. 263.
Horn Book, July 1991, p. 456.
Horn Book Guide, Fall 1991, p. 263.
Kirkus Reviews, May 1991, p. 604.
New York Times Book Review, October 20, 1991, p. 53.
School Library Journal, July 1991, p. 106.
See also *Book Review Digest,* 1992 cum.; and *Book Review Index,* 1991, p. 395; 1992.

About the Author

Commire, Anne, ed., *Something about the Author.* Gale, 1989, Vol. 57, pp. 65–68.

MacLachlan, Patricia. *Journey*

Delacorte, 1991, $13.95 (0-385-30427-7); pap., Dell, $3.50 (0-440-40809-1)

Patricia MacLachlan did not begin writing until age thirty-five, after her three children were grown. Her first book, *The Sick Day* (Pantheon, 1979, $16.95), and those immediately following were texts for picture books. Since that time, she has also produced a number of distinguished stories for the middle grades, her most famous being *Sarah, Plain and Tall* (Harper, 1985, $11; pap., $3.95; condensed in *Introducing Bookplots 3,* Bowker, 1990, pp. 23–26), which won the 1986 Newbery Medal and is based on an actual incident in the author's family history. In this 56-page novel, set in a prairie town during pioneer days, young Caleb and Anna, whose mother died when Caleb was born, are apprehensive about the mail-order bride, Sarah Elizabeth Wheaton from Maine, who has been invited to live with them and their father for one month on a trial basis. The story tells of the love that grows between these people and of Sarah's eventual decision to stay. Two other excellent novels for this age group are *Arthur, for the Very First Time* (Harper, 1980, $13.89; pap., $3.95), which tells how a shy ten-year-old boy gains self-confidence during a summer spent with his great-aunt and great-uncle; and *The Facts and Fictions of Minna Pratt* (Harper, 1988, $12), about the questions concerning growing up that beset a young girl who plays the cello and how she finds answers to some of them through her friendship with another cellist, Lucas Ellerby. *Journey* is another brief novel (only 83 pages), yet in this short text, which tells of two months in the life of the narrator, a young boy's deep feelings on the nature of loss and of families are evoked. The four novels mentioned are suitable for readers in grades 4 through 6.

Plot Summary

In the same way their father left them several years before, Liddie, mother of eleven-year-old Journey and his slightly older sister, Cat, has now abandoned them. The two youngsters have lived their entire lives with their mother and grandparents on the family farm; now a vast emptiness has entered their lives, although before leaving their mother promised to keep in touch and send money to her children.

The youngsters react to their pain differently. For Cat it is a time for action and new beginnings. She gives her camera to Grandpa and her flute to Grandma, then decides to become a vegetarian and help Grandma more faithfully in the large family garden. Journey internalizes the pain, feels he is somehow to blame for his mother's departure, and continually seeks reasons for it.

Grandpa enjoys taking photographs of the animals and places on the farm. He concentrates on snapping the members of the family in everyday situations. Even Journey begins to think there is an ulterior motive for this incessant picture-taking.

One day a letter arrives from Mama. It contains only money, no message, and no return address. That evening, to help ease the hurt, Grandma brings an old family photograph album into Journey's bedroom and shows him pictures of herself and his mother when they were his age. Grandma says that even as a child, his mother always wanted to be some other place.

The next day, Journey is visited by his best friend, Cooper MacDougal, who is baby-sitting his brother, Emmett. Cooper has a crush on Cat, even though he is still a preteenager. The youngsters look at the photo album and are struck by the family resemblances from one generation to the next. Grandpa begins playing with Emmett and reciting a nursery rhyme that evokes for Journey a vague childhood memory.

In spite of Journey's protests, Grandpa insists it is time the boy learn to drive the family car and take him into town so he can buy some special photographic equipment. His fears conquered, Journey navigates beautifully, and, of course, this momentous occasion is marked with another flurry of picture taking. When Journey tries his hand with the camera, he is not too pleased with the results, but his grandfather takes him aside and explains that in pictures, as in life, everything can't be perfect. Often we should be content with good enough. Journey wants to know if life on the farm wasn't good enough for his mother. His grandfather says that regardless of her reasons for leaving, it wasn't Journey's fault, and he must stop blaming himself. Journey asks his grandfather what has happened to the pictures of himself and Cat with their mother. He is devastated to learn Mama tore them up before leaving.

Journey is in his room one evening when he hears a scratching on the window sill. He lets in an adult cat that promptly falls asleep on his bed. Knowing his grandmother dislikes cats because they kill birds, Journey tells only Grandpa about the new arrival and says he would love to adopt her. The family has a rule that once an animal is named it must be kept; Grandpa therefore summons Grandma and announces that Journey has found a cat, whom he has named Bloom. In spite of her initial reluctance, Grandma is soon won over, particularly when the family discovers Bloom is pregnant. Of course, pictures are taken of Bloom's progress.

One day, Journey finds his cat has strayed into Mama's old room and is asleep in a box under the bed. The boy discovers the box contains the fragments of the pictures his mother shredded. He begins the impossible task of trying to piece together these remembrances of his past, but Bloom has other plans. She chooses the box when it comes time to deliver her litter. Although the pictures are ruined, four new lives have come into the world. Later, when Bloom leaves the kittens to go outdoors, Journey becomes agitated, but is assured by his sister that Bloom will return to her family.

One day, Mama phones. Although Journey is torn, he decides for the time being not to accept her invitation to visit. He explains to her that he cannot leave his cat and her new family.

It is now two months since Mama left. Grandma has made progress on the flute, and Grandpa continues his incessant picture-taking. It is Cat who explains this obsession to Journey. She says he takes the pictures to give them a sense of family and provide their future with a past. When Journey notices Grandpa spending hours in his back room in the barn, the boy creeps out one night and discovers that Grandpa has set up a darkroom and is producing, as a surprise for Journey, prints from the negatives he has found of Mama's destroyed pictures. As the boy sees a past he scarcely remembers come to life before his eyes, he reaches out and takes his grandfather's hand in his.

Thematic Material

In this touching story, the title refers both to the main character and to his journey toward acceptance of being abandoned, beginning with feelings of guilt, moving through a period of bitterness, and eventually arriving at understanding and resignation. The concept of continuity in families and time is explored, as is the theme that people and events cannot be considered as being either completely good or bad, but instead must be judged by relative standards. Love and wholesome family relationships are well portrayed, as is the simple rural life. The different reactions by brother and sister to Mama's leaving provide contrast and interesting character development. Friendship, the renewal of life, devotion, and gaining emotional maturity are also important themes.

Book Talk Material

The page preceding chapter 1, in which Mama leaves, will serve as an interesting introduction to the book. Some other passages: Cat gives up her flute and camera (pp. 2–6); Grandma shows Journey the photograph album (pp. 10–13); Journey learns to drive the car (pp. 21–26); Grandpa explains that people often must settle for something less than perfection (pp. 28–31); and Bloom arrives and is named (pp. 38–43).

Additional Selections

In Meindert DeJong's *Shadrach* (Harper, 1953, $14.89; pap., $3.95), David finds a new reason for living in his pet, a little black rabbit named Shadrach.

Set in Oklahoma during the Depression, *Red-Dirt Jessie* (Walker, 1992, $13.95), by Anna Myers, tells of a twelve-year-old girl who tries to tame a wild dog to help her father regain his will to live.

During a summer spent in a small New England town, thirteen-year-old Tracy Stewart discovers she is adopted in *Family Secrets* (Macmillan, 1992, $13.95) by Barbara Corcoran.

Retta, whose mother is dead, must take over the family responsibilities when her father works nights in *The Night Swimmers* (Delacorte, 1980, $9.95; pap., Dell, $3.50) by Betsy Byars.

In E. L. Konigsburg's *Journey to an 800 Number* (Macmillan, 1982, $13.95; pap., Dell, $2.95), Bo learns about love, loyalty, and sincerity when he goes to live with his father after his mother decides to remarry.

Ten-year-old Henry attends a school for the deaf in Pennsylvania in the early days of the automobile, and there he learns to talk and draw, in Mary Riskind's *Apple Is My Sign* (Houghton, 1981, $12.70; pap., $3.80).

In Eleanora E. Tate's *Just an Overnight Guest* (Dial, 1980, $8.95) nine-year-old Margie cannot adjust to the bratty four-year-old Ethel who has come to live with her.

About the Book

Booklist, September 15, p. 153.
Center for Children's Books, October 1991, p. 44.
Emergency Librarian, January 1992, p. 50.
Horn Book, November 1991, p. 737.
Horn Book Guide, Spring 1992, p. 69.
Kirkus Reviews, August 1, 1991, p. 1013.
New York Times Book Review, March 22, 1992, p. 25.
School Library Journal, September 1991, p. 257.
VOYA, October 1991, p. 228.
Wilson Library Bulletin, December 1991, p. 100.
See also *Book Review Digest,* 1992, p. 1235; and *Book Review Index,* 1991, p. 573; and 1992, p. 568.

About the Author

Chevalier, Tracy, ed., *Twentieth-Century Children's Writers* (3rd ed.). St. James, 1989, pp. 622–623.
Commire, Anne, ed., *Something about the Author.* Gale, 1990, Vol. 62, pp. 115–122.
Holtze, Sally Holmes, ed., *Sixth Book of Junior Authors and Illustrators.* Wilson, 1989, pp. 177–184.
Senick, Gerard J., ed., *Children's Literature Review.* Gale, 1988, Vol. 14, pp. 177–186.
Trosky, Susan M., ed., *Contemporary Authors.* Gale, 1992, Vol. 137, pp. 261–263.
Ward, Martha, ed., *Authors of Books for Young People* (3rd ed.). Scarecrow, 1990, p. 459.

Naylor, Phyllis Reynolds. *Shiloh*

Macmillan, 1991, $12.95 (0-689-31614-3); pap., Dell, $3.50 (0-440-40752-4)

As Phyllis Reynolds Naylor states in her autobiography, *How I Came to Be a Writer* (pap., Macmillan, 1987, $4.95), she began writing as a teenager.

Since then she has written about sixty books for children, among them the popular Alice series for middle-grade readers. In the first, *The Agony of Alice* (Macmillan, 1985, $13.95), eleven-year-old Alice, who wants a teacher who can be a gorgeous, poised substitute for the mother she doesn't have, is disappointed in homely Mrs. Plotkin, who nevertheless teaches Alice some valuable lessons about life. Alice has a boyfriend during the summer before entering seventh grade in the continuation, *Alice in Rapture, Sort of* (Macmillan, 1989, $13.95; pap., Dell, $3.25). Two others in the series are *Reluctantly, Alice* (Macmillan, 1991, $13.95; pap., Dell, $3.25) and *Alice in April* (Macmillan, 1993, $13.95). *Shiloh,* a somewhat more serious novel about a boy's overwhelming love for a stray dog, was awarded the 1992 Newbery Medal. The story grew out of a visit the author made to West Virginia where she met "the saddest dog I ever saw." That dog became Shiloh. It is a first-person narrative told by young Marty Preston in a frequently ungrammatical but authentic West Virginia dialect. This novel is enjoyed by readers in grades 3 through 6.

Plot Summary

Eleven-year-old Marty Preston is the oldest of the three Preston children, who live with their parents in a humble four-room house in rural West Virginia close to a small town called Friendly. Their home, situated on a wooded property surrounded by three hills, is isolated but beautiful in its peacefulness and quiet. The other children are Dara Lynn, age seven, and the baby, Becky, age three. Ray Preston, their father, is a rural mail deliverer and, although he has a steady job, much of his salary is used to support his ailing aged mother, who lives with her daughter and requires constant home care. Lou Preston, their mother, is therefore often hard pressed to run a household of five on the meager amount of money available. She often must rely on Roy's prowess as a hunter to put meat on the table. Nevertheless, it is a loving, caring household in which simple things like being polite and considerate are stressed as important guidelines by which to live.

One Sunday, after a noontime rabbit dinner, Marty takes his .22 rifle out for target practice. Marty has a great respect for living things and would never shoot an animal or bird. In the Shiloh woods he realizes he is being followed by a young beagle with black and brown spots. From its cautious, frightened behavior, Marty surmises the dog has been severely maltreated. Gradually the dog realizes he won't be harmed and allows Marty to pet and play with him. He follows the boy home and, in spite of pelting rain, remains hunched outside the house until Marty sneaks out and feeds him an egg from the hen house. Marty decides to call him Shiloh after the area where he was found.

Mr. Preston is certain the dog is Judd Travers's new hunting dog. After supper, he loads Shiloh and Marty into their Jeep to return the dog. Although Marty doesn't know Judd Travers well, he has ample reason to dislike him. He has seen Judd cheat the local general store owner out of ten dollars, and he knows Judd hunts out of season and is cruel to his hunting dogs. He also has the disgusting habit of spitting tobacco out of the side of his mouth. As Marty fears, the dog belongs to Judd, who, as a welcome-home present, gives the dog a nasty kick and promises to cut his rations until he learns not to run away. Marty is heartbroken but helpless. He plans to start earning money so that one day he will be able to buy Shiloh for his own. The next day he begins collecting bottles and cans from roadsides, hoping to make some money from deposits. The pickings are very lean, and he becomes discouraged.

The following morning, Marty hears a strange but familiar sound from the direction of the sycamore tree in the yard. It is Shiloh, who has escaped from Judd again. Marty carries him into the woods, where he puts up a four-by-six-foot pen using some fencing wire he finds in the barn and builds a little lean-to of old planks to protect the dog from the rain. He also feeds him table scraps he manages to take from the house. He feels increasingly guilty about deceiving his parents, particularly when, the next evening, Judd drives by in his pickup looking for the dog and Marty lies openly, saying he hasn't seen the dog. However, he feels that saving Shiloh's life is now his most important mission.

In the next few days, Marty's life is an agony of trying to keep Shiloh's whereabouts a secret. Once Dara Lynn almost happens on his hiding place, and on another occasion his father is asked by Judd to hunt on the Prestons' land, but luckily the request is refused. When Marty's best friend, David Howard, asks to visit and explore in the woods, Marty decides to hitch a ride to David's home in Friendly rather than face the possibility of discovery. Ironically, the man who gives him a ride is Judd Travers, who again threatens a terrible punishment on his dog when it is found.

The visit with David is fun. With the sandwich Mrs. Howard packs for his walk home and some scraps he buys from the local store with his deposit money, Marty now has enough food to feed Shiloh for the next few days.

Discovery comes quickly. Ma, who has become suspicious of Marty's eating habits, follows him into the woods and sees Shiloh. Giving in to

Marty's tearful pleas, she agrees to remain silent for twenty-four hours to see if Marty can work out a solution. However, that evening the household is awakened by loud yelping and barking from the direction of the pen. A savage German shepherd has jumped the fence and is attacking Shiloh fiercely. Marty and his father drive the intruder off, but Shiloh is badly injured and bleeding profusely. In the middle of the night Mr. Preston takes him to Doc Murphy, who stitches him up and cleans out the wounds, but the dog is unable to walk. On the way home, Marty once again begs to keep the dog. Reluctantly, Mr. Preston agrees to keep Shiloh until he has recovered. Then he must be returned to Judd.

The next day Doc Murphy brings Shiloh back to the Prestons, where he quickly captures the hearts of the entire family. Just when he is able to hobble about, Judd Travers appears at their door. Through acquaintances who saw Shiloh at the doctor's office, he has tracked down the dog. Judd refuses to sell the dog and demands that he be returned on Sunday, only three days away. Marty frantically tries to think of a way to keep Shiloh, but in vain.

Early on Sunday morning, he decides to walk over to Judd's hoping for a last-minute reprieve. On the way he sees a grazing doe and a moment later hears rifle shots. The deer falls dead, and Judd strides into the clearing to claim his illegal prize. Marty confronts him and threatens to expose him to the local game warden for hunting out of season. Judd strikes a bargain with Marty. If the boy will keep silent about the deer and do twenty hours of labor around Judd's house weeding, stacking wood, and doing odd jobs, the dog is his. Marty gets a written contract from Judd and gleefully returns home.

The family is overjoyed that Shiloh is going to become a permanent member of the household, but guilt again overwhelms Marty because he cannot tell his family the real cause of Judd's change of heart.

Each day Marty walks to Judd's to do two of his twenty hours of service, and Judd does everything he can to make the boy give up. Once he tells him the contract is invalid because there were no witnesses; on other occasions he feigns sleep, thinking Marty will steal off before his two hours are up. He also assigns him the most back-breaking chores of all—splitting large chunks of locust wood using a heavy wedge and sledge hammer. But Marty's body and spirit will not be broken, and by the last day Judd grudgingly feels something close to admiration for this gutsy boy who won't take "no" for an answer. As a parting gift, he gives Marty an old dog collar. It's pretty large, but in time, Marty knows, it will fit Shiloh snugly.

Thematic Material

This is a story of the great bond that can exist between a boy and a dog. It is also a plea to end cruelty to helpless animals and to respect all living creatures. Marty's feelings of guilt that he has to compromise his honesty, steal, and deceive his parents to save Shiloh introduce the question, "Does the end ever justify the means?" The author has captured the atmosphere of rural West Virginia and the speech patterns of the residents authentically. Solid family relationships, animal rights, the courage to fight for a just cause, and a boy's first steps to independence are other subjects dealt with in this novel.

Book Talk Material

Some interesting passages that could be read or retold are: dinner at the Prestons (pp. 11–12); Shiloh is first introduced (pp. 13–18); reasons are given why Marty doesn't like Judd Travers, and Shiloh is returned (pp. 22–27); Shiloh reappears (pp. 40–44); and Marty lies to Judd (pp. 51–54).

Additional Selections

In *Where the Red Fern Grows* (Bantam, 1992, $16; pap., $3.25) by Wilson Rawls, a young boy saves money to buy two coon dogs and is heartbroken when they die.

Two dogs and a Siamese cat set out on a perilous trek to return to their original home in *The Incredible Journey* (Bantam, 1990, $14.95; pap., $2.95) by Sheila Burnford.

Cory, the product of a troubled home, throws her love and energy into training a blind Bedlington terrier named Sterling in Lynn Hall's *The Soul of the Silver Dog* (Harcourt, 1992, $16.95).

In *Poor Badger* (Doubleday, 1992, $14) by K. M. Peyton, a novel set in the English countryside, Roz, a high-spirited girl, rescues a pony from its cruel owner but can't afford to keep him.

A boy grieves when his pet pelican is shot by a hunter in Colin Thiele's *Storm Boy* (Harper, 1978, $12.89), a story set in rural Australia.

In Jim Arnosky's *Long Spikes* (Houghton, 1992, $12.70), a yearling buck and his twin sister set out to survive in the wilderness.

About the Book

Booklist, December 1, 1991, p. 696.
Center for Children's Books Bulletin, October 1991, p. 45.
Horn Book, January 1992, p. 74.

Horn Book Guide, Spring 1992, p. 70.
Kirkus Reviews, September 1, 1991, p. 1163.
New York Times Book Review, May 10, 1992, p. 21.
School Library Journal, September 1991, p. 258.
Wilson Library Bulletin, January 1992, p. 110.
See also *Book Review Digest,* 1992, pp. 1436–1437; and *Book Review Index,* 1991, p. 662, and 1992, p. 659.

About the Author

Chevalier, Tracy, ed., *Twentieth-Century Children's Writers* (3rd ed.). St. James, 1989, pp. 710–712.
Commire, Anne, ed., *Something about the Author.* Gale, 1977, Vol. 12, pp. 156–157.
Holtze, Sally Holmes, ed., *Fifth Book of Junior Authors and Illustrators.* Wilson, 1983, pp. 227–228.
Nakamura, Joyce, ed., *Something about the Author: Autobiography Series.* Gale, 1990, Vol. 10, pp. 183–199.
Nasso, Christine, ed., *Contemporary Authors* (First Revision). Gale, 1977, Vols. 21–24, p. 634.
Olendorf, Donna, ed., *Something about the Author.* Gale, 1991, Vol. 66, pp. 170–176.
Senick, Gerard J., ed., *Children's Literature Review.* Gale, 1989, Vol. 17, pp. 48–62.
Straub, Deborah A., ed., *Contemporary Authors* (New Revision Series). Gale, 1988, Vol. 24, pp. 334–345.
Ward, Susan M., ed., *Authors of Books for Young People* (3rd ed.). Scarecrow, 1990, p. 520.

Nixon, Joan Lowery. *Maggie Forevermore*

Harcourt, 1987, $13.95 (0-15-250345-5)

Jean Lowery Nixon is extremely versatile and writes for a large range of age groups. For the teenage audience, she is best known for her fast-paced mystery novels that keep readers guessing until the last page. For middle-grade readers, one of her most successful series has been the four historical novels known as the Orphan Train Quartet, the true story of orphans sent from New York City by the Children's Aid Society in the 1860s to be adopted by parents in the West. The first part is *A Family Apart* (Bantam, 1987, $14.95; pap., $3.99) in which a young girl disguises herself as a boy to accompany her brother to his new home. In the Maggie books, the author introduces an engaging contemporary heroine in a series of lightweight but enjoyable stories. The first two Maggie books are *Maggie, Too* (Harcourt, 1986, $12.95; pap., Dell, $2.95) and *And Maggie Makes Three* (Harcourt, 1986, $12.95; pap., Dell, $2.95). In *Maggie Forevermore,* thirteen-year-old Maggie must spend Christmas in Southern California getting to know her stepmother. These novels are read by youngsters in grades 5 through 8.

Plot Summary

Thirteen-year-old Maggie Ledoux is looking forward to her first real family Christmas. It will be complete with Grandma Landry, with whom Maggie is now living in Houston, Texas; aunts and uncles and cousins; and possibly the most beautiful Christmas tree in the whole world. This is going to be a really special holiday for Maggie, as she explains to her best friend, Lisa. It will be so different from the California celebrations spent with her movie director/producer father. Why, one year, she tells a surprised Lisa, they even had a silver-and-black patent-leather tree!

However, Maggie's father is now remarried—to a twenty-year-old starlet named Kiki—and is living in a beach house in Malibu. Her father, Roger, sent her to spend the summer with Grandma Landry in Texas and Maggie begged to stay on and go to school in Houston. Roger did not object. Maggie loves her father, but, frankly, they just don't get along.

Right in the middle of Maggie's wonderful Christmas dreams, she gets a call from her father that spoils everything. He is sending her an airline ticket. He wants her to spend the holidays with him and Kiki in Malibu. He explains that his busy schedule is free right now, and this would be a good time for Maggie to get acquainted with her stepmother. Maggie protests, but to no avail. She must go and spend two weeks in California.

Maggie—Margaret to her father—and her father get off to a rather strained start. It just seems as though they are always saying the wrong things to each other, and Maggie often ends up saying things she wishes she could take back. However, to her surprise, she finds herself drawn to her young stepmother, who is casual and friendly and seems to understand Maggie's feelings about being "dragged away." Kiki tries to reassure Maggie that her father truly loves her, even though he has a hard time expressing it and seems to lose patience with her very easily.

Soon after her arrival, Maggie meets two people about her own age. Timmy Blake is a real-life star; he plays the part of Dick Dackery, who flies around in a spaceship with his father and solves crimes. Maggie thinks Blake is stuck up at first, but soon she begins to see the friendly, warm boy underneath the "star" veneer. She also meets Truly Norris, who is trying very hard to become a star in Hollywood, a town loaded with children and parents who think they have talent.

Maggie gets Kiki to agree that they will decorate an old-fashioned Christmas tree in the Malibu beach house, with her father's reluctant OK. She also invites her new friends, Blake and Truly, to join her. During the decorating party, they learn that Truly's agent is a man named Klinke, and that he demanded money before he would sign Truly as one of his clients. They also learn that Klinke apparently has not paid Truly for some small acting jobs. When Truly's father comes to pick her up that evening, Maggie's father explains to him that this agent sounds unscrupulous. Truly's father loses his temper at hearing this news. The next day he gives Klinke a black eye. The agent presses charges.

Maggie is determined to help her new friend. First she calls Grandma Landry in Texas, who is a great mystery/detective fan. Grandma suggests the only way to stop Klinke is to figure out what kind of mistake he is making. Criminals always make mistakes eventually, Grandma says.

This gives Maggie a great idea. She talks Kiki into "dressing up" as her mother and taking her to Klinke's office under the pretense of signing her up. They get an appointment and visit Klinke, who is all too willing to sign Maggie, even though she has not auditioned for him and he has no idea if she has talent or not. All he wants is several hundred dollars and a signed contract. They leave the office without signing or paying the money, but they do have a tape recording of their conversation with the unscrupulous Klinke.

Bill Hartley, a detective friend of Kiki's, tells them the tape recording will do them no good. It is against the law to secretly tape a conversation to use against someone. However, that gives Maggie another idea. On the tape Klinke incriminates himself, talking about a casting job that will pay $50 per person.

Maggie and Kiki try to persuade Truly's parents and the parents of other children who have been cheated by Klinke to join together to bring legal action. They meet opposition from parents whose only concern is to get their children into "show biz."

When Maggie asks her father to help them, he refuses and Maggie loses her temper. Suddenly she sees how much she and her father are alike in their reactions to things. Maggie calms down and apologizes. Her father calms down too, and says that perhaps there is something he can do.

He has them consult a young attorney, Jonathan Browne, who gets a summons issued against Klinke. But who will deliver the summons?

Kiki and Maggie take the summons to Klinke's office only to discover that he is "out of town." After another consultation with Grandma in

Houston, they decide to send Klinke a message through his answering service, telling him to meet Maggie's father in the Polo Lounge, where they are all going for dinner.

Sure enough, Klinke shows up. When he sees them, he turns and runs only to find his path blocked by Blake, who is coming to meet them for dinner. That slows Klinke down enough for Kiki to put the summons in his pocket.

Blake is so pleased to have done something "all by himself" that he kisses Maggie. She decides she likes it. She also decides she will look forward to her next visit to her father and Kiki and her new friends in California. She thinks that from now on, she and her father will have a much closer relationship. As she tells him, "From now on, call me Maggie . . . I *am* happy as Maggie . . . I'm going to be Maggie forevermore."

Thematic Material

A standard, fast-moving, light detective-type story set in the not-always-glamorous world of Hollywood and child stars. Maggie is an average thirteen-year-old with a tendency to become impatient, just like her father. Her genuine love for her grandmother and her growing affection for the young woman who is her stepmother are nicely drawn and realistic. Although the youngsters' ability to bring the unscrupulous agent to justice may be slightly forced, young readers should enjoy the setting and a look into the lives of the trying-to-be-famous set.

Book Talk Material

Glimpses of the lives of child stars should fascinate readers of this book. See: Maggie first meets Blake and discovers a friend beneath the "star" veneer (pp. 16–22); Maggie is hired as an elf and meets Truly (pp. 26–29); Truly talks about her agent, Klinke (pp. 33–36); Maggie and Kiki go to Klinke's office for an interview (pp. 52–59); and they meet opposition from one mother of a budding star (pp. 74–79).

Additional Selections

Thirteen-year-old Jodie finds it difficult to adjust to a new stepfamily in C. S. Adler's *In Our House Scott Is My Brother* (Macmillan, 1980, $13.95).

Sammy, a sixth-grader, thinks he knows all about women, but Becky proves him wrong in Ronald Kidd's humorous *Sammy Carducci's Guide to Women* (Lodestar, 1991, $14.95).

In *The Scariest Night* (Holiday, 1991, $13.95) by Betty R. Wright, Evin reluctantly spends a summer in Milwaukee with her foster brother and meets a medium, Molly Panca, who (perhaps) is in touch with the spirit world.

Sara has the opportunity to sabotage her mother's budding romance with the father of her disliked classmate, Adam, in *Upside Down* (Viking, 1992, $13) by Mary Jane Miller.

Eleven-year-old Ari feels that other people, including her older sister, are taking advantage of her in Francine Pascal's *The Hand-Me-Down Kid* (Viking, 1980, $12.95; pap., Dell, $2.95).

In *Dear Dad, Love Laurie* (Scholastic, 1989, $10.95; pap., $2.75) by Susan Beth Pfeffer, Laurie writes once a week to her divorced father, now a thousand miles away.

Thirteen-year-old Gilda tries to keep her siblings together when it appears her mother and father are headed for divorce in C. S. Adler's *Tuna Fish Thanksgiving* (Houghton, 1992, $13.95).

About the Book

Booklist, March 1, 1997, p. 1054.
Center for Children's Books Bulletin, April 1987, p. 132.
Kirkus Reviews, January 1, 1957, p. 61.
School Library Journal, March 1987, p. 164.
VOYA, October 1987, p. 204.
See also *Book Review Digest,* 1987, p. 1374; and *Book Review Index,* 1987, p. 567.

About the Author

Chevalier, Tracy, ed., *Twentieth-Century Writers* (3rd ed.). St. James, 1989, pp. 723–724.
Commire, Anne, ed., *Something about the Author.* Gale, 1976, Vol. 8, pp. 143–144; updated 1986, Vol. 44, pp. 131–139.
Ethridge, James M., ed., *Contemporary Authors* (First Revision). Gale, 1965, Vols. 11–12, p. 297.
Evory, Ann, ed., *Contemporary Authors* (New Revision Series). Gale, 1982, Vol. 7, pp. 363–364.
Holtze, Sally Holmes, ed., *Fifth Book of Junior Authors and Illustrators.* Wilson, 1983, p. 230.
Kinsman, Clare D., ed., *Contemporary Authors* (First Revision). Gale, 1974, Vols. 9–12, pp. 678–679.
Senick, Gerard J., ed., *Children's Literature Review.* Gale, 1991, Vol. 24, pp. 131–154.
Straub, Deborah A., ed., *Contemporary Authors* (New Revision Series). Gale, 1985, Vol. 24, pp. 344–345.

Paterson, Katherine. *Park's Quest*
Dutton, 1988, $12.95 (0-525-67258-3); pap., Puffin, $3.95 (0-14-034262-1)

Katherine Paterson is one of the most respected and admired writers of juvenile fiction. She has a remarkable ability to deal with complex themes with a compassion and understanding that touch readers of all ages. For example, in *The Great Gilly Hopkins* (Harper, 1978, $14; pap., $3.95) and *Jacob Have I Loved* (Harper, 1980, $14; pap., Avon, $2.95; condensed in *Juniorplots 3,* Bowker, 1987, pp. 85–90), she explores complicated family relationships; and in *Bridge to Terabithia* (Harper, 1977, $14; pap., $3.95; condensed in *Introducing More Books,* Bowker, 1978, pp. 38–40), she writes movingly about a young boy's adjustment to the death of a friend. She has also used her experiences in the Far East to depict Oriental thinking and culture in such novels as *The Master Puppeteer* (Harper, 1976, $15; pap., $3.95; condensed in *Introducing More Books,* Bowker, 1978, pp. 114–117). All three of these subjects—family relationships, death, and the Orient—are blended in *Park's Quest,* the moving story of a boy's search for information about a father he never knew who was killed in the Vietnam War. Park is an imaginative lad whose mind is so full of Arthurian legends that he frequently internalizes everyday experiences and transforms them into incidents of derring-do, knightly quests, and fulfillment of sacred vows. These frequent shifts in style and time within the novel give both insight into the boy's thinking and an added dimension to Park's quest. This novel is enjoyed by perceptive readers in grades 5 through 8.

Plot Summary

It is 1984, and eleven-year-old Parkington Waddell Broughton the Fifth has just learned about the imminent unveiling on Veterans' Day of the Vietnam Memorial in Washington. Park, as he prefers to be called, is unfortunately also called Pork by his mother, because even as a baby he has had a tendency toward pudginess. This, combined with his large-rimmed glasses, does not create an initial favorable impression, but Park is really a very sensitive, caring youngster who consciously helps Marty, his working mother, manage their small apartment in suburban Washington. The only serious problem in their relationship is Parkington Waddell Broughton the Fourth, Park's father, who was a bomber pilot killed in

Vietnam in 1973, when Park was only a few months old. The boy is anxious to learn about him, but Marty is steadfast in refusing to discuss the subject. She even denies Park permission to attend the dedication of the memorial. Park becomes so obsessed with learning about his father that he embarks on his own personal quest for information about this stranger whose memory his mother is denying and about the family to which he belonged. He knows him only from a wartime photograph of a smiling, handsome man in uniform that the boy had found in a book of Emily Dickinson poems that had belonged to his father. In the apartment, he finds another of his father's books, a birthday gift inscribed to "Parkington the IV" by his father, Park's grandfather. Secretly, Park begins reading this and others of his father's books, hoping to experience his father's emotions vicariously, even though at times this involves wading through the difficult, often incomprehensible prose of such writers as Joseph Conrad.

Inevitably, Park's quest leads him to disobey his mother and visit the Vietnam Memorial, where, with the help of an attendant, he finds his father's name. Filled with incredible sadness and feelings of loss, he returns home, where he tells Marty both about the visit and about reading his father's books. Once more he pleads with her to talk about his father. Marty says it is still too painful for her to discuss, but that it seems time for Park to learn about his father by visiting his grandfather, Parkington Waddell Broughton III, at his large working farm and estate in rural Strathaven, Virginia.

Arrangements are made. At the beginning of his summer vacation, Park boards a Greyhound bus and enters the next phase of his mission, a two-week stay at his father's first home. At the station, he is met by a cheerful, friendly man who introduces himself as Frank. At first Park thinks he is a hired farmhand, but later he realizes the man is actually his father's younger brother, an uncle Park did not know existed. Frank explains that Park's grandfather, whom he calls the Colonel, has suffered two debilitating strokes. As a result of the second one two years ago, he is severely paralyzed, unable to talk, and confined to a wheelchair. He is looked after by a housekeeper, Mrs. Davenport, who greets Park and shows him to his room in the family home, a once-grand mansion that now shows signs of age and neglect. Park is told that Frank lives in an adjoining house with his wife, who is expecting a baby momentarily.

Left on his own, Park begins exploring the large estate. He happens on a small wooden structure that houses a spring. While taking a drink of the refreshing water from a half coconut shell, he is accosted by a young

Oriental girl about his age who, in shrill broken English, fiercely demands that he leave. This is Park's first encounter with the wildcat known as Thanh, who he discovers lives with Frank and his wife.

Later, when he tries to help milk one of the cows under Frank's patient surveillance, Thanh unmercifully continues her taunts and hurls open insults at him because of his ineptitude. Park decides he thoroughly despises this horrible creature, whom he inwardly refers to as the Geek. The effects of Thanh's open hostility are tempered somewhat when, the next day, Frank takes Park out target shooting and teaches him how to shoot the rifle Park's father had used as a youngster.

Frank tells Park the Colonel is so physically and emotionally feeble that a meeting with him would be unwise at present. However, later that night, Park is awakened by sounds of wailing from his grandfather's room. He creeps into the bedroom and sees the old man sobbing. After running back to his bedroom, Park thinks that perhaps his quest is unwise and that his mother was right to protect him from the truth about his father. He is on the point of packing and returning home, when there are other diversions: Frank takes him out shooting again, and the Geek begins to behave a little less like an untamed hellion. Frank even allows him to meet the Colonel and wheel him out to the porch for some sunshine. Unfortunately, while Park snoozes in the veranda swing, Thanh decides the Colonel needs an outing to the springhouse and maneuvers the wheelchair halfway down the hill before Park can make a timely rescue.

When Frank's wife goes into labor and Frank takes her to the hospital, Park decides to go target shooting by himself. As he takes aim for his first shot, Thanh suddenly appears and jumps on him, proclaiming that guns are bad and should never be used. The shot goes wild and hits a crow. Accusing Park of being a murderer, Thanh runs off. Park recovers the bird and, finding that it is only wounded, takes it to the springhouse, where he intends to nurse it. Park enters Thanh's house to tell her the news and sees on the young girl's dresser a picture of his father and a Vietnamese woman, who Thanh reveals is her mother, now Frank's wife. She and her mother had lived in refugee camps for over two years after the war until Frank sent for them and later married her mother. Thanh has never been told the identity of the man in the picture. Park tells her the truth and they suddenly realize they are brother and sister.

That evening, during a phone call to his mother, further details are supplied. When his father returned from Vietnam on leave after Park's birth, he confessed to Marty his affair with the Vietnamese girl, who was now pregnant by him. Unable to accept this situation, Marty divorced him shortly before he was killed.

After dinner, Frank phones from the hospital and proudly announces the birth of his son. Thanh's reaction: "Now two big fat stupid bruzzuh."

After Mrs. Davenport goes to bed, Park and Thanh steal out to take food to the crow. Thanh decides the Colonel also needs an outing, so the two tuck him into his wheelchair and carefully maneuver it to the springhouse. While Thanh goes to feed the bird, Park is alone with his grandfather. Suddenly he feels the touch of the old man's hand on his cheek. With tears streaming down their cheeks, the two embrace, made one through guilt and grief. Thanh returns and, announcing the crow has flown off, presents the coconut shell filled with spring water. Each of them drinks as if partaking of a holy sacrament.

Thematic Material

The controversy and scars left by the Vietnam War are difficult for both adults and children. This novel explores one family's loss, grief, guilt, and the tangled relationships resulting from the war. The parallels between Park's quest and that of a medieval knight seeking the truth are well sustained even to the last scene, where the coconut shell becomes a symbol both of Vietnam and of the Holy Grail, the bitter cup of truth. The effects of war and violence on children are vividly depicted in Thanh's hostile behavior, which only masks the pathetic sorrow in her past. The adage that truth makes one free is explored in Park's growing awareness of his family's past and his mother's inability to accept her private guilt. The misgivings, identity confusion, and ego problems Park faces are convincingly portrayed. Other subjects treated include mother-son relations, family ties, friendship, acceptance of death, and the nature of injustice.

Book Talk Material

After a brief discussion of the Vietnam War and its aftermath (perhaps through mention of the memorial in Washington), Park and his particular problem could be introduced. Some passages of importance are: Park decides he must learn about his father (pp. 12–15); Park looks at his father's picture and reads his books (pp. 19–23); his trip to the memorial (pp. 29–35); meeting Uncle Frank (pp. 40–45); his first encounter with Thanh (pp. 53–59); and milking the first cow (pp. 82–84).

Additional Selections

In Theresa Nelson's *And One for All* (Orchard, 1989, $12.95), a novel that recreates the troubled 1960s, Geraldine's brother leaves for the Vietnam War while his friend becomes a war protester.

Danny, whose mother is dead, learns to survive while his father is treated for the memories that haunt him about the Vietnam War in *Danny Ain't* (Scholastic, 1992, $13.95) by Joe Cottonwood.

After a chapter on the history of the Vietnam War, Brent Ashabranner, in *Always to Remember* (Putnam, 1988, $14.95), tells about the building of the Vietnam Veterans Memorial as well as the people who fought for it and designed it.

Jenny Rutherford confronts the meaning of her mother's death in Patricia Reilly Giff's novel of family relationships, *The Gift of the Pirate Queen* (Delacorte, 1982, $11.95).

Mai, her parents, her grandmother, and her younger brother and sister flee present-day Vietnam hoping to find passage to Hong Kong in Gloria Whelan's *Goodbye, Vietnam* (Knopf, 1992, $13).

In Penny Raife Durant's *When Heroes Die* (Macmillan, 1992, $13.95), twelve-year-old Gary Boyden discovers that the uncle he adores is gay and has AIDS.

About the Book

Booklist, May 1, 1988, p. 1528.
Center for Children's Books, April 1988, p. 164.
Emergency Librarian, March 1989, p. 47.
Horn Book, July 1988, p. 496.
Kirkus Reviews, March 1, 1988, p. 368.
New York Times Book Review, May 8, 1988, p. 25.
School Library Journal, May 1988, p. 111.
Wilson Library Bulletin, June 1988, p. 109.
See also *Book Review Digest,* 1989, p. 1286; and *Book Review Index,* 1988, p. 632; 1989, p. 636.

About the Author

Chevalier, Tracy, ed., *Twentieth-Century Children's Writers* (3rd ed.). St. James, 1989, pp. 758–760.
Commire, Anne, ed., *Something about the Author.* Gale, 1978, Vol. 13, pp. 176–177; updated 1988, Vol. 53, pp. 118–129.
Estes, Glenn E., ed., *American Writers for Children since 1960: Fiction* (Dictionary of Literary Biography: Vol. 52). Gale, 1986, pp. 296–314.
Garrett, Agnes, and McCue, Helga P., eds., *Authors and Artists for Young Adults.* Gale, 1989, Vol. 1, pp. 203–214.

Harte, Barbara, ed., *Contemporary Authors*. Gale, 1970, Vols. 23–24, p. 322.
Holtze, Sally Holmes, ed., *Fifth Book of Junior Authors and Illustrators*. Wilson, 1983, pp. 236–238.
Kirkpatrick, D. L., ed., *Twentieth-Century Children's Writers* (2nd ed.). St. Martin's. 1983, pp. 603–604.
Nasso, Christine, ed., *Contemporary Authors* (First Revision). Gale, 1977, Vols. 21–24, p. 662.
Senick, Gerard J., ed., *Children's Literature Review*. Gale, 1984, Vol. 7. pp. 224–243.
Ward, Martha, ed., *Authors of Books for Young People* (3rd ed.). Scarecrow, 1990, p. 551.

7

Other Lands and Times

During the middle-grade years, youngsters are increasingly able to deal with such abstract concepts as time. They can come to appreciate and understand history and the continuity of civilization by reading about children their own age as they lived in the past. In this section there are ten novels, most of which deal with our own history from the Colonial period to World War II. Others are set in various periods in British history, and one tells of the plight of Jews during the Nazi Holocaust.

Beatty, Patricia. *Charley Skedaddle*
Morrow, 1987, $12.95 (0-688-06687-9); pap., Troll, $2.95 (0-8167-1317-0)

Patricia Beatty (1922–1991), a history major, and her first husband, a history professor, wrote many books together, such as *At the Seven Stars* (1963, o.p.) set in eighteenth-century England and dealing with the Jacobites. Her favorite subject was the American West in the nineteenth century, but she was also intrigued by the Civil War. In *Turn Homeward, Hannalee* (Morrow, 1984, $12.95; pap., Troll, $2.95), she tells how this war affected a group of Southern mill workers who were shipped from Georgia to Indiana to find work. *Charley Skedaddle* also deals with the periphery of the war and tells of a boy who flees from battle but finds the true meaning of courage in the Blue Ridge Mountains. As usual in this author's work, the material has been well researched and the settings and ambiance recreated vividly and accurately. This novel is enjoyed by readers in grades 5 through 9.

Plot Summary

At the age of twelve, Charley Quinn is a street-wise, feisty member of the Bowery Boys, the toughest gang in New York City. His older brother was killed at the battle of Gettysburg and the Civil War is still raging as Charley, who lives with his seamstress sister, fights his own battles on the mean city streets.

One day Charley gets into one fight too many, and a policeman brings him home. Charley overhears his sister's fiancé suggest that the boy might have to be sent away if he keeps getting into trouble. That night Charley decides not to wait for that indignity. He smuggles aboard a troopship leaving New York for Virginia, carrying Northern troops to battle.

In Virginia, Charley enlists as a drummer boy in the Union Army. He studies his duties with diligence because he is eager to engage in his first battle. He is also anxious to prove he is just as tough as his beloved brother and somehow to avenge his death.

Charley gets his chance to prove himself at the Battle of the Wilderness in Virginia. But it is nothing like the glory he envisioned. Caught in a Rebel trap, the Northern troops are quickly cut down. Charley watches in horror as a friend dies with a bullet hole through his forehead. In a panic, Charley picks up a loaded musket and fires at an advancing Reb. The man clutches his shoulder as blood spurts out and he falls over backward. Charley thinks he has killed his first soldier.

After the shooting, unable to deal with the fact that he has killed someone and overcome by the terrifying sounds of battle, he runs blindly from the battlefield. As he does he hears shouts of, "Charley, skedaddle. Run, ye coward Bowery bummer!"

Charley keeps running in his panic until he is captured by Southern troops. In their compassion for the young, frightened boy, they send him on his way with advice to move west, away from the fighting lest he be captured again and perhaps shot.

Charley flees into the mountains. There he stumbles on the cabin of old Granny Bent, an ornery, secretive mountain woman who distrusts him because she thinks he is a Yankee deserter. However, Granny allows him to stay with her. He helps in her garden and does whatever chores she asks of him.

Gradually the young boy and the old woman develop a friendship of sorts. She asks him what happened, and he tells her of the battle. He learns that her husband died some years before, that both of them were a link for runaway slaves on the Underground Railroad, and that Granny is also the midwife for people in the mountains.

Months pass, and the war rages on. Every time Charley thinks he might actually be starting to like the crusty old woman, she reminds him in some way that he is a deserter, and shame floods his being all over again.

One day Granny is called over the mountains to assist in the delivery of a baby. She tells Charley she will return in a day or two.

Charley spends some anxious time after Granny leaves, because there are signs the mountain lion she has spotted around the cabin has returned. Does the lion know that Charley, a novice in the mountains, is alone? In the morning, Charley takes Granny's rifle and goes out to feed the animals. He finds most of the hens have been killed. The next day, the mountain lion attacks Charley as he steps outside. Charley fires his rifle and kills the mountain lion.

Charley is pleased with himself for having saved the rest of Granny's livestock, but where is the old woman? When she doesn't return, he decides something has gone wrong, and he sets out to find her. After some searching, he finds Granny's saddled black mule, and then he sees the old woman's still body at the bottom of a ravine. The boy is certain at first that she is dead, but Granny lifts her head at his call and tells him she has hurt her leg. He wants to send the mule to her, but she says it refuses to cross water.

Charley remembers stories about blindfolding frightened animals. He blindfolds the mule and is able to rescue the old woman.

Once back at the cabin, with Granny on the mend, the news of the rescue and his killing of the mountain lion that was terrorizing so many people spreads around the area. Charley is a hero.

As spring comes and Granny returns to health, the fighting grows worse. Soon Rebel troops will be swarming over the mountains, and surely Charley will be picked up. Granny tells Charley he must head west again. But she asks if he will write to her so she will know he is safe, and perhaps, when the war is finally over, he will return to the mountains to see her.

Charley looks over the hills he has grown to love in the past months and where he has proven himself. On his own, without the help of his gang members to back him up, Charley has become his own person.

"I'll be back," he tells Granny Bent. "This ain't so bad a place for a man to settle."

"No, it ain't," she agrees.

Thematic Material

This is a tale of fiction based on fact. Many youngsters served as drummer boys in the Civil War and many, like Charley Skedaddle, faced the brutality and horror of battle. There are vivid contrasts in this tale—the rough streets of New York City's poor neighborhoods, the bewildering noise of battle, and life in the quiet rural mountain cabins of nineteenth-century America. Charley is a likable, tough young boy who is devastated when confronted with what he mistakenly believes to be cowardice on his part. But he grows to love the beauty of the mountains and learns there are many ways to display courage besides becoming a gang member or a war hero. This is an easily read tale of a young boy's growth to manhood with the backdrop of a wartime adventure.

Book Talk Material

The contrasts between New York City in the 1900s, the horror of fighting in the Civil War, and life in the mountains are nicely drawn and will serve as a good introduction to this tale of how a young boy learns the true meaning of courage and bravery. See: a policeman takes Charley home (pp. 4–9); Charley gets smuggled on the steamer (pp. 19–24); Charley trains as a drummer boy (pp. 51–62); the Wilderness battle (pp. 75–82); he meets Granny Bent (pp. 105–110); and Charley kills the mountain lion (pp. 154–159).

Additional Selections

A Tennessee boy learns about the wastefulness of war during the Civil War in William O. Steele's *The Perilous Road* (Peter Smith, 1992, $16.50; pap., Harcourt, $3.95).

Every ounce of his moral fiber is tested when a Yankee drummer boy is captured and sent to the dreaded Confederate prison at Andersonville in G. Clifton Wisler's *Red Cap* (Lodestar, 1991, $15).

In *The Root Cellar* (Scribner, 1983, $13.95; pap., Puffin, $3.95) by Janet Lunn, a twelve-year-old girl who is unhappy in her new home is transported back to Civil War days.

In Patricia Beatty's *Jayhawker* (Morrow, 1991, $13.95), set in the early days of the Civil War, a teenage Kansas farm boy becomes a Jayhawker, an abolitionist raider freeing slaves in neighboring Missouri.

In Linda R. Wade's *Andersonville: A Civil War Tragedy* (Rourke, 1991, $11.95), the largest and worst Confederate prisoner of war camp is introduced in text and pictures.

Using songs, poetry, documents, and personal recollections of the times, the emotions and events of the Civil War are recreated in Milton Meltzer's *Voices from the Civil War* (Harper, 1989, $14.89; pap., $6.95).

The reasons why and how the United States became divided, both politically and socially, and how these differences caused war are retold in Delia Ray's *A Nation Torn: The Story of How the Civil War Began* (Lodestar, 1990, $15.95).

About the Book

Book Report, November 1987, p. 21.
Booklist, November 15, 1987, p. 560.
Center for Children's Books Bulletin, October 1987, p. 22.
Horn Book, November 1987, p. 735.
Kirkus Reviews, October 1, 1987, p. 1458.
School Library Journal, November 1987, p. 103.
VOYA, December 1987, p. 230.
Wilson Library Bulletin, February 1988, p. 78.

About the Author

Chevalier, Tracy, ed., *Twentieth-Century Children's Writers* (3rd ed.). St. James, 1989, pp. 73–74.
Commire, Anne, ed., *Something about the Author.* Gale, 1983, Vol. 30, pp. 48–53.
de Montreville, Doris, and Hill, Donna, eds., *Third Book of Junior Authors.* Wilson, 1972, pp. 33–34.
Evory, Ann, and Metzger, Linda, eds., *Contemporary Authors* (New Revision Series). Gale, 1981, Vol. 3, p. 60.
Kirkpatrick, D. L., ed., *Twentieth-Century Children's Writers* (2nd ed.). St. Martin's, 1983, pp. 71–72.
Sarkissian, Adele, ed., *Something about the Author: Autobiographical Series.* Gale, 1987, Vol. 4, pp. 35–42.
Ward, Martha, ed., *Authors of Books for Young People* (3rd ed.). Scarecrow, 1990, p. 47.

Burnett, Frances Hodgson. *The Secret Garden*
(several hardcover and paperback editions available)

Since its first appearance in 1911, *The Secret Garden* has existed in countless editions, many illustrated by such renowned artists as Tasha Tudor. It has also been adapted several times for the movie screen and more recently became a hit Broadway musical. For all these many variations, it remains one of the most beloved books written for children. The author was born in Manchester, England, in 1849, migrated to America with her family, and married Dr. Swan Burnett. Her second son, Vivian, became the model for *Little Lord Fauntleroy,* the first of her children's books. It tells the story of Cedric, a New York City child who discovers he is the heir to an earldom in England presently in the hands of his grandfather, the crusty Earl of Dorincourt. In *A Little Princess,* another great success by this author, the opposite situation exists. Sara, who was born rich and privileged, must adjust to a life of poverty and deprivation. In 1908 Mrs. Burnett bought land and built a mansion on Long Island. She lived there until her death in 1924, and it was here that she wrote her most famous book, the story of Mary Lennox, Colin, and Dickon, and of the garden they bring back to life. Although the Yorkshire dialect used extensively in the book may cause some initial reading problems, most of the difficult words or expressions are explained in the context of their use. This story is enjoyed particularly by young readers in grades 4 through 7.

Plot Summary

Mary Lennox, the only child of English colonialists living in India, is both indulged and deprived. Her absentee father and social-butterfly mother have delegated child-rearing responsibilities entirely to an ayah, the Indian equivalent of a nanny, with the result that Mary has always been treated as a royal princess whose every whim is taken as a command, while at the same time she lacks the stabilizing love and discipline of a normal family life. Now approaching her tenth birthday, she is spoiled and ungovernable, lonely, and unhappy. This unhappiness shows physically; she is a thin, sallow girl, considered extremely plain.

Suddenly, life changes dramatically for Mary. A cholera epidemic strikes the compound where she lives. Separated from her ayah and frightened by the wailing she hears around her, she takes refuge in her nursery, emerging only to eat scraps of food from the kitchen. After being rescued several days later, she discovers that she is an orphan and will be sent to England to live with her closest living relative, Uncle Archibald Craven, at Misselthwaite Manor, situated on the edge of a moor in Yorkshire.

She is met in London by Mrs. Medlock, Mr. Craven's businesslike housekeeper, who explains that Mary's uncle, whom she describes as a somewhat deformed man with a small hunchback, has become a recluse and nomad since his beloved wife died some ten years before after falling from a tree in one of the many walled gardens on the property. His love for his wife was so great that he has never been able to adjust to her death and therefore rarely stays at his estate.

Her uncle is away when Mary arrives at the manor house, which contains hundreds of mostly unused rooms. It is late winter approaching spring, and the moors seem cold and forbidding to the young girl accustomed to the warmth of India.

Mary's independent and peevish ways soon alienate her from most of the help at Misselthwaite Manor, except for her young housemaid, Martha Sowerby, whose sweet disposition and quaint speech patterns intrigue Mary. Martha explains that she is one of twelve children and lives five miles away in a cottage on the moors. Her favorite in the family is a twelve-year-old brother, Dickon, who seems to have a magical ability to tame and communicate with the animals of the moor. At present, he is caring for a crow, Soot, and a fox, Captain, and has tamed a wild moor pony. Martha also tells Mary that after his wife's death, Mr. Craven locked up the garden where his adored wife fell and that since then no one has been allowed to enter it.

Mary begins exploring the many walled gardens on the property and discovers a mysterious one that appears to have no entrance. One of the gardeners, gruff Ben Weatherstaff, befriends Mary and introduces her to a robin he has tamed.

Her outdoor explorations are interrupted by several days of rain, during which she disobeys orders and ventures out of her room to explore the portrait-filled dens and living rooms as well as the lavish bedrooms. During one of these expeditions she hears strange crying sounds that she vaguely remembers hearing in her bed the previous night. Before she can search further, she is discovered by Mrs. Medlock, who denies there is any sound and orders Mary back to her nursery.

When she next goes outside, the robin greets her and lights on a newly upturned flower bed. There, half-buried in the soil, Mary finds a ring with a key attached. She is convinced it is the key to the secret garden.

Martha continues to shower Mary with kindness, compassion, and stories of Dickon and the rest of her warm, loving family. In an unusual gesture, Mrs. Sowerby, Martha's mother, who has never met Mary, spends tuppence for a skipping rope as a present for the lonely child. Gradually Mary detects changes within herself as she responds physically and emotionally to the first true friends she has ever had.

One day, as Mary is walking by the ivy-covered walls of the locked garden, a sudden gust of wind reveals a doorknob. Using the key she found, she is inside within seconds. Although it is badly overgrown, there are signs of life in the rose bushes and in the flower beds; the first green sprouts from early bulbs can be seen. Mary decides restoring the garden will be her secret project. With some money she has saved, she asks Martha to get Dickon to buy some garden tools for her. A few days later she sees an elfin-looking boy with the garden tools playing a wooden pipe that has miraculously attracted several small wild creatures. Mary is so enchanted with Dickon that she tells this unusual boy about the forbidden garden. Together they conspire to bring the garden back to life.

One day, Mr. Craven pays a sudden, brief visit to Misselthwaite Manor. Mary is summoned. During their short conversation, Mary realizes that although he tries to be pleasant, he is tortured by a terrible, all-enveloping sadness.

One night after Mr. Craven's departure, Mary is again wakened by the sound of uncontrolled sobbing. Her investigation takes her down a long corridor to a bedroom, where she finds a pinch-faced boy about her age crying inconsolably. He introduces himself as Colin, Mr. Craven's son, born shortly before his mother's accident. He was so sickly and puny as a child that doctors feared for his life. Since then, Colin has been convinced he will soon die. His preoccupation with the frailty of his body has produced a self-imposed exile and a belief that he will never be able to walk.

Surprisingly, Mary and Colin delight in each other's company, although the boy's excessively spoiled behavior, self-pity, and terrible temper tantrums at first cause severe strains. When Colin realizes Mary is as self-willed as himself and that these tricks do not impress her, the two form a true friendship.

In time, Mary introduces Colin to Dickon and eventually tells Colin about the secret garden. Colin insists on being wheeled into the garden. (While he is there, the staff is ordered to stay inside the manor, thus preserving Mary's secret.) Colin is enchanted by the garden, and as his visits become more frequent, Mary and Dickon notice many changes in him, culminating in his taking a few steps from his wheelchair to help with the gardening. In time, Ben Weatherstaff discovers their project and, as an experienced gardener, is able to offer advice and help.

Like a child learning to walk, Colin quickly progresses from faltering steps to running and jumping. Soon the frail boy has, like Mary, filled out and developed a rosy, healthy complexion. Colin wants both the garden and his ability to walk to remain a secret until his father comes home. They use many subterfuges to escape discovery, including smuggling food so their increased appetites go unnoticed. As Mary and Colin blossom, so does the garden, and by early summer it is vibrant with color and variegated greens.

Far off in Italy, Mr. Craven suddenly has a desire to return home, as though the spirit of his dead wife were beckoning him back to the garden where they had once spent many joyous hours. He arrives unexpectedly and, approaching the garden, hears voices and enters. Colin runs to welcome him, explaining that his friendship with Mary and Dickon and the magic of the garden have produced a miracle. Tenderly, Mr. Craven holds his son in his arms, and looking around at the beauty he knows the garden will never be abandoned again.

Thematic Material

Although Colin maintains the garden contains magic, it is the friendship, trust, and respect the three friends feel for each other that causes the miracle that transforms Mary into a caring girl able to receive and give love and Colin into a strong young man with a will to live. The power of love and the difficulty of accepting the death of loved ones are themes that are explored, as well as the importance of strong family relationships. The author accurately portrays the class structure and social conditions of nineteenth-century England.

Book Talk Material

Because each of the many available editions has a different pagination, the events of the beginning chapters are analyzed to indicate generally where interesting passages occur. Chapter 1 tells of the epidemic that leaves Mary an orphan; in chapter 2 Mary stays with a clergyman's family before sailing for England, where she is met by Mrs. Medlock, who tells her about Mr. Craven and Misselthwaite Manor. In chapter 3, Mary first meets Martha and then Ben Weatherstaff and his pet robin. Chapter 4 describes Mary finding the exterior of the garden, learning about its past from Martha, and hearing distant crying. Mary meets Dickon at the beginning of chapter 10 and first encounters Colin in chapter 13.

Additional Selections

In the old favorite *The Railway Children* (Peter Smith, 1988, $16; pap., Puffin, $2.25) by E. Nesbit, Bobbie, Peter, and Phyllis try to solve the mystery of their father's disappearance.

Timid nine-year-old Elizabeth Ann spends a summer with relatives in

Vermont in Dorothy Canfield Fisher's classic *Understood Betsy* (pap., Dell, $4.95).

Eleven-year-old Anne gradually wins the heart of her foster mother in Lucy Maud Montgomery's *Anne of Green Gables* (Putnam, 1983, $12.95; pap., Bantam, $2.95), the first book in an extensive series.

Pippi Longstocking (Viking, 1950, $12.95; pap., Puffin, $3.95; condensed in *Introducing Books,* Bowker, 1970, pp. 269–272) by Astrid Lindgren is the classic story of a little Swedish tomboy who has a monkey and a horse for companions. There are many sequels, such as *Pippi in the South Seas* (Viking, 1959, $11.95; pap., Puffin, $3.95).

In *Wildflower Girl* (Holiday, 1992, $14.95) by Marita Conlon-McKenna, thirteen-year-old Peggy O'Driscoll leaves famine-stricken Ireland, taking a free passage across the Atlantic to Boston in the 1850s. This story was begun in *Under the Hawthorn Tree* (Holiday, 1990, $13.95).

When, in 1903, Katharine Outwater and her family move to upstate New York, she and her brothers must adjust to a strict governess, Miss Pruitt, in Niki Yektai's *The Secret Room* (Orchard, 1992, $14.99).

Jenny Larkin and her family move from one migrant camp to another in a life where hope emerges slowly from despair in *Blue Willow* (Viking, 1940, $14; pap., Puffin, $3.95; condensed in *Juniorplots,* Bowker, 1967, pp. 69–71) by Doris Gates.

About the Author

Chevalier, Tracy, ed., *Twentieth-Century Children's Writers* (3rd ed.). St. James, 1989, pp. 159–161.

Commire, Anne, ed., *Yesterday's Authors of Books for Children.* Gale, 1978, Vol. 2, pp. 32–49.

Estes, Glenn E., ed., *American Writers for Children before 1990* (Dictionary of Literary Biography: Vol. 42). Gale, 1985, pp. 97–117.

Kirkpatrick, D. L., ed., *Twentieth-Century Children's Writers* (2nd ed.). St. Martin's, 1983, pp. 141–143.

Kuniz, Stanley J., and Haycraft, Howard, eds., *Twentieth-Century Authors.* Wilson, 1942, pp. 223–224.

Senick, Gerard J., ed., *Children's Literature Review.* Gale, 1991, Vol. 24, pp. 21–60.

Trosky, Susan M., ed., *Contemporary Authors.* Gale, 1992, Vol. 136, pp. 62–67.

Ward, Martha, ed., *Authors of Books for Young People* (3rd ed.). Scarecrow, 1990, p. 100.

DeFelice, Cynthia. *Weasel*

Macmillan, 1990, $13.95 (0-02-726457-2); pap., Avon, $3.50 (0-380-71358-6)

In addition to picture books, such as *When Grampa Kissed His Elbow* (Macmillan, 1992, $13.95), Cynthia DeFelice has written a number of fine novels for the middle grades. In *Devil's Bridge* (Macmillan, 1992, $12.95), set in coastal Massachusetts, Ben Daggett, who is still mourning his father's death by drowning, must cope with his mother dating someone new and the discovery that someone is cheating at an important fishing derby. *The Strange Night Writing of Jessamine Colter* (Macmillan, 1988, $12.95) tells of Jessie and her compulsion to write things she knows nothing about, which, she later learns, accurately predict the future. *Weasel* is set in the Ohio of 1839 and poses questions concerning moral behavior with a subtext that comments in a subtle fashion on the inhumane treatment of Indians in frontier America and how this comes back to haunt the settlers. These complex issues are treated in a story that has appeal for readers in grades 4 through 8.

Plot Summary

Although loneliness, hard work, resourcefulness, joy, sadness, and sometimes even fright have never been strangers to the hardy pioneer families of frontier America, pure terror is less often their companion. But it becomes part of the lives of eleven-year-old Nathan and his younger sister, Molly, the children of a frontier family in Ohio in 1839.

For some days Nathan and Molly have been worried about their father. He left on a hunting trip, promising to return by nightfall, but his absence has now stretched into several days, and the children fear the worst. They are alone in their cabin on their small farm. Their mother died of the fever sometime before, and now there are just the three of them—but where is Pa?

Late one night there is a knock on the cabin door. It is an odd-looking stranger. He does not speak but hands Nathan a locket. It is Mama's locket, given to her by their father the day they were married. After her death, Pa cut a lock of her hair, placed it in the locket, and wore it around his neck. He never took it off, not for anything.

The children realize the stranger knows where their father is, and although he does not speak, they understand they are to follow him, which they do, although fearfully. On the journey, they see another stranger lurking in the woods. The man who is leading them writes in the dirt "Weezl." Nathan and Molly ask if he means "Weasel," and the man nods.

The children have heard the strange tales about the wild, bloodthirsty man called Weasel. Once hired by the government to drive the Shawnee off the land, he now kills for the sport of it, preying on settlers and Indians alike. The children discover that their guide—they later learn his name is Ezra—cannot speak because Weasel cut out his tongue.

Ezra leads them to their father, who has been injured in a hunting accident. He is very weak and cannot be moved immediately. Nathan realizes he must return to their cabin alone, to feed the livestock. Although he is frightened at the prospect of traveling by himself with the evil Weasel in the area, he knows he must go. His father has taught him that if a person takes on the responsibility of animals, he must always care for them properly.

The next morning, with directions drawn in the dirt by Ezra, Nathan makes the return trip. There, to his horror, he discovers most of the farm animals have been slaughtered. He knows it is the work of Weasel. The horse and mule are missing, and Nathan figures Weasel has taken them.

After burying the farm animals, Nathan sets out to return to his father and sister. He is accosted by Weasel, captured, and made a prisoner in Weasel's mean cabin. Nathan is forced to listen to Weasel's rantings. He boasts of cutting out Ezra's tongue because Ezra, also a former Indian hunter for the government, had married a Shawnee woman. Weasel also killed her and their unborn child.

Weasel drinks himself into a stupor and Nathan is able to escape. He has a chance to kill Weasel as he lies on the floor but he does not do so. When he returns to Ezra's cabin, he finds his father is much recovered. He tells them all what happened to him and shouts his hatred for the evil man called Weasel. His father comforts him and tells him the bad time is over. He also tells Nathan he is very proud of him.

But Nathan is ashamed of himself. He had a chance to kill Weasel, who surely deserves to die, but he did not. He could have avenged the deaths of Ezra's wife and baby. But all he did was save his own skin.

Pa, Molly, and Nathan say goodbye to Ezra and ask him to come to see them. Pa doubts he ever will. Pa tells the children that long ago, he and their mother had befriended Ezra and his Shawnee wife. Ezra never forgot that kindness, and Pa says he has often thought through the years that Ezra has been keeping an eye on them and their cabin.

The three return home. Nathan still burns with hatred for Weasel and longs to kill him. His father tries to tell him that killing a man who is helpless on the ground is something only a man like Weasel would do. He is proud that Nathan would not do such a thing. But Nathan still feels someone should stop this killer. His father tells him to be patient; someone surely will.

By late February, Nathan still burns with the desire for revenge. He leaves the farm without his father knowing and heads for Weasel's cabin. When he gets there, he finds Weasel is dead; he has apparently died a horrible death, probably from blood poisoning, the result of a leg wound.

Nathan goes to Ezra's cabin and tells him what has happened. He cannot believe it when Ezra picks up a shovel. They are going to bury Weasel! Then Nathan realizes it is the right thing to do; Weasel may have been a savage, but they don't have to be.

Spring is coming; things are growing again, and one day Pa, Nathan, and Molly go to town, to a dance. Later, Molly teases her father about dancing so much with Miss Abigail Baldwin. Nathan realizes his father might someday marry again. Nothing stays the same, he knows that now.

Nathan decides he is going to learn to play the fiddle and make up songs. And part of every song he plays will be the story of what happened to Ezra and his wife and to so many of the Shawnee nation.

Thematic Material

This is a powerful, simply told tale of a young boy trying to come to grips with good and evil. Nathan is torn between his fierce desire to avenge the horrible crimes committed by Weasel and his own sense of decency and the lessons taught by his parents. The subplot of the terrible atrocities committed against the Shawnee nation serves as a quiet but vivid backdrop to this story of the harsh realities of frontier life. The story teaches an enduring lesson about the desire for revenge and the struggle to live decently and honorably.

Book Talk Material

A number of vividly drawn scenes of the harshness of frontier life in the last century will interest young readers. See: the stranger comes to the door (pp. 2–3); the man called Ezra writes Weasel's name in the dirt (pp.

12–14); Ezra leads them to their father (pp. 21–27); Nathan makes the trip back alone and finds the animals (pp. 37–43); Nathan is captured (pp. 47–48); Nathan has the chance to kill Weasel but escapes instead (pp. 55–62).

Additional Selections

In post–Civil War Texas, twelve-year-old Jo and her brother are sent to live with an uncle. In time, she finds she is protecting a bandit who has robbed their stagecoach in Willo Davis Roberts's *Jo and the Bandit* (Macmillan, 1992, $14.95).

Two youngsters fleeing the poverty of early twentieth-century Glasgow stow away to Canada in Margaret J. Anderson's *The Journey of the Shadow Bairns* (Knopf, 1980, $12.95).

A young physician's apprentice and his sister help fight the 1793 Philadelphia Yellow Fever epidemic in Paul Fleischman's *Path of the Pale Horse* (Harper, 1983, $12.89; pap., $3.95); for better readers.

Whether the son of Billy the Kid should avenge his father's death is the question posed in Harry W. Paige's *Shadow on the Sun* (Holiday, 1984, $9.95).

The oldest daughter in a Chinese family tells of her family's move from Ohio to West Virginia in the 1920s in *The Star Fisher* (Morrow, 1991, $12.95; pap., Puffin, $3.99) by Laurence Yep.

Emmy (McElderry, 1992, $13.95) by Connie Jordan Green tells of the poverty suffered by a Kentucky family living in a mining town in 1924 and of the fourteen-year-old who volunteers to work underground to keep his family together.

About the Book

Booklist, May 15, 1990, p. 1795.
Center for Children's Books Bulletin, May 1990, p. 212.
Emery Library, March 1991, p. 20.
Horn Book Guide, January 1990, p. 244.
Kirkus Reviews, March 15, 1990, p. 421.
School Library Journal, May 1990, p. 104.
VOYA, June 1990, p. 101.
Wilson Library Bulletin, May 1990, p. 8.
See also *Book Review Digest,* 1990, p. 445; and *Book Review Index,* 1990, p. 199; 1991, p. 225.

Fleischman, Paul. *Saturnalia*

Harper, 1990, $13.89 (0-06-021913-0); pap., $3.95 (0-06-447089-X)

Paul Fleischman, the son of equally famous writer Sid Fleischman (see *Jim Ugly* in this volume), began his writing career in the late 1970s with such works for young readers as *The Birthday Tree* (Harper, 1979, $13.89; pap., $4.50), about a couple who, having lost their three sons to the sea, attempt in vain to keep the fourth from also becoming a sailor; and *The Half-a-Moon Inn* (Harper, 1980, $12.89; pap., $3.50), the adventure-filled story of a mute boy who becomes lost in a blizzard and is captured by the evil Miss Grackle, owner of the Half-a-Moon Inn. His collections of poems "for two voices" have also gained high praise. *I Am Phoenix* (Harper, 1985, $12; pap., $3.95) contains lyrical poems about birds, and *Joyful Noise* (Harper, 1988, $13.89; pap., $3.95;, winner of the 1989 Newbery Medal), has fourteen verses about insects. *Saturnalia* is a historical novel intended for readers in grades 5 through 8. It deals realistically with the trials of a young apprenticed Indian boy falsely accused of a crime in Colonial Boston. The book is well researched and, in addition to telling an exciting story, gives a fascinating glimpse of Puritan life in the Colonial days. The title refers to the Pagan Roman holiday.

Plot Summary

It is the year 1681 in Boston, Massachusetts. The Colonial settlers, striving to build a new life in this strange, often harsh land, are used to keeping servants. Sometimes slaves are imported from the West Indies. Paupers and convicts become servants. Indentured servants, whose passage to America is paid in return for several years of labor, are much in demand. And many colonists use Indians as servants, although there are sometimes ambushes and raids between the settlers and neighboring tribes. The biggest battle had taken place in 1675, and the Colonials, for the most part, still fear the Indian tribes.

Fourteen-year-old William is a Narragansett boy captured in a raid six years earlier. He is apprenticed to Charles Currie, the printer, who treats William as one of his own and teaches the boy his trade. William is a bright learner and happy in the Currie household, although he often thinks of his life before his capture and wonders what has become of his twin brother.

Not everyone in the colony is happy with Indians in general and with

William's place in the Currie household in particular. Mr. Baggot, who lost his own children in an Indian raid, strides the dark streets seeing to the spiritual care of the families in his charge and secretly hoping to take out his anger on William.

Other townspeople are not so treacherous. Mr. Speke, the wood-carver, who lost his beloved daughter to a fever, roams the town at night in his grief. Mr. Hogwood, the pompous wig maker, is after the hand of a stalwart—and wealthy—widow. His indentured servant, Malcolm, is after a servant girl. Both are getting nowhere.

William receives a mysterious note, which he believes could be from his twin brother. It directs him to Flint's Alley. William knows he should not be out in the streets at night, but he is drawn to the alley to find out who sent the note. At the last moment, he changes his mind and runs home—to the chagrin of the evil Mr. Baggot, who had sent the note hoping to get William into trouble, even prison.

Although William does not find his brother, he does stumble on two servants of the cruel Mr. Rudd, who turn out to be William's own great-uncle, Michamauk, and his daughter. From his uncle he learns his twin brother is dead, shot after he tried to escape from Barbados, where he had been sent as a slave.

William vows to bring food to his uncle and cousin, who are nearly starved by their cruel master. In return, his uncle rekindles William's memories of his early life and of his family.

Mr. Baggot is dismayed to learn that the Currie family, and William, will celebrate Saturnalia around the time of the Christmas feast. On that day, marked by much merriment, servants change places with masters. Mr. Baggot is shocked by any observance of this old Roman holiday.

But in the Currie household it is met with great feasting and fun. Mr. Currie and his wife are roused from their beds early to "serve" William, the children, and the servant girl, Gwynne.

Not long after the merriment of Saturnalia, cruel Mr. Rudd's murdered body is found, his teeth clamped on a sheet of paper. The paper turns out to be a written contract for the services of Michamauk and his daughter. They are immediately accused of writing the paper and of the crime. They have never been taught to write, declares William. "But *you* have!" shouts Mr. Baggot.

William looks at the written contract and recognizes the writing as that of one of Rudd's former apprentices, who, it turns out, killed Rudd because of his ill treatment.

William is cleared of the crime, but what will become of his great-uncle and cousin? Before they can be apprenticed to another, they run off to rejoin their own people. They ask William to accompany them. He is tempted, but in the end he decides he must do the honorable thing and finish his apprenticeship to the man who has been so good to him. After that, he will decide in which world he will live. Out of love and loyalty to the Curries, he will wait until then to decide.

Thematic Material

A book for the more advanced, thoughtful reader, *Saturnalia* is rich in its prose and depiction of an early period of American history. It captures the stark contrast of good and evil, kindness and cruelty that ruled the lives of servants and slaves. William is pictured as a thoughtful boy who is caught between two worlds, feeling love and loyalty to both. This is a thought-provoking book with flashes of humor, not for every young reader but rewarding for those who will allow themselves to be transported to the often harsh reality of another time.

Book Talk Material

Several incidents capture the flavor of life in the early Boston colony. See: Mr. Baggot tests the Currie children and William (pp. 5–10); Malcolm outsmarts himself in his handling of the oranges (pp. 21–24); William is tempted by the note beckoning him to Flint's Alley (pp. 39–43); and the Currie household celebrates Saturnalia (pp. 79–83).

Additional Selections

Set in a Connecticut mill town in 1810, *The Clock* (Delacorte, 1992, $15) by James Lincoln Collier and Christopher Collier tells of the struggles of a fifteen-year-old mill worker, Annie, and her fight for justice.

Johnny Tremain (Houghton, 1943, $13.45; pap., Dell, $3.99), a Newbery Medal winner by Esther Forbes, tells the story of a silversmith's apprentice and the beginnings of the American Revolution.

Susanna and her family reluctantly become involved in the drama and horror of the 1692 Witch Trials in Massachusetts in Ann Rinaldi's *A Break with Charity: A Story about the Salem Witch Trials* (Harcourt, 1992, $16.95).

Mary Blount Christian's *Goody Sherman's Pig* (Macmillan, 1991, $12.95) is a story based on fact about a legal battle over a pig in Massachusetts during 1636 that produced massive changes in the state government structure.

During the 1830s in Massachusetts, an orphaned boy takes care of the first elephant in the United States in Carol Carrick's *The Elephant in the Dark* (Houghton, 1988, $13.95; pap., Scholastic, $2.95).

Tomboy Caddie is growing up in rural Wisconsin over a century ago in the Newbery Medal winner *Caddie Woodlawn* (Macmillan, 1973, $14.95; pap., $3.95) by Carol Ryrie Brink. A sequel is *Magical Melons* (pap., Macmillan, $3.95).

William H. Hooks uses the story of the Roanoke, Virginia, colony that disappeared completely as background for his novel, *The Legend of the White Doe* (Macmillan, 1987, $13.95).

About the Book

Booklist, May 1, 1990, p. 1702; October 1, 1990, p. 351.
Horn Book, May 1990, p. 337.
Horn Book Guide, January 1990, p. 249.
Kirkus Reviews, April 15, 1990, p. 576.
New York Times Book Review, September 30, 1990, p. 39.
School Library Journal, May 1990, p. 122.
VOYA, January 1990, p. 102.
See also *Book Review Digest,* 1990, pp. 588–589; and *Book Review Index,* 1990, p. 265; 1991, p. 298.

About the Author

Chevalier, Tracy, ed., *Twentieth-Century Children's Writers* (3rd ed.). St. James, 1989, pp. 349–350.
Commire, Anne, ed., *Something about the Author.* Gale, 1983, Vol. 32, p. 71; updated 1985, Vol. 39, pp. 72–73.
Holtze, Sally Holmes, ed., *Fifth Book of Junior Authors and Illustrators.* Wilson, 1983, pp. 114–116.
May, Hal, ed., *Contemporary Authors.* Gale, 1985, Vol. 113, p. 158.
Senick, Gerard J., ed., *Children's Literature Review.* Gale, 1990, Vol. 20, pp. 63–70.
Ward, Martha, ed., *Authors of Books for Young People* (3rd ed.). Scarecrow, 1990, p. 231.

Garfield, Leon. *The December Rose*

Pap., Puffin, 1988, $3.95 (0-14-032070-9)

Leon Garfield's first historical adventure story for young readers was published in 1965. It was *Jack Holborn* (Random, 1965, $5.99), a highly imaginative tale of piracy, shipwrecks, and murder set in eighteenth-century England. Since then he has written about thirty historical novels, many of which are somewhat vague about the exact year in which they take place, but are nevertheless well researched and convey a sense of historical accuracy without being pedantic. Several of his titles, including *Smith* (Peter Smith, 1991, $16) and *Black Jack* (o.p.), have been runners-up for the British equivalent of the Newbery Medal, the Carnegie Medal; and in 1970, he and a co-author, Edward Blishen, were given this award for a brilliant retelling of Greek myths, *The God Beneath the Sea* (o.p.). A later novel, *The Empty Sleeve* (Delacorte, 1988, $14.95; condensed in *Juniorplots 4*, Bowker, 1993, pp. 248–253) combines murder, mayhem, and the supernatural in Victorian London. This is also the setting for *The December Rose,* which was written originally as a television screenplay for the BBC and was shown here as part of the Wonderworks series. It is enjoyed by readers in grades 5 through 9.

Plot Summary

In the prologue, the reader meets Donia Vassilova, a mysterious young woman dressed completely in black who wears around her neck an unusual gold locket with a black eagle enameled on it. She has just received an important letter at the Charing Cross Post Office. Afraid she is being followed, she scurries through the twisted, crowded streets of Victorian London. That evening her pursuer—we later learn he is Inspector Creaker of the British Secret Police—traps and murders her in a deserted alley, yanking the locket from her before dumping her body into the Thames.

Ten-year-old Absolom Brown has been taken from an orphanage and illegally put to work as a chimney sweep by his "protector," Mister Roberts. Absolom is known as Barnacle because of his uncanny ability to cling to the walls of chimneys and flues. Few know what he really looks like, because his emaciated frame is always covered with soot. Living a hand-to-mouth existence with his cruel master, he has learned street survival skills that, when necessary, include lying and stealing.

One day, while perched inside a chimney, Barnacle overhears a cryptic conversation between a woman and three men, one being identified as an Inspector Creaker. They talk about an item of value and about waiting for the December Rose. Barnacle's eavesdropping is interrupted by a prod from a chimney snake wielded with such violence by the irate Mister Roberts that Barnacle falls down the wrong flue and into the room where the four people are seated around a table. Frightened and anxious to escape, he instinctively grabs some items from the table and runs out the door. Alone on the street, he examines his catch—six silver teaspoons and a strange gold locket bearing an eagle design. Unfortunately, Mister Roberts spies him, and during the ensuing chase Barnacle drops five of the teaspoons, before colliding with a stranger who helps Barnacle escape capture by hiding him under a table in a nearby pub. The stranger, a massive, kindly man, introduces himself as Tom Gosling, captain of the barge *Lady of the Lea* now docked at Broken Wharf. After forcing Barnacle to visit a public bath, from which he emerges plaster-white and totally unrecognizable, Tom and his new charge board the barge and move it downstream to new moorings only moments before Inspector Creaker appears at Broken Wharf. Through clever detective work, he has traced Barnacle and, he hopes, the locket to Tom Gosling's barge.

The next day, Creaker visits a private London club and reports his activities to a Mr. Hastymite, one of the four who witnessed the theft of the locket. They discuss a plot by foreign terrorists involving a threat to national security. It is revealed that Donia Vassilova was a foreign agent whose mission was to receive a sum of money from a messenger scheduled to arrive in a few days aboard the steamer *December Rose.* Because the missing locket is the means of identification, Hastymite commands Creaker to retrieve the locket immediately and make sure the boy does not live to tell tales.

Early that same morning, Barnacle tries to slip away while Tom Gosling is asleep. His escape, however, is prevented by a teenage girl from the next barge, who, thinking he is a thief, catches him with the hook on her barge pole. Thus he is introduced first to Miranda and next to her mother, Mrs. Clara McDipper. Since Captain McDipper's demise by drowning after a rum-drinking spree, Mrs. McDipper and her daughter now own and operate the barge moored next to the *Lady of the Lea.* They are dear friends of Tom Gosling. Later that day, Tom and the McDippers escort Barnacle to Solomon Levy's Used Clothes Emporium, where the boy is treated to a new wardrobe. Overcome by all this attention and kindness, Barnacle decides to stay and exhibits his trust by showing the precious locket to his admiring friends.

Creaker and his assistants continue to keep watch on the *Lady,* awaiting a chance to pounce. On the day of the arrival of the *December Rose,* he once again reports to Mr. Hastymite, this time at the home of the leader of the secret police, Lord Hobart. (Lord Hobart and his wife who were the other witnesses to Barnacle's unfortunate descent from the chimney.) Again,

Inspector Creaker is told to make haste, murder the boy, and get the locket.

When the *December Rose* docks close to the barge wharf, Miranda and her mother, who is a friend of the captain, Mr. O'Shea, go on board hoping to buy some Russian sable to make a cape for the young girl. There they meet a passenger, Colonel Brodsky, an imposing figure dressed completely in black. His watch bears the same eagle design as Barnacle's locket. When Miranda mentions this, he becomes extremely excited and demands to be taken to see Barnacle. On board the *Lady,* he tells Tom Gosling that he must be taken to the house where the locket was stolen and begs to be allowed to stay aboard the barge until that time.

That evening, while Tom Gosling and Barnacle set out to find Mister Roberts and, through him, the location of the house, one of Inspector Creaker's young assistants creeps onto the barge. He stabs Brodsky but, in his frightened state, leaves before finding Brodsky's money bag. When Tom and Barnacle return, they find Brodsky unconscious from loss of blood. A doctor is summoned. Tom Gosling pays the doctor with money intended for the barge rental fees. Now, Tom faces eviction unless he can replace the money.

Miraculously, Colonel Brodsky regains consciousness. Summoning all his strength, he writes a letter of introduction for Tom Gosling and Mrs. McDipper to take, along with the locket and silver spoon, to Lord Mounteagle, a prominent lawyer. Lord Mounteagle identifies the crest on the silver spoon as that of Lord Hobart, the head of the secret police. Mounteagle tells his visitors that, as feared, Hobart and his henchman, Mr. Hastymite, have been using the gullible Inspector Creaker and his assistants to kill and steal money from innocent foreigners, claiming they were secret agents.

Meanwhile, on the barges, Creaker's assistant strikes once again, but before he can stab Barnacle, Miranda knocks him unconscious with her barge pole. He falls into the river and drowns. After Tom Gosling and Mrs. McDipper return, the group exchanges news about the day's exciting happenings. Barnacle, convinced he is responsible for bringing all this misfortune into the lives of Tom Gosling and his friends, the only people who have ever loved him, decides that even though it might cost him his life, he must bring matters to a climax. He takes the colonel's money bag and steals off into the night, knowing he soon will be the target of Inspector Creaker. As expected, Creaker confronts him in a dark alley. Barnacle blurts out the story of Hobart and Hastymite's villainy and how they have duped the trusting Creaker into committing murder and theft to line their own pockets. Creaker leaves with the money bag, and Barnacle is uncertain whether the inspector believed his story. However, later that night Creaker tricks Lord Hobart and Mr. Hastymite into a confession. Conscience-stricken, he purchases the makings of a time bomb, and after luring the two criminals into a rowboat where he promises to divide the money in Brodsky's bag, detonates the bomb. All three are killed. The explosion releases Donia Vassilova's body, and it floats to the surface.

After the funeral service, Barnacle cleverly sells the locket to Lord Mounteagle for the princely sum of 200 pounds—enough to buy a sable wrap for Miranda and the *Lady of the Lea* for Tom Gosling. Barnacle, for once, feels higher than any of the chimneys in which he worked.

Thematic Material

This story of how simple people triumph over wrongdoers is effectively told in a lively plot filled with suspense and action. The author has created a vivid picture of the London of over a century ago where, in spite of poverty and squalor, positive human values were respected. Barnacle's emergence from an unthinking guttersnipe to a young man with a sense of honor and a conscience is convincingly portrayed. The power of love and kindness to bring out the best in people is shown in the generosity and integrity of Tom Gosling. Other subjects include friendship, courage, child exploitation, and the need for self-esteem.

Book Talk Material

Some exciting passages for reading or retelling are: Donia Vassilova is murdered (pp. 5–8); Barnacle escapes with the locket (pp. 9–15); he flees Mister Roberts and is befriended by Tom Gosling (pp. 19–25); he meets Miranda and Mrs. McDipper (pp. 42–47); Inspector Creaker and Mr. Hastymite confer, and Barnacle is taken to Solomon Levy's (pp. 62–71).

Additional Selections

Tim and his family solve a historical mystery when they find an old letter hidden in a model ship in Robert Westall's *Stormsearch* (Farrar, 1992, $14).

Nineteenth-century England with all its squalor is recreated in Joan Aiken's *Midnight Is a Place* (pap., Dell, $3.50; condensed in *More Juniorplots,* Bowker, 1977, pp. 75–79), in which two youngsters lose their wealth and are forced to find work in a mill town.

Twelve-year-old Winnie finds a maze that leads her back to the past in Catherine Dexter's *Mazemaker* (Morrow, 1989, $11.95).

Adolescent Jeannie is growing up on an isolated Derbyshire farm in the fine historical novel *White Peak Farm* (Orchard, 1990, $12.95) by Berlie Doherty.

Lubrin Dhu is the son of a tribal chieftain who is defending his clan against the invading Romans in Rosemary Sutcliff's *Sun Horse, Moon Horse* (Dutton, 1978, $9.95), a novel set in ancient Britain.

Kuzma, the powerful shaman of the Ghost World, invades young Ambrosi's dreams sometimes as a wizard, sometimes as a bear, in Susan Price's fantasy set in Czarist Russia, *Ghost Song* (Farrar, 1992, $15).

In 1558, while in prison, a young girl finds a secret passage that leads to an underground meeting place for Druids in Elizabeth M. Pope's *The Perilous Gard* (Houghton, 1974, $15.45; pap., Puffin, $4.99).

About the Book

Booklist, August 1987, p. 1747.
Center for Children's Books Bulletin, September 1987, p. 7.
Horn Book, November 1987, p. 742.
Kirkus Reviews, June 15, 1987, p. 924.
School Library Journal, September 1987, p. 179.
See also *Book Review Digest,* 1988, p. 615; and *Book Review Index,* 1987, p. 275; 1988, p. 292.

About the Author

Chevalier, Tracy, ed., *Twentieth-Century Children's Writers* (3rd ed.). St. James, 1989, pp. 374–376.
Commire, Anne, ed., *Something about the Author.* Gale, 1983, Vol. 32, pp. 73–79.
de Montreville, Doris, and Crawford, Elizabeth D., eds., *Fourth Book of Junior Authors and Illustrators.* Wilson, 1978, pp. 144–145.
Kinsman, Clare D., *Contemporary Authors* (First Revision). Gale, 1976. Vols. 17–20, p. 268.
Kirkpatrick, D. L., ed., *Twentieth-Century Children's Writers* (2nd ed.). St. Martin's, 1983, pp. 312–314.
Senick, Gerard J., ed., *Children's Literature Review.* Gale, 1990, Vol. 21, pp. 82–122.
Ward, Martha, ed., *Authors of Books for Young People* (3rd ed.). Scarecrow, 1990, p. 259.

Hahn, Mary Downing. *Stepping on the Cracks*
Houghton, 1991, $13.45 (0-395-58507-4); pap., Avon, $3.50 (0-380-71900-2)

This author's first book for young readers, *The Sara Summer* (o.p.), was published in 1979 and is a partly autobiographical study of a girl who is excessively tall and who is shy, insecure, and too easily influenced by others. Since then, she has written a series of well-received novels for the middle grades. Two of them are subtitled *A Ghost Story*. The first is *Wait Till Helen Comes* (Houghton, 1986, $12.95; pap., Avon, $3.50), in which Molly and Michael, brother and sister, try to save their stepsister, Heather, whom they dislike, from being bewitched by a ghost child. The second, *The Doll in the Garden* (Houghton, 1989, $13.45; pap., Avon, $3.50), tells how Ashley, a newcomer in town, and her friend Kristi explore an overgrown area and find a mysterious doll hidden in the bushes. The author also writes realistic stories such as the highly praised *Daphne's Book* (Houghton, 1983, $13.45; pap., Bantam, $2.95), the story of two girls, one a fledgling writer and the other a talented artist, who form a friendship when they work together creating a picture book for a seventh-grade contest. *Stepping on the Cracks* takes place in a small town in Maryland during World War II. It is rich in home-front Americana, with details on people's concerns and everyday items such as toys, clothing, and popular radio programs. Around this local color is woven a story of friendship and the meaning of pacifism. It is read by youngsters in grades 5 through 8.

Plot Summary

It is 1944, and World War II is ever present in College Hill, a small town south of Baltimore, Maryland, and north of Washington, D.C. For Margaret and her best friend, Elizabeth, both about to enter sixth grade, the war takes the form of stars in the window that mark the absence of their brothers. Margaret's brother Jimmy is in the Army somewhere in Europe, and Elizabeth's brother Joe is in the Navy.

The girls are well aware of the dangers their brothers face. They are reminded every time they see their older friend, Barbara, who married Butch, the star quarterback, right after high school. Now Barbara has an infant baby boy to care for—alone. Butch was killed in Italy just three months after he and Barbara were married.

Such reminders of the war are very real for the girls. So are the behavior and obvious worry of their parents. Margaret and Elizabeth are fiercely patriotic, even walking down the street shouting, "Step on a crack, break Hitler's back!" This was supposed to hurt the Nazis and bring their brothers home safely.

Yet, even with a war going on, Margaret and Elizabeth are young girls growing to womanhood, and life often seems the same as ever in College Hill. Sometimes, the more real, immediate, and threatening war is right at home in the form of Gordy Smith. He is the worst bully in the entire sixth grade. Margaret is scared to death of Gordy, but Elizabeth stands up to him most of the time. Margaret figures Elizabeth is rarely afraid of anything.

One day Gordy and the girls have a particularly nasty run-in. Not long afterward, the bully and his friends tear down the girls' private tree house. Their tree house is very special to them, and Elizabeth is determined to get even. Much against Margaret's will, she insists they follow Gordy to his hideout in the woods. Margaret knows her parents don't want her in that part of town. But, as usual, she follows where Elizabeth leads.

The girls find the hideout and leave some obvious trails of mischief to make sure Gordy knows they have been there. The bully actually quiets down for a while, but it isn't long before he returns to his nasty ways.

The girls go to the hideout a second time, Margaret as reluctantly as before. This time they make a startling discovery. Gordy and his friends are hiding someone there. They bring food and supplies to him. The girls are amazed to discover that the someone turns out to be Gordy's older brother, Stuart. He is supposed to be off fighting in the war. What is he doing hiding out?

The girls soon realize that Stuart is a deserter from the Army. They are outraged. Their own brothers are in danger somewhere in Europe and now there is a deserter right in their home town!

Gordy and his pals catch the girls spying on the cabin. In return for the girls' silence about Stu, Gordy promises he and his friends will rebuild the destroyed tree house.

Margaret is puzzled why Stu has deserted. She remembers that her brother Jimmy always liked him and defended him when others teased him. Jimmy felt sorry for Stu and the Smith family. Margaret has heard stories that Mr. Smith is a mean man given to drinking. One day the girls actually witness Gordy being mistreated by his father, and they begin to suspect that the black eyes and bruises he often shows up with at school are not just from fistfights or falling down.

Stuart becomes ill—it turns out to be pneumonia—and Margaret and Elizabeth offer to help nurse him. As they talk to gentle Stuart, they begin to understand his hatred of violence and why he felt he had to desert. The girls have to balance their patriotic fervor and worry about their brothers with a new understanding of how some people feel about war.

When it becomes obvious that Stu is getting worse, the girls enlist the aid of the only "grownup" they feel they can trust—their widowed friend Barbara, who knew Stuart in school. She comes to the rescue and takes Stu to a doctor. When the doctor diagnoses pneumonia, Barbara talks her own parents into letting the young man stay at their house.

Stu recuperates, but Gordy shows evidence of more and more abuse from his father. This prompts a visit from Margaret's mother to Mrs. Smith. But there is only so much she can do; she believes a person can only interfere so far.

The violence in the Smith family comes to a head when Stu leaves Barbara's and goes to his own home to protect Gordy. His father beats him nearly senseless. Stu is sent to a hospital, where it is discovered that he is a deserter.

This disaster gives Gordy's mother the strength to leave her brutal husband. She takes the children to her family in North Carolina. Gordy leaves without a word to the girls. They aren't sorry to see him go, but at least they have a little more understanding of what has molded him into the kind of bully he is.

No one knows what will happen to Stu when he recovers—perhaps jail, perhaps a dishonorable discharge, or perhaps the Army will take his background into consideration and go easy on him. Whatever happens, Barbara will be there for him. Stu has asked her to marry him.

Life will go on in College Hill. It will never be the same, of course, and certainly not for Margaret and her family, for they receive word that their beloved Jimmy has died in Europe. That "step on the crack" game didn't bring him back home after all.

Thematic Material

This is a wonderfully sensitive story of how the lines often blur between right and wrong, good and evil. Gordy is a bully; he doesn't change in the eyes of the girls, but they do develop some understanding of why he is as he is. The war doesn't change for them either. They are staunchly proud of the sacrifices of both their brothers, and yet they begin to have a glimmer of understanding of the "other side of the coin" as they get to know gentle Stuart. A satisfying, often humorous, sometimes sad story of young people living through a traumatic period of world history.

Book Talk Material

Several instances illustrate both the period and the girls' dealings with Gordy the bully, which are key factors in this story. See: the step-on-a-crack game (pp. 2–4); they are threatened by Gordy the Nazi (pp. 5–9); they spy on the boys (pp. 25–31); the girls meet Barbara and the baby (pp. 34–39); and Margaret and Elizabeth sabotage the hideout (pp. 53–56).

Additional Selections

Alex, age fourteen, fights his own battles on the home front while his older brother is fighting Germans during World War II in Chester Aaron's *Alex, Who Won His War* (Walker, 1992, $17.95).

In a novel set in Wales during World War II, a relocated family is befriended by an amazing baby squirrel in Nina Bawden's *Henry* (Lothrop, 1988, $13.95).

Thirteen-year-old Mattie and her family move to Oak Ridge, Tennessee, during World War II because her father has a secret job in Connie Jordan Green's *The War at Home* (Macmillan, 1989, $12.95).

In 1940, Norah Stokes and her brother, Gavin, two British evacuees, arrive in Toronto to live with Mrs. Ogilvie for the duration of the war in Kit Pearson's *The Sky Is Falling* (Viking, 1990, $15). The story is continued in *Looking at the Moon* (Viking, 1992, $12.95).

Ruthie Fox, a fifth-grader living in San Francisco in 1941, is disturbed when her friend Mitzi Fujimoto is sent to a Japanese-American internment camp in Marcia Savin's *The Moon Bridge* (Scholastic, 1992, $13.95).

Tilly forms a friendship with downstairs neighbor Mrs. McBridge during the bleak post-World War II years in England in *The Glass Angels* (Candlewick, 1992, $16.95) by Susan Hill.

The House of Sixty Fathers (Harper, 1956, $13.89; pap., $3.95; condensed in *Introducing Books,* Bowker, 1970, pp. 192–195) by Meindert DeJong takes place during World War II when China was being invaded by Japan and tells of a young Chinese boy who endures an incredible odyssey to be reunited with his family.

Interesting glimpses of life in the United States during World War II are given in Sylvia Whitman's nonfiction *V Is for Victory: The American Homefront During World War II* (Lerner, 1993, $12.95).

About the Book

Booklist, October 15, 1991, p. 436.
Center for Children's Books Bulletin, December 1991, p. 91.
Horn Book, November 1991, p. 736.
School Library Journal, December 1991, p. 114.
See also *Book Review Digest,* 1992 cum.; and *Book Review Index,* 1991 cum.

About the Author

Commire, Anne, ed., *Something about the Author.* Gale, 1988, pp. 88–90.
Holtze, Sally Holmes, ed., *Sixth Book of Junior Authors and Illustrators.* Wilson, 1989, pp. 111–112.
May, Hal, and Trosky, Susan R., eds., *Contemporary Authors.* Gale, 1988, Vol. 122, p. 209.

Keehn, Sally M. *I Am Regina*

Philomel, 1991, $15.95 (0-399-21797-5); pap., Dell, $3.50 (0-440-40754-0)

This historical novel covers a period of nine years, from 1755 through 1764, during which a young German immigrant girl is captured and raised by an Indian tribe after her father is killed in an Indian attack during the French and Indian Wars. This first-person narrative gives authentic details of life during that period as well as a fine depiction of Indian culture and society. It is enjoyed by readers in grades 5 through 8.

Plot Summary

This novel, which begins in 1755 on a small farm in Pennsylvania, is based on the true story of Regina Leininger.

Regina sailed to America from Germany with her mother, father, older sister, Barbara, and two older brothers, Christian and John, when she was just two years old. That was eight years past, and now Regina's home is a small, isolated farm in the shadow of the Allegheny Mountains of Pennsylvania. Although Regina loves her family and her farm, she is often afraid because she hears stories of terrible atrocities inflicted on the settlers by marauding Indian tribes. Barbara just laughs at her fears.

"Stop worrying about the Indians," Barbara says. "Father says they'll never come over the Allegheny Mountains."

Nonetheless, Regina is apprehensive the day her mother and sixteen-year-old John take the corn to the mill, a two-hour wagon ride. The dog,

Jack, will go with them. That makes Regina feel less safe at the farm, because Jack always warns of approaching strangers.

At noon the next day, after Mother, John, and Jack have departed, Regina's fears are realized. Two Indians appear at the cabin door. "We are enemies," they say. "You must die." They scalp Regina's father and brother and take her and Barbara captive.

So begins a harrowing tale of life in captivity for young Regina. Barbara escapes but is recaptured and then separated from her. Regina can only hope her sister will manage to escape again. Regina and a young girl taken from a nearby farm, whom she calls Sarah, are now the property of a cruel Indian called Tiger Claw.

At first, Regina lives only for escape, hoping she will find her mother and John still alive. But days become weeks and weeks become months and the months turn into years. The memories grow dim. Little by little she must accept the Indian ways in order to survive. She is given the Indian name of Tskinnak, which means blackbird, for her black hair. Sarah is called Quetit, which means little girl.

Regina knows she could not have survived this ordeal without the help of the only person who befriends her, the Indian woman called Nonschetto. This kindly woman explains Indian ways to her and helps her gather food and do her chores, thereby avoiding Tiger Claw's cruel blows. Nonschetto even rescues her when Tiger Claw tries to force her into having sex with him. She learns to speak the Indian language, to dance their dances, and she is saddened and grieves when smallpox kills off many of the tribe.

The memories of her mother and family dim until they seem a dream. But sometimes she can still remember and sing the words of the sweet song she and her mother used to sing together.

Regina also learns it is not only Indians who are given to cruelty. She is told why Tiger Claw is so vicious to white people. Soldiers killed and scalped his own father. This does not ease the bitterness in Regina's heart, but she understands him a little better.

Regina grows into young womanhood, her life made sadder by the death of Nonschetto. And then the day comes when there is talk of the end of fighting between Indians and white settlers. Those who have been captured will be released.

At last, Regina and Sarah are given their freedom. They are taken to a camp where other captives have been released, all hoping to find their families. But Regina has only fading memories of her family, and surely her own mother would not recognize her now, even if she is alive.

Regina and Sarah travel to Fort Pitt in the shadow of the Allegheny

Mountains. She watches others being reunited, but she begins to think her own situation is hopeless. She cannot even remember her own language.

One day Regina chances on a Bible. She remembers her family had one. Although she can no longer speak the white people's tongue, she can read the words in the Bible. The next morning she is told that a woman with hair the color of snow wishes to see her. The woman saw her the night before in the fort and thinks perhaps she knows her. But when Regina sees the woman, whose face is kind, she is forced to say she does not recognize her. The woman turns away, and a young man comes to comfort her.

Then Regina hears the woman sing a song, and suddenly Regina answers her with the words of the song her mother taught her so long ago. Her mother takes her in her arms, and the young girl says haltingly, "I am Regina."

Regina and her mother and brother John were reunited in 1764. With Sarah, they went home to a cabin in Pennsylvania. It is not known if sister Barbara ever joined them, but she did escape from the Indians after being a captive for more than three years.

Thematic Material

This is a sobering tale of cruelty and misunderstandings on both sides of two clashing cultures, but also of love and warmth and friendship. It is given more poignancy by the fact that it is based on a true story. Regina is portrayed as a young girl of great inner strength and understanding, who learns to love and respect those of her captors who show her kindness and caring. There are subtle lessons about bigotry and the need for understanding between different peoples.

Book Talk Material

Regina's capture and the first days of her harsh new life make a powerful introduction to this tale of great sorrow and bravery. See: the abduction (pp. 22–26); Regina meets Sarah (pp. 34–35); Barbara escapes and is captured (pp. 47–54); Nonschetto shows her kindness (pp. 77–81); and Nonschetto tells Regina she will survive (p. 90).

Additional Selections

Matt learns Indian survival techniques when he is left to guard his family's wilderness home in eighteenth-century Maine in Elizabeth George Speare's *The Sign of the Beaver* (Houghton, 1983, $12.70; pap., Dell, $3.50). By the same author, *Calico Captive* (Houghton, 1957, $13.45; pap., Dell, $3.50; condensed in *Juniorplots,* Bowker, 1967, pp. 119–121) tells of

Miriam's life as an Indian captive during the 1750s and her eventual sale to the French in Quebec.

In Conrad Richter's *Light in the Forest* (Knopf, 1966, $21.95; pap., Bantam, $3.99), a young white boy is captured by Indians and, after becoming a true tribe member, is suddenly returned to his parents. A companion volume, *Country of Strangers* (o.p.), tells of similar experiences from a girl's point of view.

In *Where the Buffaloes Begin* (Viking, 1989, $14.95; pap., $5.99), Olaf Baker retells the American Indian legend of a boy who led stampeding buffalo away from his people.

Told in alternating chapters by two young Taino Indians, *Morning Girl* (Hyperion, 1992, $12.95) by Michael Dorris is the story of the idyllic life they led on a Bahamian island in 1492.

James Houston's *The White Archer: An Eskimo Legend* (Harcourt, 1990, $8.95) tells how an Eskimo slowly resolves his hatred of American Indians.

In Betty Baker's *Walk the World's Rim* (Harper, 1965, $13.89), an Indian boy has adventures with the doomed Naivaez expedition in the 1520s to find Cibola, the City of Gold.

About the Book

Booklist, July 1991, p. 2040.
Center for Children's Books Bulletin, April 1991, p. 198.
Horn Book Guide, Fall 1991, p. 275.
Kirkus Reviews, June 1, 1991, p. 730.
School Library Journal, June 1991, p. 108.
VOYA, August 1991, p. 172.
See also *Book Review Digest,* 1992 cum.; and *Book Review Index,* 1991, p. 487; 1992 cum.

Lowry, Lois. *Number the Stars*

Houghton, 1989, $12.70 (0-395-51060-0); pap., Dell, $3.99 (0-440-40327-8)

Lois Lowry is usually associated with contemporary family stories, such as the humorous series chronicling the growing pains of Anastasia Krupnik or the more poignant *Rabble Starkey* (Houghton, 1987, $12.70; pap., Dell, $3.95; condensed in *Juniorplots 4,* Bowker, 1993, pp. 71–76), which deals with a young girl growing up with a talented mother who works as a housekeeper. *Number the Stars,* the 1990 Newbery Medal winner, represents a change in time, locale, and mood. It takes place in World War II Denmark during the terrible days of the Nazi occupation when the Danish Resistance fighters were gallantly committing acts of sabotage and the Nazi roundup of Jews for export to death camps was beginning. In an afterword, the author details the historical sources used and which incidents and characters are based on fact. The title comes from Psalm 147, which is read by Peter Neilsen during the supposed wake for Great-Aunt Birte (pp. 86–87). The significant lines are:

> O praise the Lord . . .
> It is he who heals the broken in spirit
> and binds up their wounds,
> he who numbers the stars one by one.

Although the story is written in the third person, the events are seen entirely through the eyes of the young heroine, Annemarie Johansen. This novel is appropriate for readers from grades 4 through 7.

Plot Summary

It is September 1943, and Copenhagen is enduring its third year of Nazi occupation. Ten-year-old Annemarie Johansen is racing home after school with her friend and neighbor Ellen Rosen and Annemarie's five-year-old sister, Kirsti. They are stopped by two German patrolmen, who engage in some bullying tactics before allowing them to continue on their way. All three are shaken by the experience, and at home both Annemarie's mother and Mrs. Rosen warn them to avoid that street in future. The Johansens (mother, father, Annemarie, and Kirsti) live in the same apartment building as their friends and neighbors the Rosens, a Jewish couple who have only one child, Ellen. Annemarie remembers her beloved older sister, Lise, who was killed less than three years ago at age 18, on the eve of her wedding to Peter Neilsen. Her parents rarely mention her death except to say it was caused by an automobile accident. Her unworn wedding dress has been carefully stored in a never-opened trunk in the room Annemarie and Kirsti now share. Young Peter is still part of their lives. He occasionally delivers a copy of the underground newspaper *De Frie Danske, The Free Danes,* to the Johansens. Annemarie is convinced he is a member of the gallant freedom fighters who make up the Danish Resistance movement.

Everyday life is difficult under the occupation. Food, clothing, and fuel are very scarce; even young Kirsti is forced to wear shoes made of fish skins. However, Annemarie is fortunate in having loving, patient parents who do their best and hope for a better future. Occasional gifts of food from Mrs. Johansen's bachelor brother, Uncle Henrik, a fisherman who lives on the north coast, also help.

They begin to notice indications of increased persecution of Jews. All shops owned by Jews are closed, including the tiny button shop run by their friendly neighbor, Mrs. Hirsch. At Jewish New Year, the Rosens' rabbi tells his congregation that Jews will soon be rounded up for deportation. That evening, Annemarie's mother announces that Mr. and Mrs. Rosen have been called away suddenly and that Ellen will be spending a few days with them.

In the middle of the night, the Johansens are awakened by German soldiers who want to search the apartment for Jews. As they enter the girls' bedroom, quick-thinking Annemarie snatches an incriminating Star of David from Ellen's neck. Ellen is introduced as daughter Lise, and when the officer questions the fact that she has dark hair when the rest of the family is fair, Papa Johansen cleverly shows them a baby picture of Lise from the family album, who, luckily for them, had been born with a temporary head of rich dark-brown hair. Reluctantly, the soldiers leave.

The next day, Annemarie overhears a mysterious conversation between Papa and Uncle Henrik with references to good fishing weather and a carton of cigarettes. Soon, the three young girls and Mama Johansen are on a train headed north to visit Uncle Henrik in the tiny fishing village of Gillelege, only a few miles from the coast of Sweden. To avert suspicion, Papa stays behind in Copenhagen.

After a close brush on the train with more suspicious Nazis, they arrive safely and walk to the promontory on which Uncle Henrik's home and small farm are located. Kirsti, Ellen, and Annemarie are enchanted by the house, by a little kitten they find whom Kirsti names Thor, and by the luxury of real cream and butter courtesy of Henrik's cow, Blossom.

The next day, Mama announces that in the evening a casket containing the body of recently deceased Great-Aunt Birte will arrive and that a wake is to be held at Uncle Henrik's. Annemarie knows there is no Great-Aunt Birte but remains silent.

The casket is placed in the living room, and soon the "mourners" appear. First, there is a young couple with a tiny baby, followed by an elderly man. Soon they are joined by another couple, Mr. and Mrs. Rosen! When Peter Neilsen also appears, Annemarie realizes this is part of an elaborate and dangerous rescue plan. They will use her uncle's boat to transport the fugitive Jews to neutral Sweden and safety.

The mock wake is interrupted by loud banging on the door. German soldiers enter. They are suspicious and demand that the coffin be opened. Ingeniously, Mama tells them that Birte died of a very infectious form of typhus and that the attending doctor had insisted the coffin remain closed. After they leave, Peter opens the casket—it is filled with warm clothing, which is distributed to the refugees. Peter also gives Mr. Rosen a small package that he says must be delivered to Henrik at his boat. Peter leaves for the boat with the first group, and twenty minutes later Mama leaves with the Rosens. The rocky, root-covered path is extremely treacherous in the dark.

When Mama's return is long overdue, Annemarie sees her in the distance, crawling painfully toward the house. She has fallen and broken her ankle. Annemarie also sees on the ground the package Mr. Rosen was to deliver. He obviously has accidentally dropped it. After making her mother comfortable, Annemarie sets out alone to deliver the package. After cleverly outwitting Nazi guards, she reaches the boat in which her friends are now safely hidden. The package contains a special formula that will deaden the sense of smell of the guard dogs the Germans use to sniff out humans hidden on fishing boats. Because of Annemarie's bravery, the boat is able to leave safely for Sweden.

The war ends, and Denmark is awash in celebrations, but for Annemarie sorrow is mixed with joy. Some months before, Peter Neilsen had been caught and executed. She has also learned that her sister Lise was in fact a martyr in the Resistance movement. She will never forget their sacrifice, but now she awaits the return of her friend Ellen and the opportunity to give back the tiny necklace she has looked after for her.

Thematic Material

This is not only a stirring re-creation of a bleak period in Western history but also a moving tribute to those who sacrificed themselves to save their friends and restore their country's liberty. Its child's-eye view enables young readers to understand the war and identify with those innocents caught in it. It also explores the meaning of courage and how even the young can perform acts of heroism and selflessness. Another theme is the power of friendship between individuals and families and how this can influence important moral choices even to the point of jeopardizing one's personal safety. Good family relationships, the terrible consequences of prejudice, the Holocaust, and everyday life in occupied Denmark are all well portrayed in this suspense-filled, simply written novel.

Book Talk Material

This novel contains a number of exciting passages to read or retell: Annemarie and Ellen are stopped by soldiers on their way home from school (pp. 1–4); Mrs. Hirsch's store is closed (pp. 19–22); Kirsti and her fish shoes (pp. 28–30); German soldiers raid the Johansen apartment (pp. 43–49); and the train ride to Uncle Henrik's home (pp. 54–56).

Additional Selections

The Man from the Other Side (Houghton, 1991, $13.45) by Uri Orlev tells how Marek and his family hide a Jewish man in the days before the Warsaw Ghetto uprising.

An entire French town becomes involved in trying to save some Jewish refugee children during World War II in Michael Morpurgo's *Waiting for Anya* (Viking, 1991, $13).

A young Jewish girl tells of years of hiding from the Nazis during their occupation of Holland in World War II in *Hide and Seek* (Houghton, 1991, $13.95).

During World War II, a young Jewish boy takes refuge in the Soviet Union after being driven from home in Poland in Tamar Bergman's *Along the Tracks* (Houghton, 1991, $14.95).

In *The Upstairs Room* (Harper, 1987, $14.89; pap., $3.95; condensed in *More Juniorplots,* Bowker, 1977, pp. 95–99) by Johanna Reiss, two young Jewish girls are hidden for over two years in the home of a simple Dutch peasant during the German occupation. A sequel is *The Journey Back* (Harper, 1992, $17.89; pap., $3.95).

During World War II, Lisa and other teenage Jews become involved in a resistance movement during the German occupation of Denmark in *Lisa's War* (Scribner, 1989, $13.95; pap., Scholastic, $2.75) by Carol Matas.

Anne Frank's life before she went into hiding, the events recorded in her diary, and her subsequent deportation and death are told in Gene Brown's *Anne Frank: Child of the Holocaust* (Blackbirch, 1992, $14.95; pap., $7.95). Older readers might like to read Anne Frank's actual diary, *Anne Frank: The Diary of a Young Girl* (Doubleday, 1967, $21.95).

About the Book

Booklist, March 1, 1989, p. 1194.
Center for Children's Books Bulletin, March 1989, p. 176.
Horn Book, May 1989, p. 371.

New York Times Book Review, May 21, 1989, p. 30.
School Library Journal, March 1989, p. 177.
See also *Book Review Digest,* 1989, p. 1027; and *Book Review Index,* 1989, p. 508; 1990, p. 503; 1991, p. 565.

About the Author

Chevalier, Tracy, ed., *Twentieth-Century Children's Writers* (3rd ed.). St. James, 1989, pp. 610–611.
Commire, Anne, ed., *Something about the Author.* Gale, 1981, Vol. 23, pp. 120–122.
Estes, Glenn E., ed., *American Writers for Children since 1960: Fiction* (Dictionary of Literary Biography: Vol. 52). Gale, 1986, pp. 249–261.
Holtze, Sally Holmes, ed., *Fifth Book of Junior Authors and Illustrators.* Wilson, 1983, pp. 198–199.
Metzger, Linda, ed., *Contemporary Authors* (New Revision Series). Gale, 1984, Vol. 13, pp. 333–336.
Olendorf, Donna, and Telgen, Diane, eds., *Something about the Author.* Gale, 1993, Vol. 70, pp. 134–137.
Senick, Gerard J., ed., *Children's Literature Review.* Gale, 1984, Vol. 6, pp. 192–197.
Ward, Martha, ed., *Authors of Books for Young People* (3rd ed.). Scarecrow, 1990, p. 451.

O'Dell, Scott. *My Name Is Not Angelica*

Houghton, 1989, $14.45 (0-395-51061-9); pap., Dell, $3.50 (0-440-40379-0)

Scott O'Dell (1903–1989) was one of the great masters of the historical novel for young readers. His *Island of the Blue Dolphins* (Houghton, 1990, $18.45; pap., Dell, $3.99; condensed in *Juniorplots,* Bowker, 1967, pp. 47–50) won the 1961 Newbery Medal and tells of the adventures of an enterprising girl, Karana, who is accidentally left behind by her California Indian tribe when they abandon their jinxed island. In a sequel, *Zia* (Houghton, 1976, $14.95; pap., Dell, $2.95), Karana's niece, living safely at the Santa Barbara Mission, dreams of rescuing her aunt from her island prison. *My Name Is Not Angelica* was the last novel O'Dell completed before his death. It takes place on the island of St. John, which was then part of Denmark and is now part of the U.S. Virgin Islands. It is based on accounts of an actual slave revolt during 1733–1735. The author depicts with harsh reality the suffering of the slaves and the dehumanizing effects of slavery on both master and slave. It is suitable for readers in grades 5 through 7.

Plot Summary

Sixteen-year-old Raisha's ordeal begins when she is stolen from her home in Africa and carried across the sea in a plague-ridden slave ship. Among those captured with her is Konje, the man she is supposed to marry in three years. Dazed and terrified, Raisha finds herself standing on a platform in the slave market on the Danish-owned island of St. John in the West Indies.

The time is the early 1730s. The island of St. John was discovered by Christopher Columbus in 1493 and occupied by Spain, the Netherlands, England, and France until 1717, when the Danes settled there. In the 1900s, Denmark would sell the island to the United States.

Raisha, Konje, and their friend Dondo are sold together to the plantation of Jost von Prok. Raisha becomes a house servant of Jost's wife, Jenna. All the slaves' names are changed. Raisha becomes Angelica.

Raisha, or Angelica, is one of the lucky ones. She is not treated cruelly or harshly by either Jost or Jenna von Prok. Many of the less fortunate slaves endure horrific punishments and degradations.

Not long after their enslavement, Konje manages to tell Angelica he is going to escape. He has heard that runaway slaves have gathered at a place called Mary Point. He promises he will return to rescue Angelica.

Konje does return but only to tell Angelica that the governor of the island will be coming for a talk with the planters about runaway slaves. He will be bringing powder and bullets. Konje wants Dondo to steal what he can for the escaped slaves. He tells Angelica the time is not right for her rescue.

An angry Governor Gardelin arrives on the island. With him is Preacher Isaak Gronnewold, a friend to the captured slaves. The governor has heard about a slave revolt planned by a leader called Apollo, which is the name the white owners gave to Konje. In retaliation, the governor proposes a new set of laws governing the treatment of slaves. They allow horrible cruelty and torture, tactics not used on the island before.

The von Proks try to get Angelica to tell them what the drum signals that they hear nightly can mean. Angelica pretends not to know. When von Prok promises her freedom, Angelica says she can be free only if he frees all the slaves on the plantation. In reply, he revokes his promise.

There are more and more rumors of a coming slave revolt. The von Proks and other whites are fearful. It is decided to send Jenna von Prok to the island of St. Thomas until the trouble blows over. Angelica is to go with her. Angelica acts as though she will comply, but she knows that she will never leave St. John and Konje.

Dondo is caught trying to help a young boy escape a cruel punishment. For that he is to be tortured, and all the slaves are brought out to watch. Isaak Gronnewold tries to interfere. The governor's soldiers knock him down and return to the torture. But it is already too late. Dondo has escaped his punishment by dying.

Angelica takes this opportunity to escape herself and makes her way to Konje's camp. She is amazed and proud to find how well run the camp is, how strongly Konje leads his people. Many of them are armed now with stolen rifles and gunpowder.

When Preacher Gronnewald comes to the camp to warn them what the governor will do, he marries Angelica and Konje.

Some months later, Gronnewald returns with news that the governor is sending many armed men to put down the threatened revolt. He tells them the governor will not stop until there are no runaway slaves left on the island. And if he fails, Denmark's king will only send another governor to succeed. There is no way the slaves can win.

The armed ship that pulls into the harbor is not Danish but French. The captain, Dumont, sends a message that all runaways must surrender. Gronnewald tells Konje that Governor Gardelin had sent to the island of Martinique to ask the French for help in putting down the rebellion.

Konje asks to talk to the French captain, but soon the slaves realize the French have not come to talk. They will be killed unless they surrender to their fate.

The slaves choose freedom instead of bondage. One by one, two by two, they leap over the cliff to their death.

When Konje takes Angelica's hand, she hesitates. Angelica is carrying their child, and she cannot jump to her death. Konje and Angelica look at each other, and then he leaps over the cliff.

Angelica, now Raisha once again, is taken by the French captain to the island of Martinique, where she cares for his children until her daughter is born. In a year, the French set the slaves free, including Raisha and her daughter.

Thematic Material

This somber but well-paced and easily read story is based on an actual slave revolt on the island of St. John in 1733. Although not graphic in its depiction of slave treatment, it presents a clear picture of the horrors of slavery, its dehumanizing aspects, and the bravery and courage of individual slaves and of the few whites who abhorred these cruel practices. Raisha is shown as a young woman of great courage and endurance. Good readers in this age group will be moved by this story.

Book Talk Material

A number of scenes can lead to a discussion of slavery and its evils and the dignity and courage of the human spirit. See: Raisha's capture (pp. 12–15); the slave market on St. John (pp. 20–25); Konje tells Angelica he is escaping (pp. 33–35); the governor sets down new laws for slave treatment (pp. 49–53); and Dondo's death (pp. 84–91).

Additional Selections

The 1733 St. Jan slave rebellion in the Virgin Islands is described by an actual participant in Ellen Howard's *When Daylight Comes* (Macmillan, 1985, $14.95).

Thirteen-year-old Jessie Bollier becomes an unwilling cabin boy aboard a slave ship in the Paula Fox's Newbery Medal winner *The Slave Dancer* (Macmillan, 1982, $13.95; pap., Dell, $3.50; condensed in *More Juniorplots*, Bowker, 1977, pp. 82–86).

Ann Petry in *Tituba of Salem Village* (Harper, 1964, $14.89; pap., $3.95) tells the story of Tituba and her husband, John Indian, from the day they were sold as slaves in Barbados until the tragic Salem witchcraft trials.

A father and his son are kidnapped in West Africa and sold as slaves to plantations in Jamaica, where they are separated in a story of slavery in the 1820s by James Berry, *Ajeemah and His Son* (Harper, 1992, $13).

In James Lincoln Collier's *Jump Ship to Freedom* (Delacorte, 1981, $13.95; pap., Dell, $3.50), a fourteen-year-old slave in 1787 wants to buy freedom for himself and his mother by cashing in notes received from his father, who fought in the Revolution. There are two companion volumes: *War Comes to Willy Freeman* (Delacorte, 1983, $13.95; pap., Dell, $3.25) and *Who Is Carrie?* (Delacorte, 1984, $14.95; pap., Dell, $3.25).

A contemporary black girl travels back to the days of slavery in Belinda Hurmence's *A Girl Called Boy* (Houghton, 1982, $14.45; pap., $4.70).

Based on an 1861 autobiography, Mary E. Lyons's *Letters from a Slave Girl: The Story of Harriet Jacobs* (Scribner, 1992, $13.95) tells the story of a girl in hiding on a Southern plantation.

Virginia Hamilton uses such documents as slave narratives and autobiographies to tell the history of slavery in America, the resistance to it, and eventual freedom in a book touchingly illustrated by Leo and Diane Dillon, *Many Thousand Gone: African Americans from Slavery to Freedom* (Knopf,

1993, $16). For older readers, use Walter Dean Myers's *Now Is Your Time! The African-American Struggle for Freedom* (Harper, 1991, $17.95; pap., $10.95; condensed in *Juniorplots 4,* Bowker, 1993, pp. 361–365).

About the Book

Book Report, March 1990, p. 33.
Booklist, November 15, 1989, p. 674.
Center for Children's Books Bulletin, October 1989, p. 40.
Horn Book, March 1990, p. 208.
Horn Book Guide, July 1989, p. 76.
Kirkus Reviews, October 15, 1989, p. 1533.
New York Times Book Review, January 25, 1990, p. 29.
School Library Journal, October 1989, p. 135.
VOYA, December 1989, p. 280.
Wilson Library Bulletin, September 1990, p. 14.
See also *Book Review Digest,* 1990, p. 1354; and *Book Review Index,* 1989, p. 613; 1990, p. 609.

About the Author

Block, Ann, and Riley, Carolyn, eds., *Children's Literature Review.* Gale, 1976, Vol. 1, pp. 145–149.
Commire, Anne, ed., *Something about the Author.* Gale, 1977, Vol. 12, pp. 161–164.
Estes, Glenn E., ed., *American Writers for Children since 1960: Fiction* (Dictionary of Literary Biography: Vol. 52). Gale, 1986, pp. 278–295.
Fadool, Cynthia, ed., *Contemporary Authors.* Gale, 1976, Vols. 61–64, p. 402.
Fuller, Muriel, ed., *More Junior Authors.* Wilson, 1963, pp. 161–162.
Kirkpatrick, D. L., ed., *Twentieth-Century Children's Writers* (2nd ed.). St. Martin's, 1983, pp. 588–589.
Metzger, Linda, ed., *Contemporary Authors* (New Revision Series). Gale, 1984, Vol. 12, pp. 346–347.

Sutcliff, Rosemary. *Flame-Colored Taffeta*
Farrar, 1986, $14 (0-374-32344-5); pap., $3.50 (0-374-42341-5)

Rosemary Sutcliff is generally considered to be the foremost writer of historical fiction for young people. Her novels deal primarily with English history and span the years from the Bronze Age through the eighteenth century, with a heavy concentration on the Roman period, including her favorite novel, *The Eagle of the Ninth* (Oxford, 1987, $20); and on Anglo-Saxon times, including *The Shining Company* (Farrar, 1990, $14.95; pap.,

$4.95; condensed in *Juniorplots 4,* Bowker, 1993, pp. 263–268). *Flame-Colored Taffeta* begins in 1750 in England during the reign of George II. The abortive invasion by Bonnie Prince Charlie and his Jacobite followers occurred five years before, and the English still look with suspicion and hostility toward France. The setting of the novel is the Selsey Peninsula on the coast of Sussex only a few miles from the city of Chichester, an area that during this period was infested with smugglers anxious to make a few pounds bringing contraband liquor, tobacco, and fabrics into the country from the Continent. The novel is enjoyed by better readers in grades 5 through 8.

Plot Summary

The previous summer, twelve-year-old Damaris Crocker and her dear friend Peter Ballard, the thirteen-year-old son of the local vicar, discovered an abandoned, half-ruined cottage in the woods that has become their secret hiding place. Damaris romantically nicknamed it Joyous Gard after Sir Lancelot's mythical castle, but the more realistic Peter calls it Tumbledown. Now, the following spring, it is fulfilling two purposes. In addition to being their favorite meeting place, it is housing a young vixen they are nursing back to health after one of her paws was shattered in a hunter's trap.

On her faithful pony, Snowball, Damaris is now riding to Joyous Gard carrying hidden kitchen scraps to feed Lady, the vixen. On the way, she notices that a chalk cross has appeared on her father's barn; and on the road, she hears Shadow Mason, an old one-eyed sailor, playing sea shanties on his fiddle as he walks the countryside. Although only twelve, Damaris already knows these are the telltale signals that there will be a smuggling run by the so-called Fair Traders tonight. With high tariffs, smuggling has become a profitable part-time occupation for many in the neighborhood. John Crocker, her father, is an honest man who does not engage in smuggling, but like others in the area he fears reprisals if he doesn't cooperate—in his case, by leaving his barn door open so that his horses can be used to carry the contraband.

When she gets home to Carthagena Farm, she is greeted by her father and Aunt Selina, who has been their housekeeper since her mother died years before. That night after dinner, Damaris, in her room, repeats a wish to the starlit sky that some day she will own a beautiful petticoat made of flame-colored taffeta similar to one she saw on a gypsy girl two years before. As she drifts off to sleep, she hears pistol shots far in the distance.

The following morning, in the woods, Damaris finds an unconscious young man with a large bullet wound in his left leg. She summons Peter, and after hiding the stranger in Joyous Gard, they contact Genty Small the Wise Woman in the village. Through her use of herbs, charms, home-grown medicines, and incantations, she has gained the reputation of being half-healer and half-witch. She agrees to accompany the two youngsters and, at the cottage, removes the embedded bullet using crude surgical instruments. She places healing poultices on the wound and feeds the stranger medicinal herbs.

Although her frequent, unexplained absences are causing problems at home, Damaris continues to visit the stranger whenever possible. She trusts him instinctively and finds, when he is able to converse with her, that he is both charming and well educated. She tells him about herself and how she often wishes for a flame-colored taffeta petticoat. He smilingly promises that on her wedding day, he will find a way to give her one. The young man calls himself Tom Wildgoose, and although he claims to be neither spy nor smuggler, he is secretive about his past. Damaris notices that around his neck he carries a strange oilskin packet. At first, he tries to keep it from her sight. Later, when he realizes she has seen it, he hides it somewhere in the cottage.

In time, the health of both Tom and Lady improve. Soon Lady is well enough to be free, and Tom is now alone in Joyous Gard except for regular visits from his three friends.

One day, while Damaris is in the cottage with Tom, they hear the sounds of a hunting party and the baying of hounds in the distance. It is the local squire, Mr. Farrington, and his friends. In the clearing before the house, a terrified Lady appears. Damaris and the vixen hide in the cottage while Tom confronts the hunters. He pretends to be a French sailor who has missed his ship. Farrington claims he is a spy and forcefully drags him off to his compound.

In desperation, Damaris runs to get help from Genty. The witch tells Damaris to contact Matthew Binn, the chief guard on the Farrington estate, and tell him that she will place a life-threatening curse on him unless he provides an opportunity for Tom to escape. To emphasize her point, she gives Damaris a waxen heart pierced by five dark thorns to present to Binn. It works. In the middle of the night, Damaris leads Tom to Genty's house and, she hopes, safety. Guiltily, Damaris sneaks back home.

The next day, the girl arrives at Genty's home to check on Tom at the same time as a squad of customs officials, searching for hidden contraband. Damaris is petrified, but miraculously Tom is not found. When the officers leave, Genty pulls back a hearth rug, revealing a trap door to the basement storeroom where she has hidden Tom.

Tom now reveals that he is a Jacobite, a follower of the defeated Young Pretender Bonnie Prince Charlie, and that he is on a mission to deliver some letters to his lord's supporters in London. He assures Damaris these letters are not treasonous in content but merely acknowledge the cause is now lost. With the help of Damaris and Peter, Tom returns to Joyous Gard to retrieve the documents. Horses are secured so Tom can be taken to Chichester, where he will catch a coach to London. In a moving farewell, Tom bids Damaris goodbye and kisses her gently on the forehead.

Five and a half years pass, and Damaris is busy preparing for her wedding to Peter when, unexpectedly, she finds a package addressed to Mistress Damaris Crocker, for her wedding. Inside is a flame-colored taffeta petticoat.

Thematic Material

The author has beautifully re-created an area and time in English history that was rife with lawlessness and political intrigue. In a tight, intricately developed plot, she combines a series of tense and suspenseful incidents with an atmosphere as colorful as the book's title. Details concerning food, clothing, and everyday life in eighteenth-century Sussex produce a feeling of authenticity. In addition to being a rousing adventure, this is also a story of how courage and resourcefulness triumph and trust and friendship are rewarded.

Book Talk Material

A brief description of the setting of the story and a retelling of the plot until Damaris finds Tom should interest readers. Some specific passages for retelling or reading are: Damaris realizes a smuggling run is imminent (pp. 5–7); Damaris wishes for her petticoat (pp. 11–13); she finds Tom and seeks help for Peter (pp. 21–25); Genty removes the bullet from Tom's leg (pp. 36–40); and Tom slowly recovers (pp. 55–61).

Additional Selections

In the courtly world of a wealthy kingdom, the search is on for a princess who will match the prince's good looks, riches, and intelligence in Katherine Paterson's *The King's Equal* (Harper, 1992, $17).

Set in Japan around 1600, Lensey Namioka's *The Coming of the Bear* (Harper, 1992, $14) is the story of two lordless young samurai, their problems with colonialists who are at war, and the mystery of a bear that attacks settlements.

Lucy's younger sister, Sarah, is accused of being a fairy child, a changeling, in a novel set in seventeenth-century Yorkshire, *The Half Child* (Simon & Schuster, 1989, $13.95; pap., $4.95) by Kathleen Hersom.

During the Norman conquest of England in 1066, Juliana, an eleven-year-old, loses her home and parents in Eloise Jarvis McGraw's *The Striped Ships* (McElderry, 1991, $15.95).

Thirteen-year-old Tymmon finds an animal friend when he flees into the forest after his father, a court jester, is abducted in Zilpha Keatley Snyder's *Song of the Gargoyle* (Delacorte, 1991, $14.95).

An old lady remembers the exciting times of Bonnie Prince Charlie in Scotland in *Quest for a Kelpie* (Holiday, 1988, $12.95) by Frances Hendry.

In Tamora Pierce's *Alanna: The First Adventure* (Macmillan, 1983, $14.95; pap., Knopf, $3.25), a young girl living during the Middle Ages changes places with her brother so she can become a knight. A sequel is *In the Hand of the Goddess* (Macmillan, 1984, $14.95; pap., McKay, $3.50).

About the Book

Booklist, November 15, 1986, p. 518.
Center for Children's Books Bulletin, December 1986, p. 77.
Horn Book, March 1987, p. 213.
Kirkus Reviews, November 1, 1986, p. 1650.
School Library Journal, February 1987, p. 95.
VOYA, February 1987, p. 287.
See also *Book Review Digest,* 1987, pp. 1818–1819; and *Book Review Index,* 1986, p. 703; 1987, p. 742.

About the Author

Block, Ann, and Riley, Carolyn, eds., *Children's Literature Review.* Gale, 1976, Vol. 1, pp. 182–192.
Chevalier, Tracy, ed., *Twentieth-Century Children's Writers* (3rd ed.). St. James, 1989, pp. 938–940.
Commire, Anne, ed., *Something about the Author.* Gale, 1986, Vol. 44, pp. 188–197.
Fuller, Muriel, ed., *More Junior Authors.* Wilson, 1963, pp. 200–201.
Harte, Barbara, and Riley, Carolyn, eds., *Contemporary Authors* (First Revision Series). Gale, 1969, Vols. 5–8, p. 1119.
Kirkpatrick, D. L., ed., *Twentieth-Century Children's Writers* (2nd ed.). St. Martin's, 1983, pp. 744–746.
Ward, Martha, ed., *Authors of Books for Young People* (3rd ed.). Scarecrow, 1990, p. 683.

8

Interesting Lives

YOUNG readers are interested in people and enjoy reading about their favorite heroes and villains. In this section, four interesting lives are explored. Two are biographies of writers who are popular with youngsters: One was a pioneer who settled in the Midwest with her husband, and the other grew up in a China beginning to open up to foreigners. The other two represent contrasting cultures and times: the first was a Confederate general in the Civil War and the second a black musician and entertainer who left his indelible mark on American jazz.

Anderson, William. *Laura Ingalls Wilder: A Biography*
Harper, 1992, $15.89 (0-06-020114-2)

In 1932, the first of the Little House books was published. It was *Little House in the Big Woods* (Harper, 1961, $15; pap., $4.95), which tells about Laura Ingalls Wilder's earliest days in a little gray house in the Big Woods of Wisconsin. Eight books later, these delightful, often moving remembrances of the author's past ended with *The First Four Years* (Harper, 1971, $15). This series has become a recognized classic in the field of American children's literature and continues to be read and loved generation after generation. William Anderson has, in turn, written an enjoyable biography of the author that relates Wilder's life in language suitable for the youngsters who are presently reading her books. He fills in gaps left by the individual books and complements the text with sixteen pages of photographs. The first half of the biography deals with the author's childhood, and the second with her adult life. This well-researched, interesting book is suitable for readers in grades 4 through 7.

Plot Summary

Laura Elizabeth Ingalls was born on February 7, 1867, near the town of Pepin, Wisconsin, to Charles and Caroline Ingalls. She was their second daughter, Mary Amelia having been born two years earlier. Their only neighbors in the Big Woods of wilderness Wisconsin were Henry and Polly Quinner and their three children. Laura remembered her father as strong, fearless, and jolly, and her mother as quiet, gentle, and comforting.

In 1868, the family decided to sell their land in the Big Woods and travel west. The story of that trip into the state of Kansas in a covered wagon was later told in Laura's book, *Little House on the Prairie.* She was too young to remember much of the trip, but her parents told her about it later.

Baby Carrie was born in 1870, and the following spring the family made the long trek back to Wisconsin because the man who had bought their land did not want to finish paying for it and wanted them to take it back. Laura's and her family's experiences back in the Big Woods of Wisconsin are contained in her book, *Little House in the Big Woods.*

Papa Ingalls sold the farm again in 1873, and the Ingallses trekked to Minnesota. They settled on the Minnesota prairie at Walnut Grove. Lots of pioneer families began arriving, and a school was started. The Ingalls girls attended. Laura later wrote of those times in *On the Banks of Plum Creek.*

In 1875, a new baby arrived—Laura's first brother, named Charles Frederick. But the sickly infant lived less than a year and died in 1876.

Once again, the Ingalls family was on the move, this time to Burr Oak, Iowa. But by the following year, Pa's restless feet had them back in Walnut Grove. In 1879, Mary, Laura's older sister, came down with an illness that eventually left her blind. Laura became her sister's link to light and color and action, describing what she saw in the outside world.

The 1880s found the Ingalls family in Dakota territory, and Laura was growing up. When Mary turned sixteen, she went to the Iowa College for the Blind. Laura helped Mary with many of her studies, gaining an education herself. When she became sixteen, she took a teacher's examination and was qualified to teach school. She had not, herself, graduated from high school.

In 1885, Laura married her long-time friend Almanzo Wilder, whom she called Manly. He was nearly ten years older than she. Their daughter, Rose, was born in 1886. Their second child, a boy, died in 1889.

The Wilders seemed to share the Ingalls family wanderlust. After a short trip to Florida, they went back to South Dakota and then decided to head for Missouri and the "Land of the Big Red Apple." A friend asked why they traveled so much, and Laura replied, "We want to see the world!"

The Wilders settled in Mansfield, Missouri, on what they called Rocky Ridge Farm. At last, they were home.

In February 1911, Laura published her first article in a magazine. At the age of forty-one, her writing career began. Soon she became a recognized expert on farm life. She encouraged women to become equal partners in the work and life of the farm.

By June of 1931, Laura's first book was in the making, and she and Manly made a trip back to South Dakota. They visited friends and saw Laura's sister Carrie, who had married a mine owner and lived near Mount Rushmore.

Little House in the Big Woods was published in 1932. At sixty-five, she was famous. *Little House on the Prairie* was published in 1935. Laura Ingalls Wilder's books won her many honors and a growing audience.

In 1949, at the age of ninety-two, Manly died of a heart attack. They had been married for sixty-four years. Laura decided to stay on at Rocky Ridge. In 1951, she was awarded one of her highest honors: the Laura Ingalls Wilder Library was dedicated in Mansfield, Missouri.

Despite her loneliness without her husband, Laura continued to enjoy a happy, productive life. She took her first airplane ride at the age of eighty-seven. She lived to be ninety years old. She died three days after her birthday, on February 10, 1957.

This pioneer, wife, farmer, mother, and author left a rich harvest of wonderful words as a lasting memorial.

Thematic Material

The biography of Laura Ingalls Wilder reads much like one of her own books. It conveys a sense of the restless pioneer spirit and love of the land that kept so many Americans in the 1800s on the move across this vast land. The biographer conveys the deep sense of family love and loyalty that the Ingallses, Wilders, and other pioneer families displayed. He also points up the loneliness and sadness when illness and death struck and could not be prevented. But through all the hardships, the true sturdiness of the American pioneer shines, and young readers will enjoy this warm and very real picture of life in America more than a century ago.

Book Talk Material

Many scenes in this book give a true picture of the harshness of life in the wilderness, yet also convey the hardiness of spirit that kept families together. See: families stick together in the Big Woods (pp. 20–29); the trip into Indian territory (pp. 33–41); Laura discovers books (pp. 43–45); life along Plum Creek (pp. 51–61); the year in Ohio (pp. 62–75); and school-days in Walnut Grove (pp. 78–88).

Additional Selections

Two other recommended biographies of this author are Patricia Reilly Giff's *Laura Ingalls Wilder: Growing Up in the Little House* (Viking, 1987, $10.95) and, for a younger audience, Gwenda Blair's *Laura Ingalls Wilder* (Putnam, 1981, $6.95).

Laura Ingalls Wilder's *West from Home* (Harper, 1974, $14; pap., $3.95) is a collection of letters the author wrote to her husband in 1915 when she visited San Francisco at the time of the Panama-Pacific Exposition.

The life of another writer beloved by young readers is told in Angelica Carpenter's and Jean Shirley's *L. Frank Baum: Royal Historian of Oz* (Lerner, 1992, $15.95).

Beverly Gherman has written a well-researched, respectful, and loving biography of the creator of *Charlotte's Web* in *E. B. White: Some Writer!* (Macmillan, 1992, $13.95).

In an oversized, well-illustrated book, the famous author-illustrator of children's books, Bill Peet, who worked for many years at the Walt Disney Studio, tells his story in *Bill Peet: An Autobiography* (Houghton, 1989, $16.45).

Arlene B. Hirschfelder and Beverly R. Singer have collected an excellent group of poems, songs, and stories that span the years 1887–1990 by talented young Native Americans in *Rising Voices: Writings of Young Native Americans* (Scribner, 1992, $12.95).

The life of William Shakespeare is chronicled with a guide to his major plays plus beautiful illustrations in Diane Stanley's and Peter Vennema's *Bard of Avon* (Morrow, 1992, $15).

Marion Dane Bauer's *What's Your Story?* (Houghton, 1992, $13.45) is a practical young person's guide to fiction writing that explores such elements as plot, dialogue, and characterization.

About the Book

Booklist, December 15, 1992, p. 728.
Center for Children's Books Bulletin, December 1992, p. 105.
Kirkus Reviews, November 1, 1992, p. 1371.
School Library Journal, December 1992, p. 1115.

Collier, James Lincoln. *Louis Armstrong: An American Success Story*
Macmillan, 1985, $14.95 (0-02-722830-4); pap., $5.95 (0-02-042555-4)

To most young readers, James Collier is known as a writer of novels with a contemporary setting, such as *Outside Looking In* (Macmillan, 1987, $13.95; pap., Avon, $2.95; condensed in *Juniorplots 4,* Bowker, 1993, pp. 19–23), about the journey of a fourteen-year-old boy and his younger sister when they leave their hippie parents and set out to find their grandparents. He is also the familiar author of several excellent historical novels in collaboration with his brother, historian Christopher Collier. An example is *My Brother Sam Is Dead* (Four Winds, 1984, $14.95; pap., Scholastic, $2.50; condensed in *More Juniorplots,* Bowker, 1977, pp. 79–82), a heartbreaking story about a family whose loyalties are divided by the American Revolution. Adult readers known him best as a writer on jazz topics, including biographies of Benny Goodman and Duke Ellington. In 1983, *Louis Armstrong: An American Genius* (pap., Oxford, 1983, $12.95) was published. From it came an abridged version, *Louis Armstrong: An American Success Story,* written for a young audience from roughly grades 6 through 10. Although this is a complimentary biography, it does not shy away from the seamy side of Armstrong's life, particularly his childhood. Because of the amount of background material included, it is also valuable for its data on the rise and development of jazz in America.

Plot Summary

He would grow up to become one of the greatest of all jazz musicians. He would be loved as one of the most famous entertainers of all time—known, respected, revered, and admired by kings and queens, presidents and sheikhs, rich and poor, adults and children the world over. And yet he barely knew his parents; he never knew his birthdate; he grew up in a shack with no bathroom; he did not advance beyond the third grade and could read and write only poorly. He was born in the South at a time when nothing much was expected from a dirt-poor, uneducated black man and nothing much often materialized. But he was different. Although he was too poor to own a musical instrument until he was seventeen and didn't learn to read music until he was past twenty, he and his cornet would change the music of his country and of the world. He was Louis Armstrong, known the world over with great affection as Satchmo. A true American success story.

Louis Armstrong was born in New Orleans, Louisiana, in 1898. He spent his youth in the ghetto. His father, Willie, ran off and married again before Louis started school. Willie only lived a few blocks from Louis, but he never came to see him.

Louis's mother, Mayann, moved out when he was about a year old, leaving the young boy in the care of his grandmother, Josephine Armstrong. She took in white people's laundry for a living, and they were dirt poor. When Louis was seven, his mother took him to live with her in her apartment on Perdido Street in New Orleans. Perdido Street was a tough place, but it was in the black entertainment district. Music became one of the few good things in his life.

From a young age, Louis knew he wanted to be a musician. But how could he possibly get money for an instrument? He began to sing in the streets for change. During the next several years, he played and sang in New Orleans honky-tonks, growing up with jazz, hustling for money, getting himself into trouble now and again, and continuing to learn the cornet. By 1922, he was getting a reputation as a hot musician. King Oliver, considered to be the best jazz man in New Orleans until he took his band to Chicago, heard about young Louis and sent for him to play second cornet.

Louis Armstrong spent the next seven years in Chicago. He was almost as happy to be joining the band as he was to be living in his first apartment with a private bath. This was luxury!

In 1924, Louis married Lil Hardin, a pianist with Oliver's band. She urged him to go out on his own, but gentle, shy Louis always refused. Finally, in 1925, he went to the Okeh recording studios in Chicago and cut some records that started his fabulous career, including his first big hit, "Heebie Jeebies."

By 1928, Louis was recognized as being in a class by himself as a jazz musician. In 1929, with a white man, Tommy Rockwell, as his new manager, Louis went to New York City, to the Savoy, and became a smash hit. His marriage broke up in 1931, although he and Lil remained good friends all their lives.

Louis Armstrong went on to greater and greater glory. His life was not always easy, however; talented or no, he was still a black man in a largely white and often prejudiced society. But his fame grew steadily, and so did his loving fans. Through all this he played with a painfully battered lip, which he had ruined playing his instrument incorrectly in his early years.

In 1942, Louis married Lucille Wilson, a dancer at Harlem's Cotton Club. They had a long and happy marriage. After 1947, when his "Blueberry Hill" hit the charts, Louis's career rose steadily. By 1963, he was known the world over, especially after his smash hit "Hello, Dolly!" Louis Armstrong was at the top of the world of popular music.

Satchmo died on July 6, 1971. His funeral was attended by show business celebrities and dignitaries from all over the country. In New Orleans, fifteen thousand people gathered to hear jazz played in his honor.

Louis showed his country that a poor, uneducated black boy from the South could make it to the top and still keep his artistic integrity and his decency as a person. He left a wealth of music for Americans and others all over the world to enjoy for centuries to come. He also left his mark as a human being of worth, respect, and dignity. Louis Armstrong is truly an American success story.

Thematic Material

This is an easily read, highly interesting biography of a fascinating and talented entertainer whose name is familiar to most Americans. Even young readers with scant knowledge of jazz will find interest in the rise of Louis's career. His demeanor, shyness, and courtesy through many trying times of his life stand as a strong role model for young Americans, black and white, showing what you can accomplish if you find the strength to persevere.

Book Talk Material

The simple facts of Louis's young years will serve as an excellent and sensitive introduction to the genius of Louis Armstrong. They also paint a vivid and sad picture of prejudice and bigotry, ignorance, and poverty in America. See: Louis's first years (pp. 3–12); Louis's first music (pp. 14–20); Louis gets into trouble and is sent to the Colored Waifs' Home (pp. 24–33); Louis and King Oliver (pp. 50–64); and Louis in Chicago (pp. 65–77).

Additional Selections

Two other biographies of the jazz great who rose from poverty in New Orleans to the musical heights are Sam Tanenhaus's *Louis Armstrong* (Chelsea, 1989, $17.95); and, for a younger audience, Genie Iverson's *Louis Armstrong* (o.p.).

In *Black Music in America: A History through Its People* (Harper, 1987, $15.89; pap., $6.95; condensed in *Juniorplots 4,* Bowker, 1993, pp. 357–361) by James Haskins, there is a history of black music told through the lives of the black people who made it, from slaves to such contemporaries as Tina Turner and Wynton Marsalis. A companion volume is *Black Dance in America* (Harper, 1990, $15; pap., $6.95).

The story of the black Texan who became a great composer of ragtime is told in Barbara Mitchell's *Raggin': A Story about Scott Joplin* (Carolrhoda, 1987, $9.95; pap., $5.95).

In *Fiddler to the World: The Inspiring Story of Itzhak Perlman* (pap., Betterway, 1992, $5.95), Carol H. Behrman tells the story of the amazing Israeli violinist who overcame a crippling attack of polio at age four.

James Haskins presents brief biographies of twelve black Americans who have achieved success in such areas as art, business, and medical research in *One More River to Cross: The Stories of Twelve Black Americans* (Scholastic, 1992, $13.95).

For better readers, Studs Terkel gives biographies of several jazz greats in *Giants of Jazz* (Harper, 1992, $16.89).

An excellent book for both browsing and reading is Susan Altman's *Extraordinary Black Americans from Colonial to Contemporary Times* (Childrens Pr., 1989, $30.60), which contains eighty-five short biographies.

About the Book

Booklist, October 1, 1985, p. 219.
Center for Children's Books Bulletin, November 1985, p. 44.
Horn Book, July 1988, p. 462.
Kirkus Reviews, March 1, 1985, p. 520.
School Library Journal, October 1985, p. 169.
VOYA, December 1985, p. 330.
See also *Book Review Digest,* 1986, pp. 322–333; and *Book Review Index,* 1985, p. 134; 1986, p. 161.

About the Author

Chevalier, Tracy, ed., *Twentieth-Century Children's Writers* (3rd ed.). St. James, 1989, pp. 223–234.
Commire, Anne, ed., *Something about the Author.* Gale, 1977, Vol. 8, pp. 33–34.
Evory, Ann, ed., *Contemporary Authors* (New Revision Series). Gale, 1981, Vol. 4, pp. 149–150.
Holtze, Sally Holmes, ed., *Fifth Book of Junior Authors and Illustrators.* Wilson, 1983, pp. 78–80.
Kinsman, Clare D., ed., *Contemporary Authors* (First Revision). Gale, 1974. Vols. 9–12, p. 179.

Olendorf, Donna, and Telgen, Diane, eds., *Something about the Author.* Gale, 1993, Vol. 10, pp. 39–42.
Senick, Gerard J., ed., *Children's Literature Review.* Gale, 1987, Vol. 3, pp. 44–49.
Ward, Martha, ed., *Authors of Books for Young People* (3rd ed.). Scarecrow, 1990, p. 224.

Fritz, Jean. *Homesick: My Own Story*

Putnam, 1982, $14.95 (0-399-20933-6); pap., Dell, $3.99 (0-440-43683-4)

In recent years, Jean Fritz has become best known for her lively, often humorous (but always accurate) re-creations of the lives of famous Americans in history. Even the titles foretell an amusing look at the subject. For example, in *Will You Sign Here, John Hancock?* (Putnam, 1982, $6.95), she tells of the flamboyant Boston dandy with the gigantic signature who first signed the U.S. Constitution. She has also written several fine historical novels, usually dealing, again, with American topics. One of these, *Early Thunder* (pap., Puffin, 1987, $4.99), set in Colonial Salem, is the story of young David and his exploration of where his political allegiance should lie. In *Homesick,* Jean Fritz re-creates her life growing up in China during the 1920s. These early experiences are compressed into an account that covers two years, 1925–1927, when the future path of Chinese politics was being determined through the leadership of Sun Yat-sen. However, this is basically a family story and the first-person account of a girl's aspirations, fears, and yearnings. The text is complemented by seven full-page drawings and twenty-three family photographs. It is enjoyed by readers in grades 4 through 7.

Plot Summary

The book takes place from October 1925 to September 1927. Young Jean has discovered a number of things. For one, she is an American on the wrong side of the world. She is in China with her missionary parents, even though she definitely feels American at the British school she attends. When the British children sing "God Save the King," Jean keeps her mouth shut. She also discovers that even though she is an American, she can never become president of the United States because she wasn't born there. The U.S. Constitution says the president must be American-born. Actually, Jean already knows she doesn't want to become the president; she wants to be a writer . . . but still . . .

Young Jean has more to worry about than not becoming president. This is a period of turmoil in China, as Communists fight for control of the country. Foreigners are becoming more and more unpopular. At any time, foreign women and children might be sent out of the country.

As much as young Jean worries and as much as she is often homesick for America, she loves China, and most of her days are spent just being a curious, lively, fun-loving little girl. There are many wonderful things to do. There is her beloved amah, the Chinese woman who take cares of her. Li Nai-Nai teaches her embroidery, and young Jean teaches her English. Sometimes Jean has a little fun with the lessons. When Li Nai-Nai asks her what she should say if she meets an American on the street, Jean replies, "You say 'sewing machine.' "

Jean also has wonderful adventures with her best friend, Andrea. Like Jean's family, Andrea's works for the Y.M.C.A. Although Jean and Andrea have become used to being insulted and called "foreign devils" when they walk about town, they know the situation is worsening when one day they are stoned by young boys. They aren't hurt, but they certainly are frightened.

Finally, the revolution begins in earnest as strikes break out all over the country. Occasionally there are riots. The trouble means Jean and her family cannot go to the ocean at Peitaiho where they usually spend their summers. Her father is afraid for their safety. Instead they go on a trip to the mountains, and Jean spends two beautiful days traveling on the Yangtze River, a trip she will never forget.

During this period, Jean's baby sister is born. She is named Miriam; Jean had been hoping for Marjorie. But the baby soon dies of unknown causes.

When the family returns from their trip, they are nearly killed by a mob but are saved by ricksha coolies. Jean writes to her grandmother that she was so scared her knees were actually shaking. As tension mounts and anger against foreigners increases, Jean and her family begin to worry about their return to America—about getting there at all. They are due to return in April. It is now October, and Jean's British school has not opened this year because the teacher has returned to England. Jean's mother, a former Latin teacher, decides to become her daughter's tutor.

In March, word comes that a new man is being sent to the Y.M.C.A. to take her father's place, so the Fritz family makes plans for their own departure. But in late March, her father comes home with the news that they have about three hours to pack. All women and children are ordered to leave the city immediately. There is terrible fighting between the Communists and the Nationalists. The journey is arduous and frightening, but at long last on April 26, Jean and her family board the *President Taft* for the long journey home.

Jean is on deck when the steamer pulls into San Francisco harbor and she thinks, "This is my own, my native land!" She has her first American soda—chocolate! Then they begin their drive across the United States and young Jean first sees her country. It is a never-to-be-forgotten experience. When they finally arrive at her grandmother's in Pennsylvania, Jean hears the words she has been waiting for all her life—"Welcome home."

Thematic Material

This a straightforward account of two years in the life of a normal, fun-loving American girl who just happens to live in China. There is nice contrast between the familiar antics, joys, and worries of any youngster in adolescence, and the fears and turmoil of a land in upheaval. Young Jean Fritz exhibits qualities of courage and strength, along with the innocence of childhood. A good read for boys and girls of this age group with an interest in foreign lands. The colorful insights into China in the early part of the century are especially interesting.

Book Talk Material

The strangeness of being a youngster growing up in a foreign land will serve as a good introduction to this highly readable biography. See: Jean and "God Save the King" (pp. 11–13); amah and the English lesson (pp. 17–18); Jean visits the Hulls (pp. 32–34); Jean and Andrea under attack (pp. 42–43); the revolution begins (pp. 53–56); and the trip on the Yangtze (pp. 61–66).

Additional Selections

In a companion to *Homesick*, Jean Fritz has written for slightly older readers, *China Homecoming* (Putnam, 1985, $15.95), an account of her return to her hometown, Hankow, after an absence of about forty years.

For better readers, Jean Fritz has also written a compelling account of the Communist army's incredible journey across China in 1934 and 1935 in *China's Long March* (Putnam, 1988, $15.95; condensed in *Juniorplots 4*, Bowker, 1993, pp. 351–356).

The early history of China, its culture, people, and contributions are given in the well-illustrated *The Chinese* (Silver Burdett, 1991, $16.98) by Pamela Odijk.

Peggy Ferroa's *China* (Marshall Cavendish, 1991, $21.95) introduces the history and geography of China but emphasizes cultural topics and how the people live.

Barbara Mitchell writes about another famous author who spent years in China in *Between Two Worlds: A Story About Pearl Buck* (Carolrhoda, 1988, $9.95).

In the 1950s, a young Korean girl survives first the Japanese and then the Russian occupation of North Korea before escaping to the south in the novel by Sook Nyul Choi, *The Year of Impossible Goodbyes* (Houghton, 1991, $13.45; pap., Dell, $3.50).

The China of over 100 years ago in the days of the Taiping Rebellion is re-created by Laurence Yep in *The Serpent's Children* (Harper, 1984, $13.89), the story of Cassia and her brother, who, after their mother's death, are increasingly ignored by their father.

In the novel *The Bombers Moon* (pap., Farrar, 1992, $4.50) by Betty Vander Els, two children of missionaries are evacuated to escape the Japanese invasion of China. A sequel is *Leaving Point* (Farrar, 1987, $15).

About the Book

Booklist, September 1, 1982, p. 42.
Center for Children's Books Bulletin, July 1982, p. 206.
Horn Book, December 1982, p. 649.
Kirkus Reviews, September 1, 1982, p. 1002.
New York Times Book Review, November 14, 1982, p. 41.
School Library Journal, September 1982, p. 120.
See also *Book Review Digest,* 1982, pp. 536–537; and *Book Review Index,* 1982, p. 185; 1983, p. 193.

About the Author

Chevalier, Tracy, ed., *Twentieth-Century Children's Writers* (3rd ed.). St. James, 1989, pp. 363–364.
Commire, Anne, ed., *Something about the Author.* Gale, 1982, Vol. 29, pp. 79–84.
de Montreville, Doris, and Hill, Donna, eds., *Third Book of Junior Authors and Illustrators.* Wilson, 1972, pp. 94–95.
Estes, Glenn E., ed., *American Writers for Children since 1960: Fiction* (Dictionary of Literary Biography: Vol. 52). Gale, 1986, pp. 156–167.
Evory, Ann, ed., *Contemporary Authors* (First Revision). Gale, 1985, Vol. 5, pp. 201–202.
Kirkpatrick, D. L., ed., *Twentieth-Century Children's Writers* (2nd ed.). St. Martin's, 1983, p. 303.
Metzger, Linda, and Straub, Deborah A., eds., *Contemporary Authors* (New Revision Series). Gale, 1986, Vol. 16, pp. 125–129.

Riley, Carolyn, ed., *Children's Literature Review.* Gale, 1976, Vol. 2, pp. 79–83.
Sarkissian, Adele, ed., *Something about the Author.* Gale, 1986, Vol. 2, pp. 99–109.
Senick, Gerard J., ed., *Children's Literature Review.* Gale, 1988, Vol. 14, pp. 102–123.
Ward, Martha, ed., *Authors of Books for Young People* (3rd ed.). Scarecrow, 1990, p. 249.

Weidhorn, Manfred. *Robert E. Lee*

Macmillan, 1988, $14.95 (0-689-31340-3)

Historian Manfred Weidhorn was born in Austria but left for the United States when Hitler rose to power. He began his writing career with a series of novels, moved on to scholarly, historical works for adults, and then switched to biographies for a younger audience. His first, *Napoleon* (Macmillan, 1986, $16.95), was published in 1986, followed two years later by *Robert E. Lee.* This biography re-creates the life of a brilliant military strategist who could also inspire great loyalty from his men. Although this account of the Confederate general concentrates on his years as commander of the Army of Northern Virginia, it also tells of his early life and his time as a college president after the Civil War. The inclusion of interesting anecdotes and several black-and-white photographs bring additional reality to the narrative. It is read by youngsters in grades 5 through 8.

Plot Summary

Robert E. Lee based his life on three all-important factors; he was a gentleman and an American, but most of all he was a Virginian. And because he was first and foremost a Virginian, he wept but turned down President Abraham Lincoln's offer to lead the Union Army in the Civil War. He would not fight for slavery or to secede from the Union, but he would defend his family, his friends, and his Virginia against an invading army. This is the key point in his great military genius, and he was loved and respected by the men he sent into battle.

Lee, who always signed his name as R. E. Lee, was born on January 19, 1807, to Ann Hill Carter and Harry Lee. His mother was from one of Virginia's richest families. She was much younger than, and the second wife of, his father, known as Light-Horse Harry for his heroic deeds in the American Revolution and his dashing personality.

Even though his father left the family for the Caribbean and died while

Lee was still a young man, he seems always to have had a military career in mind. He entered the United States Military Academy at West Point in 1825. After graduation he went home to care for his dying mother, with whom he had a special bond and who is credited with turning him into a man of decency and integrity.

In 1830, after his mother's death, Lee married Mary Randolph Custis, whom he had known all his life. She was the great-granddaughter of Martha Washington. Lee would prove to be a loving father to the three sons and four daughters who were born to the couple.

Although Lee had a fine and respected early military career, during which he proved he was not only an outstanding soldier but an excellent administrator and engineer, by the time he reached his middle fifties, he was gray of hair and somewhat depressed with the ordinariness of his military life.

And then came the terrible years that tore the country apart and caused this decent and honorable man to agonize over his refusal to accept President Lincoln's request that he head the Union Army in the Civil War. According to Lee's wife, he wept "tears of blood" when he turned down the president. If Lee could place his own state above his country, why could he not place his moral doubts about slavery above his own state? Probably because Lee, like so many others of the time, regarded slavery as a traditional institution.

As commander of Virginia's military forces, with the rank of major general, Lee faced a formidable task putting together an army. And he faced a formidable foe. The North had almost three times the population of the South, a far greater industrial capacity, and the sympathy of the world.

In May of 1861, Richmond, Virginia, was named the capital of the Confederacy, and Jefferson Davis became the president of the Confederate States of America.

The Confederates won the first big battle of the war, at Bull Run (or Manassas). Lee deserves the main credit for this victory for it was his strategy that succeeded. Although there would be defeats and drawbacks in the months ahead, President Davis steadfastly backed his military leader, and Lee proved his genius.

In June 1862, Lee assumed command of the Army of Northern Virginia. In the so-called Battle of the Seven Days that followed, Lee would change the character of the war. The North expected a quick victory with their overwhelming forces. But Lee's counteroffensive tactics changed that. The confederate general showed his qualities of leadership, risk-taking, intelligence, aggressiveness, and a deep caring for the men who would fight with him. He was gracious in victory, never arrogant, and incorruptible. Respect, love, and admiration for this great leader grew throughout the South.

Through the bloody battles that followed—Second Manassas, Antietam, Fredericksburg, Chancellorsville, and the turning point of Gettysburg—even Lee's brilliance could not stop the inevitable victory for the Union's superior forces. And so, on April 9, 1865, near Appomattox Courthouse, Virginia, General Robert E. Lee surrendered his forces to General Ulysses S. Grant of the Union Army.

After the war, with his military career ended, Lee, his wife, son Custis, and three surviving daughters moved into the Virginia countryside. Although he tried to write his memoirs, he never succeeded. In August 1865, he took on his last major assignment, as president of Washington College in Lexington, Virginia. Today, we know it as Washington and Lee University.

No mere figurehead president, Lee worked hard at his job and revived the school by increasing enrollment, upgrading the course of study, and bringing in much-needed funds. He died on October 12, 1870, after suffering a stroke. He is remembered as a gentleman and a military genius, perhaps a rare combination.

Thematic Material

This is a very readable account of a very likable historical figure. The qualities of decency, honor, truth, and compassion shine through in this story of the adult life of one of the greatest of U.S. military leaders. Lee is shown to be, first of all, a decent human being, and young readers can easily relate to the gentleness and courage of this man who lived his life according to his moral values, even in the midst of one of the bloodiest of wars.

Book Talk Material

The qualities that helped mold Robert E. Lee into a great commander and leader make a good introduction to this book about one of America's most interesting lives. See: Lee's views on slavery and his refusal of Lincoln's offer (pp. 23–27); Lee's relationship with Jefferson Davis (pp. 31–36); Battle of the Seven Days (pp. 42–54); Gettysburg (pp. 78–91); and the surrender to Grant (pp. 114–124).

Additional Selections

Zachary Kent's *Ulysses S. Grant* (Childrens Pr., 1989, $17.27; pap., $6.95) is an account of the life and career of the Civil War hero who became president. Another of this author's books about the Civil War is *The Story of the Surrender at Appomattox Court House* (Childrens Pr., 1987, $13.27; pap., $3.95).

In Jean Fritz's *Stonewall* (Putnam, 1979, $15.95; pap., Puffin, $4.99), she tells of the amazing Southern general who was nicknamed Stonewall after his stand at Bull Run during the Civil War.

In his well-illustrated Newbery Medal-winning biography, *Lincoln: A Photobiography* (Houghton, 1987, $16.95; pap., $7.95), Russell Freedman gives a balanced, accurate account of the Civil War president.

The battle of Gettysburg is told from two different viewpoints, that of a Confederate lieutenant and that of a Union corporal, in Jim Murphy's *The Long Road to Gettysburg* (Houghton, 1992, $15.95).

In addition to explaining the causes of the war, James I. Robertson Jr.'s *Civil War! America Becomes One Nation* (Knopf, 1992, $14) gives a year-by-year account of events.

In the novel *Becca's Story* (Scribner, 1992, $14.95) by James D. Forman, letters from two young men in the Union Army to a girl living in Michigan describe the life of soldiers during the Civil War.

The life of a young Union soldier and spy during the Civil War in the West is told in the Newbery Medal-winning novel *Rifles for Watie* by Harold Keith (Harper, 1957, $14.95; pap., $3.95; condensed in *Juniorplots*, Bowker, 1967, pp. 40–42).

About the Book

Book Report, September 1988, p. 44.
Booklist, March 1, 1988, p. 1188.
Center for Children's Books Bulletin, May 1988, p. 192.
Kirkus Reviews, March 1, 1988, p. 371.
School Library Journal, June 1988, p. 128.
VOYA, August 1988, p. 152.
See also *Book Review Digest,* 1989, pp. 1744–1745; and *Book Review Index,* 1988, p. 855; 1989, p. 866.

About the Author

Commire, Anne, ed., *Something about the Author.* Gale, 1990, Vol. 60, pp. 198–199.
Kinsman, Clare D., ed., *Contemporary Authors.* Gale, 1975, Vols. 53–56, p. 575.

AUTHOR INDEX

Asterisks denote titles that are featured as main entries.

TITLE INDEX

Asterisks denote titles that are featured as main entries.

SUBJECT INDEX

This listing includes only those titles fully summarized and discussed in this book. Additional titles relating to these subjects can be found in the "Additional Selections" that accompany the discussion of the books listed here. Unless otherwise noted with the label nonfiction, the subject headings refer to fictional treatment of the subject.

CUMULATIVE AUTHOR INDEX

This index lists all the titles fully discussed in *Introducing Books* (IB), *Introducing More Books* (IMB), *Introducing Bookplots 3* (IB3), and *Middleplots 4* (M4).

IB = Introducing Books; IMB = Introducing More Books;
IB3 = Introducing Bookplots 3; M4 = Middleplots 4

IB = Introducing Books; IMB = Introducing More Books;
IB3 = Introducing Bookplots 3; M4 = Middleplots 4

IB = Introducing Books; IMB = Introducing More Books;
IB3 = Introducing Bookplots 3; M4 = Middleplots 4

CUMULATIVE TITLE INDEX

This index lists all the titles fully discussed in *Introducing Books* (IB), *Introducing More Books* (IMB), *Introducing Bookplots 3* (IB3), and *Middleplots 4* (M4).

IB = Introducing Books; IMB = Introducing More Books;
IB3 = Introducing Bookplots 3; M4 = Middleplots 4

CUMULATIVE SUBJECT INDEX

This index includes only those titles fully summarized and discussed in *Introducing Books* (IB), *Introducing More Books* (IMB), *Introducing Bookplots 3* (IB3), and *Middleplots 4* (M4). Additional titles relating to these subjects can be found in the "Additional Selections" that accompany the discussion of the books listed here. Unless otherwise noted with the label nonfiction, the subject headings refer to fictional treatment of the subject.

IB = Introducing Books; IMB = Introducing More Books;
IB3 = Introducing Bookplots 3; M4 = Middleplots 4

IB = Introducing Books; IMB = Introducing More Books;
IB3 = Introducing Bookplots 3; M4 = Middleplots 4

IB = Introducing Books; IMB = Introducing More Books;
IB3 = Introducing Bookplots 3; M4 = Middleplots 4

Fantasy